ch 1, 2, 3, 5

Dani

ONLY MUSLIM

EMBODYING ISLAM IN TWENTIETH-CENTURY FRANCE

NAOMI DAVIDSON

CORNELL UNIVERSITY PRESS
Ithaca and London

First published 2012 by Cornell University Press
First printing, Cornell Paperbacks, 2012

Printed in the United States of America

Library of Congress Cataloging-in-Publication Data

Davidson, Naomi, 1976–
Only Muslim : embodying Islam in twentieth-century France / Naomi Davidson.
p. cm.
Includes bibliographical references and index.
ISBN 978-0-8014-5091-4 (cloth : alk. paper)
ISBN 978-0-8014-7831-4 (pbk. : alk. paper)
1. Muslims—France—Ethnic identity. 2. Muslims—France—Social conditions—20th century. 3. Islam—France—History—20th century. 4. France—Ethnic relations. I. Title.
DC34.5.M87D38 2012
305.6'970944—dc23 2012005181

Cornell University Press strives to use environmentally responsible suppliers and materials to the fullest extent possible in the publishing of its books. Such materials include vegetable-based, low-VOC inks and acid-free papers that are recycled, totally chlorine-free, or partly composed of nonwood fibers. For further information, visit our website at www.cornellpress.cornell.edu.

Cloth printing 10 9 8 7 6 5 4 3 2 1
Paperback printing 10 9 8 7 6 5 4 3 2 1

To my parents, Miriam and Jeff Davidson

Contents

Acknowledgments

It is a pleasure to be able to thank the people and institutions who have contributed in so many different ways to this book. First and foremost, I want to recognize the constant support of Leora Auslander, without whom this project simply would not have been. Our conversations over the last decade have challenged, excited, and pushed me farther than I imagined I could go. I appreciate her qualities not only as an engaged scholar but also as a human being and friend (and hiking and cooking partner). Katherine Taylor helped someone with little background understand how to think about architecture and what we do with it, including walking through the Mosquée with me to map it out in experiential terms. Michael Geyer's urgings to think comparatively and transnationally have enriched my thinking. I would also like to thank Dipesh Chakrabarty and Holly Shissler for their support and interest in my research. Finally, Joan W. Scott's enthusiastic encouragement as the dissertation became a book was very welcome.

I am grateful for the generous financial support of the institutions that made it possible to complete the research for this project from 2002 to 2007: the University of Chicago's Kunstadter and Cochrane Travel Grants, as well as FLAS funding for the study of Arabic in Morocco, the Georges Lurcy Charitable Trust, the German Marshall Fund, and the Social Science Research Council. An additional year of funding was made possible by the Charlotte W. Newcombe Dissertation Fellowship. Finally, the University of Chicago Center in Paris was an anchor for three years, and I am grateful not only for the luxury of having had an office there but also for the indispensable support of its staff.

I would like to thank the archivists and librarians at the following institutions, many of whom went above and beyond the call of duty in helping me locate relevant documents: in Rabat, the Archives nationales; in Paris and its suburbs: the Archives Nationales, the Archives du Ministère des Affaires Etrangères et Européennes, the Archives de la Préfecture de Police (special thanks to Rémy Valat), the Archives de l'Assistance Publique/Hôpitaux Publics, the Société historique de l'Armée de terre, the Archives départementales de Seine-Saint Denis, the Archives of the Vicariat de solidarité, the Archives of the Archdiocese of Paris, the Archives départementales des Hauts-de-Seine, the Archives of Association Génériques (special thanks to Naïma Yahi), the Archives of the Institut des Etudes Politiques, the Bibliothèque Nationale de France, the Bibliothèque historique de la ville de Paris, the Bibliothèque administrative de la ville de Paris, the Institut du Monde Arabe, the Bibliothèque de documentation internationale contemporaine, and the Bibliothèque du Centre culturel algérien. Working at the Archives Nationales d'Outre-Mer was a true pleasure. The archivists at the Archives départementales de l'Allier were gracious enough to send me photocopies of the documents I requested.

I thank Ghaleb Bencheikh for sharing his memories of the Mosquée during the 1980s and Bernard Godard for giving me insight into the Ministry of the Interior's Muslim policies.

I have been grateful for the chance to present versions of this project to different audiences, beginning with my peers at the University of Chicago. I would like to thank the members of the Modern Europe Workshop, the Anthropology of Europe Workshop, the Modern France Workshop, and the Workshop on the Built Environment. In Paris, Patrick Weil and Jean-Claude Monod's "Laïcité, sécularisation: l'impact des migrations sur les modèles nationaux en Europe et en Amérique du Nord" seminar introduced me to French colleagues who greatly enriched my work. In later stages, comments from colleagues at meetings of the Society for French Historical Studies, the French Colonial Historical Society, the American Anthropological Association, and the Council for European Studies and at talks at the Rutgers Center for Historical Analysis and the Freiburg Institute for Advanced Studies were very useful.

Friends and colleagues have provided guidance at different moments over the course of this project, and their intellectual companionship has made my work richer. I, of course, am solely responsible for any mistakes. I would particularly like to thank Raberh Achi, Kimberly Arkin, Josh Arthurs, Josh Cole, Angéline Escafré-Dublet, Mayanthi Fernando, Liz Foster, Béatrice de Gasquet, Elizabeth Heath, Choukri Hmed, Eric Jennings, Ethan Katz, Charles Keith, Erez Levon, Mary Lewis, Amelia Lyons, Dejan Lukić, Heather Murray, Ben Nickels, Clifford Rosenberg, Ryme Seferdjeli, Todd Shepard, Daniel Sherman, Emmanuelle Sibeud, Paul Silverstein, Judith Surkis, Mohamed Telhine, Meredith Terretta, Helen Veit, Patrick Weil, Naïma Yahi, and Michelle Zancarini-Fournel. Members of the Rutgers Center for Historical Analysis and the Rutgers University History Department welcomed me for a wonderful postdoctoral year. *Merci* also to my colleagues and students in the History Department at the University of Ottawa.

At Cornell University Press, I have been privileged to work with John G. Ackerman, whose enthusiasm, calm, and clear insight have been much appreciated. I am also grateful to my two anonymous readers for their insightful comments and queries. Karen M. Laun has shepherded me through the editing process with ease, helped by Martin Schneider's careful copyediting.

I thank earlier teachers who taught me ways of thinking about the past, and of writing about it, in more than one language: Madhavi Kale, Stephan Miescher, Jeannette Eisler, Carole Powers, and Gill Cook.

I have been lucky to have been surrounded by a circle of people who provided me with warm friendship in Paris when I was far from home. I especially want to thank Eli Ben-Haim and Roland Bost, my Parisian family, who have supported me (in both the French and English senses!) without fail since the beginning.

Kimberly Arkin, Eli Ben-Haim, Roland Bost, Richard Delacy, Laura Etherden, Sarah Ezzy, Abigail Jacobson, Heather Murray, Jonathan Ripley, Cindy Skema, and Hadas Shintel have put up with this project for many years. I cannot thank them enough for their sympathetic ears, but also, more importantly, for their reminders of the world outside: hikes, travel, elaborate meals, and endless conversations. I wish we were on the same continent, let alone in the same place, more often. Special thanks are due to Kimberly Arkin and Heather Murray for their unflagging ability to read and re-read, ad nauseam, without ever losing their edge.

I want to thank my parents, Miriam and Jeff, whose love and strong faith in me have been a source of great encouragement. I am also very appreciative of the way they handled many thankless administrative tasks with good cheer while I was living abroad. My brother Ezra and I shared the pleasures of graduate student existence, such as they are, and his support was especially meaningful for that reason. My sister-in-law Evelyn's stress-reduction suggestions were always welcome, and both Ezra and Evelyn indulged me with depressing movies and red velvet cake during weekends in New York. My brother Sam inspires me with his commitment to social responsibility, as unpretentious and unassuming as it is sincere. Colomba and Philippe Greppo have cheered me on, and now they can see in English what I've been talking about in French over countless dinner conversations.

Enfin, Sébastien Greppo sait tout ce que je lui dois. His patience, attention to detail, and technical skills have saved the manuscript on more than one occasion. Sébastien can cite entire passages of this book from memory and is happy to debate French politics with me until all hours, but I am most grateful for his wicked humor and his love.

Note on Translation and Transliteration

Unless otherwise noted, all translations are mine. I refer to institutions and associations by their French names, for the most part, but translate them into English. *Islam français,* or French Islam, appears in French throughout the text. *Indigène,* which shares the connotation of the English *native,* is used in French, as is *laïcité* and its adjectives *laïc* and *laïque,* which correspond to the French *secularism* and *secular.*

I have chosen to use the French transliterations of Arabic words for continuity with the language used in my sources. To give but a few examples, the Muslim reformist association known in some literature as the *Ulama* or *Ulema* appears here as Ouléma. Likewise, two major holidays in the Muslim calendar that are often written as *Eid* in English appear here as *Aïd el Kébir* and *Aïd el Seghrir.*

Abbreviations

The following abbreviations will be used to refer to archival collections:

AAP	Archives de l'Archdiocèse de Paris, Paris
AAP/HP	Archives de l'Assistance Publique/Hôpitaux Publics, Paris
AD S-SD	Archives départementales de Seine-Saint Denis, Bobigny
AIEP	Archives de l'Institut des études politiques, Paris
AMAEE	Archives du Ministère des affaires étrangères et européennes, Paris
AN	Archives Nationales, Paris
ANOM	Archives Nationales d'outre-mer, Aix-en-Provence
APP	Archives de la Préfecture de Police, Paris
AVS	Archives du Vicariat de la solidarité, Paris
BAVP	Bibliothèque administrative de la ville de Paris, Paris
BDIC	Bibliothèque de documentation internationale contemporaine, Nanterre
BHVP	Bibliothèque historique de la ville de Paris, Paris
BNF	Bibliothèque nationale de France, Paris
CCA	Bibliothèque du Centre culturel algérien, Paris
SHAT	Société historique de l'Armée de la Terre, Vincennes

ONLY MUSLIM

Introduction

Muslims only as Muslims

Abdelhak Eddouk, the president of the Muslim association of the Paris suburb of Grigny II, astutely observed in the aftermath of the fall 2005 unrest in many French suburbs that "for years, one dealt with Muslims only as Muslims, one saw only their religion."[1] Given the centrality of *laïcité,* or secularism, to French republican ideology during the twentieth century, Eddouk's placement of Islam at the center of debates about social exclusion might seem puzzling. Why would the universalizing state that passed a law in 1905 formally separating church and state administer a particular population exclusively on the basis of its religious affiliation? Why would the citizens of a secular republic identify certain of their fellow citizens only as members of a religious community? Another version of the same question might ask why, over the course of the twentieth century, the secular French Republic was able to make its peace with (most) Catholics, Protestants, and Jews but not with Muslims? Part of the answer to this question lies in the creation of what I call French Islam, or *Islam français.* French Islam was a system that blended French secular republicanism with distinct embodied practices and aesthetics drawn from the French imaginary of orthodox Moroccan Islam. It was elaborated by French politicians, colonial officials, social scientists, architects, urban planners, and *indigénophiles* in the years surrounding the First World War. This particular vision of Islam, though quite distinct from the heterodox Islam(s) practiced by some immigrants from France's Muslim-majority colonial territories, was nonetheless used as the basis for metropolitan French understandings of Islam and Muslim.

I argue that the reason the French state treated immigrants from North Africa "only as Muslims" is that French Islam saturated them with an embodied religious identity that functioned as a racialized identity. The inscription of Islam on the very bodies of colonial (and later, postcolonial) immigrants emerged from the French belief that Islam was a rigid and totalizing system filled with corporeal rituals that needed to be performed in certain kinds of aesthetic spaces. Because this vision of Islam held that Muslims could only ever and always be Muslim, "Muslim" was as essential and eternal a marker of difference as gender or skin color in France. The argument that Muslimness, because of the embodied nature of Islam, was innate and immutable is what made *Islam français* different from French Catholicism, Protestantism, and Judaism. All three faiths had been forced to make some compromises with *laïcité*. Yet in spite of the anti-Semitism that was brutally displayed during the Dreyfus affair and the Vichy years, Jews, alongside Protestants and Catholics, could all be both French and members of their religious communities. This book is an explanation of why and how French policy makers and intellectuals racialized Islam and Muslims and what the consequences of the transformation of a "religious" identity into a racialized identity were for immigrants from North and West Africa.

I explain the paradoxes of *Islam français* in twentieth-century metropolitan France by tracing out the destiny of the site that did the most to define it, the Mosquée de Paris (Paris Mosque), which was inaugurated in 1926.[2] The Mosquée's placement in the center of Paris's urban landscape, in the very heart of its historic university district, proclaimed loudly that Islam's civilization and intellectual heritage were of the same stature as those of France. Yet the site's *hispano-mauresque* architecture reiterated that Muslim believers could only live out the tenants of their rigorously demanding faith with its many embodied practices in a particular aesthetic space. The Mosquée as a physical site reflected but also helped constitute French perceptions of Islam and Muslim practices. By examining the tensions embodied by the Mosquée de Paris, the contradictory impulses of French Islam become clear and, in turn, offer us a nuanced understanding of the tangled relationship between race and religion in colonial and postcolonial France.

Embodying Islam

Why did the proponents of *Islam français* draw such clear distinctions between modern, secular French subjects and Muslims and make such reductive claims about the identities of people from the Maghreb and West Africa? How was it possible to suggest that "Algerian" and "Muslim" were synonymous, while never suggesting that "French" and "Catholic" were? To answer these questions, we must consider first the issue of the saturation of "Muslims" with Muslimness, and second, consider the ways in which Catholics and Jews were exempt from a similar logic. In attending to the question of saturation, it may be useful to use two analogies: the saturation of women with their gender and of colonial peoples with their "primitivism." For in the minds of many influential French politicians and intellectuals, Muslims had a different kind of personhood than they themselves did as rational individuals, and that irrational personhood was inscribed in their very bodies.

The embodied Muslim self, like the female and colonial self, was not the same as the male, bourgeois, French self. As Joan Wallach Scott and Gary Wilder have pointed out, embodying a particular identity such as one's gender or colonial subjectivity makes it impossible for one to be a republican abstract individual.[3] In the case of Muslims, their subjectivity as fundamentally religious individuals kept them from becoming republican subjects according to this model. Yet the problem of the saturation of Muslims with Muslimness goes beyond the question of republican belonging and ultimately has to do with a larger production of embodied difference. Historically, this kind of bodily difference has most often been associated with women and peoples Western Europeans considered to be less civilized than themselves. As Wendy Brown explains, shifts in gender distinctions during the nineteenth century produced "a pervasively sexed body, a body that produced a new foundation for subordination rooted in putative difference."[4] Her language in describing this process is helpful in understanding how *Islam français* saturated Muslims with Muslimness: "difference was understood to saturate the . . . body, mind, and soul . . . that is, to exhaustively define their respective identities, subjectivities, and potential public personae."[5] Unlike late nineteenth- and twentieth-century white women, who were able to participate in their respective public spheres to a greater or lesser extent in spite of (and sometimes because of) their difference, people identified as Muslim were not able to do so for much of the twentieth century.

The other analogy that may help us understand how "Muslimness" worked is that of racial difference itself.[6] While some varieties of twentieth-century race thinking have emphasized phenotypes and visible physical difference, a strain of viewing race as "nature" or "culture" has been equally strong since the nineteenth century. Arthur de Gobineau's midcentury writings on the inequality of peoples classed races in a hierarchy of appearance and intelligence, with the "Aryan" races at the top and the "melanin variety" at the bottom. Yet by the late nineteenth century, French thinkers like Hippolyte Taine and Ernest Renan used *nationality* and *race* interchangeably to stand for "cultural" qualities that were innate and essential.[7] Pierre-André Taguieff has argued that contemporary racism has replaced the "biologization" of peoples with their "culturalization" or, in other words, that while racist discourse once held that groups' characteristics were defined by their biology, it now makes a similarly reductive claim in which peoples are defined by their cultural environment.[8] Yet I argue that the saturation of Algerians with Muslim identity actually represents the opposite phenomenon: rather than masking classical "biological" racist claims about the innate laziness, violence, and lawlessness of Algerians with "cultural" critiques of Islam, French officials *created* the reductionist, totalizing religio-cultural category "Muslim" out of the notion of embodied Islam. The French belief in Islam's domination of the Muslim's physical self was less a cultural argument than a biologized one. The distinction between a corporeal logic and a racializing logic is important to maintain, for as we will see, the saturation of "Muslim" immigrants with this embodied identity was selective, and not all Muslims were identified equally as Muslims.

Finally, we must ask why the proponents of *Islam français* would choose to emphasize embodied rituals as the particular proof of Muslim difference. I borrow here from the work of scholars of religion, anthropology, and philosophy on how modern, liberal Westerners have tended to think about themselves as opposed to members of "traditional" societies.[9] In a collective essay by Adam B. Seligman, Robert P. Weller, Michael J. Puett, and Bennett Simon, the authors describe the commonly accepted model that suggests that "modern" society is made up of autonomous individuals who make conscious choices to accept norms and customs. "Traditional" societies, on the other hand, are seen as governed by ritual, or unquestioned forms of authority that regulate individual lives. They suggest that this model is fundamentally flawed and instead propose a model in which the opposite of "ritual" is not "individual autonomy" but "sincerity." The "sincerity" model posits that modern subjects prize above all else an authentic self whose truth is expressed transparently through coherent actions—whereas ritual, with its constant repetitions and restrictions, is seen as masking the authentic self or, worse, revealing that such a self does not even exist.[10] French obsession with Muslim ritual hinged in large measure on the belief that it precluded the "sincerity" of which French subjects were capable.

Yet how was it the case that Muslims alone were considered incapable of letting go of the rituals that were the outward symbol of their innate nature, why were they alone incapable of "sincerity"? Although Protestants deny the importance of physically embodied practices, it is clear that in the early decades of the twentieth century, when *Islam français* was created, practicing Jews and Catholics were still observing alimentary restrictions, which, at least in the case of Catholics, were respected in "secular" spaces.[11] Some historians have argued that the law of 1905 actually produced a resurgence of Catholic theology and practice, including a growth in Marian cults and processions, sometimes against the wishes of municipal authorities.[12] Jews, in addition, obeyed sartorial codes as well as mandates concerning hygiene and sexual relations, all of which were also profoundly corporeal. Jewish religious observance in metropolitan France during the interwar years was strongest among more recent immigrants from Eastern Europe than among more assimilated French Jews, and the Jews of North Africa tended to follow laws about dietary restrictions in even greater numbers.[13] Some Catholics and Jews in metropolitan and colonial France continued to perform, publicly and privately, religious practices with their bodies by eating or not eating particular foods, by parading in particular places at particular times, or by ritually washing themselves.

It is important to consider, of course, that Jews in particular have a long history of being represented as racially and religiously different over centuries of French history. Steven Kruger argues that bodies and corporality were central to the depiction of the Jew as alien to Christianity as early as the medieval era.[14] For Christian thinkers, the two religions were distinguished by an "opposition between Jewish corporeality and Christian spirituality," and Jewish theologians were thought to produce "readings of scripture [that were] overly literal, corporeal denials of the 'true spirit' of the text."[15] More recently, over the course of the nineteenth century, Europeans began to consider Jews as a race rather than a nation. As Wendy Brown has argued in her discussion of the "tolerance" of Jews, "race was inscribed in every element of the body and soul" and thus persisted even if the trappings of Jewish identity fell away. In other words, "race allowed (or required) a Jew to be a Jew no matter how fully assimilated."[16] Yet by the twentieth century, of these minority religious communities, Muslims were the only ones whom most French scholars and policy makers argued were unable to free themselves from their faith's domination of their very bodies. This held true across different political regimes, ranging from the left-leaning Popular Front to Pétain's Vichy regime to postwar Gaullist administrations and into the Mitterrand years.

Bodies and Spaces

The French fascination with Muslim bodies and the spaces in which they moved pushed me to think about how and why visible expressions of Islam were so central to French Muslim policy. I argue that the saturation of Muslims with Muslimness described above informed, and was in turn reinforced by, French architects' and intellectuals' representations of the "Muslim" built environment and "Muslim" religious practices. Crucial to my attempt to demonstrate the tension between the ostensibly religious definition of immigrants from North Africa and the embodied or corporeal logic that in fact underlay those assumptions is an examination of the "Muslim" built environment as conceived by French leaders and Muslim community actors and the social practices performed in and around Muslim religious and community sites. By "built environment," I refer to the physical sites of Muslim religious practice and sociability, principally the Mosquée de Paris but also the other buildings or public spaces that were associated with *Islam français* (such as cemeteries, hospitals, *halal* slaughterhouses, provincial mosques, and social service agencies) and with Islam in France (independently organized places of prayer, cafés, workers' dormitories, and outdoor festival sites). I follow the arguments of anthropologists and urban and architectural historians who suggest that the built environment is not only a reflection of social forms but also an attempt to reproduce those very forms.[17] As I suggest below, the French architects who designed the Mosquée were dedicated to just such a task.

It is not coincidental that the earliest theoreticians of the "Muslim city" or of "Muslim urban planning" were French: the Marçais brothers launched what came to be known as the "school of Algiers" in the late 1920s.[18] As urban historian André Raymond explains, the Marçais brothers and their colleagues were strongly influenced by the belief that just as Islam structured the lives of Muslims, it was also the engine that drove the growth of "Muslim" cities. Raymond rightly highlights these early urbanists' disappointment with what was perceived as the disorganization and stagnation of the Muslim city and its lack of resemblance to the clean lines of the ancient Roman cities it had replaced. The members of the Algiers School overemphasized the centrality of the city's mosque, rather than seeing it as one piece of a total built environment.[19] In my analysis of Paris's "Muslim" built environment, I have been inspired by historians of colonial urbanism, specifically in the context of French North Africa but also by work on religious architecture and material culture.[20]

The Mosquée's French proponents were convinced that the sensations evoked by moving through the site's different spaces represented an integral element of the embodied nature of Islam.[21] It was for this reason that the complex's architects, Maurice Mantout, Charles Heubès, and Robert Fournez, tried to recreate the smallest details of their Moroccan models so as to reproduce, as faithfully as possible, the same physical sensations that would have been produced by a visit to a mosque in Fez.[22] The experience of *being* in the Mosquée (smelling the flowers of its "Arab" gardens, hearing the splash of water in its fountains or the muezzin's call to prayer, touching one's forehead to prayer rugs, scrubbing off dead skin in the *hammam,* sipping hot, sweet mint tea in the café) all produced understandings of Islam and of being Muslim in Paris. As Maurice Merleau-Ponty has explained, not only do all five senses communicate to produce our perceptions of objects around us, but there is also no real experiential distinction between the body's act of perception and the objects it perceives: the mosque was the object that would allow Islam to be perceived.[23]

The Mosquée de Paris thus provided the means for the proponents of *Islam français* to instantiate their ideas about the innate physicality of Islam in a site in the middle of Paris. The programs national and local authorities organized there and at other Parisian Muslim sites under the Mosquée's authority emerged out of their belief that the most important element of Islam was its embodied practices. One of the first institutions to emerge in this schema was the Hôpital Franco-Musulman in the Parisian suburb of Bobigny in 1935. After its inauguration, Muslims were funneled there, often against their will. They were denied access to the public hospitals open to French citizens and sent instead to the hospital designed to spare them the "disorienting" experience of non-Muslim hospitals. Later, in the midst of the Second World War, the government set up a special food distribution program for the celebration of Aïd el Kébir, one of the most important holidays in the Muslim calendar. In spite of the severe food shortages that characterized the war years, the Ministry of Supplies nevertheless acquired and distributed couscous, mint tea, and mutton to Muslims in Paris and provincial cities. There is, of course, a distinction to be made between the state *offering* Parisian Muslims the option of treatment in a Muslim hospital, or foods associated with the celebration of a religious holiday, that would otherwise have been unavailable to them, and *compelling* them to accept it. But in repeatedly directing Muslim immigrants toward specific services and away from those designed for other immigrants or French citizens, the state did not offer North Africans much of a choice. For if it was accepted that Islam defined their lives to the point that their very physical bodies were Muslim, the state was in fact doing Muslim immigrants a service in using the language of *Islam français* to administer them in ways deemed to be culturally sensitive to Muslims' needs. I suggest that the racializing *Islam français* that emerged in the 1920s would ultimately influence not only French state attitudes toward Muslim immigrants but also self-identifications of some members of France's diverse Muslim communities.

Pure Islam, Degenerate Islam: Marking Islam as Moroccan and Algerians as Muslim

In order to understand the important role *Islam français* played in the marginalization of colonial populations, this book makes two central arguments. First, I argue that at the moment of its creation, *Islam français* emerged exclusively out of French perceptions of orthodox Moroccan Islam rather than out of the many forms of Islam practiced from Dakar to Djerba. My second argument, which I elaborate below, is that the saturation of nominally "Muslim" immigrants from North and West Africa in the colonial and postcolonial metropole was not, in fact, uniform, in spite of the universalizing tendencies of *Islam français.* The use of Moroccan Islam as the basis for *Islam français* was not a haphazard choice but rather one that reflected the nature of France's differentiated relationships with its North and West African Muslim territories and its subsequent valorizations of their Islams. As historians of French colonialism have long noted, Morocco had never been part of the Ottoman Empire, and its royalty claimed descent from the Prophet, guaranteeing it an important stature in the Muslim world. As an independent state that had resisted European incursions in the past, Morocco and its "pure" Islam represented the greatest challenge to France's presence in Muslim Africa.[24] In West Africa, Islam was seen as a way of encouraging the cooperation and collaboration of local leaders, but it was not considered to be as developed as Moroccan Islam. Colonial officials and ethnographers claimed that their deep knowledge of what they called *Islam noir* (an Islam associated with "black" Africans, which was said not to be far removed from paganism) and *Islam maure* (an "orthodox" Islam associated with Arabic-speaking "whites") enabled them to better govern the West African federation.[25] Algeria, however, unlike the colonies of French West Africa[26] or its neighboring protectorates of Morocco and Tunisia[27] was a settler colony[28] from early on and an integral part of France itself.[29] The site of a long and harsh process of colonization going back to 1830, much of Algeria's Muslim infrastructure was virtually destroyed over the course of the nineteenth century.[30]

French historian Jacques Frémeaux explains that from the earliest days of the conquest, colonial policy in Algeria rested on the "conviction that Algeria had never been a state, nor the Algerians a nation."[31] In other words, Algeria was a blank slate whose territory could be used as a settler colony as well as a site for the deportation of political opponents and a testing ground for theories of urbanization, medicine, and hygiene.[32] French insistence on Algeria as a "tabula rasa" also justified the almost complete annihilation of Muslim sites and socio-religious structures. The administration quickly took over management of all Muslim institutions, closing mosques and meeting sites of Sufi brotherhoods, confiscating *habous* (property owned by religious institutions), and disrupting religious education.[33] This policy emerged out of a colonial assimilationist ideology that sought to eliminate indigenous practices to allow colonial subjects to become French citizens eventually.[34] The reorganization of Algerian Muslim life under French control both confirmed and reified the French perception that there was no Algerian Islam worthy of respect.

Morocco, whose culture represented the height of North African Muslim civilization in the French imagination, became a protectorate in 1912. Tunisia had become a protectorate in 1881, and, eventually joined by Morocco, was put under the authority of the minister for foreign affairs who was represented by the resident-general. While the establishment of both protectorates met with some resistance, it took place without the widespread violence of the Algerian conquest. Unlike in Algeria, the bey of Tunisia and the sultan of Morocco officially maintained sovereignty over their respective protectoral territories, and their governments, the Beylik and the Makhzen, remained in place.[35] As Maréchal Louis-Hubert Lyautey,[36] Morocco's most important resident-general, explained, the goal of the protectorate was to allow the "association and close cooperation of the native race and the protecting race in mutual respect and in the scrupulous safeguarding of traditional institutions."[37] Lyautey's administration sought to "preserve" Moroccan Islam on several different registers, many of which had to do with space and place. More than any other colonial official, Lyautey promoted the French belief in the centrality of spatial organization and aesthetics in Muslim lives; his architects and urbanists were charged with "preserving" the protectorate's medinas not only for their aesthetic value but also in order to maintain the gendering of public and private space. Thus, for example, no construction could be undertaken that would allow someone to see into a neighbor's inner courtyard and thus violate the privacy of the family's women.[38] Lyautey was also responsible for making it illegal for non-Muslims to enter mosques, a measure that did not "preserve" Moroccan Islam, as this prohibition had no historical basis, but rather acted to reiterate the French belief that Muslims' lives were structured around their physical environments to a far greater extent than secular French or French Catholics, Protestants and Jews.

The choice to define *Islam français* as "Moroccan" signaled an acknowledgment of Morocco's power and prestige, an utter disregard for Algeria, and an ignoring of Tunisia and West Africa. This choice carried even more meaning because of the demographics of early twentieth-century immigration to the metropole. As will be discussed in greater detail in chapter 1,

French Islam and the Paris Mosque could be characterized as Moroccan precisely because there were so few Moroccans in the metropole: Moroccan immigrants represented a tiny proportion of those men who crossed the Mediterranean looking for jobs. While the vast majority of immigrants throughout the century would come from Algeria, it would be French imaginings of Moroccan Islam that would define what it meant to be Muslim in France. This mobilization of the practices and aesthetics of orthodox Moroccan Islam was yet another element in the erasure of Algerian forms of Islam.

The racialized French Islam embodied in the Paris Mosque based in French understandings of Moroccan orthodox Islam spoke of Islam and Muslims as a unified entity. Yet, as I mentioned earlier, my second argument in this book concerns the differentiated ways in which "Muslimness" was associated with different immigrant groups in France. I suggest that the category "Muslim," as imagined, constructed, and maintained by French officials and thinkers, ultimately came to be a synonym for "Algerian." The particularly violent and long nature of French rule in Algeria and Algerian resistance to the colonial project produced a distinctive French-Algerian relationship, distinct from French relationships with Moroccans, Tunisians, and West Africans (see chapter 5). Yet this particularity had to be reconciled with the shared "Islamic" character of France's African colonies and protectorates. I argue that this complexity was resolved by conflating "Algerian" with "Muslim," which effectively transformed a religious identity into a racialized one. Moroccans, Tunisians, Senegalese, and other colonial subjects and protégés who were also ostensibly "Muslim" remained outside this logic. The French state's relationship with Moroccan and Tunisian protégés was less conflictual than with its Algerian subjects during most of the twentieth century. West Africans, whose bodies were perceived to have been broken and emasculated after centuries of enslavement, no longer held the same menace as Algerian bodies in the French colonial imagination. It is not a coincidence that the visual representation of colonial valor in the French army is the grinning *tirailleur sénégalais,* whose face still adorns the Banania breakfast drink package.[39] This domestication was not applied to the figure of the *tirailleur algérien,* whose military prowess was argued to be more impressive than that of the West African units but whose role in French victories in two world wars is overshadowed by Banania's mascot.[40] Algerians were not brought into the realm of French domesticity, even in a subaltern position, and remained outside the boundaries of French national culture.[41] The equation of "Muslim" with "Algerian" in metropolitan France accomplished important political work: by identifying Algerians solely as Muslim, the French state at once denied them a potential political identity that threatened its authority

(Algerian) while at the same time making it impossible for them to lay claim to a different one (French), because of their innate "religious" identity.

As I discuss in this book, immigrants from North and West Africa were certainly subject to racism in France, sometimes horrifically so. By focusing on the sublimation of racial difference by religious difference, I am not suggesting that "visible" race did not matter. Rather, I am suggesting that we need to understand the ways in which "invisible" religious difference came to function in the same way as "visible" racial difference seems to work in other circumstances. In other words, I argue that in France, it is more productive to think about "Muslim" as a category of racial difference rather than as one of religious difference. That not all Muslims were equally Muslim in the eyes of the French state forces us to rethink the ways in which racial, religious, and national difference mattered in twentieth-century France. Further, it suggests that the "Muslim exception" to *laïcité* is only one way of understanding the historical exclusion of Muslims from membership in the French Republic.

Writing Beyond the Muslim Exception

It is now a commonplace that metropolitan and colonial histories cannot be written independently of one another; as Gary Wilder argues, we need to "displace conventional oppositions between the French colonial empire and national republic, racism and universalism, the national and the transnational."[42] Although most of the sources, textual and visual, on which this book's arguments are based are drawn from metropolitan French archives and libraries, I have tried as much as possible to construct a narrative that moves back and forth between the Parisian center and the metropolitan and colonial peripheral cities that played such important roles in shaping *Islam français*. In writing this transmediterranean account of French Islam, I am trying to reshape the ways historians have thought and written about the question of Muslim difference in France, both before and after decolonization.

One of the major challenges facing French historiography is how to think about race. I suggest that in the case of colonial subjects, racial difference must be thought about in tandem with religious difference. Important work has been done on the construction of race in the colonies, but its implications on racial attitudes and perceptions in the metropole are still being considered.[43] The logic of French republicanism, which denies that race is at all determinant in one's life experience, has obscured the role that race played in French attitudes toward nominally Muslim immigrants to the metropole when articulated together with religion. The tension between the homogenizing agenda of French republicanism and the saturation of certain individuals with other identities has been successfully explored in the realms of gender and colonialism,[44] but not yet adequately in that of religion, which has so often been a code for race. Todd Shepard rightly argues in his important work on the role that the decolonization of Algeria played in the creation of France that "neither racial, ethnic, nor religious criteria entered into official definitions of Algerians with local civil status, as they did in other colonies. Nonetheless . . . assumptions about the inferiority of Algerian 'Muslims' joined continued assertions that France needed to respect the attachment of 'Muslims' to their Koranic . . . law status as explanations for the continued exclusion of most from full citizenship."[45] Yet this argument for exclusion is based on the familiar trope of the incompatibility of Islam with French citizenship, not racial inferiority. I seek to show how racial difference was encoded in the language of religion, producing a hidden logic of exclusion.

To begin to translate the coded language of religion and race, this book also aims to provide a more complete understanding of French *laïcité*'s historical trajectory, one in which race and culture are implicit in articulations of religion, as well as an interrogation of the notion of the "Muslim exception" in French secularism. Scholars working on colonial legal and political history have inserted the latter question into the history of *laïcité* to reveal the ways in which secularism's boundaries were at once rigid and porous. Raberh Achi and James McDougall's work on the legal structures in place in Algeria after the law of 1905 challenges the idea that secularizing laws simply did not apply in Algeria.[46] While it is vital to understand how these laws were negotiated in the colonies, it is perhaps more important to consider Islam's largely *non-exceptional* legal status in the metropole during the twentieth century in order to understand why it was so often argued to be "exceptional."[47] Ultimately, this book's aim is to question the usefulness of *laïcité* as a category for understanding the history of Islam in France.

This book is organized chronologically in order to focus on certain key moments in the development of French Islam. Following the introduction, chapter 1 focuses on the intellectual and ideological contexts in which the perceived impossibility of separating people identified as Muslim from their religious practices had two important consequences during the first decades of the twentieth century. I argue that the inability of Muslim subjects to divest themselves of their religious identities and practices was used as an explanation for the refusal to extend full citizenship rights to the vast majority of colonial nationals and that the argument that this embodied Islam was the defining characteristic of the majority of colonial subjects in North and West Africa made the joint management of Islam as a religion and Muslims as subjects essential. I suggest that French understandings of Islam created racialized difference, and the accommodations made for Muslim religious practices served to underline that difference, particularly in comparison with Catholics and Jews.

In chapter 2, I explore the articulation of *Islam français* by investigating the planning and construction of the Mosquée de Paris and Institut Musulman, the institution that embodied this new vision of Islam. I argue that the architectural and aesthetic distinctions made between the Mosquée and the Institut served to define the two sides of *Islam français*: the French orientalist architecture of the Mosquée was designed to reflect the ancient traditions and rituals of Islam, while the Institut, located in the Latin Quarter, instead embodied Islam's fundamental compatibility with French secularism, universalism, and republicanism.

Chapter 3 investigates how the *Islam français* embodied by the Mosquée came to serve as the almost exclusive medium for the French state to manage its interactions with its Muslim subjects residing in the metropole. I suggest here that the social service and policing programs developed by the local and national administrations, in using Islam as the basis for their differential treatment of North Africans, set up the pattern in which the segregation of immigrants from the Maghreb was portrayed as protective and as preferential treatment based on religious difference. In other words, it was the panoply of social programs that emerged during the same period as the Mosquée's creation that helped establish Muslims as only and eternally Muslims.

In the fourth chapter, I address the sea changes *Islam français* underwent during the resolutely antisecular Vichy years and the legacies of this period for the postwar creation of provincial Muslim religious sites. I argue that the state's evacuation of the secular and republican content of French Islam and its strong emphasis on embodied Muslim practices was not merely a reflection of the antisecular regime but also of the racializing practices that characterized the period. In the provinces, an Islam *in* France rather than *Islam français* characterized the new religious sites built with state assistance. This Islam did not take French values as its reference point and was not intended to bring Muslims into the realm of secular public space.

The fifth chapter addresses another period of crisis, that of the Algerian War (1954–1962) and its immediate aftermath. Here I examine the competing visions of Islam proffered by the French state and by the French Federation of the FLN (the nationalist group that led the Algerian Revolution) and each entity's attempt to impose its vision on the Muslim population of Paris. In spite of the incredible ruptures produced by this long and violent war, I argue that both *Islam français* and *Islam algérien* maintained the strong link between Algerian-ness and Muslimness established during the colonial period. The French state's and the FLN's visions of Islam mirrored each other in many respects, for neither was able to consider truly the possibility that Algerians could divest themselves of their Muslimness.

In the sixth and final chapter, I investigate the ways in which the interplay among race, culture, and Islam was made visible in the 1970s, an era of changed immigration policy and a new direction in the state's management of "Muslim" immigrants. Typically assumed to be the decade of "*Islam social*" (social Islam), I argue that while there was nothing novel about the state's decision to use Islam as the medium for managing its relationship with populations presumed to be Muslim, what was new about the 1970s, with its social housing mosques and factory prayer rooms, was the explicitly racial and cultural terms of the debates over access to Muslim religious sites. The conflation of racial, national, and cultural identities with Islam at a time when most Muslims and non-Muslims agreed that religious practices were on the wane demonstrates the staying power of the central tenet of *Islam français*: that Muslims could only ever be Muslims.

Chapter 1

Religion and Race in the French Mediterranean

According to the internal logic of *Islam français,* all Muslims should have been equal and equally Muslim, but French politicians and social scientists in fact made many careful distinctions between subjects who were all nominally "Muslim" over the course of the twentieth century, on both shores of the Mediterranean. These categories, as I suggested in the introduction, were shaped by French perceptions of Islam and structured by the administration of Islam in its different colonial territories. Yet no matter what "Muslim" practices colonial subjects may actually have performed and despite the sometimes wildly divergent French analyses of these practices as declining or increasing, Islam was understood by *islamologues* as based in embodied practices and as dominating all aspects of daily life. In this chapter, I argue that the perceived impossibility of separating people identified as Muslim from their religious practices had two important consequences during the first decades of the twentieth century; they set in motion a pattern that would last for many decades to come. First, the inability of Muslim subjects to divest themselves of their religious identities and practices was used as an explanation for the refusal to extend full citizenship rights to the vast majority of colonial nationals; and second, the argument that this embodied Islam was the defining characteristic of the majority of colonial subjects in North and West Africa made the joint management of Islam as a religion and Muslims as subjects essential. In the early twentieth century, French understandings of Islam created racialized difference, and the accommodations made for Muslim religious practices served to underline that difference, particularly in comparison to Catholics and Jews.

"The Word 'Religion' Does Not Mean the Same Thing for Muslims": Constructing Islam as a Totalizing System

French perceptions of Islam were the product of contemporaneous French and European intellectual debates and of imperial fears and rivalries; these ideas about Islam influenced policy decisions about the status of "Muslims" in the colonies and metropole. During the first decades of the twentieth century, France's position as a political power in the Muslim world was challenged by England's imperial interests in the Middle East. French politicians argued that the country needed to reassert its own authority in the Muslim world. "If England is numerically *the largest Muslim power,* France, in its origins, is *the greatest Muslim power,*" as one lobbyist put it.[1] In order to maintain its position as the world's premier Muslim power (*puissance musulmane*), the French government had to articulate a Muslim policy (*politique musulmane*) that would allow it to maintain its hold on its empire. One of the bodies charged with this task was the Interministerial Commission on Muslim Affairs (Commission Interministérielle des Affaires Musulmanes, CIAM), created by decree on 25 June 1911 and presided over by the minister of foreign affairs with members drawn from the Ministries of the Interior, Colonies, and War.[2] The CIAM was to address the problem of the incoherence of France's Muslim politics during a period when France was beginning to imagine an entity called "the Muslim world," thus embodying the intimate relationship between political interests and knowledge of Islam. It was a consultative body designed to synthesize the knowledge produced about Muslim laws, practices, and societies produced in the colonies and protectorates as well as at the Université de Paris and the Collège de France. The CIAM, as a major voice in the articulation of French Muslim policy, would play a role in the early days of the Mosquée's planning.[3]

Yet as many scholars have argued, France's *politique musulmane* was by no means as coherent or unified as the members of the CIAM may have wished. It was the product of cooperation between special interest groups and colonial lobbyists, intellectuals, and members of several ministries, groups that often had competing aims. The fruit of this collaboration was "a heterogeneous collection of ideas" rather than a clearly defined, empire-wide vision of how best to administer France's Muslim subjects and protégés.[4] Furthermore, the dilemma of how to best manage Islam and Muslims became a trans-Mediterranean problem rather than an exclusively North and West African one, as colonial workers began to arrive on French shores and colonial soldiers fought alongside metropolitan soldiers in the French army. Colonial and metropolitan politicians had to refine their *politique musulmane* in light of Islam's place in "the France of tomorrow."[5] It was thus essential to define what Islam was (and was not) as well as who Muslims were (and were not) in order to determine what kind of Islam the French state should be defending.

Many of the French colonial administrators, orientalists, architects, and urban planners involved in articulating France's *politique musulmane* respected and admired particular elements of Muslim philosophy, literature, aesthetics, and architecture. Some of them, most famously Morocco's resident-general Lyautay, were troubled by the potential annihilation of Islam through the colonial encounter.[6] Yet at the same time, they feared Islam's potential as an alternative, and oppositional, worldview to counter a French Catho-secular modernity.[7] As Henry Laurens, a French historian of the Muslim world, has explained, debates about Islam had become so important that by the turn of the twentieth century, Paris had become a major center for *islamologue* research in the humanities and social sciences.[8] The École des langues orientales vivantes was renovated in 1873; it educated many France's most well-known islamicists. Alfred Le Châtelier, a military career man turned academic, created the chair in sociology of the Muslim world at the Collège de France and in 1907 also launched the *Revue du monde musulman,* one of the field's most important journals. Representing the intimate ties between France's political aims and its intellectual production, the chair at the Collège de France was financed by the Moroccan Protectorate.[9] One of the first non-state-sponsored institutions dedicated to the study of Islam was the Collège libre des sciences sociales, founded by the Positivists in 1895. Believing that Islam was the religion that came closest to "the positive state" that led to emancipation, Auguste Comte's disciples had "total respect and sympathy for Islam." The French positivists were especially proud of the many Muslim intellectuals who came to give lectures and lead conferences at their institution.[10] At the same time, a small group of men interested in Muslim issues but not part of the Orientalist or Islamologist establishments founded the *Revue d'Islam,* believing that Islam, Muslims, and the Muslim world were subjects too important to be left exclusively to a small coterie of intellectuals. The *Revue* advocated a republican and anticolonial *politique musulmane,* and its contributors hoped to "defend Muslim interests in Europe."[11] The Parisian community of intellectuals engaged with Muslim issues was thus large and somewhat diverse and often had strong, if sometimes contestatory, connections to the colonial administrations. These scholars were instrumental in the production of France's Muslim policies in the early twentieth century.

Islam français, which sought to marry French perceptions of Moroccan Islam combined with classically "French" values such as liberty and fraternity, emerged out of this turn-of-the-century intellectual and political environment. Its attempt to bridge the gap between the civilizations separated by the Mediterranean was not completely foreign to contemporary French thinking on Islam. As an editorial published in 1903 in the *Revue de deux mondes* opined that

> Nothing in [Muslim] rites is in opposition to the religions of the West. In fact, there are only five obligatory practices: the profession of faith [the *Shahada*], the five daily prayers and ablutions, the giving of charity, the Ramadan fast, and the pilgrimage to Mecca for the rich exclusively . . . nothing is thus incompatible with Christian morality. We could conceive that the idea of a rapprochement between Islam and Christianity might not be entirely chimerical, as long as it is understood that it must not lead to conversion nor to absolute assimilation.[12]

However, the practices emphasized most explicitly in French Islam, discussed in detail in chapter 2, were those which had to do with the body: ablutions to be performed before prayers, the consumption of *halal* meat, and the burial of corpses in accordance with religious law, among others. Critics of Islam and its admirers alike were drawn to its embodied rituals. As ethnographer Arnold Van Gennep wrote after his travels in Algeria in 1911 and 1912, "There are few religions which impose . . . so much self-restraint, exterior calm, and dignified allure. The gestures of prayer are slow . . . requiring a majestic attitude; the small acts of detail, for example, the ritual manners of prostration, of sitting on one's toes, of purifying one's hands with water, with sand, or with a big, smooth pebble, they need a measured, very rhythmic, suppleness."[13] In focusing so intently, even admiringly, on the physical gestures of French Islam, the rhetorical arguments about the philosophical common ground between Islam and French society tended to fade into the background. For while they insisted on the compatibility of Islam with French values, the proponents of *Islam français,* Muslim and non-Muslim alike, were never able to abandon the idea that Islam remained a fundamentally foreign entity. What marked Islam as irrevocably different from secular French civilization in the imaginations of French Islam's proponents was their belief in Islam's immutable physicality and in the embodied nature of the Muslim everyday experience. What marked *Muslims* as irrevocably different from secular French subjects, in the eyes of French policy makers and intellectuals, was the French perception that this bodily discipline was part of a totalizing system that controlled all aspects of Muslim daily life. Or, as a brochure written by Renault management and reprinted in a 1956 issue of *Cahiers nord-africains* intended to help employers understand their Muslim workers explained, "The word 'religion' does not mean the same thing for Muslims as it does for us. The Islamic religion is in fact in addition to a doctrine and religious rituals in the strict sense, an entire ensemble of customs and ways of living in society."[14] By this logic, French Catholics, Jews, and Protestants, then, did not have "ways of living in society" that structured their everyday interactions as well as their private, innermost lives—only Muslims did.

The French belief in the totalizing, systemic discipline of Islam was hardly unique in its time. The so-called rigidity of Islam was taken for granted by nineteenth-century European scholars, as Tomoko Masuzawa reminds us: "The concept of Islam as the epitome of stifling rigidity, intolerance and fanaticism was . . . in the public domain; it had become a familiar theme, mechanically repeated by one treatise after another, in flagrant disregard of the diversity and obvious malleability evidenced in the vast domain of the actual Islamic world."[15] French orientalists located the origins of the rigid discipline of Islam in its sacred text. As nineteenth-century politician and republican theorist Edgard Quinet explained in a lecture at the Collège de France in 1845, "The [Muslim] religious tradition does not grow, it is complete from the very beginning, in the pages of the Quran."[16] Emerging from their understandings of the pervasive influence of Islam's central religious text, French *islamologues* moved on to investigations of what they believed to be the rigid, deeply codified, and purely physical rituals that constituted Muslim religious practice.

It is important to emphasize that Muslim theology does in fact explore the importance of the body; its religious rituals involve both inner (mental or emotional) actions and external (physical) ones. Yet generations of Western scholars of Islam, including the French *islamologues* cited earlier, argued that the religion relied not on inner reflection or devotion but on rigid adherence to codified daily rituals in which one's physical self was profoundly implicated. More recent scholarship has tried to "recuperate" ritual by arguing instead that embodied practices are simply the outward manifestations of an internal, spiritual process. In this view, Islam comes to resemble more closely Christian religious practice with its emphasis on an internal quest for communion with the divine, as scholar of premodern Muslim religious law Paul Powers argues.[17] Powers makes a compelling case for the idea that neither the "empty" ritual of earlier Orientalists nor the "spiritual" one of contemporary scholars reflects an accurate understanding of the relationship between *niyya,* or "intent," and corporeal practice in Muslim law. He cites the eleventh-century jurist Abu Ishaq al-Shirazi's discussion of purification (*tahara*) as an example of a practice made up of several different bodily practices (wet ablutions, dry ablutions, and bathing), each of which is to be completed with its accompanying *niyya.* Anthropologist Saba Mahmood, in describing women's pietist movements in contemporary Egypt, has focused on women's constructions of selfhood through embodied practice. She explains their practices by using the fourteenth-century Muslim scholar Ibn Khaldun's definition of *malaka*: "firmly rooted qualit[ies] acquired by doing a certain action and repeating it time after time."[18] I borrow from Powers's and Mahmood's discussions of premodern and modern Muslim practice in order to demonstrate that the French emphasis on Muslim bodily practices, so central to their imaginings of Islam and Muslims, did not emerge entirely out of French imaginaries of Islam. Practices related to the body, such as alimentary restrictions, do indeed play an important role in Islam, for their "observance . . . is a strategic component of well-being because [they] demand the subjugation of physical appetites and passions."[19] However, for many French scholars of Islam, embodied practices were only identified as arcane and as lacking spiritual significance. Furthermore, these practices were said to be so integral to Muslims' everyday lives that they could not possibly accommodate the distinction between private and public lives that twentieth-century *laïcité* required. Unlike the bodily practices of Jews and Catholics, then, those of Muslims were indissociable from their very being and could not be confined to the private sphere; they would by definition impinge on Muslims' actions in public.

Many influential French politicians and intellectuals in the late nineteenth and early twentieth centuries were incapable of imagining North Africans as anything but Muslim. While some early nineteenth-century observers held out hope for the possibility of the assimilation of Muslim peoples, by the twentieth century colonial policy makers and ethnographers were beginning to wonder if such a thing was possible. Thus, at the moment of the Algerian conquest, colonial administrators and military leaders preached the exposure of Muslims to French civilization, which would eventually allow them to move beyond the "tenacious" grasp of race and tradition.[20] Alexis de Tocqueville noted in 1837, before being formally commissioned to conduct an investigation of the French colonial project in 1841, that "nothing . . . indicates to me that there is any incompatibility of temperament between the Arabs and us. . . . During peacetime, the two races mingle painlessly and as they get to know each other better, they grow closer . . . all the young Arab generation of Algiers speaks our language and has already adopted some of our manners."[21] In this vision, Muslim subjects could slowly become French through carefully designed policies that would enable them to evolve into modern individuals and leave behind their traditional practices, religious and otherwise. Yet decades later, Louis Massignon, whose career led him from the Collège de France to a series of diplomatic postings in the Muslim world, would question the likelihood of Tocqueville's predictions, arguing that "we must consider the extent to which western social order can associate itself with Muslims in the social defense of their traditional society, in the rules of their communal life, of their patrimony as believers."[22]

What was the "traditional society" that Massignon feared would be so impenetrable? In the case of Algeria, some turn-of-the-century *islamologues,* such as Le Châtelier, claimed that signs of Muslim observance were becoming less visible. Le Châtelier reported that the acceptance of European sartorial codes, the smoking of tobacco, and the drinking of alcohol signaled a decline of religious sentiment. Increasingly, Muslims were educated in French rather than Quranic schools, which he claimed meant that many people remained relatively ignorant of basic religious principles and of classical Arabic. Patronage of *confréries* (Sufi brotherhoods) and *marabouts* (Muslim religious leaders or teachers) was on the wane. For Le Châtelier and his colleagues, this was clear proof that "'fanaticism' was declining and the light of reason was penetrating Muslim Algeria."[23] Yet as French historian Charles-Robert Ageron reminds us, the observations of Le Châtelier must be contextualized: he and his peers were men whose political and professional lives depended on the successful assimilation of Muslim populations to *laïc* French values.

In the first decades of the twentieth century, when *Islam français* was created, France's North and West African territories were diverse spaces whose populations' varied practices of Islam took many forms. It seems unlikely, however, that Le Châtelier's conclusions were correct in reference to Algeria or any of France's other African territories. A more apt description may come from Clifford Geertz's analysis of Moroccan Islam in the 1960s as "the Islam of saint-worship and moral severity, magical power and aggressive piety."[24] Scholars of Islam working in North and West Africa at the turn of the century such as René Basset, Edmond Doutté, and Alfred Bel spoke of an Islam on the rise. They argued that the advent of Christianity served only to increase Algerians' devotion to Islam and encourage a veritable Muslim renaissance in rural and urban areas among both Berbers and Arabs. Practices such as the use of prayer beads, the public recitation of prayers, pilgrimages to the graves of particular saints, and local feast days and sacrifices were widespread. Again, as Ageron points out, these observers were hardly in a position to analyze these practices as a response to French colonialism and the encounter with Christianity because they had no means to compare them to precolonial customs. He argues that this school of analysis, in which all Algerians lived an Islam that was "paganism badly disguised in Quranic clothes" and that revolved around colorful local folk practices, was as misguided as the one that identified Algerian Muslims as entirely *laïc* subjects.[25] Ageron suggests that we should neither "overestimate the very selective evidence of religious indifference which was particular to the rare case of Frenchified urban dwellers, nor should we believe in a marked progress of orthodox Islam."[26]

Ageron's insistence on contextualizing the interested observations of French *islamologues* and rejection of an image of predominantly secular or predominantly orthodox North Africans is appropriate, yet it ignores the "saint worship" Islam of which Geertz wrote, which could be said to represent the religious beliefs and practices of many Maghrébins during the early part of the twentieth century. The distinction between "folk" and "orthodox" Islam was of great concern to French observers. Edmond Doutté, a professor at the Faculty of Letters in Algiers, succinctly summarized the commonplace distinction made between these two Islams in Algeria and Morocco:

> Morocco, closed in upon itself, isolated until now from [Christianity], conserves the type [of Muslim civilization] almost unchanged, after centuries. Maybe it is not even an exaggeration to consider this country as that which has kept the purest Muslim civilization. Algeria offers us the experiment which is taking place before our eyes, the contact of Islam with a superior civilization and their mutual co-penetration.[27]

Yet even in "pure" Morocco, Doutté admitted, "the old beliefs still exist," giving rise to the carnivalesque celebration of Achoura, the Muslim new year, rather than the mourning rituals prescribed by Orthodox Islam.[28] The distinction between "folk" Islam and "orthodox" Islam could be quite tenuous: in Morocco, for example, sacrifice rituals and feast days often centered on the sultan, whose status as a descendant of the Prophet conferred *Baraka*, or intense "supernatural powers."[29] Morocco's theologians and religious scholars participated in the celebration of the person of the sultan, bringing *Baraka* into the realm of "official" practice as well. Doutté's explanation for the phenomenon of saint worship lay in the fact that "Allah is too far from the believer; he is separated by an abyss and the Muslim seems like a toy in his God's hand." In addition, he argues, the Maghreb has always, since ancient times, engaged in a "veritable adoration of man, of anthropolatry," which naturally evolved into the worship of local saints and the acceptance of marabout leadership.[30]

In West Africa too, older rituals continued to be performed, whether designated as Muslim practices or not. Thus Mouloud, the holiday that celebrates the Prophet's birthday, was observed as Tabaski, a Wolof fetishist holiday. The consultation of sorcerers and the wearing of amulets continued. Burial practices in particular conserved a distinctly local, pre-Islamic character rather than conforming to the Muslim rituals of North Africa and the Middle East: other than in Saint-Louis, Senegal, graves were not oriented towards Mecca and marked with stones.[31] The role of Sufi brotherhoods, disparaged by Algerian reformers and French observers alike, was also a source of French concern in West Africa. Marabouts, Sufi Muslim religious leaders, were seen by the French colonial administration as potential partners in governance but also an internal menace. Marabouts were accused of fomenting dissent and encouraging supernatural beliefs and peddling magical objects to credulous believers. Yet at the same time, this non-Orthodox form of Muslim religious practice was a comforting bulwark for the French against the threat of a more doctrinal form that was beginning to emerge elsewhere in the Muslim world. As Governor-General William Ponty wrote in 1911, "Luckily the Islam of our West Africa still retains a rather special character which we have the greatest interest in preserving. Our Muslims have not yet accepted the pure Coran, whatever their devotions they have wanted to preserve their ancestral customs."[32] What Ponty was not able to understand or acknowledge was that the "ancestral customs" that the marabouts were said to encourage among West African Muslims were deeply imbedded in the Sufi brotherhoods (such as the Qadiriyya and the Tidjaniyyah) that spread across North and West Africa. Furthermore, the Islam of many West Africans in the early twentieth century was a *chosen* Islam. As French historian of West African Islam Jean-Louis Triaud explains, unlike the majority-Muslim Maghreb, West Africa saw enclaves of Islam surrounded by peoples practicing other religions.[33] Those who followed marabouts were drawn to Islam largely because of the men themselves. Marabouts functioned as leaders, religious guides, healers, and teachers, and, like the sultan of Morocco or like saints, they were full of *Baraka*.[34]

Sufi leaders and their followers troubled not only French administrators in some cases, but also Muslim reformers. The Algerian villagers who described their former harvest festivals with some discomfort to French historian Fanny Colonna in the 1970s explained that Muslim scholars had taught them to turn away from such practices. As one villager told her, "Common people don't know how to distinguish [between the licit and illicit], and need men of culture and religion to tell them."[35] The "men of religion" to whom her informant referred would most likely have been members of the Ouléma, an Algerian reformist group that sought to restructure Algerian society through a rejection of French modernity and a "return" to orthodox, scriptural Islam.[36] The Ouléma's criticisms of the forms of Islam practiced by most Algerian Muslims were almost as scathing as the remarks of French *islamologues* dismissing their practices as folklore: the Islam of Algerian peasants was identified as degenerate. As Colonna points out, "What the reformists called *ignorance* covered more or less the religion and the ordinary way of life of peasants in those years . . . of the ways of celebrating life and death."[37]

The Algerian reformers who were so dismissive of popular religious practice were trying to reform a doctrinal Islam that they believed had seriously declined in their country. Led by Cheikh 'Abd al-Hamid Ben Badis, the best-known Sunni Muslim reformist in North Africa, the Ouléma mounted cultural campaigns designed to renew Muslim Algerian society through instruction in Islam and Arabic and through connections to religious reformers in the wider Muslim world. In his classic work on the Ouléma, historian Ali Merad identifies the isolation of Algerian Islam not as the result of the French presence but with a rupture between Algeria and the rest of the Muslim world. Algerian Islam, Merad writes, "was almost closed to any regenerating influence" and depended exclusively on the three official *médersas*, or Muslim religious schools, which sought to "renew traditional Islamic education by enriching it with modern acquisitions and methods."[38] The reformist movement, given new blood by visits from Egyptian theologians, attracted attention throughout Algeria's different Muslim communities during the interwar years. Ben Badis and the Ouléma led campaigns against marabouts and Sufi brotherhoods and were furiously disappointed when local Muslim leaders sought and received permission from French authorities in Constantine to organize a *zarda* in a cemetery.[39] He expressed grave disapproval in a letter published in a French-language local newspaper, arguing that "the cemetery is a sacred place of prayer and contemplation, which must not be turned into a place of celebrations which are not in conformity with the Muslim religion."[40] Advocates of reform included individuals like Ibnou Zekri, a Kabyle Muslim scholar, who saw the opportunity to reform the *zaouias* (Sufi brotherhoods) in Kabylie, which he argued were at the heart of the divisions within Kabyle society:

> For a long time Kabyles have resigned themselves to submitting (after consenting on the basis of their traditions and their beliefs) to the marabouts in general, and to the personnel of the *zaouia* like the

> *moqaddem* and the *chioukh* of diverse religious orders in particular, and to venerate and protect sacred places.
>
> The *zaouia* . . . serve as places for orientation and counsel . . . they are the Mecca of the Kabyles. They do not hesitate to confide their confidences, their wishes, their problems. The *walis* and the other magicians play the role of supreme prophets, they believe deeply in all the declarations and magical practices of their "*sufis*" who are in fact nothing other than ignoramuses and heretics.
>
> The Kabyle *zaouia* are often the sites of horrible spectacles, the satanic preachings of their imams often create internal disputes and battles inside the *zaouia* and provoke a general flare-up in villages and other tribes. In short, the flames of heresy have always generated a climate of tension between Kabyle tribes.[41]

Ibnou Zekri's disdain for the nondoctrinal forms of Muslim practices among his Kabyle peers was echoed and expanded in the Ouléma's condemnation of Arab Algerian urban proletarians' slow abandonment of orthodox practices and embrace of metropolitan vices like alcohol and prostitution. James McDougall argues that there was nothing new about the Ouléma's attempt to impose moral authority over Algeria's Muslims, but their innovation lay in their attempt to become the unique arbiter of moral and religious authority over all members of the community.[42] The Ouléma's struggle to reform Algerian Islam has been argued to be foundational for Algerian anticolonial nationalism by some historians and a purely religious movement by others.[43] While this book does not seek to write the history of Algerian nationalism or Muslim reformist movements, it is nevertheless important to recognize the link that Ben Badis and the Ouléma created between Algerian identity and a reformed Islam. This association would later be taken up by the FLN during the Algerian War, as we will see in chapter 5.

From the reformist Islam of the Ouléma to the "folkloric" Islam its leaders criticized, most French observers agreed that Islam dominated all aspects of individual existence. Doutté put it succinctly when he wrote, "The expression 'Muslim civilization' is justified because in this civilization religion is preponderant: it invades public *and* private life."[44] He argued that everything from the arts to agriculture to state structures is based on Muslim belief. If, as Doutté argued, "religious prescriptions cover all actions, and man is incapable of behaving well using only his own reason . . . the State intervenes in private life" to ensure adherence to Muslim law.[45] Thus whether individual metropolitan and colonial administrators and academics may have disagreed over developments in Muslim religious beliefs and practices in any given

French territory, they all believed firmly that Islam was a faith in which the private and public sphere were inextricably linked.

While it is difficult to speak authoritatively about the practices and beliefs of North and West African Muslims in the first decades of the twentieth century, it is clear that their Islams, as opposed to those of the scripturalist reformers, bore little resemblance to the *Islam français* of the Mosquée de Paris. Some of their practices, especially the rituals surrounding saints' tombs or seasonal processions, were indeed associated with embodied rituals that needed to be performed in particular times and places. Yet they certainly did not suggest a rigid adherence to orthodox practices. Throughout the twentieth century, there was a chasm between the *Islam français* of the Mosquée de Paris and the Islams practiced (or not) by immigrants from North and West Africa, as will be demonstrated in the chapters to come. In the 1920s, Moroccan Islam was taken as the model for *Islam français,* yet the working-class immigrants living in the suburbs of Paris did not conform to this orthodox vision. As a Moroccan colonial official who conducted sociological research in that particular community in 1930 reported to his superiors in Rabat, "All these Berbers who are in France, we can't tell them they're not Muslim. They are, and they say they are. But their religion is 'on the back burner.'"[46] By the late 1940s, French observers were anxious about a decline in Algerian Muslims' religious practices, which they viewed as a negative development, for it was accompanied by the adoption of undesirable "Western" practices such as the consumption of alcohol. West Africans arriving in France in the late 1960s and 1970s practiced an Islam that was seen by French social workers as so unorthodox that it required much effort to "recognize the Black Muslim as the Arab Muslim's brother."[47] The diverse practices associated with the peoples of North and West Africa did not, in fact, inform the designating of some groups of colonial immigrants as "Muslim."

Religion, Race, and Rights: Muslim Immigrants in the French Melting Pot

Muslim individuals, like Islam itself, occupied different spaces in the French juridical sphere across North Africa. A small minority of the non-European residents of North and West Africa were French citizens, but the vast majority of them were French subjects. They had French nationality with none of the attending rights of citizenship. With the exception of the Four Communes of Senegal, whose residents were automatically naturalized in 1848,[48] Muslims in North and West Africa were subject to the so-called Code d'indigénat, or Native Code, and did not have access to French law. The

Native Code was not, in fact, an empire-wide systemic code for the administration of subject populations. Rather, each territory's administrators devised their own regulations, including identifying crimes and their punishments. This ad-hoc judicial system for subjects of the French empire would remain in place until 1928 in Algeria and 1946 in the rest of the empire.[49]

In Algeria, the initial Royal Ordinance of 1834 proclaimed after the new colony's annexation to France made Muslims and Jews French subjects, though subsequent legislation would distinguish between Muslims and "Arabs of the Jewish faith."[50] The Sénatus-Consulte of 1865 confirmed that Algerian Muslims were French nationals governed by Muslim law, rather than French citizens governed by French civil law.[51] It was argued that Muslim law was incompatible with French law, especially with respect to marriage and divorce, and thus Muslims could not possibly be considered eligible for citizenship.[52] The decree created the possibility for Algerians to become naturalized French citizens, yet this was conditional on their rejection of their Muslim personal legal status, which was unthinkable for many people.[53] Only 371 Muslims were naturalized between 1865 and 1875. In contrast to their Muslim fellow nationals, Algerian Jews were given citizenship *en masse* five years after the Sénatus-Consulte. The Crémieux Decree of 1870 thus created a firm distinction between Algeria's indigenous Muslims and Jews and confirmed the argument that Muslims were not capable of French citizenship. The next significant legislation to attempt to define the legal status of Algerian Muslims was the law of 4 February 1919 that enumerated a new series of conditions for requesting French citizenship, for which all but a tiny minority of Muslims continued to be ineligible.[54] Those *indigènes* who qualified for full citizenship but refused to abandon their Muslim personal status, however, were now identified as indigenous citizens, a "demi-naturalized" status in between citizen and subject.[55] This law implicitly acknowledged that most Algerians, although French nationals, would never become French citizens and as such laid out a program for their political representation. Certain civic rights normally associated with citizenship were extended to Algerians as French nationals, including representation in Algeria's assemblies by elected members and access to government posts.[56] The Blum-Viollette project of 1936, designed to stave off nationalist agitation, promised to expand the possibilities offered by the Law of 1919 by offering the right to vote to a larger proportion of Algerians as well as proposing French citizenship without having to renounce one's Muslim status.[57] But the Popular Front's project to encourage the integration of Muslim elites failed due to conservative opposition in the metropole and Algeria (including opposition from some Algerian nationalists and religious leaders).

For Moroccan Muslims living under the French protectorate, there was initially no special legislation that identified them as nationals or citizens.[58] Muslims, like Jews, continued to be subject to Muslim and Jewish religious law rather than French civil law, and both remained formally under the authority of the Makhzen rather than the French colonial administration.[59] Under the Tunisian protectorate, on the other hand, Muslims had slightly more access to the rights of French citizenship. An 1887 law granted citizenship to those who provided services to France (in the army or in public office), and automatic naturalization was granted in 1923.[60] In French West Africa, only residents of the Four Communes of Senegal, which occupied a unique place within the federation, were nominally French citizens. Laws passed during the French Revolution (and again in 1848 and 1871) allowed them to elect deputies to the National Assembly and to be judged in the French justice system.[61] Thus when the federation's justice system was established in 1903, it stipulated that French law would apply only to non-Muslims in the Communes and other major cities, while African "customary" law would apply in rural areas to regulate the lives of African subjects. However, the 1903 code also permitted French justice to intervene in the "customary" sphere when practices clearly violated the principles of French republicanism, such as engaging in slavery.[62] For those residents of Afrique occidentale française (AOF) who were not residents of the Communes, a law passed in 1912 made it possible for certain "exceptional" Africans to acquire French citizenship on the basis of their assimilation to French culture and proven loyalty to the colonial state.[63] Nationality and citizenship, then, did not often coincide in the French empire.

Muslims who immigrated to the metropole were thus both more and less French than other immigrants to France during the first half of the twentieth century. While they may have possessed French nationality, it was easier for European immigrants to acquire French citizenship than it was for colonial subjects.[64] The second-tier status of immigrants from North and eventually West Africa would shape most aspects of their daily lives as immigrants to the metropole over the course of the twentieth century. While elite Muslims had long come to France as tourists or temporary residents, working-class Algerians, the metropole's earliest Muslim immigrants, began to arrive in numbers large enough to register shortly after the turn of the century.[65] Most estimates suggest that as early as 1912 there were approximately three thousand Algerians working in Marseille, Paris, and in the North. In 1913, France abolished the travel permit formerly required of Algerians, which allowed them to circulate freely between metropole and colony. The advent of the First World War meant that in addition to workers immigrating independently, the Ministry of War brought colonial workers to the metropole to compensate for labor shortages through the Organizational Service for Colonial Workers (Service d'organisation des travailleurs coloniaux, SOTC).[66] Over the course of World War I, approximately eighty thousand workers from Algeria lived in France,[67] though the authorities repatriated the workers (and soldiers) who had been brought to France by the SOTC after the Armistice. Yet because Algerians were still allowed to circulate freely across the Mediterranean, men continued to immigrate to France, seeking jobs in the reconstruction effort. Approximately twenty thousand men emigrated in 1920, but by 1924 that figure had increased to seventy thousand.[68] By November of 1924, the French state limited Algerian mobility in response to concerns that the colony's workforce was being depleted by emigration. But these restrictions, in the form of additional requirements such as work permits, medical visits, identity cards, and other measures did not halt illegal immigration: the Algerian population had risen as high as 85,568 by the early 1930s.[69] In spite of the quasi-legal nature of much of this immigration, the interwar years saw the creation of a colonially inspired (as well as former colonial officer–staffed) surveillance and social assistance apparatus designed to keep the North African population distinct from the French one. It also saw the flowering of Paris-based Algerian nationalist movements, such as Messali Hadj's Étoile Nord-Africaine (North African Star), which opposed the colonial management of North Africans on both sides of the Mediterranean, as will be discussed in chapter 2.

Islam and *Laïcité*

The law of 1905 is often considered to be the hallmark of French *laïcité,* which is said to have no direct equivalent in English but is usually translated as "secularism."[70] The controversial law was not the first to legally dismantle certain powers of the Church in the regulation of public life in France; earlier legislation had already provided for free secular public education and secular hospitals. Yet it is credited with ushering in a new era of state management of religion and creating a firm boundary between the public and private spheres in France. However, even after the law of 1905 this boundary was still somewhat porous concerning state funding for religious sites, religious associations, and religious education. Nor was the law of 1905 applied uniformly across French territory: it was neither applied in Alsace and Lorraine, which at the time were German possessions, nor, more importantly, was it applied in the same manner in Algeria as in metropolitan France.[71] I have argued earlier that although the relationship between the French state and Muslims was often mediated through the language of religion, ultimately Islam was a marker of racialized rather than religious difference for North Africans. Nevertheless, it is essential to understand the historical trajectory of secularism in France as well as the place it occupies in French national mythology in order to understand why debates about Islam were shaped as they were.

The Concordat between the Pope and the French state of 1802 is often viewed as the first step toward *laïcité.* The Concordat applied to Catholicism, Reformed Protestantism, and Lutheranism (it did not apply to Judaism until 1808), which were known as the *cultes reconnus,* or officially recognized religions.[72] The agreement between France and the Vatican stated that as Roman Catholicism was the religion of the large majority of French citizens, the government of the republic would guarantee its free exercise in France

and that it would be "public" as long as it conformed to police regulations. Thus Catholicism, Protestantism, Lutheranism, and Judaism theoretically existed together in a newly neutral public sphere, and religious pluralism, at least at the official level, was celebrated. Each religion's clergy were identified equally and salaried as "*ministres du culte,*" even though the roles they played in each faith were quite different.[73] Judaism, France's other "foreign" minority religion, was fitted into the logic of *laïcité* differently than Islam. Judaism entered the Concordat in 1808 thanks to three decrees signed by Napoleon; this inclusion also involved the creation of the Grand Sanhédrin, an intermediary body designed to represent the Jewish community to the state and to regulate its internal affairs. It was at this moment that Judaism was transformed into "*israélitisme,*" which is to say that Judaism was reduced to a denomination, like Catholicism, and robbed of its power to regulate other aspects of life.[74] Jean Baubérot also emphasizes the shaping of Judaism to fit a Catholic mold, arguing that at the time of these decrees "religion" was commonly understood as "Catholicism."[75]

The law of 1905 dismantled the Concordat system of *cultes reconnus* in its second article, which stated that the Republic did not recognize or subsidize any faith. The law did not deny churches' right to exist, it merely signaled a departure from the Napoleonic tradition. Churches were no longer public institutions and could no longer intervene in the functioning of the state. What seemed straightforward in the language of the law itself was considerably more complicated in its application, particularly as regarded *associations culturelles* and *associations cultuelles.* The law of 1901 made it possible for any legally declared *cultural* association to receive aid from the French government at national and local levels. The law of 1905 created the "*association cultuelle,*" which was exclusively religious and thus ineligible for any kind of state support. However, the law of 1907 permitted 1901 cultural associations to be religious as long as that was not their only defining characteristic (so a Catholic sports association, for example, could be subsidized in all legality). As will be discussed in the following chapter, these juridical distinctions made it essential to change the status of the Société des Habous, the transnational association of elite Muslims that was technically responsible for the administration of the Mosquée, from that of an association registered in Algiers under Muslim law to one registered in France as a 1901 cultural association eligible for state funding.

Another important consideration was the juridical status of religious sites after 1905. The law of 2 January 1907 transferred all religious buildings (and their contents) constructed before 1905 to the *commune*. The sites were to be given permanently and freely to the members of the religion and their clergy for their use, but no construction or renovation could be done without the agreement of the *commune* that owned the site. Religious buildings constructed after 1905, however, were the private property of the religious community that had built it. Thus *communes* were financially responsible for the maintenance and conservation of sites built before 1905 but could not legally finance any repairs for those built after 1905.[76] Yet it was still possible for the state, the *département,* or the *commune* indirectly to finance the construction of religious edifices through the *bail emphytéotique,* a long-term lease for a building of up to ninety-nine years that confers legal rights to the leaseholder. The rent for such leases is almost always symbolic; it was usually one franc per year.

Thus the separation of church and state as enshrined in the law of 1905 was not as firm as it first appeared, as funding for religious schooling and places of worship, as well as for associations with a religious character, was still permitted under certain circumstances. The story of *laïcité* in the case of Islam and the Mosquée de Paris is further complicated if we take into account the regime of exception to the law of 1905 that was enacted in Algeria. Prior to 1905, the policy of the French administration was, theoretically, to protect and preserve Muslim religious practices. The incorporation of Muslim religious patrimony, known as *habous* (including mosques, land, and libraries), into the public domain in order to finance religious activities also placed France in the position of providing allocations for Muslim religious practices. As in the metropole prior to 1905, the state played an active role in the management of religious affairs, and the law separating church and state should have had a strong impact on Islam in Algeria after 1905. Yet what remained somewhat ambiguous in the metropole was applied even more ambiguously in Algeria. Article 43 of the law of 1905 states that "public administrative rulings will determine the conditions under which this law will be applicable in Algeria and the colonies." The *décret* of 27 September 1907, which was created precisely to clarify the conditions referred to above, stated that the governor-general could, "in the public and national interest, allocate temporary indemnities" to *ministres de culte* handpicked by him. The *décret* set limits to these temporary subventions,[77] but a series of subsequent decisions prolonged these "temporary" exceptions repeatedly.[78] After the passage of these laws and decrees, French colonial administrators could no longer directly nominate men for various posts within the Muslim religious establishment, nor could they be directly responsible for the maintenance of Muslim religious sites. Informally, however, departmental authorities continued to play a significant role in shaping Muslim religious affairs. Article 13 of the 1907 decree provided for the creation of religious associations for managing Muslim life in Algeria, and in many cases legal stewardship over mosques and shrines was granted to these Muslim associations, whose budgets depended on that of the colony. James McDougall has suggested that for French colonial leaders, "the creation of the *cultuelles* [religious associations] was an attempt to respect the letter of the law while retaining effective control," including the right to veto troubling candidates.[79] Yet at the same time, he argues that the Algerian Muslim notables who held lay or religious positions of authority within the associations "were not simple *beni oui-oui* ('yes-men'), administration stooges lacking caliber or interests of their own" and that some of them were able to turn the associations into spaces of "ungovernable local politics."[80] As Raberh Achi has argued, the gulf between state neutrality with regard to religion as promised in the law of 1905 and the administrative reality of the regime of exceptions of the 1907 decree also allowed the Oulèma to mobilize for a genuine separation of church and state in Algeria that would allow other Muslim associations to hold the powers currently claimed by official clerics.[81]

The common misperception that the law of 1905 was simply not applied in Algeria thus needs to be clarified, as does the consequences of the law for the development of Muslim religious life in the colony: what was applied was a version of the law with built-in exceptions that did not exist in the metropole. There were tensions involved in the application of the law of 1905 in Algeria: at stake was the continuity between republican ideology in metropole and colony; the fear that the law would stigmatize only Catholicism but leave Islam untouched; and finally, the political consequences of withdrawing state funding for Catholic churches given that "foreign" clergy (naturalized Italians and Spaniards) would continue to receive financial support from their home countries. However, the overwhelming consideration was that complete neutrality in the realm of state intervention in religious affairs would constitute a dangerous risk for French authority over Islam and hence over Algeria.[82]

The migration of colonial subjects to the metropole beginning at the time of the First World War meant that the management of Islam in the secular republic needed to be considered in the larger context of French debates about labor immigration. American historian Elisa Camiscioli argues that "while Jews, colonized people, and white immigrants alike were racialized in early twentieth-century France, the weight assigned to this racialization was not the same."[83] The same is true, I would argue, of the modes of racialization: for only in the Muslim case would it be that religion would form the basis of that racialization. Camiscioli cites Marcel Paon, the head of the Ministry of Agriculture's Labor and Immigration Service, who claimed that "religious background is quite secondary in our country, which is profoundly liberal on this subject. . . . A much greater fixity is to be found in the immigrant's racial background."[84] Paon's words provide an interesting window into the contradictions of French immigration policy: while republican logic should have been equally blind to the religious *and* racial origin of potential immigrants, both of these factors played a role in the French state's decision about whom to let in, and when. The government's attitude toward Islam and Muslim immigrants must be considered not only in light of its treatment of other immigrants of different backgrounds but also with respect to its policies toward the religious communities already in France.

France was already a country of migrations, both internal and external, during the nineteenth century. It was during the interwar years, however, that France opened its borders to immigration from all over Europe and the empire in the hopes of resolving two major crises: the fears of depopulation that emerged after World War I and the ever-increasing need for workers. Yet politicians, social scientists, and employers were not willing to accept *any* immigrants: the question of repopulating France was too important not to require an immigration policy that would encourage the immigration of peoples judged to be racially compatible with the French. As the influential Dr. René Martial, the immigration specialist at the Institut d'hygiène de la Faculté de médecine de Paris, explained, xenophobic attacks on immigration were misguided. In a France ravaged by depopulation, he argued, immigration was essential for the country's very survival. The question for him was simply how to define "desirable" immigrants based on their racial characteristics, their cultural proximity to French society, their health, their intelligence, and their morality.[85] As Camiscioli explains, the need to generate French offspring meant that questions of immigration could not simply be considered in light of labor needs: while colonial workers could help with France's labor shortage, they were not appropriate candidates to renew a dwindling population. Italians, Poles, and Spaniards were promoted as the ideal immigrants to respond to both of France's needs, and they made up about 60 percent of the total immigrant population in 1931, thanks to treaties the French government had signed with the leaders of the respective countries to regulate labor immigration to France. Less desirable were Armenians, Greeks, and Eastern European Jews, who were said to be "very different" from the French and thus less easily assimilated. North Africans, however, were to be avoided at all costs as permanent immigrants, for their assimilation was said to be "nearly impossible," according to a natalist demographic survey.[86] This impossibility stemmed not only from racial difference but also from religious difference: Martial explained that "a Muslim's every gesture, every thought, is grounded, however distantly, in religion."[87]

Yet as French historian of immigration Ralph Schor has argued, that Italians, Poles and Spaniards were European and Catholic did not necessarily lead them to assimilate as easily as natalists suggested they should. Their Catholic practices were not identical to those of their French neighbors and colleagues, and they often attended services at their "own" churches rather than at the local church. Furthermore, it was sometimes the case that immigrants who were not particularly religious ended up in a staunchly Catholic neighborhood, or, on the other hand, a group of deeply observant Catholics arrived in "Catholic" France to find themselves surrounded by non-practicing French. Foreign Catholics who did engage in daily and holiday religious practices were sometimes able to pray at their own "national" church but other times made use of a small area of the local church that a priest had allowed them to use when available. Their employers, especially large companies, sponsored the voyages of religious leaders from their employees' home countries, constructed and maintained religious sites, and paid priests' salaries.[88]

In some ways, the experience of Muslim immigrants to France in the twentieth century mirrored those of Catholic, Protestant, and Jewish European immigrants. Muslims, too, often had to pray in someone else's sacred space and were sometimes led in prayer by an employer-sponsored clergyman. The crucial difference, however, is that no other immigrant religious sites were financed by the state, only Muslim ones. The French government was not willing to compromise the law of 1905, which prohibits the state's funding of religious institutions, for European Catholic immigrants. Nor did it finance the construction of synagogues; these were built with funds from France's Jewish communities. I argue that this is a reflection of the fact that European Catholics, European Protestants, and even European Jews were ultimately considered as potential secular French people: should they choose to engage in religious practices, they were free to do so with their own resources. Muslims, on the other hand, did not have the potential to become secular and thus required a different commitment from the French state. This commitment was born not only of the French belief in the immutable physicality of Islam but also of the different relationship with Muslim immigrants: North Muslims were under the "protection" of the French imperial republic in a way that European Christian and Jewish immigrants were not. The question of how to accommodate Muslim religious practice after the separation of church and state was intimately tied to debates about immigration.

I have argued in this chapter that in the early part of the twentieth century Islam and Muslims occupied liminal spaces in French law and immigration politics, especially compared with other religious "minorities" in the French empire and with non-French immigrants to the metropole. This liminality was based in the perception that Islam's embodied practices fashioned Muslims into people whose difference was in fact innate, even though it appeared to be based in religious practices. The location of this racialized difference in Muslim identity would engender debates about the "Muslim exception" to secularism after the passage of the law of 1905 in the early discussions of the plan to build a mosque in Paris during the First World War, as we will see in the following chapter.

CHAPTER 2

Un monument durable: Building the Mosquée de Paris and Institut Musulman

The Mosquée de Paris and Institut Musulman were first conceived as a war memorial to be built in the shadow of Les Invalides, but they ultimately became a temple to *Islam français,* built in the heart of the Latin Quarter. Locating the complex near France's shrine to its military victories was intended to reflect the sacrifices made by North and West African colonial soldiers during the First World War, as well as to render the complex easily accessible to elite Muslims visiting Paris. The architecture of this "durable monument" was expected to conform to the "artistic demands" of a grand capital.[1] The Mosquée's proponents hoped that the permanence of such a gesture was intended to differentiate the project from the army's makeshift mosques and prayer sites, which had been built in hospitals and military camps. Unlike these sequestered, temporary sites invisible to those outside the encampments, the Mosquée de Paris was to be one of the capital's landmarks.

When the ground for the construction site was broken six years later, in the 5th *arrondissement* across from the Jardin des Plantes, the site had been reimagined as a reproduction of a mosque in Fez that would be built alongside French civilization's most hallowed institutions of learning rather than the shrine to its military successes. The Mosquée de Paris and Institut Musulman were the fruits of contentious collaboration involving the Ministry of the Interior, the Ministry of Foreign Affairs, the Ministry of War, the city of

Paris, and the colonial and protectoral administrations of Algeria, Morocco, Tunisia, and French West Africa. In addition to the metropolitan and colonial administrations, a group of elite Muslims from the Maghreb participated in the elaboration of this project.

The placement of the Mosquée's complex in the 5th *arrondissement,* the cradle of French civilization, and its "Muslim architectural character" signaled visually the tension between its role as a secular cultural and religious institution that defined the paradox of *Islam français.* In this chapter, I argue that the Mosquée was designed to embody "*Islam français,*" the particular vision of Islam that blended Muslim and French civilizations. *Islam français* inscribed Islam firmly within a French republican and *laïc* model, yet it simultaneously maintained Islam outside the boundaries set by *laïcité.* The architectural and aesthetic plans for the Mosquée, as well as the events that marked the milestones in its development, were essential to the creation and diffusion of *Islam français.*

Wartime Gestures: Islam and Colonial Soldiers

The Mosquée, ostensibly a memorial to recognize the sacrifices of France's Muslim colonial soldiers, was the culmination of a wartime *politique musulmane* in whose elaboration the army played a major role. The predominance of the army in debates about the management of Islam in the empire followed from the integral place soldiers from France's North and West African colonies occupied in the French army during the conflict.[2] Although there was huge participation from Algeria (and, to a lesser extent, Morocco and Tunisia) the symbol *par excellence* of the colonial soldiers in French culture has often been the *tirailleur sénégalais.*[3] Yet the symbol chosen to demonstrate public gratitude for the sacrifices made by these colonial subjects was given a distinctly Moroccan aesthetic character rather than a West African one. Although the image of the *tirailleur sénégalais* may have been used in advertising campaigns, the sacrifices made by these soldiers were not inscribed visually in the site that was, in theory, designed to commemorate their losses.[4] This erasure of West Africa and celebration of North Africa (Morocco, to be precise) reflected the French belief that Moroccan Islam was more civilized than Algerian Islam, not to mention Sub-Saharan African Islam. The celebration of "Moroccan" aesthetics in the Mosquée, as we shall see, was essential to the creation of *Islam français.*

Colonial soldiers were not only subject to a different disciplinary regime than their metropolitan fellow soldiers, but their difference was signaled visually in their uniforms. The *tirailleurs'* khaki uniforms stood out, in their color and their form, from the blue uniforms of the metropolitan *poilus*: colonial soldiers wore long tunics and knee-length puffed pants. Rather than standard headgear, they wore *chechias* that often included a crescent or a crescent and a star.[5] Visible physical differences were thus reinforced by uniforms that were based in Orientalist imaginings of African warriors rather than clothing appropriate for conducting modern warfare. The headgear for colonial soldiers also identified Islam as the main symbol of their difference by using the crescent on their hats, thus conflating racial and colonial otherness under the sign of religion. Tyler Stovall has argued that in "spite of the unprecedented presence of Muslims on French soil . . . religion does not seem to have played a role in the racial violence of World War I."[6] While it is certainly possible that actors engaged in violence against colonial workers or soldiers would not have claimed to be motivated by religious factors, I argue that the conflation of Islam with racial difference embodied and made visible by the soldiers' uniforms complicates Stovall's conclusion, which clearly separates religion and race. "Religion" as such may not have played a role in racial violence, but the racialization of nominally Muslim colonial subjects as "Muslim" through their segregation in the military was an important moment in the creation of *Islam français*.

The gestures made by French army leaders toward their colonial soldiers, such as the construction of a mosque at the military hospital at Nogent-sur-Marne were largely staged around Islam. Thus Muslim burials were performed, imams were brought to minister to recovering soldiers, and North African dishes were prepared according to Muslim dietary law to the extent that it was possible. Of course, not all efforts focused on religion; there were a multitude of other gestures, such as the June 1917 Journée de l'armée de l'Afrique et des troupes coloniales, designed to honor colonial soldiers as well as huge divisional celebrations with music and dance. Colonial soldiers were also given the opportunity to learn French, although North African soldiers were taught formal French while West Africans quickly realized that what they were being taught was pidgin French.[7]

The two most important gestures from this period that were designed to maintain France's preeminent role in the Middle East and North Africa were the construction of a mosque on the grounds of a military hospital at the Jardin Colonial (Nogent-sur-Marne) and the creation of the Société des Lieux Saints de l'Islam, an association of Muslim notables charged with facilitating French subjects' and protégés' participation in the annual pilgrimage to Mecca. The military mosque was a direct response to the threat that German propaganda posed to colonial soldiers' loyalty. As officials at the Quai d'Orsay argued, Germans had built a mosque in their POW camp, giving captured Muslim soldiers "all the facilities necessary to conform to the precepts of their religion," something that was not easily available to them in their own army.[8] The CIAM pronounced its support for the construction of a mosque at the military hospital at its meeting on 2 December 1915, and the Ministries of Foreign Affairs and War also appeared to support such a project. Putting it into practice was another matter, as neither ministry was especially willing to take financial responsibility for the wooden mosque, mortuary room, and sanitary facilities, whose cost was estimated at eight thousand francs. The Ministry of Foreign Affairs was willing to contribute four thousand francs on the assumption that the Ministry of War would make up the difference. The minister of war, however, was wary of providing financial support for the construction of a "religious edifice in a French hospital," as it could potentially constitute a precedent for people of other faiths to make similar demands. He suggested that the Ministry of Foreign Affairs take full responsibility for the project and identify it as overseas propaganda or that the money be requested from the governments of Algeria, Morocco, and Tunisia. This discussion continued, with the minister of foreign affairs arguing that outsourcing the funding for the building of a mosque in France would undermine the project's purpose: to manifest the metropole's recognition of the sacrifices made by Muslim soldiers. He agreed, however, that it would be "inconvenient" for the funding for a religious establishment to come directly from an official budget and that he would thus take it from the "special expenses" section of his ministry's budget. In the end, the Ministry of War was pressed into paying the other four thousand francs necessary for the mosque's construction.[9]

The issues raised by this exchange, including the fear of breaking the relatively recent law of 1905 by providing financial support for a Muslim religious site in the metropole, would come up again on a larger scale in the debates around the construction of the Mosquée de Paris. Yet in spite of the disagreements over the Nogent-sur-Marne project among metropolitan officials, there was general agreement that such a project was not only beneficial but also essential. The specter of the law of 1905 was less an ideological question, it seems, than a purely practical and economic one: the argument was not that the mosque should not be built because it violated the separation of church and state, merely that the funding for it would have to be negotiated in such a way so that it did not *appear* to be a violation of the law of 1905.

The contestation of this project from the other side of the Mediterranean was based on different grounds. The Moroccan position was that such a project undoubtedly held "a foreign policy interest" for the French state but that it would do nothing to create loyalty to France among Moroccan Muslims. The argument advanced by Lyautey's delegate to the minister of foreign affairs was essentially that if a mosque was to be built, its "prestige" would require "a certain atmosphere that would perhaps be missing at Nogent-sur-Marne." In addition, previous experience in Algeria showed that Muslims do not accept mosques built by French hands with French money. This would be the fate of a mosque at the Jardin colonial, he argued; worse, "Would not our indigenous soldiers, who have been able to contemplate the magnificence of our cathedrals, feel themselves to be very poor relations?" The gesture would do more harm than good.[10] Again, the Moroccan resident-general's opposition to a plan devised almost exclusively by metropolitan politicians, colonial lobbyists, and Parisian *indigènophiles* would figure prominently in the planning of the Mosquée. What was at stake, in both cases, was a conflict about who had ultimate authority over decisions regarding Islam in Morocco, whether in the center or on the periphery, and also about what Islam in fact was, could be, or should be.

The creation of the Société des Habous des Lieux Saints de l'Islam emerged from similar preoccupations and involved many of the same actors who played a role in the construction of the mosque at Nogent-sur-Marne. It was the Société des Habous that would be charged with the creation and management of the Mosquée de Paris and Institut Musulman. Created in Algiers in 1917 (and registered under Muslim rather than French law), the association was charged with the acquisition of two hotels in Mecca and Medina to lodge North African Muslims performing the *hajj.* The Société des Habous was overseen by Si Kaddour Ben Ghabrit, a Tlemcen-born Muslim who was serving as the chief of protocol for the Moroccan sultan, who would eventually become the Mosquée's first *recteur.* Its members included Muslim dignitaries from Morocco, Tunisia, and Algeria, with a few members drawn from West Africa. In choosing this Muslim association to be officially responsible for running the Mosquée's affairs, the French state hoped to create the illusion that the project was entirely designed by and intended for its Muslim subjects with almost no intervention from the government.

The CIAM, arguing that "the North African Muslim *indigènes* have a strong desire to see the law providing for the construction of an Institut Musulman in Paris" put into action, thus estimated that it was in France's best interests to move quickly.[11] Yet it was not only the CIAM that lobbied for the Mosquée's construction.[12] Plans to build a mosque in Paris had been afloat since the late nineteenth century, especially around the turn of the century. As early as 1895, the Comité de l'Afrique française began lobbying for such a project, even going so far as to select the building's architects. Paul

Bourdarie of the *Revue Indigène* explained this initiative's failure by noting that "it seemed that North Africa's Muslim question was not yet well-known enough in France, and that France's politics in Algeria created even bigger obstacles."[13] The circle of *indigènophiles* who made up the *Revue Indigène* and a number of Muslim dignitaries began to revisit this question during the war, eventually forming a committee whose existence was approved by the CIAM. This committee, headed by Senator Edouard Herriot, consulted with eminent Muslims such as the Jeunes Algériens (Young Algerians) Emir Khaled (Khaled ben El Hachemi), who was the grandson of the Algerian leader Emir Abdelkader; and Dr. Benthami Ould Hamida, a pharmacist who would go on to play an important role at the Franco-Muslim Hospital in Bobigny.[14] The Jeunes Algériens, whose name echoed other modernizing movements in the Arabo-Muslim world, sought equality for Muslim Algerians within the colonial framework, and Herriot, whose sympathy for the Young Algerians was well known, sought to collaborate with members of the French-educated Muslim elite interested in association with France.[15] Herriot's committee also reached an agreement with an architect interested in designing the Mosquée, a certain Tronquois. In this original plan, the complex containing the Mosquée would include not only the prayer site but also a memorial fountain, a war museum, a library, a medrasa, and a guest house.[16]

Although members of the North African Muslim elite were involved in the initial plans for the Mosquée, the real push to create such an institution was primarily metropolitan with some colonial administrative participation. Metropolitan politicians may have seen this plan as an attempt to coordinate an empire-wide *politique musulmane,* but the involvement of the colonial administrations challenged their exclusive authority to articulate what this should be. These early projects were designed to define a particular *politique musulmane* but not expressly with the aim of creating a French Islam. This would be the work performed by the Mosquée complex itself.

Institut Musulman Vs. Mosquée de Paris: *Laïcité* in Question

The proponents of the Mosquée de Paris and Institut Musulman made both rhetorical and aesthetic distinctions between the Mosquée and the Institut, and these differences offer a way to understand the tensions that underlay the creation of French Islam. I argue that the rationale behind the distinction between the Mosquée, a religious site that would come to be identified with a particular "Moroccan" aesthetic, and the Institut Musulman, an intellectual center for cross-cultural exchanges set in the heart of Paris' Latin Quarter, was not a political ruse to avoid charges of violating the law of 1905.

Certainly, such criticisms were made in the Senate and in the press, and the Mosquée's proponents performed plenty of verbal gymnastics in responding to them. But the true significance of these discussions lay in the attempt to define an Islam that was French, republican, and *laïc* and at the same time based in a set of elite Moroccan religious and aesthetic norms. The site of the Mosquée de Paris and the Institut Musulman was the physical manifestation of the attempt to reconcile these two elements into a new French Islam.

What is most intriguing about the discussions of *laïcité* and the Mosquée's construction is that legally speaking, as we have seen, there was in fact no violation of the law of 1905 in the state's and the city of Paris' attribution of funds to the Société des Habous for the institution's establishment. The delicate maneuverings that surrounded the construction of the Mosquée de Paris were necessary in the sense that as far as the public understood, the French state was paying for the building of a mosque in Paris after the passage of a law prohibiting exactly that. It is for this reason that Herriot, among others, took pains to emphasize that what was actually happening was completely legal and within the realm of accepted practices: the French state was subsidizing a group registered under the law of 1901, which was in turn planning the construction of a multifunctional site that was primarily educational but that would also have a place of worship attached. Herriot's finessing of the *laïcité* question by making a distinction between the Mosquée and Institut Musulman cloaked a more important, and ultimately more contentious, debate about the nature of French Islam.

Although there was overwhelming support for the construction of a mosque in Paris in metropolitan political circles, there were, in the colonial lobby and in the popular press, still strong critiques made on the grounds that state support for a religious institution was a violation of the law of 1905.[17] Some of this opposition came from Catholics, such as this protest in the *Bulletin religieux du diocèse de Bayonne*:

> Among our anticlericals, not a single voice rose up to protest the subsidies, monument, ceremony or government participation [in the ground-breaking ceremony of the Mosquée]. What will become of the state's *laïcité* in this affair? It is outrageously violated . . . and the blows of the pickaxe on the grounds of the minaret are blows to intangible laws. Ah! If it had been a question of a Catholic church, what an uproar there would have been![18]

Similar views were expressed in the Senate during the discussion of the passage of the law of 1920 approving a subsidy to the Société des Habous. After Senator Raphaël-Georges Lévy's impassioned plea to support a law that "does not require financing the entire cost of the construction" of a mosque in "the only large capital which has no mosque," royalist Senator Dominique Delahaye took the floor to defend the rights of Catholics:

> I will not raise my voice against a subsidy for Muslim congregations, because we have Muslims in our protectorates. But in terms of Catholics, we're dispossessing them of their property. . . . It's high time that we started to treat Catholics as well as we treat Muslims.[19]

These critiques reflect not a desire for total neutrality of the state with regards to funding for religious institutions, but rather, that the state fund Catholic institutions in the way that it was perceived to be funding this Muslim institution. Delahaye's statement also speaks to the question of reconciling the law of 1905 in the metropole and in the colonies.[20]

The institutions' supporters responded to critiques voiced openly in the language of *laïcité* on the same grounds, as did Edouard Herriot during the debate at the Assemblée nationale. He argued that "there is no contradiction" inherent in the state's decision to finance the institution. Herriot made his argument in two registers that seem, on the contrary, to be entirely contradictory but ultimately reveal the attempt to reconcile the two halves of *Islam français*. On the one hand, he argued that what the government was sponsoring was not a mosque but an institute which "would be called to study all questions relative to Muslim interests and to the relations between metropole and Muslim colonies or protectorates." Herriot suggested that investing in this type of institution was far more modern and efficient than leaving the regulation of France's Muslim affairs to well-meaning but ill-equipped French functionaries. This argument builds on Bourdarie's original vision of the institute as a scholarly center that would allow for the study of Muslim civilization, law, and history and Arab grammar as well as a site for the exchange of knowledge among Muslim elites, North African colonial administrators, and metropolitan officials. The Institut Musulman as thus described in no way infringed on the law of 1905, since there was no question of funding a religious site. The institute would be a completely secular entity in which questions of religion would be addressed purely on an intellectual level.

Yet on the other hand, and with no apparent difficulty, Herriot also argued that the proposed law would also provide funding for a mosque and that this was perfectly acceptable because "the French state recognizes the right of French citizens in the colonies to practice their religion, whatever it may be. There is no flaw in giving Muslims a mosque, since we very legitimately give churches to Catholics, temples to Protestants and synagogues to Jews."[21] By describing a particular juridical regime in Algeria and using that to stand in for the administration of religion in "the colonies," Herriot sought to justify the state's decision to fund a religious institution. Yet he completely elided the issue of this particular institution's setting in the metropole rather than in the colonies and did not elucidate why the exception made to the law of 1905 in Algeria should be extended to the metropole. Herriot clinched his argument that the state was not violating the law of 1905 by reminding his fellow politicians that the French government was neither directly funding nor administering the Mosquée: the law provided funds to the Société des Habous, who would be legally responsible for the institution. Again, Herriot passed over the complicated legal proceedings that obliged the Société des Habous to change its status from an association governed by Muslim law to a French cultural association under the conditions of the law of 1901 so that it could legally accept funding from the French state.[22] The emphasis on the distance between the state and the Muslim administration of the Mosquée echoes the Comité de l'Institut Musulman's wish that the Institut be the work of "Muslims, friends of Muslims, and the government" but that the Mosquée be "what Muslims themselves choose to make of it."[23] Of course, neither the Institut nor the Mosquée would be what the Muslims themselves made of them; the metropolitan and colonial administrations would be implicated in their management at every level, from the very beginning.

But the question of whether or not the state was violating the laws of *laïcité* was not what truly animated these debates, for the objections on these grounds were relatively few. The real debates occurred among historical actors who took for granted that the state should play an active role in the management of Islam, though they forcefully disagreed on what that role should be. The tensions between metropolitan and colonial ideas of how best to nurture an Islam compatible with their own interests can be seen in the debates over the funding of the institution and the discussions of the construction of the actual site.

The struggle to bring together the money required to finance the project made visible the power struggles among the various French ministries, colonial administrations, and North African notables and portended the future negotiations over the ownership of the Mosquée. Although no one was enthusiastic about providing financial support, once the site's construction was under way, these same actors identified the project as theirs and as a credit to their own relationship to Islam.

Partial funding for the project came from the Assemblée nationale (500,000 francs) through subsidies to the Société des Habous. In addition, the city of Paris donated 1,620,000 francs in the form of the donation of a parcel of land in the 5th *arrondissement,* on the grounds of the former Hôpital de la Pitié.[24] Yet as Si Kaddour continuously reminded anyone who would listen, this amount was not nearly enough for the construction, let alone the upkeep, of the Mosquée-Institut complex. Additionally, it was vital that the Mosquée not be seen to have been constructed by and for the French but by and for Muslims. Thus he argued that the financial support should also come from Muslims, most importantly those in French territories.[25] Si Kaddour, as representative of the Société des Habous, thus waged a difficult campaign with the help of the Ministries of Foreign Affairs and of the Interior to raise money from the North and West African administrations. Meanwhile, Si Kaddour also traveled throughout North Africa meeting with local Muslim leaders to collect "donations" from their communities. As he wrote in a Moroccan newspaper, "The faithful of Morocco, Algeria and Tunisia should give a show of force in donating their individual contributions to help the completion of this grand and noble project" to assure its Muslim character.[26] Yet he also acknowledged the "current economic crisis and the heavy burden of taxes" that weighed down on Muslims in the colonies and consulted with the French administration's financial officers to get an "informed" opinion of the financial status of Moroccan Muslims and their ability to contribute.[27]

Gathering money from the colonial administrations was no less difficult and involved continuous negotiations. Although the Algerian, Moroccan, and Tunisian administrations agreed to devote 150,000, 100,000, and 30,000 francs respectively to the Mosquée in their 1922 budgets, these figures were only agreed upon by playing different administrators against each other.[28] The minister of colonies also wrote to the colonial governor-generals, including the amounts already pledged by other administrations, and went on to say that:

> It seems to me that the French colonies cannot stay on the sidelines of this manifestation, whose goal is the strong affirmation of Franco-Muslim fraternity, already sealed on the battlefields. In addition, I hardly need to emphasize the political importance of this foundation destined to prove French gratitude to Muslim eyes.
>
> I draw your attention to the utility of assuring your deeply needed support for this project of national importance, and I would be very much obliged if you could let me know the extent you which your colony will be able to contribute to the expenses of the Institut Musulman.[29]

This particular letter was sent to the governor of French West Africa, whose response indicated that he understood that he would be required to devote funds to the Mosquée's construction and that the "request" was a demand. However, he did protest the imposition of this Parisian project in saying that the contribution of the French West African Federation would "not be very high" mostly because "our subjects will hardly benefit from this Parisian establishment" but also because in the request for an initial donation was hidden the expectation of an annual contribution for its upkeep. These things considered, the governor was not willing to contribute a large sum.[30]

The question of whether Muslims living in the colonies would actually derive any benefit from the construction of the Mosquée was one that worried colonial administrators as much as the financial burden of participating in the project. Their concerns bring us back to the questions of how the building's use was imagined by metropolitan and colonial leaders and how *Islam français* was understood on both sides of the Mediterranean. There was no unified position on these issues across North and West Africa. The strongest response came from Lyautey, who has always been described as the Mosquée's staunchest defender by French historians of French Muslim policy. In fact, he was deeply critical of the plan to build a complex containing a mosque *and* a Muslim institute in Paris for a variety of reasons, all of which spoke to his concerns about the contours of Islam on both sides of the Mediterranean. Lyautey fully supported the construction of a mosque in the heart of the metropole, which arose from the "legitimate need to make a gesture of recognition of the Muslim soldiers who fell gloriously for France." He believed that such an institution had only benefits to offer and would present no danger whatsoever to the French state. As Lyautey saw it, the public nature of the Mosquée de Paris would make its surveillance easy; in addition, he felt that "Muslims will not go there very often for many reasons, not least of which is that it was not built in Muslim territory and thus, being the work of infidel hands, will always bear the stigmata of its origins." However, it would still be a beautiful building that will "flatter" the sentiments of North Africans, so France would have succeeded in making the gesture its leaders wanted to make.[31]

What he objected to, however, was the danger inherent in "the pairing of the words 'Mosquée and Institut Musulman.'" This pairing, in Lyautey's eyes, was nothing but a "cunning" maneuver on the part of metropolitan politicians hoping to avoid controversy on the grounds that they were funding a religious establishment. Although a mosque was harmless, a Muslim institute entailed perils for which the metropolitan administration was unprepared. The problem lay in the suggestion that it was in the French state's interest to provide Muslim subjects with access to Muslim education (as mediated by French interlocuters). An Institut Musulman in Paris would expose young students from North Africa pursuing their studies across the Mediterranean to all sorts of "worldly and social influences" from which Lyautey would be unable to protect them. He argued that in his Morocco, he aimed to "open their minds to progress in helping them to evolve [within] their religion, their family traditions and their country's institutions."[32] A mosque would fall within the realm of this policy, while an educational institution that could potentially serve as a breeding ground for subversive political action would not. He opposed the plan for a dual-natured complex in order to preserve his particular vision of Islam (emphatically not *French* Islam) and also on the grounds that precisely that exposure of Islam to French ideas would be profoundly detrimental to young Moroccans in France. The possible transmission of such an Islam across the Mediterranean was deeply disturbing to Lyautey.

Embodying *Islam français*

The play between the Institut and the Mosquée was not merely a bit of political sleight of hand, as Lyautey believed, but an active attempt to imagine an Islam that was both French and Other at once. This *Islam français* was occasionally articulated explicitly but was more often defined implicitly, in the discussions of where the complex housing the Mosquée and the Institut Musulman should be built and how they should be decorated. It was the physical site, with its ambiguously public and private spaces, that served as the grounds for negotiating what this Islam would look like.

As I have argued, French proponents of the Mosquée were convinced that Islam was a religion that invaded all aspects of everyday life in the private and public spheres and that the everyday rituals of Islam needed to be performed in a particular space decorated in a specific way. Thus the choice to use a mosque to embody their vision of Islam physically was a logical one. However, visual representations do not occupy the same space in Muslim religious belief as they do in this French imagining. Art historian Oleg Grabar has argued that "traditional Islamic culture has identified itself through means other than the visual" and that there is no "Islamic" style of architecture.[33] Muslim ritual does not require a sacralized space, nor is there a ceremony to sacralize or desacralize the space of a mosque.[34] Yet the Mosquée de Paris was not merely a religious site, it was a monument to France's power in the Muslim world, built to reflect its vision of Islam and Muslims. As such it was a "repositor[y] of meaning" where a wide range of events inscribed France's relationship with its Muslim subjects on a daily basis.[35] It is instructive to compare the construction of the Mosquée de Paris to the building of synagogues a century earlier. Dominique Jarrassé argues that because Jews did not have a particular architectural tradition, it was necessary to invent one: French Jews, struggling to balance assimilation with traditional Judaism, constructed their houses of worship as Jewish equivalents to Catholic churches.[36] The synagogue was "the very image of the Jew in the *cité,* the building was the reflection of his condition, and thus the investment in architectural luxuriousness was meant to symbolize progress, equality, patriotism. . . . The identification of [Jews] with the edifice . . . meant that society and public authorities tended to project their image of the Jew on the building . . . [thus obliging the Jews] to construct 'windows' to fulfill these expectations."[37] The Mosquée was also a *vitrine,* a window display, and was often referred to as "*la vitrine d'Islam*": yet it was a window constructed by the state and elite Muslims, not by a large autonomous Muslim community.

Islam français, a system of belief and ritual that was at once particular to Muslim civilization but compatible with French republican ideals and *laïcité,* was thus to be instantiated in the site of the Mosquée de Paris. For the French *indigènophiles,* it was in Morocco that this "rejuvenated Islam" originated from an Islam magnificent in "its isolation, its archaism, which . . . brings it closer to the purest [Muslim] belief." This purest form of Islam existed in a country that, through its encounter with "modern life," was "adapting to progress" with France's help.[38] Lyautey argued that this encounter was possible because Morocco and France were both civilizations that respected their ancient traditions while being open to progress. Like the French, he explained, the Moroccans had "an enlightened bourgeoisie . . . very concerned with progress, most especially economic progress."[39] But in addition to these similarities between elites on both sides of the Mediterranean, proponents of the Mosquée argued that Islam and French republicanism shared many traits. Si Kaddour asserted that "respect for morality" and the "glorification of charity" were principles dear to both Islam and a French civilization whose greatest concern was equality.[40] President Doumergue made the link between the philosophical underpinnings of French and Muslim culture more explicit:

> [Equality] . . . of human consciences and of their sincere impulses, is the mark of our democracy; the Muslim savants, as we know, have exalted the respect of individual dignity and human liberty. They have called for . . . the reign of a large fraternity and of equal justice. Democracy has no fundaments other than these.[41]

There was a clear attempt to identify Islam as compatible with democracy, tolerance, equality, and individual liberty. What would become more apparent in the debates over the construction of the site was how this related to French republicanism. I suggest that it lay in the attempt to make Islam compatible with *laïcité* by making it simultaneously secular and religious, public and private.

Although the Mosquée's proponents originally hoped that it would be built near Les Invalides, it was eventually constructed in the 5th *arrondissement* on land donated by the city of Paris. This was because the city land that became available happened to be located across from the Jardin des Plantes; it was not a deliberate decision to place the Mosquée complex there.[42] The eventual construction of the Mosquée in this spot was due to the Conseil municipal's refusal to donate land directly to the Société des Habous on the grounds that it had always refused to make donations to foreign associations. The Conseil proposed instead the traditional *bail emphyéotique* to the Société with a rent of one franc per year for ninety-nine years. Si Kaddour refused this offer, explaining the Société's wish to possess rather than rent the land on which the Mosquée would be built, making it a truly Muslim site. Finally, the Conseil agreed to allocate 1,500,000 francs to the Société so that it could purchase the available land on the grounds of the Hôpital de la Pitié, which had closed its doors in 1911. The land belonged to the Service de la Santé publique, was purchased with a subvention from the city of Paris, and then became the legal property of the Société des Habous.[43]

Once this decision had been made, it was argued that situating the complex "from which French thought shines" would be the only suitable way to "illuminate Islam with the benevolent virtues of French civilization."[44] It was in such a locale that "Muslim thought and beauty, far from losing their luster on borrowed soil, will develop, through their contact with France, the fecund originality of their own genius!"[45] As Emile Dermenghem, a renowned scholar of Islam, noted in an article on Muslims in Paris, the Mosquée's location near the Jardin des Plantes was "curiously predestined" and that rue Mouffetard, known as "rue Moukhtar" among the Muslims who seemed "drawn" to the neighborhood, was where Muslim ambassadors promenaded during the epochs of François I and Louis XVI.[46] The location of the Institut Musulman became another way to argue for the fundamental compatibility between French and Muslim civilization. Or, as the préfet de la Seine explained, "Are we not right next to the Pantheon? . . . Do not the works of the Persian Saadi and the Arab Averroès appear on the shelves of the library consecrated to . . . intellectuals? Finally, are we not in the heart of the university neighborhood, renowned for centuries, where so many studious generations have been formed by the most illustrious savants?"[47] This reference to these Muslim philosophers underscores that the Institut Musulman was intended to be a site for the study of "Quran, theology and traditions, Muslim law, [and Arab] linguistics"; in other words, it was to maintain its cultural specificity even as it blossomed through its encounter with French thought.[48] This was essential in working toward an elaboration of a secular French Islam, for it made clear that becoming compatible with French values did not necessitate abandoning Islam. Furthermore, compatibility with *laïcité* could not be better expressed than by making the Institut Musulman a completely public space in which Muslims and non-Muslims could interact as individuals in the public sphere rather than religious subjects in the private sphere. It is not a coincidence that the institute never fully materialized as it was planned, that it was only the strangely public privacy of the religious site that came fully into being.

It was the Mosquée, rather than the Institut, that did the work of remaining bound to "Muslim" tradition as filtered through French perceptions of Moroccan Muslim aesthetics and practices. The Mosquée was supposed to be a private space for Muslim religious observance, yet in fact it was a public-private sphere. The observance of Muslim religious rituals and practices that took place in it and were observed by a non-Muslim French audience was integral to the publicness of *Islam français*. When its proponents discussed the Mosquée's creation, they did not situate it in the heart of Paris's university district: that was the space occupied by the Institut Musulman, whose Islam was intellectual, modern, and compatible with French republicanism but whose physical design was never described. The Mosquée, on the other hand, was not discursively located in a particular part of Paris, other than in its center. Although it was necessary that the site be visible to visitors in Paris' landscape, its geographical location was far less emphasized than its design. Its aesthetic character was of primary importance because the Mosquée represented an Islam that its French proponents believed had a "hold on its faithful" and controlled all aspects of their lives. It required of its believers that they perform certain practices in particular settings because of the inextricable link between religious practices and daily life.[49] Its architects hoped to ensure the Mosquée's appeal for Muslims by designing it in a "Moroccan" style that would respond to their aesthetic ideals, although contemporary observers were quick to point out its appeal to Parisian and other tourists, comparing it both to tourist attractions in North Africa and metropolitan expositions and fairs.

Nowhere is this tension between the Institut built near the Pantheon and the Mosquée modeled on a Moroccan mosque more evident than in

FIGURE 1. Promotional illustration of the Institut Musulman de Paris, from *L'Institut Musulman et la Mosquée de Paris*, undated promotional brochure distributed by the Société des Habous des Lieux Saints. Personal collection of author.

the drawing distributed with a commemorative brochure for the Mosquée's inauguration.

In the drawing, the Mosquée's complex occupies a virtually empty space. It is far larger than the few buildings pictured immediately adjacent to it, and it could be in any part of Paris. It also features elements that were not actually part of the final architectural plans, such as two imposing Moroccan arched gates that would have cut through rue Geoffroy Saint-Hilaire to rue des Quatrefages along one side of the Mosquée. By the time this drawing was distributed, it was clear that these gates would not be constructed, so the choice to include them in the illustration emphasizes the Moroccan character of the site at the expense of reality. The confusion engendered by this visual description of the Mosquée complex is made even more complicated by the legends at the bottom of the illustration: on the left-hand side, it states, in French, "the Paris Muslim Institute," while on the right side, in Arabic, it reads "The Paris Mosque and Muslim Institute." In the illustration there is nothing to signal an institute, much less an institute dedicated to creating links between the French and Muslim civilizations. What is signaled, not least by the prominent minaret towering over the complex, is a religious site whose design does not suggest that it belongs in Paris.

This was exactly the aim of the Mosquée's architects, who chose to give the building the "traditional hispano-mauresque" style in vogue among Lyautey's Service des Beaux-Arts architects.[50] It was in Morocco, critics agreed, that "a new architecture [was] born . . . [a] collaboration between French science and intelligence with indigenous craftsmanship and tradition."[51] Si Kaddour met with architects who specialized in buildings with "Muslim character" in Rabat in October 1920 in order to prepare the preliminary plans for the Mosquée and its annexes.[52] A few months later, he reported back to the Ministry of Foreign Affairs that the Moroccan members of the Société des Habous had unanimously decided that the Mosquée should have "an African architectural character" and, more specifically, that it should be modeled on Fez's fourteenth-century mosque-madrasa Bou Inania. Sultan Abou Inan hoped to reorient the city's religious geography by building the complex near the boundary between the old and new cities and thus drawing people away from some of the older mosques. Yet although the Inspecteur des Beaux Arts wrote that the site was "undoubtedly the biggest and most sumptuous [mosque] of all Morocco," its decoration was not as refined and artistic as that of Fez's older mosques.[53] The sources that refer to the decision to use Bou Inania as the model for the Mosquée complex mention the physical beauty and renown of the Fassi site but do not refer to its founder's attempt to remake his city's religious landscape or to the site's relative aesthetic weakness compared to older mosques. It would be intriguing to know whether they were conscious of the ramifications of their choice of this particular institution as a model for Paris's mosque. Finally, Bou Inania was a "mosquée-cathédrale," which is to say that it was large enough and constructed in such a way as to accommodate crowds for Friday's noon prayer service. This cathedral model would also be copied in the Mosquée de Paris.

Once this model had been chosen, the French architects were given blueprints of this famous institution to inspire their first attempts at plans for the Parisian mosque, whose layout is clearly based on that of Bou Inania.[54] This resonated with metropolitan architectural critics, one of whom noted approvingly that "Muslim constructions, unlike ours, have not evolved and must, on the contrary, remain traditional."[55] Lyautey's Morocco was a virtual laboratory for modernist architecture and urbanism in a colonial setting, as Gwendolyn Wright has argued. Under his residency, the Service des Beaux Arts instituted an energetic campaign to preserve entire districts, virtually freezing Moroccan medinas in time, and to "restore" and "reproduce" monuments and other sites that had fallen into disrepair. Wright also argues that the Service, especially under the leadership of Tranchant de Lunel, "oriented itself towards charming streetscapes that would appeal to French residents and tourists."[56] The architectural style of the Mosquée and the fact of it being built to recreate, as closely as possible, a specific Moroccan religious site at once identified Islam as immutable and unchanging and turned the building into a spectacle to be enjoyed by non-Muslim Parisians.[57]

The discussions about the way the space of this "traditional" Muslim religious space was to be used, and by whom, help us to understand how a nominally private religious site and the faith practiced there were to be rendered public. Mantout, one of the Mosquée's architects, provided the Ministry of Foreign Affairs with a thorough verbal description of their plans for the complex, which would contain the religious site and the Institut Musulman as well as the other features, such as the *hammam* and the restaurant. This document serves as a verbal tour of the grounds, and it indicates which elements of the complex were particularly important for the architects. The image below shows the drawing of the site that accompanied this report.

The Mosquée complex was built on 7,500 square meters, of which 3,500 were destined for the planting of "Arab gardens." It was bounded by rue Geoffroy Saint Hilaire (which separated it from the Jardin des Plantes), rue Daubenton, and rue Quatrefages.[58] Two entrances, one for pedestrians and one for cars, were to be built on rue Geoffroy Saint Hilaire and the place du Puits de l'Ermite, respectively, although neither of these entrances would come to be constructed in the manner in which they were planned.[59] Upon entering, the visitor found herself immediately in an Arab garden whose "mosaic patterned alleys led to the different sets of buildings which surround the garden." On one's left were the guest houses, with "comfortable and modern" rooms that would host "noteworthy visitors or Muslim delegations." Another important piece of the complex dedicated to physical comfort and hospitality was the restaurant, which would be "accessible to all Muslims and to the Parisian public, where only Arab cuisine prepared with the greatest care will be served." Mantout promised that "everything will be of the purest Arab style in composition, construction, and furnishing, while keeping in mind modern comfort and the special dispositions the Parisian climate requires." Of course, the "Arab" nature of the cuisine and the decor was in fact "Moroccan," as imagined by French architects. The two references to Paris suggest awareness of the possibility that the Mosquée would have a certain potential as a non-Muslim destination, making it thus essential to depart somewhat from the "pureness" of the Arab style that would otherwise have characterized it. It is interesting to note that unlike the guest rooms, the two lodgings designated for the mufti and imam[60] were designed "in the architectural form and tradition of Arab houses," with no adjust-

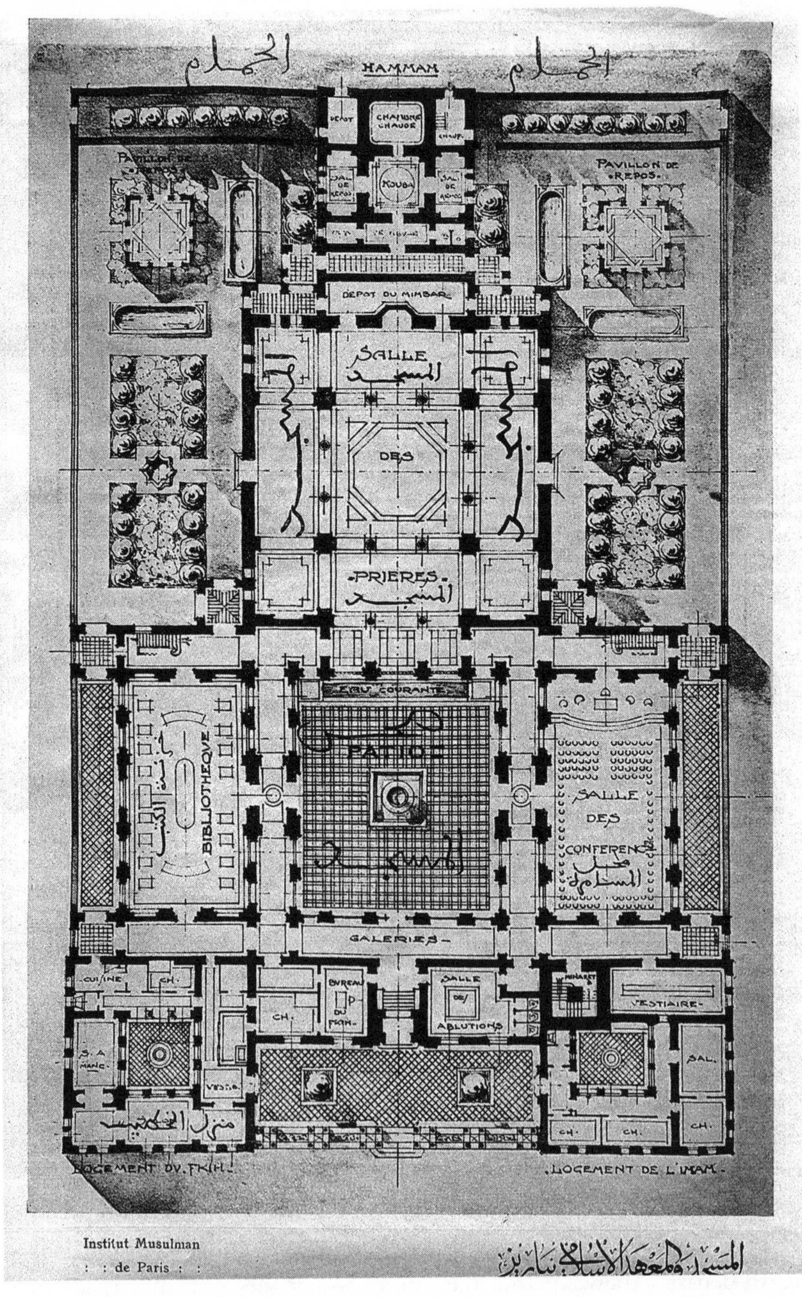

FIGURE 2. Architectural illustration of the Mosquée de Paris, from *L'Institut Musulman et la Mosquée de Paris*, undated promotional brochure distributed by the Société des Habous des Lieux Saints. Personal collection of author.

ments made for the Parisian locale. This can perhaps be explained by the fact that these positions, unlike Si Kaddour's, were to be filled by men sent from North Africa for temporary assignments and were thus not expected to acclimate to Parisian styles or interact with a non-Muslim audience. Their lodgings, which would not form part of the Mosquée's guided visit, could thus remain "traditional" without modification.

The minaret, which was always foregrounded in any visual illustration of the Mosquée (including those used in promotional material by the Mosquée's lobbyists and those disseminated in the architectural and popular press),[61] barely makes an appearance in Mantout's description, which immediately raises the question of why its physical and symbolic centrality was downplayed. All that Mantout says about the minaret is that it is "26 meters tall and 6 meters wide [and] built according to North African custom, with a square tower with an interior staircase with large steps, which the muezzin will climb to call the faithful at the hours for prayer." In this case, it is described as North African rather than Arab, which is more appropriate but still not fully accurate, there being wide regional variation among (and within) the architectural styles of the three countries of the Maghreb.[62] The reference to the muezzin's call to prayer is one of many references in this document to specific practices that, it was imagined, would take place in particular spaces in the Mosquée. What goes unstated is that unlike elsewhere in the Muslim world, the call to prayer of the Mosquée de Paris would be audible only within the confines of the complex, not even in the neighboring streets.[63] For a French secularist, the minaret is perhaps the physical symbol *par excellence* of the absence of a clear line between religious and secular spaces. According to this logic, an amplified call to prayer breaks down any barriers between communal, public, temporal space and the private realm of religion. Yet the Mosquée's founders recognized the visual and rhetorical importance of a highly visible minaret, and they wanted the auditory performance associated with it to be accessible to the Muslims and non-Muslims visiting the site. Its audibility in the truly public sphere, however, would have been understood as an aggressive challenge to the Catholic-inflected secularism of the French public sphere in which audible church bells do not violate *laïcité*—but a muezzin most certainly does. This created a paradoxical situation typical of *Islam français* in which the call to prayer must be heard in the "public" private sphere but not in the truly public sphere, whose secular space was reserved for Catholic ritual.

Immediately following the description of the minaret is that of the adjacent gardens that lead to the vestibule before the *salle de prière.* Mantout, in describing the vestibule, with its door "inspired by the most beautiful specimens of Moroccan architecture," provides his audience with another example of a religious practice that would take place in this setting: next to the vestibule was the *salle d'ablutions* "installed according to ritual, and destined for the purification of the body before prayer."[64] This room led to a large open patio (350 square meters) decorated with marble, mosaics, faience, and wood "conforming to the most beautiful traditions of Muslim architecture." The patio preceded the *salle de prières*, the beating heart of the Mosquée. This "vast room, with 56 columns and measuring 500 square meters, [could] hold between 500 and 600 worshippers." The decorations for this room include Oriental rugs, which again mixes the "Arab," "North African," and "Moroccan" elements of the design. Mantout mentions that the room is oriented toward Mecca, as indicated by the *mirhab*.[65] On either side of the room are changing rooms so that "Muslims dressed in European clothes can change into ritual clothing for prayer."[66] The lighting for the *salle de prières* would be provided by "chandeliers and lamps made in Muslim lands whose light will be sufficiently discreet so as to preserve mystery and meditation." This reference to the "mystery" of Muslim religious experience and its expression in aesthetic forms was a major trope for Orientalists, one highlighted by the popular press, which touted the Mosquée's touristic interest. The *salle de prières* was, like the minaret, an architectural element that straddled the public and private divide. Its use was reserved for Muslims at prayer, and non-Muslim visitors could merely peek into the room from the threshold. The room and the practices performed within its walls were nominally private but were in fact public and visible.

Finally, Mantout describes the *hammam*, "entirely construed according to North African custom," which would be open to the "Muslim public" and large enough to accommodate about twenty people at a time. It would also include individual massage chambers and a small *café maure* to provide refreshments. Management of the *hammam* would be "assigned to a Muslim proven specialist." It is interesting to note that the architects did not originally conceive of the *hammam* as a site that non-Muslim Parisians would consider using, though they did think that the restaurant would interest them.[67]

The popular press, as well as Orientalist journals, on the other hand, quickly touted the tourist potential of the Mosquée. One observer wrote in the Catholic journal *En Terre d'Islam* of the "veritable enchantment" of the Mosquée de Paris: "in penetrating these courtyards and richly decorated rooms, one has more of an impression of visiting a museum than of entering a place of prayer."[68] The reference to visiting a museum is important, for despite the intentions of the Mosquée's founders that the site serve a purely pedagogical function, many Parisians viewed it as a site for the display and consumption of Islam. In fact, the Mosquée also bore some resemblance to the colonial expositions, although unlike the exhibits constructed there, the Mosquée was set in Paris's landscape permanently and could be visited again and again. The very mosaics used to adorn the Mosquée had appeared at the Moroccan pavilion at the 1922 Exposition coloniale in Marseille, as a gift from Lyautey.[69] One newspaper promised its readers, in its review of the Mosquée, "It will provide a change for Parisians from the cardboard boxes with which one pretends to convey, in expositions, the splendor, the mysterious charm of the intimacy of African houses."[70] *L'Illustration* urged those who had traveled in the Muslim world to visit the Mosquée in order to experience anew their memories of the food and decor they had so enjoyed.[71] From the beginning, the Mosquée's founders planned to charge admission to the site from non-Muslim visitors, which contributed even more to the idea that it was an exhibit to be consumed publicly. Fresh from their success, the Mosquée's architects would go on to design both the North African pavilions of the 1931 Exposition coloniale and the Hôpital Franco-Musulman in Bobigny, which would open in 1935, whose façade greatly resembled the Mosquée's aesthetics. Clearly, in many peoples' minds, the Mosquée was a highlight in a set of sites around the capital that provided visitors with an exoticized image of Islam and Muslims.

The organizers of the 1931 Exposition coloniale believed as firmly as the Mosquée's architects that it was essential that the buildings "should reflect as exactly as possible *indigènes'* spaces," so it was imperative to have access to varied materials. These materials—"colonial woods, all the exotic cloths, all the twine, all the Arab or Asian tiles, all the raffia or bamboo decorations"—were not only essential to reconstruct the colonies accurately in Paris but also to demonstrate the strength and diversity of colonial production.[72] While Mantout planned the hospital in Bobigny, it was Fournez who designed the Moroccan pavilion at the 1931 expo. His plan included a palace built in the "spirit" of Moulay Hassan's Marrakesh palace as well as a "beautiful garden lined with cypresses and traversed by a canal, like the riads of Fez, surrounded by *indigène* boutiques and *cafés maures*."[73] Although the report makes clear that Moroccan artisans had completed much of the decorative work, French artisans had also been involved. Everyone involved in the Mosquée's construction emphasized that its artisans as well as its materials had been brought from Morocco. Their participation was supposed to ensure the building's authenticity.

Yet the Exposition coloniale was designed to showcase not only architecture from the empire but also the cultural practices of colonial peoples, at least those that might interest French audiences. Mahieddine Bachetarzi, the tenor who sang at the Mosquée's inauguration, described the experience of performing there:

> On September 3 [1931] we gave a concert at the Exposition coloniale. That, well, that is a less pleasant memory. Oh, not on our account, we were only there for an evening, our concert was like all the others, and we garnered our usual success. But there was something very humiliating about seeing all these Africans and Asians brought there to satisfy the taste for exoticism of their conquerors, in the comfort of their own home, exposed like strange beasts to a public not immune to idiocy and often unconscious of its insolence. But . . . at that time, our only choice was among various humiliations.[74]

Bachetarzi did not consider his role in the inauguration as something intended to satisfy a French desire for exoticism, yet it is difficult not to read some of the ceremonies and events organized to mark important developments in the Mosquée's development as remarkably similar to those of the Exposition coloniale.

The events organized by the French state in collaboration with Si Kaddour and the colonial administrations contributed to the creation of a "secular" Islam in the sense that "religious" events were folklorized, rendered public, and emptied of their original significance, all the while ostensibly occupying the central space of the Mosquée's activities. The ceremonies surrounding the Mosquée's landmark moments (the groundbreaking, orientation, and inauguration) served as a way to mark both the place of the complex in Paris's geography of significant monuments and the relationships among metropolitan, colonial, and Muslim dignitaries. In addition to these landmark events associated with milestones in the Mosquée's construction, other occasions also served as opportunities to shore up metropolitan and colonial relations, particularly with Morocco. A note from the police dated 26 June 1930 reports that a "Fête de charité 'Nord-Africaine'" would take place in the Mosquée's confines the following day, under the patronage of the wife of Morocco's resident-general. The soirée was designed to raise funds for the Red Cross's work with the *indigènes*.[75] The Mosquée was also a privileged site for drawing the Moroccan elite, especially the young generation, closer to France. Even before the site was completed, it was an important stop during tours of Paris taken by Moroccan students. During the 1923 visit, the students followed an "interesting" visit to the museum at the Jardin des Plantes with a tour of the construction site led by Mantout. The group's leader noted that "we recognized many of Fez and Meknes' master mosaicists, who offered us mint tea." By 1925, the students were apparently "thrilled" with "this corner of Morocco, completely charming with its patios, gardens, water jets, beautiful galleries" and proud that "European visitors do not hide their admiration."[76]

The inaugural festivities, for which the guest of honor was the sultan of Morocco, involved a parade through the city's landmarks first with the French president, then with an escort made up of the sultan's guards. With the president, the route ran along the Faubourg St-Honoré, Marigny, Champs-Elysées, Avenue Georges V, where the escort was formed, and then continued to the Mosquée via François 1er, Georges V, Champs-Elysées, Place et Pont Concorde, Boulevard St-Germain, rue Danton, Place St Michel, quais Rive Gauche, rues des Fossés St-Bernard, de Jussieu, Linné, Geoffroy St-Hilaire, Daubenton, and Quatrefages.[77] This route through the heart of Paris signaled the importance of the event while inscribing France's role as a Muslim power throughout the city, not merely in the area immediately surrounding the Mosquée. This route not only displayed Paris's wonders to the Moroccan sultan but also displayed him to Paris, as the guest of the French republic, which was in the process of consolidating its power in his country. David Harvey has written of the importance of spectacles and parades in order to mobilize support of state power and of Haussmann's talent in organizing events to commemorate everything from the opening of a new boulevard to the visit of a foreign dignitary to the Hôtel de Ville.[78] The spectacle provided by this inauguration did similar work.

Bachetarzi described the inauguration as taking place on a beautiful sunny day, under a blue sky "worthy of Algeria":

> Welcomed by Si Kaddour Ben Ghabrit, who was waiting in front of the grand entrance of the brand new, sparkling white mosque, His Majesty Moulay Youssef made his entrance with his three sons, surrounded by his African Guard, and followed by dignitaries from all the islamic countries, Caucasians, Hindus, Afghans, Iranians, Egyptians, Turks, Tunisians, Moroccans, Algerians, Sudanese.
>
> The instant the Sultan crossed the threshold, his Guard, lined up in the courtyard, launched into the Cherifian anthem. What a sumptuous spectacle, one Paris had never seen and would most likely never see again!
>
> It was a cavalcade of embroidered caftans, multicolored djellabahs, burnous, fez, chechias, and turbans.[79]

The show of respect for the sultan was carefully orchestrated both to provide the "sumptuous spectacle" Bachetarzi describes, full of colorful costumes and song and also to make important political points. The emphasis on the sultan's visit and participation at this event was linked to particular events currently taking place in Morocco, and much less attention was paid to other Muslim dignitaries who crossed the Mediterranean to attend the festivities. Yet when the bey of Tunis visited Paris in 1923, a carefully orchestrated reception was planned for him at the Hôtel de Ville, which was attended by all of the people who took part in the Mosquée's inauguration. He was not paraded through the city in a *cortège* like the Moroccan sultan, however. His visits to sites around Paris, such as the Tomb of the Unknown Soldier and the Mosquée itself, were accompanied only by those officials who were in some way connected to Tunisia.[80] Both visits, however, took place immediately surrounding France's national holiday, which was yet another opportunity to combine a celebration of France's power with a celebration of its relationship with Islam.

The events designed to showcase the Mosquée also highlight that it was built in the French capital during a period in which metropolitan-colonial questions were particularly fraught. Nowhere is the local battle to place Paris at the heart of the French empire more evident than in Pierre Godin's campaign in the Conseil municipal de Paris in support of the city celebrating the centenary of the conquest of Algeria. Although his omission of the Mosquée itself as a site contributing to Paris's importance in the colonial Muslim world is shocking, his comments about the relationship between the city and the North African colonies are important to understand the space the Mosquée occupied in the city as a synecdoche of France. For, as Godin argued, "Algeria is not only . . . a province of French thought, but an enthusiastic department of Parisian thought. And Paris is enchanted by its animating influence."[81] Although he was primarily interested in bringing groups of students to Algeria to witness French progress in action, Godin also hoped to create Parisian venues for the exhibit of Algerian art, crafts and architecture, and literature. The celebration of the Mosquée as a credit to Paris's cachet as the heart of the Muslim certainly supports Gary Wilder's suggestion that we see Paris as "a fundamentally imperial city" in a metropole that was itself "the very center of an empire of which it and its colonies were integral parts."[82]

The Mosquée de Paris, then, was the product of collaboration among the French state, colonial administrations, and North Africa's Muslim elite. It was very much a product of its time: fears of being eclipsed by England and Germany as a power in the Muslim world propelled France's metropolitan and colonial administrators into providing tangible evidence of their *politique musulmane.* The Muslim elites who acted as intermediaries between Muslims and the colonial administrations saw their participation as a way to prove their loyalty to France and increase their own prestige. Yet what began as a fairly straightforward political move in response to external threats quickly became something much more complex. The Mosquée de Paris became the physical embodiment of a secular Islam, *Islam français,* compatible with the principles of *laïcité* while rooted in "traditional" Moroccan Islam. Although it was originally described as a gesture of recognition for the sacrifices made by colonial soldiers, a war memorial of sorts, chance dictated that the Mosquée would come to be built not near Les Invalides but in the heart of the Latin Quarter. This allowed the Mosquée's proponents to use the site as a theater for the display of *Islam français*: the Institut Musulman, whose intellectual character perfectly suited it for the neighborhood, celebrated the similarities between French and Muslim civilizations, while the Mosquée's Moroccan-style architecture guaranteed the authenticity of the practices that would be performed in the building. The deeply rooted French belief that Islam was a religion in which materiality mattered much more than in any other faith made the choice of embodying this vision of Islam in a mosque a logical one.

Yet the idea that Muslim practice was intrinsically physical and invaded all aspects of everyday life, confounding the public and private spheres, also implied that the metropolitan and colonial administrators who favored the Mosquée's construction did not believe that it was possible for Muslims to become *laïc* subjects. The state that separated church and state in the law of 1905 insisted on identifying its colonial subjects and protégés as inevitably and only Muslim. As we will see in the following chapter, the ambiguity at the heart of *Islam français* informed the policy and social assistance programs designed contemporaneously with the Mosquée to cope with the North African immigrant population of Paris.

CHAPTER 3

To Monitor and Aid: Muslim Bodies, Social Assistance, and Religious Practices

The construction of the Mosquée de Paris and the Institut Musulman gave body to the vision of *Islam français* as imagined by its proponents, but the question of how government support for French Islam would affect the lives of the primarily male, working-class North African residents of the capital was unclear.[1] The Islam practiced by many of these men was not recognized as "true" Islam by metropolitan and colonial proponents of *Islam français*; their religious observances were characterized as akin to paganism. Nevertheless, North Africans quickly learned upon their arrival in Paris that they would be counted, professionally oriented, and healed as Muslims rather than simply as immigrant workers. With the Mosquée as the central site of Muslim authority, the national and local administrations created a city- and suburban-wide network of Muslim sites designed to structure the lives of North African immigrant workers. Sites like the Bureau de la rue Lecomte, at once a social assistance office and a surveillance center, or the Hôpital Franco-Musulman in the northeastern suburb of Bobigny were part of a network of separate social assistance services centered on Muslim religious identity created for North African immigrants.

The foundations for the French policy of administering North African immigrants almost exclusively as Muslims were laid at the same time as the creation of the Mosquée itself. The tension between the promise of openness embedded in the logic of *Islam français* and the restrictiveness of Parisian

Muslim institutions symbolizes the paradox at the heart of French Islam. Although all immigrant workers during this period were subject to different legal regimes than were French citizens, the programs designed for North African Muslims set them apart from other immigrants, even other colonial immigrant workers.[2] The rationale for this segregation was corporeal: the French belief in the centrality of embodied practices in the lives of Muslims meant that the kinds of services that were designed to assist North African immigrants took for granted that Muslim bodies had different demands than non-Muslim ones. The Hôpital Franco-Musulman is the example *par excellence* of the state's contradictory impulses: while the construction of this hospital effectively "protected" Parisian public hospitals from what were seen as disease-ridden North African male bodies, some of its proponents also sincerely believed that they were providing Muslims with the space to engage in Muslim practices safely and securely. This corporeal logic of the 1920s and 1930s, couched in the language of religious protection, would take on a more explicitly racialized tinge during the Vichy period.

Furthermore, the disregard of metropolitan and colonial officials and social scientists for the Muslim practices of certain North African immigrants in the Paris region was essential to their defense of *Islam français*. Because French observers believed that the "pagan" observances of Parisian Muslims did not require a particular kind of aestheticized space and did not demand particular embodied behaviors, these "folkloric" practices were not viewed as "real" Islam. The Islam of Algerian and Moroccan immigrants during this period was in some cases linked to nationalist activity; in others, to social solidarity and mutual aid societies; in others still, to cultural activities. But the possibility of Islam's multiplicity, of different ways of being Muslim, was foreclosed from the very beginning of the articulation of *Islam français* until the 1970s, when, as we will see in the final chapter, the French state began to acknowledge that a unitary vision of religious identity and practice was not tenable.

Colonial Immigrants and Others: Foreign Workers in the Interwar Years

European and colonial immigrant workers were subject to different administrative regimes from the beginning of the labor recruitment associated with the war effort during World War I. The government's management of the French labor market as of 1915 brought the racialized logic of contemporary social scientists to the realm of employment. The state directed particular populations toward certain kinds of labor, such as Africans for manual labor, and also allowed private employers to request workers of a particular race.[3] The distinctions made between immigrants from elsewhere in Europe and those from the colonies were accentuated in the interwar years. The workers recruited from France's empire, as well as from China, were expelled at the war's end. French officials sought to replace these less desirable immigrants with European ones. To this end, the Ministry of Labor used the Service de la main-d'oeuvre étrangère to issue identity cards and make placement decisions for immigrant workers in agriculture and industry.[4]

While certain European immigrants were seen as necessary additions to the French workforce and sometimes to the French nation as well, interwar immigration policies did not take into account the costs of providing social welfare services to these workers. In 1926, for example, the *département* of Bouches-du-Rhône (with Marseille's many immigrant workers) devoted 17.7 million francs to free medical care for all of its residents, of which 4.6 million was taken up by Italian immigrants alone.[5] Private social assistance agencies had to step in where the state failed to provide adequate care, or when resources were strained too tightly. One such agency was the Service social d'aide aux émigrants, the French branch of the Organisation internationale d'assistance, whose traveling social workers and nurses were often the spouses or daughters of wealthy men who considered it their Christian duty to assist those in need. The Catholic Church was also instrumental in providing services to immigrant workers, and some priests lobbied against the expulsions and immigration restrictions. Protestant leaders created their own agency, CIMADE, in 1939.[6] Among the Jewish community, more than half of the immigrant population belonged to *landsmanshaftn*, or mutual-aid societies, on the eve of World War II. These self-help groups were sometimes federated under larger organizations, such as the Zionist and bourgeois Fédération des sociétés juives de France, or the communist Union des sociétés juives de France.[7]

All of these religiously affiliated social service associations, however, existed *in addition to* the aid provided to immigrant workers by the French state. While such assistance may at times have been lacking, European immigrants had access to both state public welfare programs and help from religiously affiliated associations. This was not the case for North Africans, who were denied the resources available to European migrant workers and were directed toward specialized social service agencies exclusively for Muslims. Their recruitment and travel was arranged differently from European immigrants, and once they arrived on metropolitan soil they learned that they did not share the same rights, especially as pertained to their medical care. One of the major differences between European and Algerian immigrants during the interwar years was access to *allocations familiales,* or funds to support one's family. Initially, the state let employers decide whether or not to provide their workers with these funds, but a 1932 law required companies to provide these subsidies for parents with children living abroad. Because Algeria was technically French, Algerian workers were not able to obtain financial support for their children living on the other side of the Mediterranean.[8]

The differentiated management of immigrant populations was in part the result of what French political scientist Patrick Weil describes as a veritable boom in the "science" of immigration in the 1930s. Immigration scientists cobbled together a blend of "eugenics, racial studies, biology, anthropology, sociology, criminology and psychology, or indeed psychoanalysis" to make their arguments.[9] One of the best-known experts of this burgeoning field of study, Georges Mauco, created a system for judging the chances for successful assimilation among given national or ethnic groups based on research he conducted with French factory directors. Mauco's judgments were based on several criteria, such as physical aptitude, discipline, and French comprehension. Arabs were at the very bottom of his scale (with a score of 2.9 out of 10); at the top were Belgians, Swiss, Italians, Spanish and Poles, in descending order of assimilability.[10]

The French state's attitude toward European immigrants was not especially coherent, and it tended to fluctuate according to the needs of the labor market and shifting political tides. At the beginning of the 1930s, the agricultural labor market was almost completely unregulated in terms of immigration restriction, and industry also applied immigration controls rather loosely. A few years later, however, a series of decrees attempted to regulate these flows, which resulted in forced repatriations. The arrival of the Front populaire to power temporarily loosened these restrictions, but then Léon Blum's government instituted a new kind of surveillance of immigration designed to distinguish between desirable immigrants and far less desirable European refugees. Although Italian, Russian, and Armenian political refugees were already present in France, the "refugees" cited in the discourse of immigration specialists in the mid-1930s were Jews fleeing Germany, Austria, and Poland. Mauco, for example, argued that while a carefully selected labor immigration was necessary for France, the state should not accept all refugees blindly. What France needed, Mauco argued, was a *complementary* immigration of workers and peasants, not a massive influx of Jewish refugees practicing the liberal professions in direct competition with French citizens.[11] New and old anti-Semitic arguments were voiced by the French far right by 1933, who claimed at once that Jews were German spies and that they would force France into a war with Germany. Although voices from the center and left were raised to counter these claims, historians such as Esther Benbassa argue that the fate of the Jews of France was already sealed before the war broke out.[12]

Unlike Jews during this period, Algerians were not necessarily considered racially undesirable; indeed, some immigration experts considered Algerian Kabyles to be white.[13] Algerian Arabs, on the other hand, were not considered "good" immigrants and were judged lazy and potentially violent. The needs of the French labor market as well as the situation in Algeria made it unrealistic to consider halting all Algerian immigration; furthermore, Algerians were French nationals and had the right to circulate freely between metropole and colony. To solve the problem of bringing Europeans in and keeping Algerians out, a series of legal restrictions was passed in 1924. While travel permits for Algerians had been abolished for a decade, the new law required an identity card with a photograph (the photo was not required of other foreigners). This sharply curtailed legal immigration, but as men began to figure out how to maneuver around the new restrictions, illegal immigration increased sharply.[14] In the eyes of local and national officials, the increasingly large population of Algerians, with smaller communities of Moroccans and Tunisians, required a new kind of immigration control. These policies would emerge from the *politique musulmane* of the war years and would continue to use *Islam français* as the channel for administering North African workers.

Islam as "Special" Treatment: A Prehistory

The history of French authorities using Islam as a medium for their interactions with North and West African subjects is an old one. As we have already seen, the army took great pains to ensure that Muslim soldiers had the means to practice their religion during World War I. As early as 1915, Muslim doctors were brought from Algeria to treat wounded fellow Muslims, at the urging of Ben Thami, an Algerian doctor serving in the French army. Ben Thami's request that imams from Algeria be sent to provide religious services for hospitalized soldiers, however, was more controversial because the Algerian administration sent representatives of the official clergy, in whom army officials said the Algerians had no faith.[15] The minister of war issued a series of instructions to the Direction des Troupes Coloniales and the Service de l'Organisation des Travailleurs Coloniaux en France ordering them to provide workers wishing to fast during Ramadan as much leeway as possible to observe the holiday. Managers were not to dock wages during the month and were also ordered to allow fasting workers to take care of their own dietary needs. In addition to allowing Muslim workers to be responsible for their own religious observance, military authorities were supposed to "take the initiative" in having all workers celebrate the beginning and ending of the Ramadan period with celebrations that reflected "a noticeable amelioration of the ordinary."[16] Not only was the observance of holidays to be respected, so were the religious rules that constituted everyday life and life cycle events. The Ministry of War ordered the Public Health Service to make special provisions for "Algerians, Tunisians, Moroccans, or other Muslims" whenever possible in their hospitals. These included putting them together in one room; setting aside a separate lard-free kitchen for their use; allowing one of them to supervise the preparation of their meals;[17] providing them with a room in which to perform their ablutions; and ensuring that they never had the impression that anyone was trying to convert them (thus no non-Muslim clergy was allowed to enter their rooms, nor was army leadership to distribute any medals or icons that could be perceived as religious in nature).[18]

The army's commitment to its Muslim colonial soldiers stands in marked contrast to that of its Jewish soldiers, whether of European or North African origin. Jewish military chaplains, like their Catholic and Protestant counterparts, performed the traditional duties of tending to the ill and dying, performing religious burials, and leading prayer services. A Hebrew-French prayer book for daily and holiday services was assembled by one of the Jewish chaplains and distributed to Jewish soldiers. Yet soldiers could not hope to recite these prayers in a synagogue provided by the French army like the temporary mosques built for Muslims soldiers. Instead, they prayed "in such and such a barn, or village school . . . or in some subterranean shelter."[19] More fundamentally, it seems that although some Jewish soldiers consumed foods that were either traditionally associated with or religiously mandated during certain holidays (such as Passover), these foods were not provided by the French army. Jewish magazines reported that soldiers were able to eat matzah during Passover in 1915 and 1916, yet at least in 1915 this was the result of a community initiative championed by the Consistoire in which rabbis exhorted their congregations to provide funding to send matzahs to soldiers.[20] Another report from 1916 mentions a group of Algerian Jewish soldiers preparing a "traditional" meal to break the fast on Yom Kippur. While the author praises the captain for allowing the men leave to prepare and celebrate the holiday, he does not imply that the special foods were provided by the army.[21] It is clear that although observant Jewish soldiers also had alimentary practices or restrictions associated with particular holidays, the French state did not feel the need to provide them with the means to perform their religious duties as it did with Muslim soldiers.

I believe that this different treatment derived not from any realization on the army's part that national Jewish organizations would accomplish this task themselves but from a belief among French politicians and military leaders that Muslims were in thrall to their embodied practices in a way that Jews were not. Jews, as secular subjects, could choose to perform religious rituals, or not, within the confines of their own community. Muslims, on the other hand, could not.

It is difficult to know how Muslim soldiers viewed the army's gestures. Individual men may or may not have identified themselves as Muslim, may or may not have actively practiced their religion. Even for those who did want to perform their daily religious obligations, there is little evidence that would allow us to know whether they appreciated the French army's involvement in their spiritual life. According to French historian Gilbert Meynier, Islam was a vitally important element in the lives of Algerian soldiers stationed in the metropole. These soldiers followed Quranic strictures more closely than their countrymen serving in Algeria; he explains that for these men far from home, "faith was the ultimate defensive bastion."[22] In the interviews he conducted with former soldiers, all the men recounted their disgust at being forced to drink strong liquor to "heat them up" before battle; if given the choice, they drank coffee rather than wine and spent their free time in the cobbled-together *cafés maures*. In their letters home, they wrote of their anguish in not knowing whether their rations were truly *halal* or not, or whether, in a land without sun, they were orienting themselves correctly toward Mecca when they prayed. Meynier argues that these soldiers, however concerned they were with fulfilling the duties required by their religion, were completely uninterested in "the official Islam" provided by the army with its makeshift mosques and imported imams. Soldiers recovering at the hospital of the Jardin colonial at Nogent-sur-Marne performed their prayers outside on the hospital grounds rather than use the mosque the army had built for their use.[23] The tension between a certain population's interest in incorporating Muslim religious practices into everyday life and the French state's desire to provide the means to do so would of course be played out again with the creation of the Mosquée. The army's gestures toward its Muslim soldiers' religious practices, however, went hand in hand with discriminatory treatment. North and West African soldiers were regularly denied leave while metropolitan soldiers were given theirs, and French soldiers were encouraged to report any suspicious conversations overheard among colonial soldiers. Arab and Africans' letters were censored more heavily than their French colleagues' missives home. Finally, military camps designated for use by colonial soldiers were frequently overcrowded and lacking in basic hygiene.[24] While they were accorded religious privileges that Jewish soldiers, for example, were not, Muslim colonial soldiers were denied the basic rights of their French counterparts.

Muslim Bodies in the City

The army's policy of providing Muslim soldiers with the means to observe their religious obligations while treating them as a second-class population found its postwar echo in the services and agencies designed to monitor the activities of North African workers created by both the national government and the city of Paris. As we have already seen, European immigrants were subject to different legal regimes than French workers and were not always welcomed with open arms even when they were judged desirable and assimilable. However, the possibility of equal French citizenship was open to them, and they had access to the same services available to French citizens. Religious organizations provided similar services, which they could use in addition to or instead of those provided by the French state, but they were not required to avail themselves of medical care or other aid from Catholic, Jewish, or Protestant groups. Not only were North African immigrants administered separately from other foreigners (even though Algerians were in fact French nationals, if not French citizens), but they were administered as religious subjects. On the one hand, the state could be commended for providing them with religious services that may otherwise have been unavailable to them since there simply was not a longstanding Muslim community capable of providing religious sites for new immigrants. Yet on the other hand, by requiring them to make use of separate Muslim services, the French state made it impossible for Muslim immigrants to be anything but Muslim.

The Ministry of the Interior simultaneously helped finance the salary of an imam to serve Paris's North African population[25] and created a complex network of techniques for managing those same people. During the war, the minister of war oversaw the Service de surveillance des coloniaux (created in 1916), which was transferred one year later to the minister of the colonies. The following year saw the creation of the Commissariat général des militaires et travailleurs africains, yet these three services were all closed down at the war's end. In the years immediately following the war, however, they resurfaced in two forms: the Service de contrôle et d'assistance en France aux indigènes des colonies (CAI), created in 1923, and the Service des Affaires indigènes nord-africaines (SAINA), created in 1928. The CAI was designed to manage the West African and Southeast Asian colonial populations of France, with a particular goal of stamping out any nascent nationalist movements taking root in French soil. The SAINA, controlled by the Préfecture of the Seine and the Préfecture of Paris, was directed exclusively at the capital's North African population. The cornerstone of these services was known as the Service de la rue Lecomte, or, as it was officially called, the Brigade nord-africaine.[26]

Rue Lecomte was, to a large extent, the result of one man's obsessive campaign to bring the lessons he had learned as a colonial official in Algeria to bear on the administration of North African immigrants in Paris. Pierre Godin, a member of Paris's Conseil municipal (and its president from 1926–1927), began his career in Algeria as a clerk and went on to become a police officer and eventually a *sous-préfet.* Godin believed that a understanding of the "native mentality" was essential to the proper management of the capital's North African populations, and indeed rue Lecomte was directed by a former official from the French administration in Algeria: Adolphe Gérolami, who had been chosen for his knowledge of the "Algerian Muslim."[27] Although the Bureau de la rue Lecomte was described as a resource center for North African Muslim workers, it was primarily a site designed to monitor the movements and activities of the Maghrébin population in the city and suburbs. Godin, who was also one of the Mosquée's main proponents, explained in his report to the Paris municipal council:

> A recent and sensational crime—the murder of two poor women . . . by an Algerian Kabyle . . . has focused the anxious attention of public opinion on the invasion of France by foreign or colonial elements, especially North African emigrants. [Public opinion] is beginning to wonder if some prudent measures wouldn't be in order, to discipline, maybe even limit, this invasion. . . . We do not know exactly how many Algerian or African *indigènes* there are in Paris. . . . Algerian *indigènes* travel freely [the *permis de voyage* having been eliminated in 1915] and thus it is very difficult to follow this errant work-force in its peregrinations.[28]

The Service de la rue Lecomte was designed to respond to this free-floating anxiety about the presence of these "timid men from the mountains" transformed into "urban workers" and living among the French.[29] Godin minced no words about the service's dual purpose: to "monitor and aid" the city's North Africans. He presented it as a moral imperative, for "these 'primitives' are among us. These 'mountain dwellers,' these 'barbarians' heard civilization's call and are tasting the charms of the City. With them, old Africa opens itself up and comes to us. It is Islam, approaching."[30] The equation of "old Africa" with "Islam" in this formulation is instructive. What is most important to note about rue Lecomte is the way its programs were structured around a conception of these workers as simultaneously Muslim and North African. For Godin and the other authorities involved in the management of North African immigrant populations, "Africa" arriving on France's doorstep was really the approach of Islam. Thus national identities were replaced with a religious one.

The rue Lecomte site was located in a former school building in the eastern part of the 17th *arrondissement.* Initially, it consisted only of a labor placement and information office for North African workers' use. North African immigrants to Paris were required to register their presence at the office and occasionally to renew their identity papers. Rue Lecomte employees[31] also promised aid with locating jobs, translation, legal paperwork, the shipment of one's earnings to family in North Africa, and other services. The complex also featured a cafe, which, along with the other resources, was largely ignored by the city's Muslims, as Gérolami sadly reported to a colonial official visiting from Morocco.[32] The following year, in 1926, the Municipal Council inaugurated the dispensary, which provided basic care and minor surgery. Medical professionals concerned with public health noted with relief that the clinic also featured special services for those afflicted with tuberculosis and venereal diseases, which were thought to be endemic to North Africans.[33] In 1927, an eighty-bed hostel, or *foyer,* also opened as part of the rue Lecomte site. Gérolami hoped to extend his and his institution's authority beyond the walls of the rue Lecomte complex and to do a better job of winning the loyalty of the city's Muslim workers. Another *foyer* was built in the suburb of Gennevilliers, which featured a prayer room, "*hammam* and café," and dormitories, and the rue Lecomte's director hoped to see similar *foyers* develop all over the city and suburbs.[34] Ultimately, only five others would be built in a joint arrangement between and a private company in areas with significant North African populations: Boulogne-Billancourt, Asnières, Saint-Ouen, Charenton, and Colombes.[35] Gérolami believed that his agency and other Parisian Muslim institutions needed to create deeper connections with the city's Muslim communities and that the best way to do this was through the creation of mutual aid societies, which would work through the idiom of Islam. He tried to launch a "fraternal association of . . . Muslims in Paris, a sort of mutual assistance society, whose first project would be the construction of the wall of the Muslim cemetery of Paris."[36] Gérolami's Muslim mutual aid society, however, met with as little success as his café, for Muslims continued to rely on their own associations rather than pay a monthly membership fee to join rue Lecomte's association.

Managing North African immigrants thus revolved around two poles: social assistance and policing. The trio that oversaw Paris's "Muslim" institutions, Si Kaddour, Gérolami, and Godin, was implicated in providing the conditions for the "proper" observance of Muslim life cycle events, particularly illness and death.[37] The Paris municipal council and the Préfecture de Police were instrumental in managing end-of-life issues for North Africans, religious or not, during this period. The links connecting the SAINA, the Mosquée, and the Hôpital Franco-Musulman in the eastern suburb of Bobigny were extremely close.[38] The CIAM pronounced itself in favor of the following projects: standardized regulations concerning the burial of Muslims in the Département de la Seine; the setting aside of plots in suburban graveyards, "where they can be buried according to their beliefs and rituals," in addition to the expensive Muslim area of Père Lachaise; the formation of an association to provide indigent Muslims with religious burials; and, finally, the creation of an Office of Muslim Beneficence.[39] The question of Muslim cemeteries was being considered at the same time that decisions about health care and *foyers* for North African workers were being made.[40] The CIAM dedicated a meeting early in 1931 to debating how and where a cemetery for Paris's Muslims could be created, with testimony from Si Kaddour, Pierre Godin, and Gérolami. The issue had been raised because Si Kaddour had addressed the préfet de la Seine directly to support the establishment of such a site, who in turn consulted the minister of the interior about the legality of such an undertaking.[41] Si Kaddour presented the issue as something that concerned Paris's Muslims "because of the religious character attached to Muslim funerals. If, in death, they find themselves far from Muslim lands, they attach an even greater value to having a cemetery reserved for members of their faith."[42] The préfet de la Seine, whose hesitation in the face of this request was based not only in his concerns about legality but also in fears that in giving Si Kaddour a positive response, "we would expose ourselves to reclamations in the same style from Protestants [and] Jews."[43] Yet as Si Kaddour explained in person at the meeting, "As for the objections on legal grounds which have been put forward, they were also true for the Institut Musulman and the Mosquée de Paris, which were nevertheless created. Thus we need only follow an analogous procedure" to establish a cemetery. Godin's solution to this problem was to suggest that the Hôpital Franco-Musulman contribute land for the creation of a Muslim burial ground, as hospitals could legally build cemeteries serving particular populations on their grounds. The CIAM accepted this compromise, and the burial ground was eventually constructed in Bobigny.[44]

In the debate over this issue, Si Kaddour was asked who would be buried in such a site. He responded that it would be primarily soldiers, "since the bodies of Muslim notables who die in Paris are usually repatriated to their country of origin by their families." Si Kaddour's assertion that a Muslim cemetery in Paris was of interest to Muslims the world over was probably an exaggeration, but it was certainly a point of interest to French diplomats and functionaries in the Muslim world who were concerned with the religious observances of the Muslim elite. As a French diplomat stationed in Cairo explained, although "the Orientals who travel to France belong to the fortunate classes who don't go to mosques," the Mosquée de Paris had still been used for the funerals of two Egyptians who, though not observant at all, still wanted a Muslim burial. He was strongly in favor of the creation of a Muslim cemetery, as "a 'believer' can not pray, he can be treated in a public hospital with no problem, but he cannot face the idea of being buried right next to non-Muslims."[45]

While creating areas where Muslims could be buried according to the precepts of their religion was a priority for those making Muslim policy in the Paris region, their medical care was also a huge concern. As Clifford Rosenberg and others have shown, there were great fears of venereal disease among the population of single North African men who arrived in France as laborers in the 1920s and 1930s. Policies segregating this population to Muslim dispensaries and hospitals were based in these fears, yet were couched in the language of cultural sensitivity. The dispensary of the Mosquée de Paris itself was formally placed under the control of the Office of Social Hygiene of the Préfecture de la Seine in 1928.[46]

The real centerpiece of North African healthcare in Paris, however, was the Hôpital Franco-Musulman de Bobigny, one of whose architects was none other than the Mosquée's Maurice Mantout. The hospital was voted into existence by Paris's Conseil Municipal on 11 July 1929 and came under the authority of the Département de la Seine in 1930. Its location was a source of great tension between the various Paris-area politicians involved in its creation, and it was eventually decided to construct it in the communist suburb of Bobigny as an attack on its leadership.[47] Like the policing agencies, it was supposed to protect North African *and* French populations by isolating Muslim workers and providing them with separate services. During the period in which the Hôpital was conceived, constructed, and inaugurated, Paris's public health care system was in a disastrous state. The public hospitals served only Parisians whose incomes fell below a certain level, and its health care services were entirely free.[48] Outdated and overpopulated, the city's hospitals were increasingly unable to cope with the demands of the city's population. In the face of these poor conditions, many local politicians objected to spending money on health care for immigrants, even though, statistically speaking, foreigners made up only a small percentage of the city hospitals' overall patients.[49]

The Hôpital Franco-Musulman was designed to give North Africans access to a health care center big enough to cope with an increasingly large population (the Rue Lecomte and Mosquée clinics having become too crowded). The arguments made in favor of this health care regime, which were echoed in the medical press, concerned not only anxieties about "African pathology which demands doctors and nurses with specialized education" but also social welfare concerns about a population that felt "unmoored, isolated" in French hospitals. North Africans treated in Paris's public hospitals "found none of the traditions and customs which are so important to them and to which they are so faithful. Everything, the staff, the other patients, was strange to them."[50] The Hôpital Franco-Musulman would allow them to feel at home again "during a time when, touched by illness, they are particularly sensitive."[51] Although the hospital contained all of the most modern medical technologies, its façade was designed to signal its special North African character. The medical press was not insensitive to the display: "This monumental door, in pure mauresque style, produces a beautiful effect. . . . It's very 'local color', one finds oneself in a very evocative atmosphere. . . . If one had to formulate a critique, it would be that it is too well done . . . a bit too luxurious for a clientele who, doubtless, will not appreciate it, nor understand it, nor take pleasure in it."[52]

FIGURE 3. Façade, Hôpital Franco-Musulman de Bobigny. Photo taken by Sébastien Greppo.

Aside from its "Muslim" aesthetic, the daily administration of the hospital was structured around Muslim religious requirements. The statutes of the hospital decreed that a number of Arabic-speaking doctors, preferably those "familiar . . . with Muslim natives and their customs," would be recruited and that Arabic-speaking staff would receive bonuses. Freedom of religion would be respected within the hospital's walls, but "the Mosquée de Paris's imam or a Muslim clergyman designated by the Institut Musulman [would] have access to patients who seek their assistance." Furthermore, the site would feature not only "a *salle de prière* for the patients and Muslim personnel" but also a space for the "slaughter of animals according to Muslim ritual."[53] The hospital's Muslim personnel were given the day off on Muslim holidays, and during the month of Ramadan, patients' meals were served at sunset.[54]

Although much care was taken to describe the hospital as a place designed to cater to Muslim religious needs, it was also a place to quarantine foreign bodies suspected of harboring dangerous diseases that might easily spread to French citizens. Or, as the president of the *département* of the Seine's Conseil général explained at the hospital's inauguration, "We needed to protect, but also police, because undesirable individuals had been mixing with healthy elements."[55] The full ambiguity of the French state's position lies in its attitude toward Muslim bodies: they were considered a danger to public health but were also taken seriously as having particular religious embodied practices that needed to be provided for in a hospital setting if patients were to have any hope of recovery. While those who celebrated the hospital's creation claimed that "the population truly appreciated" the special treatment the hospital afforded them, even if they could not fully understand the attention that went into its aesthetic planning,[56] many North Africans did everything in their power to avoid receiving treatment at the Hôpital Franco-Musulman. In 1937, for example, one third of admitted patients refused to be treated there.[57] The special committee of the Haut-Comité Méditerranéen, a group of French experts on the Muslim world established under Léon Blum's Popular Front government, was disturbed to report that Muslims had to be forced to go to the Hôpital Franco-Musulman against their will. The HCM's observers were surprised to find that "in spite of the excellence of the medical care, which incidentally demands a very significant budgetary contribution from the state, some North Africans prefer to be treated in other hospitals."[58] A member of the Seine Conseil général went further in his observations of the missteps of the state's attempt to provide Muslims with appropriate health care. "I must say," Léon Mauvais explained, "that Arabs have come to complain that they have been forced to go to this Franco-Muslim hospital and that the Parisian hospitals did not want to admit them."

Mauvais also noted that "some North Africans did not want to follow the special alimentary regime" used at the hospital "because they are now used to French customs, even [when it comes to food]."[59] Immigrants' refusal to be segregated on the basis of religion suggests that they were fully aware that they were being denied access to the services available to everyone else, even as they were being offered special privileges. Their desire to be treated at French public hospitals may have stemmed in part from fears about the quality of care at the Hôpital Franco-Musulman, but certain Muslims were also rejecting their involuntary assignation to the categories "Muslim," "Arab," and "North African." In other words, they were rejecting a regime that kept them outside of the boundaries of the French public sphere, supposedly for their own comfort, on the basis of their presumed religious identity.

Pagans on the Periphery

The refusal of some Parisian Muslims to be exclusively categorized as Muslim by the French state reflected a larger problem in *Islam français*: the religious observances of working-class North African immigrants who were practicing Muslims were not considered "real" Islam in the eyes of French observers. Paul Bourdarie, one of the Mosquée's earliest proponents, had argued that the embodiment of *Islam français* was designed to appeal to both the elites and the masses. As he explained, "If the creation of a Franco-Arab Institute will deeply interest our Muslim elite, the erection of the Mosque will touch the masses in the depths of their religious sentiment."[60] However, the only Muslims who sometimes made use of the complex in its early days were members of the elite. The population of Muslims living in Paris during the war years and the 1920s was mostly made up of workers who were not expected to settle permanently in France. The idea of creating a living institution devoted to religious practice for a large, vibrant community is quite different from creating an institution primarily intended to negotiate a difficult relationship with a colonial population.[61]

Reconstructing the religious and social practices of North African workers living in Paris during the late 1920s and 1930s is difficult not only because of the relative scarcity of sources but also because the archival evidence that does exist comes from colonial officers sent to the metropole to report back to their administrations on the activities of their nationals living in Paris and its suburbs. What does seem apparent, even when filtering through for the colonial lenses that color the reports, is that "Islam" was but one of many ways that North African workers structured their worlds. Even when Muslim religious activities were an important part of Muslims' daily lives, they were not the most important factor in their identities or in the way they constituted their social relations with one another. Social solidarities seemed to have much more to do with place of origin than a common-feeling of being Muslim. Lt-Col Justinard, head of the Section sociologique de la Direction générale des affaires indigènes (Morocco) reported to his superiors that "there is a spontaneous solidarity among these immigrants . . . which is very beautiful."[62] This solidarity was manifested in money sent home to relatives, aid to new arrivals and collections to repatriate sick countrymen or bodies for burial. Justinard notes that "this socialism . . . means that they can quite easily pass up social welfare services," which he viewed as a positive development, for he believed that too much dependency on the French state would encourage North African populations to group themselves exclusively around social service centers, while if they were left to their own devices, they would be less concentrated and thus less dangerous. The Moroccans among whom Justinard found his informants lived in Gennevilliers, Asnières, Grezillons, Argenteuil, Saint-Denis, Puteaux, Courbevoie, Nanterre, Stains and Villetaneuse; almost all were Soussis, from the Souss region of Morocco.[63] The Soussis "do not like the Algerian *indigènes* and do not befriend them," a sentiment echoed by colonial administrators on both sides of the Mediterranean when observing the interactions of North African colonial subjects and protégés. This evidence that local, regional, or national identities trumped a shared Muslim identity among many North African immigrants did not change the French perception that these workers were first and foremost Muslims.

Yet at the same time, Justinard observed among the Soussis living in the Paris region an attachment to the "pagan" Islam cited earlier to describe the religious practices of immigrants in the capital. He wrote that "this Berber society transplanted to Paris has groups which form spontaneously in a very curious manner which one could call '*inflas.*'"[64] The religious leaders who organized these gatherings were "marabouts . . . often with no other employment, criss-crossing the country, praying over the dead, and officiating at funerals. They are well-known and easy to find." Justinard acknowledged that his knowledge of these practices often came from informants, "the clever ones who have made their fortune and are now owners or managers of buildings, cafes and stores," rather than personal observation.

Based on the information he collected during his fieldwork, Justinard concluded that the Soussis living in the Paris region "do not have any religious centers. We've heard of the Tidjanniya *zaouïa.* In reality, in a house on rue de l'Espérance inhabited by Moroccans in Gennevilliers, there is a room where people meet to pray together."[65] The implicit judgment that such a room could not be considered a "religious center" is clear. The Islam of these workers is described in both police records and the writings of some contemporary scholars as a collection of folkloric customs as performed by poverty-stricken rural villagers, highly unorthodox and bearing little resemblance to orthodox Islam.[66] The préfet de la Seine warned the Ministre des Affaires etrangères when describing his concerns about the health of North African workers immigrating to Paris that these men were certainly not the "avant-garde" of Islam as celebrated by the Mosquée's founders. Rather, theirs was a "very particular Islam, with its sheen of paganism, its laws, its marabouts, its everyday life material habits . . . in short, an Islam on the margins of the Quran."[67] This was also the conclusion of visiting researchers sent by the Moroccan administration to complete a sociological study of Moroccan immigrants in the Paris suburbs. The report was blunt: "All these Berbers who are in France, we can't tell them they're not Muslim. They are, and they say they are. But their religion is 'on the back burner.'"[68]

The *ziaras*, gatherings led by visiting religious leaders, among the Moroccan community in France (particularly, but not exclusively, in Paris) continued to concern colonial officials, who by 1938 began to argue that they needed to be stopped. According to one report, during one summer six major *ziaras* took place in France, with the largest sums being collected in Paris. French observers contended that the Moroccan communities in France participated in these events halfheartedly, even against their will, and donated their hard-earned money out of fear of reprisals or consequences for their families back home rather than a desire to participate. The money was collected during *ouâdas,* "meetings which generally take place among Chleuh in a Moroccan café on a religious holiday . . . or when it's necessary to come to the aid of a Moroccan in need or to permit him to pay for his trip back to Morocco if he is poor or sick." The *ouâdas* in and of themselves were not objectionable to French officials, it was the perceived "hijacking" of these meetings by religious figures who pillaged those who "work so hard to put a bit of money aside." When *ouâdas* were organized independently of the *ziaras,* observers noted, they cost the attendees "less than the cost of a trip to the movies and give far more pleasure; they eat couscous together, drink mint tea; listen raptly to stories . . . ; hear musicians, singers, and dancers who, dressed in traditional garb, entertain them for long hours."[69] Yet as with all the "religious" events that took place outside of the confines of the Mosquée, French observers had difficulty identifying these practices as Muslim. The line between communal life and mutual aid and religious observances was further blurred by the *ouâdas*.

Just as colonial and metropolitan authorities were concerned about whether and how North African immigrants in the Paris region organized their religious lives, the Ouléma were also worried about the effects of immigration on the religious lives of their Algerian countrymen. The Ouléma established a mission in the working-class 20th *arrondissement,* which had a large Algerian population, called the *nadi al-tahdhib,* or the "educational club." The *nadi* soon expanded, holding meetings in several locations in the Paris region, offering courses in Arabic and Islam, and proposing alcohol-free cafés. For as the leader of the Parisian club said to an audience in Algiers in 1937, Algerian immigrants in France "are straying further and further from the precepts of the Qur'an, but they must be forgiven, for they have among them no scholars or qualified men to show them that they are deviating from the true faith. The colonialists profit from this, and seek to complete their perdition, by furnishing them with opportunities to drink alcohol. . . . All in an effort to destroy Islam!"[70] The Ouléma also clearly understood that the Islam they sought to promote in Paris had to compete not only with the Islam of the Mosquée and the "pagan" practices of Muslim immigrants themselves, who were becoming increasingly "corrupted" through their encounter with France, but also the nationalist temptation provided by more radical movements like the Étoile Nord Africaine.

Of course, not all of North African immigrants' social lives revolved around religious practices or nationalist political activity. In spite of the small size of the population, concerts of Arab music attracted full houses when performed in spaces that were socially and economically accessible to North African workers. While non-Muslim Parisian audiences were not enamored of performances by North African singers and musicians on tour from Algeria or Morocco whose repertoires were entirely classical Arabic music, the same concerts found huge success among Paris's Algerians. Bachetarzi recalls his first performances in 1924 in front of a French audience at the Olympia, which "was not a great success" when compared to a show with his troupe El Moutribia in the *mairie* (city hall) of the 10th *arrondissement* in which his "Algerian brothers" spread the word and filled the house.[71] The Algerian singer wondered, before organizing and embarking on a tour of France "to bring a little 'breath of air from the homeland'" to immigrant workers in France, whether such a venture was a good idea:

> This Algerian public whom we wanted to reach, would we even be able to contact it, to inform it of our tour, to bring it to the concert hall . . . assuming someone gives us one. And would these workers,

> scattered across factories, exhausted by a miserable life, even be interested in our songs and dances?
>
> I had already sung in Paris . . . but not at all under the same conditions. At the "Olympia" and the "Empire" I did not have to attract the public, they were there every week, for other shows, and they looked at me a bit like a strange animal with my "exotic" songs. You could count the Algerians who came to see me on the fingers of one hand: just some friends who wanted to pass backstage to congratulate me. This did not prove the existence, only the possibility, of an "Arab Public."[72]

But Bachetarzi, having managed to find his "Arab Public," organized a tour in Paris, with shows at *mairies* and newspaper offices. Although his troupe of musicians did not undertake much publicity, "it happened on its own, by word of mouth, in the Algerian milieu. Just like at home, the 'Arab telephone' worked!" Algerians from Clichy, Saint-Denis, Nanterre, Gennevilliers, and Billancourt mobbed all the shows put on by the troupe.[73] El Moutribia's final performance, however, held at the restaurant of the Mosquée, was not destined for the workers in "exile" who were so grateful for a taste of home but rather for the "entire North African elite of Paris, as well as many French including many 'Officials.'"[74] Thus while the majority of the Paris region's North African workers did not have economic or social access to the big French concert halls in which visiting musicians performed, nor did they apparently have access to North African cultural offerings performed at the Mosquée, they did consume Algerian music and dance whenever they could.[75]

Much of the religious and cultural life for the Paris region's Muslims took place far from the confines of the Mosquée de Paris. Of the Parisian site, "near the Jardin des Plantes," Justinard wrote that Moroccans living in the suburbs "hardly ever go there, and no one has done anything up till now to attract them. It is far from their neighborhoods. It is expensive for their budgets. The *hammam,* the café and the restaurant attached to the Mosquée are luxurious spaces destined for Parisians or for foreigners looking for exotic thrills and in which the shabby clothes and worker's helmets would be a sorry sight." A Catholic priest, after visiting a Moroccan neighborhood in Gennevilliers, recounted a conversation about the relationship between the immigrant community and the Mosquée's personnel:

> "Have you ever gone to see la Mosquée de Paris?"
>
> "Once, monsieur."

This was a shopkeeper who earned money and could thus afford the trip. But most of his comrades have never gone.

> "And the marabout of Paris, does he come visit you from time to time?"
> "Not often, monsieur. He came once or twice this year, no more than that."[76]

Far from bemoaning this situation, in which Paris's actual Muslim population was excluded from the one central religious site recognizable to outsiders, Justinard thought that the Mosquée's direction and the French state "should be congratulated." His fear was that the Mosquée could, in spite of its luxuriousness and inaccessibility, become an authentic religious center and a site of hostile propaganda.

Performing Islam at the Mosquée

Justinard was right to fear that the Mosquée might somehow be associated with nationalist protest, but these demonstrations did not have much impact on the daily administration of the site during the interwar years. National and local administrations, with the cooperation of the colonial governments and the Mosquée's leadership, maintained tight control over the site's religious programming. Muslim festivities provided occasions for the multiple actors concerned about Muslim religious life in Paris to use the Mosquée to rehearse their visions of what Muslim religious practice should look like. A key feature of the Mosquée's practices was their visibility to the French public and to French authorities, as opposed to the relatively "invisible" forms practiced elsewhere in the city. Both the police and agents from the Quai d'Orsay took careful note of the goings-on at the Mosquée's celebrations and of those in attendance. An official report of an Aïd el Kébir ceremony at the Mosquée in 1934, for example, mentions that "the crowd was considerable," with five thousand faithful taking part.[77] Its author noted that most participants came directly from the military barracks in Paris, Compiègne, Senlis, and Chalons-sur-Marne. The heavy contingent of soldiers and the fact of their arrival en masse most likely having been organized by their military leaders of course raises questions about the personal choices involved in their presence at the Mosquée. It is not clear whether, left to their own devices, these soldiers would have chosen to attend the services at the Mosquée or elsewhere or would have chosen not to observe the holiday religiously at all. However, because the holiday fell on a Monday, "a large number of Muslim workers from the Capital, detained by their work, were not able to come accomplish their devotions." That workers' schedules made it impossible for them to attend Aïd observances cannot be debated, but of course what can be questioned is whether they would have chosen to attend had they had the choice. The observer believed that their absence could be explained entirely by the physical impossibility of being in two places at once, suggesting that "it would be very desirable for the Parisian factory owners employing North African personnel to give their Muslim workers the morning off for Aïd Séghir [*sic*] and Aïd El Kébir, the third . . . holiday, Mouloud, being celebrated at night." Such a gesture, he argued, would be advantageous for France's image among its North African subjects and protégés. Si Kaddour was apparently of the same opinion, for he proposed to contact the direction of the Paris region's Citroën, Panhardt, and Renault[78] factories personally.[79]

The official's report on the gathering at the Mosquée is more notable for its list of personalities, Muslim and French, in attendance, than for its description of the religious observances that took place. Most accounts of these practices come from similar sources, so it is difficult to gauge the extent to which these holidays served as carefully choreographed displays of France's regard for Islam rather than as "genuine" religious observances, both for those officiating in religious capacity and for those in attendance, whether Muslim or not. In the entire report, the observations of the actual religious content of the day's activities were summarized as follows: "The 'Khotba' was pronounced, in the *salle des prières,* by the Algerian imam Si Ali Yahyaoui. . . . In the *salle de réception,* . . . abundant refreshments and pastries were served. . . . Following custom, the . . . soldiers stayed behind at the Mosquée where they were served a generous 'diffa,'"[80] or feast. Even in this brief description of the religious observance of this holiday, much of the focus is on the "cultural" aspects of the event, such as the expansive offerings of refreshments. Immediately following this description, the observer concludes that "to summarize, [it was] an important manifestation of Muslim unity, on our soil, . . . in which French prestige [was evident]." This description does, however, suggest that we can read this Aïd celebration as an attempt to recreate an "authentic" North African observance of the holiday for Muslim residents of Paris and its environs, but also for French observers. As it was essential to the public nature of *Islam français* that these rituals be transparently visible to non-Muslim French, the celebration of Aïd as a "manifestation" of France's relationship with its Muslim subjects was important.

Media coverage of the events at the Mosquée often emphasized the exoticism of the Muslim crowds that filled its halls, even though such "crowds" were quite small. In an article about the observance of Aïd El Seghir in 1930, a journalist reported that "all the Muslims of Paris" were there, which police reports on attendance at other holidays suggest was highly unlikely.[81] Although the funeral of the former shah of Persia fell on the same day and was performed at the Mosquée, the author referred only to the presence of Muslims who were there to observe the holiday. For this journalist, this event took place in an exhibit-like setting that did not quite fit into Paris's landscape: "Sadness of the Orient, reduced to singing in Paris under a soft February sky!" The author described the Mosquée's design as the "improvised stucco [of an] exposition," which, combined with the reference to the incongruousness of such a site under a Parisian sky, reminds us of the Mosquée's role in a Paris designed for tourism and spectacle. In this *tableau vivant,* however, there were still distinctions to be made between the elite and proletarian Muslim populations of the capital. Those of certain means were "shod in lemon yellow babouches and draped in white linen, others . . . to distinguish themselves from impure Europe, [wore] a red fez." Yet "most" of the Muslims in question were "manual laborers from the quays at Javel or Billancourt, dressed in honest workers' overalls, only their soul in its Sunday best."[82] The wearing of "traditional North African" clothing by North Africans in France was remarked on by journalists from the Catholic journal *En Terre d'Islam* reporting on the Moroccan and Algerian communities in Paris's suburbs in the 1930s. They were thrilled to find a laborer in Nanterre clad in a *chéchia,* or brimless head covering, and forlornly asked his cap-wearing neighbors, "Why don't you wear your *chéchia* anymore? The cap isn't beautiful, it's flat, but the *chéchia* is great, it keeps your head warm, it's chic. . . ." Their subjects responded, "Da cap, good for work, *chéchia* beautiful, but not here." As the disappointed Catholic reporters explained, "The cap really disfigures them. They wear it awkwardly, it makes them look like apaches. But oh well, they want to be like everyone else!"[83] The choice to wear items of clothing associated with different regions of North Africa was intimately tied to one's social status. The elites dressed in babouches (slippers) and djellabas (long tunics) at the Mosquée during holidays were equally at home in European tailored suits, including Si Kaddour himself. The North African proletariat, however, seems to have dressed like their French colleagues and rarely, if ever, cloaked themselves in the Maghrébin clothing.

The elite nature of the Mosquée was but one of the critiques launched against it. North African nationalists pronounced it the "advertisement Mosquée," a piece of propaganda for Parisian entertainment built by colonial officials whose hands were red with Muslim blood. Exchanges of letters between Si Kaddour and the police's Service des Affaires indigènes in the days leading up to holidays or other major events often expressed fears that nationalists and other militants would choose such occasions to protest France's role in North Africa and would use the Mosquée as the ideal place to voice those critiques. Si Kaddour was conscious of the significance of the nationalists' decision to hold protests at the Mosquée, for he defined himself as "not Moroccan but French" and his role at the Mosquée as the protector of "our work and more precisely the policy it represents."[84] Fears of nationalist opposition were well founded, as the Mosquée did in fact frequently serve as a site to contest French authority.[85] The Étoile Nord-Africaine (North African Star, ENA) was founded in Paris in 1926 by a small group of Algerian men closely affiliated with the French Communist Party.[86] In his memoirs, Messali Hadj, the ENA's leader, would remark on the coincidence of the founding of his anticolonial movement with the defeat of the Emir Abdelkrim in Morocco's Rif War to suggest that the working-class North African immigrants in Paris would take up the nationalist cause.[87] The founding of the ENA and Abdelkrim's defeat also, of course, almost coincided with the inauguration of the Mosquée.[88] Messali Hadj derided the building as "an Oriental cabaret, made for tourists, lowlifes, and hookers . . . built with money from workers, who are excluded from it . . . an insult to Islam."[89] The Arabic-language journal of the French Communist Party, *El Amel,* echoed this critique, emphasizing in particular the activities organized at the Mosquée that had nothing to do with Muslim religious practices:

> Yes, of course, last June 15th Princess Aage of Denmark abandoned the Chapelle Saint Ignace for once to bow down before "the representative of Islam," His Traitorship Si Kaddour Ben Ghabrit. It's just that in these sorts of circles, they all get along. The Moroccan of this holy site is not a savage, a coward, a rebel against whom one needs to send . . . bombs; he is the man worthy of respect, the writer full of praise for civilizing France, the manager of sites of worship who received, at the *mirhab,* even these bimbos in their nudity!
>
> It seems that the day of the 15th was joyous, with couples traipsing through the courtyard, the garden, visiting the different sections one by one. You could find them in every corner. It was really everything that's delicious about love *à la orientale.*
>
> The Mosquée is now blessed, there's no need to disturb Cardinal Verdier—oh, excuse me—the Sultan of Morocco—because it's a Muslim mosque. The high-class girls and high society gentlemen have already drunk to that.[90]

This critique refers not only to the cultural divide between those for whom the Mosquée was said to be constructed and those who actually used it but also to the other kinds of social events that took place in the Mosquée.

It could be argued that in providing immigrant workers from majority Muslim countries with health care designed to respond to Muslim sensibilities or the means to celebrate major holidays at a mosque located in the center of the city, the French state was being more generous to its colonial subjects than it was to its metropolitan citizens (a charge often leveled against the founders of the Hôpital Franco-Musulman, for example). Certain politicians working at the municipal and national levels truly believed that they were responding to a desperate need on the part of Muslim immigrant workers. Yet it is essential to remember that the discourse of providing Muslims with "special" medical or employment services masked the fact that they were kept in a parallel social universe, separated not only from the French but also from other immigrants. Having defined their vision of *Islam français* in the form of the Mosquée, the next step for those involved in its administration was to use that "Islam" as the medium for all interactions with North African immigrants, thus reducing their multifaceted socio-cultural lives to a single element. Their own religious sentiments were dismissed as unorthodox at best and illegitimate at worst.

The decision to structure social assistance programs for North African immigrants along Muslim lines set the pattern for the state's interaction with these communities. Rosenberg argues that by "treating North Africans so differently from other immigrants, by segregating them and subjecting them to an often brutal surveillance regime, republican authorities helped entrench what had been an unexceptional anti-'Arab' sentiment and reinforced a critical distinction between nationality and citizenship."[91] While not disagreeing with this conclusion, I would suggest instead that the separate regime designed for North African immigrants, particularly in the case of Algerians who were in fact French nationals, was more significant in that it legitimized segregation on religious grounds in the name of cultural sensitivity. The local, national, and colonial politicians involved in the creation of the apparatus that policed the capital's North Africans acted out of complex motives; perhaps they sincerely believed that they were providing their colonial workers with services they wanted. Judging their motives, however, is less important than recognizing the fact that French politicians believed Islam's embodied demands to be such that Muslims required separate hostels and hospitals and could not be assimilated into the larger immigrant population, let alone the French population. This trend, begun during the interwar years, would gain added strength during the Vichy years, in which the racializing logic of Pétain's regime coincided with the embodied logic of *Islam français*.

Chapter 4

Islam français, Islam in France: Forms of Islam in Paris and the Provinces

The Vichy regime, under the leadership of Maréchal Philippe Pétain, drastically changed secular France's religious landscape, bringing religious education back into public schools and restoring property to the Catholic Church. In this decidedly antisecular climate, the questions of what exactly it meant to be Muslim and whether it meant different things in Paris and in the provinces preoccupied French officials. An administration committed to bringing Catholicism back into the public sphere had to consider what its role in supporting Muslim practices in the metropole should be.[1] As North African immigration to the metropole increased, workers began to settle in larger numbers in provincial cities, compelling national and local administrations to consider what kinds of Muslim services should be provided to immigrant communities outside the immediate orbit of the Mosquée de Paris. These questions were considered in the light of two distinct but intimately linked issues: the space of Islam and the place of Islam. By the *space* of Islam, I mean the aesthetic and architectural frames for particular embodied practices. The *place* of Islam, on the other hand, refers to the geographical location of these Muslim spaces: in the center of the city or on its outskirts, in a "Muslim" neighborhood or in a "French" one, in the capital or in a provincial city.

For the first time, French management of Muslim religious practice in the metropole reflected an interrogation of whether the state should be supporting *Islam français* (and if so, which kind) or Islam *in* France. It is important to examine how the republican and *laïc* "Frenchness" of the Mosquée's *Islam français* lost currency even as the site continued to serve as a central, embodied representation of Islam for a metropolitan audience. Certain Parisian Muslim sites, as well as some provincial places of worship, embodied an Islam imported almost "intact" from North Africa (even though they were often staffed with members of the local Muslim community), one that made no attempt to position itself in relation to French values. The spaces of alternative Parisian and provincial Muslim sites did not share the Mosquée's opulent *hispano-mauresque* style; their decor was more subdued and their scale far more modest. Nor did they share the centralized placement of the Mosquée de Paris: these Muslim sites were not located in city centers easily accessible to non-Muslim visitors. Because these sites were intended for exclusive use by Muslims, there was no need for them to serve, additionally, as representations of Islam, so the practices that took place within them did not need to be made visible or transparent.

Questions about the potential secularism of Islam and Muslims were posed again, not only because of the Vichy regime's resolutely antisecular stance but also due to the climate marked by the racialization of those considered to be non-French others that characterized this period, such as Jews. People who had been *israélites* became members of the "Jewish race" under Vichy. The existing French tendency to overemphasize Islam's physicality was only reinforced by contemporary discourses about the innate nature of race and culture. North African immigrants were not the victims of the vicious and lethal racism that targeted French Jews.[2] But it was nevertheless during the Vichy years that the tendency to characterize Islam as inherently physical, a central element of *Islam français,* was given full rein. The representation of particular embodied rituals took on a greater importance than ever in the display of *Islam français* to the non-Muslim French at the expense of a counterbalancing emphasis on Islam's compatibility with French culture and civilization. The maintenance of the space and place of the Mosquée de Paris was thus of paramount importance to national and local administrations, for the Muslim religious site's setting was considered essential to the proper observance of these rituals.

The difficulties of the war years do not seem to have unduly affected the everyday affairs of the Mosquée de Paris, which serves as a testimony to the gravity of its mission in the eyes of the French state. The Mosquée's annual budgets show ever-increasing revenues from entrance fees and postcard sales, and the number of tour guides (as well as their salaries) continued to rise. This suggests that there was a steady and indeed growing public seeking out the Mosquée's display of Islam. During the war years and in the decade that followed, Parisian associations and the national administration took great pains to provide for relatively sumptuous celebrations of holidays, complete with "traditional" foods. At the Mosquée, the celebration of Muslim holidays such as Aïd es Seghir and Aïd el Kébir took place in two phases, which reflected the dual nature of *Islam français*: a "strictly religious"[3] morning ceremony took place in the intimacy of the *salle de prières* for Muslim worshippers, and an afternoon "reception" drew numerous French officials and dignitaries as well as Muslim elites to the Mosquée's public open spaces so that the holiday could still be celebrated and observed by a French audience.

The complicated shifts in the *Islam français* of the Mosquée, however, were only part of the landscape of Islam in Paris and in the metropole. At the same time as the centrally located Mosquée continued to engage in public displays of Muslim religious practices, alternative religious sites used by the Paris region's increasingly large immigrant community came to occupy an important space in the city's Muslim geography. One such site located in the northern suburb of Gennevilliers, the Moroccan-directed Maison de Bienfaisance (known as "Dar es Sultan"), often boasted greater attendance at its religious and cultural celebrations than did the Mosquée. More importantly, the Islam celebrated at Dar es Sultan was not the *Islam français* of the Mosquée in any of its instantiations: rather, it was the "folkloric" Islam derided by observers like Justinard in the 1930s.

It was not only in Paris that such a split occurred. During the 1940s the Ministry of the Interior and the General Government of Algeria embarked on an ambitious program to establish a network of smaller provincial religious sites (under the authority of the Mosquée de Paris) designed to serve North African immigrant laborers. Unlike their parent institution, these regional sites were not sumptuously decorated buildings designed to be visible in their respective cityscapes. They were often not even mosques but modest prayer rooms or cemeteries, and they were not usually located in city centers. The difference lay in the fact that provincial places of worship were not temples to *Islam français,* nor were they used for the interests of the non-Muslim French.

It was its presence in Paris that signaled the Mosquée's importance. The Mosquée was but one monument in a collection of monumental architectural sites in the French capital, and it was its inclusion among such noteworthy sites which gave the institution its power and authority. The Muslim site was of course not the only Parisian monument to French power. The Place de la Concorde's obelisk also commemorated a certain kind of French-Muslim relationship, while the Arc de Triomphe celebrated Napoleonic victories.

The arch may have been a more obvious representation of French power, but the Mosquée was nevertheless visible proof that the state considered its authority over Muslim lands to be secure. This site thus needed to be built not only in the capital but also in its very heart, in order to show that France was truly a *puissance musulmane* and to be visible to elite Muslims from French territories as well as curious French visitors. Few observers from Algiers or Rabat, or even from elsewhere in France, would have gone to visit a mosque in Saint-Etienne, for instance. The Mosquée's monumental nature also depended on its uniqueness. The sites conceived by members of a transnational Muslim elite living in France as similarly luxurious spaces to display Islam to French elites, such as the mosques of Nice and Vichy, were never actually built. A "cathedral mosque" in the provinces would have diminished the power of the capital's premier Muslim site to project an image of Paris as the center of the Muslim world.

Administering Islam during the War and After: Rupture or Continuity?

The Vichy years were characterized by stunning reversals by Maréchal Pétain of the law separating church and state of 1905, marking the Occupation as a period of profound rupture with preceding decades. As early as December 1940, Pétain opened the door to the teaching of religion in public schools, and a few months later, in February 1941, his administration restored religious edifices to the ownership of the Catholic Church. A law passed on Christmas of 1942 decreed that state donations for buildings dedicated to religious use, whether classified as historic monuments or not, would not be considered subsidies. This final law, which was a direct violation of article of the law of 1905 that made it illegal to subsidize religious activity, was never abrogated after Liberation; it is still in force to this day. Under Pétain's leadership, the Vichy regime undid much of what the Third Republic had done to make France a secular country. As Catholicism was reintroduced in force during the Occupation and Jews were deported, Muslims occupied a liminal space with respect to their religion and identity.

The full story of the Vichy regime's relationship to Islam and Muslims on both sides of the Mediterranean is one that largely remains to be written. A series of laws passed during the Vichy years nevertheless suggests that the régime's *politique musulmane* bore more than a passing resemblance to Lyautey's Moroccan protectoral regime, with its gestures toward the "protection" of Islam. In Algeria, departmental *associations cultuelles* that gave Muslim religious leaders some autonomy over their own religious sites (which still belonged to the state) were founded in 1943, and the law of 27 October 1941 made it illegal for Muslims to consume alcohol as well as for anyone to sell alcohol to Muslims. French historian Jacques Cantier argues that during Vichy, the government "maintained a privileged alliance with the traditional elites" based in part on the "many affinities between the hierarchized vision of society articulated by the *Révolution nationale*, Pétain's political program, and the conservative discourse which celebrated a rural and patriarchal Algeria held . . . by the conservative forces of Muslim Algeria."[4] Yet contemporary analyses of Algerian socio-religious realities paint a different picture, of a society whose "traditional cadres" had been "strongly undermined." The famous Islamicist Jacques Berque wrote a report entitled "La Société musulmane algérienne" for the Ministry of the Interior in which he argued that since 1920, and especially between 1936 and 1945, "the hereditary social authorities, aristocrats, and marabouts lost part of their prestige."[5] The blows to traditional social structures, Berque explained, created a country of "*déracinés*" susceptible to all kinds of nationalist propaganda.

Though perhaps not for the reasons Berque identified, Algerian and other North African nationalist activity did indeed flower during World War II and the years that immediately followed. The religious reformist movements, such as the Ouléma, lost ground to different political organizations such as the Amis du Manifeste de la Liberté (AML), founded by Ferhat Abbas in 1944, which drew different political currents together in support of his manifesto (sent to the governor-general in March 1943). In addition to calls for national self-determination, the manifesto demanded religious freedom and the application of the law of 1905 to Algeria.[6] It was the AML that organized the peaceful demonstrations in favor of Algerian independence in Sétif on 8 May 1945, which ended in violent repression by the French army as V-E Day was celebrated in Europe. The Sétif massacres were yet another indication of the need to rethink France's management of its colonies, particularly in Algeria. The Organic Law of 20 September 1947 was intended to address some of the concerns of Algerian nationalists while maintaining Algeria firmly within the French empire. While proclaiming all Algerians equal with regard to race or religion, the law nevertheless maintained separate European and Muslim electoral colleges. In addition, Muslims had to choose between maintaining their Muslim personal status and becoming French citizens, which was only possible under certain restrictive circumstances. This last issue was particularly important for Muslims who immigrated to France: living in a country where the principles of the law of 1905 were actually applied showed them that one should not have to choose between one's religious and civil status.

These dangerously "uprooted" Muslims conversant with the language of *laïcité* and equality threatened both the metropolitan and colonial governments, and it was for this reason that they worked together to manage the Muslim religious experience in France. At the war's outbreak, the Ministry of War was deeply opposed to the idea of creating a special corps of Muslim clergy to serve Muslim soldiers, arguing that imams from the Mosquée de Paris should be able to cope with their needs. The ministry argued this case on religious and pragmatic levels. First, it was suggested that "the Muslim religion does not allow for any intermediary between the created and the creator; thus it does not have a clergy like most other religions." In addition to the lack of clergy, most Muslim rituals "are performed by [the Muslim] of his own initiative and without the control or intervention of another party." For those rituals that are performed in a group, such as the Friday noon prayer or funeral prayers, the person unanimously chosen as the best qualified, it was posited, simply leads his fellow Muslims in worship. Finally, Ministry of War officials argued that it would be impossible to constitute a corps of Moroccan or Tunisian imams, since in the protectorates it would be seen as an unwelcome intrusion into the religious sphere, still ostensibly managed by the sultan and bey, respectively. In addition to these religious considerations, the ministry raised the practical question of guaranteeing the safety of these clergymen as the Geneva Convention did not recognize "Red Crescent" symbols as designating clergy or medical teams. The one exception was the Turkish medical corps, but identifying the French army's Muslim staff with the symbol acknowledged to represent Turkey was hardly an option.[7] Finally, the question of whether the French army's Muslim soldiers would even appreciate such a gesture was generally answered in the negative.

The Ministry of War's early opposition to the creation of Muslim chaplains is surprising, given that it had provided space and resources for Muslim religious practice during World War I, as already noted. The return to the army's role as facilitator of Muslim life for colonial soldiers was signaled by the *décret* of 14 May 1940, which created a "Service d'Assistance religieuse pour les militaires musulmans." This decree provided for a corps of fifteen imams recruited from Algeria, Morocco, and Tunisia, whose nominees were subject to the approval of the Ministre de la défense nationale et de la guerre. The Service d'Assistance was a temporary measure, designed only to last the duration of the war. Unlike Catholic, Protestant, and Jewish army chaplains, the fifteen imams had no contract with the military and were not issued military uniforms or ranks.[8] Their tasks included providing religious assistance at military sites and hospitals as well as managing Muslim burials.[9]

The military, however, was not the only agency responsible for providing Muslims living in the metropole with religious personnel. A 1935 policy issued by the General Government in Algeria decreed that in order to "represent Algeria at the Mosquée de Paris, a Muslim *agent du culte* from the Colony will henceforth be designated every year for four months."[10] Thus in 1938, Si Kaddour asked the governor-general to designate the mufti of Bône's mosque to serve in the same capacity at the Mosquée de Paris for a period of four to five months. This individual, El Hadj Mohamed Djebli, had been selected for "his age, his experience in Muslim religious questions, his fidelity, and his loyalty toward France."[11] The administration in Algiers cooperated with the Vichy regime to ensure the continuation of this exchange of trusted Muslim religious figures over the course of the war.[12] In June 1941, Si Kaddour was able to arrange for the passage of five imams (two Algerians, two Moroccans, and a Tunisian) under this scheme from Marseille to occupied Paris without German travel documents, a feat that later aroused suspicion about his relationship with the German authorities.[13]

With the war's end, however, a more permanent solution needed to be found for staffing Muslim religious sites in Paris and the provinces. The question of which government ministries would be financially and otherwise responsible for these sites hinged on juridical and financial considerations in addition to political ones about where the ultimate authority for administering Islam in the metropole lay.[14] Muslim religious personnel paid by the Algerian colonial administration were sent from Algeria to work in France, though they continued to be subject to the legislation governing Muslim clergy in Algeria. As the governor-general explained to the minister of the interior in April 1945, the *décret* of 27 September 1907 gave the governor-general the power to subsidize clergy "temporarily" if it was deemed to be in the public interest.[15] This system of subsidies rested on *circonscriptions cultuelles* (parishes, dioceses, Jewish or Protestant *Consistoires*, and Muslim religious districts) that were supposed to reflect the religious needs of Algeria's territories. Because clergy subsidized by the Algerian administration had to come from within the official *associations cultuelles* associated with the *circonscriptions*, staff sent to the Mosquée had to be drawn from Algeria. The governor-general hoped to reorganize this procedure, arguing, "Would it not be opportune to prepare a new set of rules concerning Islam in the Metropole which would allow us to confront local needs?"[16] He was willing to increase his administration's subsidy to the Mosquée to circumscribe the need to provide a salary for Algerian religious figures working in the metropole.

There seemed to be agreement between the Ministry of the Interior and the administration in Algiers that it was in everyone's interest to staff France's

Muslim religious sites with a mixture of Algerian and local religious figures. The decision to recruit, at least partially, local metropolitan Muslims did not, however, mean that the governor-general would play a less active role in metropolitan Islam. Even local recruits would still be selected by the Mosquée's leader, who, in turn, reported to both Algiers and Paris. Si Kaddour was behind this two-pronged solution to the problem of responding to local needs in Paris and the provinces. It was he who suggested to the minister of the interior that the governor send imams to serve in six-month increments at the Mosquée. The imams, who would serve in the "metropole's major centers for North African labor," would be chosen by the Mosquée's leadership from the local Muslims "exercising a professional activity and having sufficient diplomas."[17] The governor-general agreed to have the Algerian préfets select potential imams, "showing all guarantees of knowledge and loyalty"; they would be paid by his administration and would serve at the Mosquée de Paris. In addition, he arranged for an additional subvention of 150,000 francs to be paid directly to the Mosquée to choose imams from the local population.[18] This was the procedure Si Kaddour followed in the Nord Pas-de-Calais region. He suggested to the Moroccan miners that "they choose imams from among themselves," since the role of imam "can very easily be filled while continuing a full-time professional activity."[19] The residencies of Morocco and Tunisia contributed 50,000 and 25,000 francs, respectively, to "permit Muslim workers in the metropole to practice their religion."[20] The extent to which any given site's religious personnel (whether brought over from North Africa or chosen from among the metropole's residents) influenced the kinds of Islam practiced in different religious sites in Paris and the provinces is not clear. The Mosquée, it seems, was staffed primarily with figures brought primarily from Algeria (though also from Morocco and Tunisia), while provincial sites were usually served by local Muslims. As we shall see, the kinds of practices as well as the very conception of "Islam" differed in their enactment in these varied sites. Sources, however, do not allow us to determine the ways in which these differences were the result of the French state's differentiated management of the Parisian and provincial sites or of a concerted effort by local or foreign staff to put their own visions of Muslim religious activity into practice in their institutions.

It is important to note that the Ministry of Labor was also involved in the financing of Muslim religious practice during and immediately after the war. This particular ministry's early involvement in the elaboration of a national program of staffing and maintaining Muslim religious sites belies the perception that Islam came to play a role in the workplace as late as the 1970s. It also indicates that *Islam français* has long been associated with the Muslim working classes living in Paris and the provincial capitals. The *décret* of 11 November 1945 transferred the "social works" that had formerly been the responsibility of the now-defunct Bureaux des affaires musulmanes nord-africaines to the Ministry of Labor. In the debates about what kinds of sites should be built in which cities, the issue of whom these religious institutions were meant to serve would become vitally important. Finally, the early participation of the Ministry of Labor in the financing of Muslim religious practice in France proves that the boundaries between the management of religion and the administration of potentially "dangerous" proletarian populations, particularly racially othered ones, is not a new feature of French *laïcité*. As we shall see, a similar blurring of boundaries existed in the sphere of social services, where religious entities such as the Mosquée were charged with providing crucial services to needy Muslims that in other circumstances would have been provided by the state. It is certainly true that Pétain was not the first French leader to use Islam as the backbone of social service programs directed at North African immigrants, for this pattern had been established in the two decades before he came to power. What was different about *Islam français* under his regime, and what would linger on in the decade to follow, was the evacuation of its secular *content* even though the *laïc*-compatible *format* of Muslim religious practice at the Mosquée de Paris was maintained by continuing to hold public and private religious observances, as will be explored in the section that follows. This continuity is important less in terms of what it suggests about the antisecular Vichy regime than in what it reveals about the not entirely secular policies pursued by Vichy's republican predecessors and successors.

Celebrating Tradition at the Mosquée: Black Market Sheep, Couscous, and Mint Tea

In spite of the privations that characterized the war years and the reconstruction period, government agencies and private organizations on both sides of the Mediterranean made it a priority to provide the city's Muslims with what they saw as the appropriate foods to celebrate the major religious holidays of the Muslim calendar. Although a holiday food distribution program to individual needy families was not entirely successful, as both government officials and Parisian Muslims observed, the rations provided to the Mosquée itself always arrived at their destination. This attention to food was part of a program in which the holidays served as occasions to render public and visible the state's relationship with its Muslim subjects. To this end, there were two celebrations of each holiday: those attended by French and colonial officials and those reserved for Muslims exclusively. The mise en scène of Muslim religious observance at the Mosquée rested on two elements: a heavy emphasis on alimentary rituals and the paired public/private celebration of Muslim holidays. Both were integral to the shifting definition of *Islam français* embodied by the Mosquée during this period: Islam was increasingly tied to particular "traditional" restrictive bodily practices rather than to principles compatible with *laïcité,* but its rituals were still performances to be observed by a French public.

The celebration of Aïd el Kébir in 1941 took place on 29 December, after intensive preparation by Si Kaddour, the Préfecture de Police, and the Secours National, Vichy's social assistance agency.[21] The SAINA of the Préfecture de Police began planning for the celebration in November, in cooperation with the Ministry of Supplies (Ravitaillement) and with a credit of 50,000 francs from the Secours National. These agencies provided for the organization of free couscous dinners in North African restaurants and the distribution of both provisions and ration cards for mutton to poor families. In addition, they procured two hundred sheep for the Mosquée itself to use as its leadership saw fit. By 1941 the problem of acquiring *halal* meat (meat from animals slaughtered according to Muslim law) had been resolved to Si Kaddour's satisfaction. The préfet de la Seine provided Muslims with an abattoir at La Villette, in the 19th *arrondissement,* to slaughter animals according to their dietary law. However, the German authorities forbade this practice when they occupied Paris, claiming (according to Si Kaddour) that their motivation was humanitarian, out of concern for the animals' pain. Si Kaddour complained that this meant that Paris's Muslims could not consume meat for several months. Finally, Si Kaddour ordered the abattoir's manager to resume slaughtering animals "according to Quranic instructions" while being careful not to be caught in the act. This he did, and the Germans eventually closed their eyes to the practice. Of course, we have only Si Kaddour's word that Muslims stopped eating meat during this period at all, or, if meat consumption did decrease or stop, whether this was in fact due to the knowledge that their source of *halal* meat had been compromised. I have not been able to find evidence to allow me to characterize North African workers' individual consumption of *halal* meat before this period, with the exception of the army and the Hôpital Franco-Musulman, where meat was prepared in accordance with dietary regimes. When descriptions are given of the meals served in workers' *foyers* during this period, it is not mentioned whether the meat was *halal* or not.[22] These "liberalities" at a time when everyone in Paris was hungry were taken "in favor of North African Muslims for the celebration of their ritual holiday." The state's decision to risk severe criticism by providing a specific group with particular kinds of food while many others went hungry underlines the extent to which "traditional" foods were made into artifacts so important that they needed to be provided to Muslims in France at any cost.[23] As Si Kaddour threateningly reminded the secretary of supplies, France's North Africans had "always been satisfied" during the war when it came to making "exceptions" to provide them with "food products which are traditionally part of the ritual meals of our coreligionists."[24] This exchange suggests that it was Si Kaddour himself or other member's of the Mosquée's staff who took on the responsibility of informing the authorities which foods constituted the "ritual meals" that were part of these holidays' celebrations.

Si Kaddour refers at once to "tradition" and "ritual," which are, of course, not interchangeable. It is true that the foods in question, couscous and mutton, would in fact have been consumed by many North African Muslim families with the means to do so to celebrate Aïd el Kébir. However, this meal of mutton couscous was in no way a religious obligation, nor was it a meal that was consumed by Muslims from other regions with their own culinary habits. Si Kaddour's conflation of rite and tradition in terms of food confirmed French administrators' stance that Islam was a demanding religion when it came to everyday practices and served to justify their misplaced emphasis on alimentary practices in Muslim everyday life. What was not emphasized in the discussions of these food distribution programs was the one aspect of food consumption that actually *is* a requirement of Muslim dietary law, namely, that meat be slaughtered in ritual fashion. Journalists at *Er Rachid,* the Paris-based journal of the anti-Semitic, pro-German Comité musulman de l'Afrique du Nord, accused Si Kaddour and the Mosquée's leadership of laxity in terms of dietary law at the Muslim abattoir at La Villette and even alleged that pork, forbidden by Quranic dietary law, was consumed within the very walls of the Mosquée.[25] Si Kaddour's skillful blurring of the line separating rite and tradition in which the actual ritual content of Muslim food restrictions was evacuated allowed him to demonstrate that Islam did have "traditions" that were different and exotic from French ones but not completely alien. After all, Catholics did not eat meat on Fridays, so why shouldn't Muslims have their own dietary habits? His emphasis on food performed important ideological work for the French administrators involved in managing *Islam français,* for it allowed them to focus on a relatively "harmless" element of cultural difference that could be not only tolerated but also celebrated. Other, more potentially dangerous challenges to French authority, such as Muslim law codes, would be more difficult to integrate.[26]

The French obsession with Muslim alimentary traditions (if not necessarily restrictions) grew out of the belief that Muslim practices were corporeal and moreover were linked to particular spaces. In concentrating only on holiday celebrations and rituals, French officials did not consider the question of *time,* instead focusing on *space,* which is what distinguished Islam more sharply from French secularism or French Catholicism. The Vichy state was not interested in making Islam compatible with *laïcité,* but its management of Muslim holidays did bring it into the realm of Catholic time. That observant Muslims' everyday was marked by five prayers at different points during the day was not emphasized in the Mosquée's programming, but the distinctive practices associated with particular holidays, exceptions to the everyday, were given much attention. Thus even the Vichy regime was not able to imagine a Muslim everyday that was truly distinct from a Catholic, or secular, everyday. This failure shows that the attempt via *Islam français* to make Islam compatible with French values was not completely transformed by the Vichy period. During the war years, the French state did not try to show the links between Islam and *laïcité,* as it had during the secular Third Republic. Rather, it made Islam compatible with the Catholic religious calendar, which conformed to contemporaneous representations of French values.

The celebration of the holiday itself was given relatively little attention by the authorities in comparison with the preparations for the distribution of "traditional" foods. All that was reported by the police in 1941 was that a ceremony gathering one thousand worshippers took place at the Mosquée from ten a.m. until noon; it was also attended by the former Turkish sultan and representatives from different branches of the Ministry of Foreign Affairs. A brief reference was made to a special dinner and an "Oriental concert" organized by the Section nord-africaine de la Ligue Française in the 13th *arrondissement* by some of the dignitaries who had also attended the Mosquée celebration.

Si Kaddour relied on the cooperation of the Parisian police and other agencies devoted to managing the city's Muslim population in organizing the observance of Ramadan, Aïd es Séghir, and Aïd el Kébir. Officials from these agencies as well as the national administration were sometimes welcome at the Mosquée's observances, but not always. The complicity between Si Kaddour and the préfet de Police and the extent to which the complex of SAINA services were implicated in Muslim life were revealed during the course of the Aïd es Séghir celebrations in 1942, for which only 150 people came to the Mosquée. Si Kaddour explained that "the ceremony, which had been set for Monday, 12 October, was moved one day forward at the last minute and a large number of the Paris region's Muslims could not be alerted of this change in time."[27] Si Kaddour's strategy to notify Muslims of the time change was to have the police publicize it in all of SAINA's centers in Paris and the suburbs. Although this collaboration did not result in a large number of people participating in the Mosquée's ceremony, it does illustrate the close partnership between Si Kaddour and the city's Muslim agencies. In 1942, the ceremony itself was "reserved exclusively for the Muslim world and no invitation was extended to officials." The only explanation given for this decision was a vague reference to "the circumstances."[28] This distinction does not seem to have been made during the celebration of Aïd es Séghir in 1943, which, according to the police, gathered 1,100 Muslims (mostly North Africans): Si Kaddour again received all the dignitaries after the religious ceremony, but no reference was made to their having been expressly forbidden to attend prayers. In 1943, unlike the previous year, a meal was served at 12:30 in the Mosquée's restaurant to three hundred Muslims who were either "needy" or "without family." This meal appears to have been sponsored by the Ministry of Supplies, whose minister attended the lunch and made a speech in honor of the occasion that was broadcast over the radio the following day.[29] Yet two months later, when Aïd el Kébir was celebrated on 8 December, no officials were invited to attend the ceremony.[30]

After the war, however, Aïd el Kébir was observed on 26 November 1944 with 2,220 people (including "many Muslim soldiers") in attendance and a stronger showing of French officials, who were not excluded from the religious ceremony with its "procession and songs" and a "short speech" in Arabic by the imam. The Ministry of the Interior informed the Parisian police in August 1945 just before Ramadan was about to begin that "in order to facilitate the observance of [the] religious customs [of the Muslims of your *département*]," they should allow restaurants to remain open later during Ramadan and authorize the consumption of coffee or coffee substitutes until closing time.[31] The question of appropriate alimentary practices for Aïd el Kébir proved to be a more difficult problem to resolve: the police reported a healthy black market trade in sheep bought by Muslim butchers with the support of the Mosquée de Paris. The director of the Economic Sector of the Police suggested that given the importance of sheep for the religious holiday, the best solution would be to have the minister of supplies pay the seller the going wholesale rate of 25 francs per kilogram directly.[32] The celebrations of these holidays seemed to revolve entirely around alimentary concerns rather than spiritual ones, and no emphasis on the ties between France and Islam was made during these events.

The French authorities' emphasis on ritual, particularly its alimentary aspect, continued in the years immediately following the war. Holidays were also observed with religious services attended exclusively by Muslims followed by a public display of Muslim religiosity at receptions held at the Mosquée. In 1947, Aïd es Séghir was celebrated by two thousand people between 10:30 a.m. and noon, including representatives of many Arab states. No French officials were present "because this observance was of a strictly religious nature." The president, however, visited the Mosquée the next day at 4 p.m. along with other French officials, and this pattern would continue for the next several years for both Aïd es Séghir and Aïd el Kébir.[33] These brief visits (about forty-five minutes) by French officials that took place after the religious services were also called "ceremonies" by the government functionaries who described them, which was the same word used to describe the morning's prayer services. By 1952, however, the forty-five-minute "ceremony" at 4 p.m. had become a two-hour event, beginning instead at 5 p.m., and involving "French and Muslim personalities." In addition, the morning's religious ceremonies were immediately followed by visits from French officials who were received by Si Kaddour. The afternoon's festivities, where cakes and drinks were served, were attended by representatives of the colonial administrations in Paris as well as the ministries involved in the running of Muslim affairs as well as influential members of Paris's Muslim community, particularly businessmen and journalists.[34] The Ministry of the Interior's reports indicate that in 1950, Aïd el Kébir was celebrated with both a morning ceremony for Muslim worshippers (including Lebanese, Afghan, Egyptian, Saudi, and Jordanian diplomats) and an "intimate reception" in the afternoon for some Muslim dignitaries and French national, colonial, and local officials involved in the management of North African populations.[35]

The two-tiered observance of holidays and the combination of "ceremonies" and "receptions" for Muslims and non-Muslim French observers represented the most crucial link between the *Islam français* of this period and that of the Mosquée's earlier years. One *indégenophile* described the sensation of being present at an Aïd el Kébir celebration in particularly emotive terms:

> Under the low grey sky, the Mosquée stands in its whiteness, but its adorable gardens seem out of place. A few djellabahs, fez, and chéchias give off a few colorful sparks among the sadness and monotony of European clothes and dripping umbrellas. . . . Si Kaddour receives, as always, and everyone penetrates the *salle de prière*; songs rise, grave and mysterious, slow and nostalgic. Then the Imam, Si Larbi Ben Souda, gives a very elevated and thoughtful sermon.[36]

Clearly, the combination of exotic spectacle and "profound" religious difference continued to fascinate Parisian observers. By sometimes holding two separate events, the Mosquée's leadership was able to give the impression that there were some aspects of Muslim religious observance that were too intimate to be transgressed by outsiders but that other elements could, and should, be appreciated and shared by non-Muslim French. Thus *Islam français,* though no longer necessarily compatible with republicanism, was still, in many ways, a representation of Islam to be consumed by Parisians who also ate couscous and bought "North African" home décor. Another French dévoté of the Mosquée's ceremonies wrote, "One noticed a very large number of Christians. . . . The Mosquée de Paris is open to all believers, and the Muslim religion knows how to distinguish between its friends and those curious for exoticism."[37] This not-disinterested remark was challenged by a Muslim observer at the same Aïd el Kébir observance, who wrote that the holiday at the Mosquée de Paris is "always the occasion for a 'Hollywood-esque' mise-en-scène. Nothing is missing, neither press, nor radio. . . . Those who we see the least of are Muslims come for the sacrifice."[38]

After the war, however, the authorities of the newly republican government were equally uninterested in characterizing the site as republican or *laïc.* Unlike the 1920s and 1930s, they paid almost no attention to the rhetorical or political dimensions of rituals at the Mosquée. Instead, French officials focused on the everyday religious practices, which they argued defined the Muslim experience of these holidays and were integral to maintaining the goodwill of Muslims on both sides of the Mediterranean. When the minister of the interior asked the general secretary for supplies in 1947 that provisions "necessary for the celebration of the Muslim holiday Aïd es Séghir in the Paris region" be released in spite of rationing restrictions, he reminded him that "for several years similar [exceptions] have been made for the major Muslim holidays." The maintenance of this "tradition" of "solicitude," the minister argued, was especially important given the current discussions about Algeria's status.[39] The government did indeed dispense food to particular agencies charged with organizing the distribution of these goods to the Muslim community, such as the Commission d'Assistance aux Nord-Africains.[40] But staples were also distributed to North African grocers and restaurant owners during Ramadan to allow them to meet the needs of their clients during the weeks of early breakfasts and late dinners. This procedure did not run smoothly, as is apparent from a letter signed by five restaurant owners from the 11th and 13th *arrondissements* addressed to the Service de Ravitaillement. These men contacted the service directly to ask for a shipment of couscous during Ramadan since their "clientele was exclusively [made up of] North African workers" and because the distribution of staples to groceries was "irregular," leaving most North African workers empty-handed, an arrangement that benefited only "a few privileged people."[41] These dealings were already the source of some criticism during the war; *Er Rachid*'s journalists also commented on the illicit dealings that characterized the food distribution program, saying that the operation would have taken place fairly were it not for the fact that "everyone wanted to have his word. . . . The Sub-Direction of Algeria [at the Ministry of the Interior], rue Lecomte, the Mosquée, everyone gave their advice, every service had its own preferred middleman."[42]

An exasperated Bureau social Nord Africain director from Saint-Etienne, M. Bourgeois, wrote the Ministry of Labor to complain about the national administration of the food distribution program. Although he referred to the specific case of Saint-Etienne, the issues raised by his letter are essential to understanding the role food played in the definition of the French state's vision of *Islam français*:

> The Muslim, in his overhasty desire to be considered French in order to enjoy all the rights of a Frenchman, simultaneously clamors to be recognized as Muslim to benefit from these donations in a totally extravagant fashion, while our miners make 600 francs a day. . . . [The Muslims] do a terrible black market business with all the provisions they receive. . . .
>
> The Algerians . . . themselves have said that the misery rations given by the Supply or the Government are nothing but provocations. . . . We must finish with these bad habits and make the Minister of Supply face up to his responsibilities, for he is truly playing with the destiny of France!
>
> In 67 days it will be Aïd el Kébir. The Supply should put reasonable quantities in place now, and not wait until the last minute, like last time . . . namely, one kilo of couscous per worker, and at least 250g of mutton, otherwise, at unanimous request, not distribute anything else, since they need to stop provoking [the Algerians]!!![43]

Bourgeois shared the widespread assumption that providing Muslims with reasonable amounts of the foods associated with holidays had major political consequences for the French government and for France's "destiny." He took for granted that these food items were an indispensable part of Muslim religious practice and considered that the objections voiced by Algerians about the donations stemmed not only from greed but from wounded national or religious pride. Bourgeois also seemed to assume, along with his colleagues, that alimentary traditions could stand in for all Muslim religious practices and that providing workers with these foods would be enough to allow them to fulfill their religious obligations. This assumption rested at once on a refusal to acknowledge those elements of Islam that were more encompassing of everyday life (such as Muslim law) and on the belief that all North Africans identified themselves primarily as Muslims and wished to be treated as such by a paternalist, non-*laïc* administration.

To avoid mishaps that could have costly political ramifications, the Commission des fêtes musulmanes was created to oversee the alimentary aspects of the celebration of Muslim holidays in the Paris region, among other duties.[44] The commission's president, a man named Morard, had long been a player in Paris Muslim politics. Its other members included, among others, Si Kaddour, representatives of the Offices of Morocco and Tunisia, the person responsible for North African labor at the Ministry of Labor, a representative of the SAINA,[45] and several social workers. The commission's main task seems to have been assembling funds from varied sources to ensure that enough appropriate food be available to Paris's Muslims. In 1947, for example, the Ministry of Labor and an association called Entre'aide Française were not able to make their annual contributions, so the commission had to request additional funds from the administrations in North Africa, all of which complied; this was in addition to the annual contribution from the *indigènophile* association Amitiés Africaines. On the other hand, that same year, the Préfecture de la Seine took over the responsibility for financing all the food distributions to take place in SAINA's centers as well as the distribution of food items to individual families. The total cost for the distribution of food to individual families, *foyers,* and hospitals was 375,000 francs.[46] In 1948, the CFM built on its successful distribution from the previous year by expanding its operation to two factories in Boulogne-Billancourt and Saint-Ouen, in addition to student hostels in Paris. The Mosquée was thus at the center of a network of local and national agencies dedicated to providing the Paris region's Muslims with the means to celebrate major holidays "traditionally." This emphasis on alimentary authenticity as a mark of proper religious observance served to recall the physicality of Muslim bodies but also signaled a blurring of boundaries between the Mosquée as purveyor of Muslim religious experience and the Mosquée as dispenser of social services.

A l'Ombre de la Mosquée, or Sending Postcards from the *Hammam*

Celebrating Muslim holidays was not the only reason to go to the Mosquée. The site's physical space continued to display a particular image of Islam and North Africa to a Parisian audience during the Vichy years and in the decade that followed, and it remained an essential element in defining *Islam français*. The site was valuable because it was the embodiment of the relationship between state power and Muslim subjects; even the Nazi administration in Paris realized the propaganda value of disseminating photographs of German officers visiting the Mosquée in the company of Si Kaddour.[47] The Mosquée complex was of course also an important space for the display of North Africa without leaving Paris, in a cityscape where "Algerian" and "Moroccan" sites destined for the entertainment of non-Muslim Parisians began to multiply in the late 1940s and early 1950s. In spite of the economic difficulties most Parisians encountered during the war, the Mosquée's budgets show that the revenues from entrance fees rose from 1939 to 1944.[48] In 1939, the Mosquée made 52,000 francs combined from entrance tickets and postcards, while in 1944 entrance fees alone brought in 76,250 francs, in addition to 10,000 francs from postcard sales. Interestingly, fewer entrance tickets sold in 1945 (60,000 francs), but an additional tour guide was hired, bringing the total number of guides to four. The Mosquée leadership as well as the metropolitan and colonial administrations that funded it seemed to appreciate the importance of built space in displaying Islam, for the complex's budget also included three scholarships for Muslim students pursuing degrees in engineering or architecture.

While non-Muslim Parisians continued to show interest in visiting the Mosquée and touring its gardens and rooms, they did not show the same enthusiasm for the *hammam,* restaurant, or gift shop (other than postcard sales); Muslims were no different. The manager of the *hammam* was no longer able to pay the rent he owed to the Mosquée for use of the space.[49] Sources do not indicate how much entry to the *hammam* cost, or how many entries were recorded at any given time, which makes it difficult to determine who did and did not use the *hammam.* The *hammam,* unlike the small fountains outside the *salle des prières* used for ablutions before prayer, had no religious function. Its importance was both hygienic and social, serving as a bathing and meeting place for both men and women. In France, "*bains à l'orientale,*" or Turkish baths, became popular in the nineteenth century. At the same time, starting in 1898, the city of Paris opened a number of municipal *bains-douches.* One of the municipal baths constructed during this period was on rue Lacépède, immediately across the street from the Mosquée. The site was constructed in "a very old neighborhood where aside from a few rare new buildings, the houses have no bath fixtures" and housed a population who needed easy, affordable local access to bathing facilities.[50] It is unfortunate that sources do not allow us to compare the use of the *bain-douche* and the *hammam,* which were situated across the street from another, to determine what use, if any, neighborhood residents made of the Mosquée's site. Evidence seems to suggest that Muslims did not come to the Mosquée from other neighborhoods to use the *hammam,* and many of the public *bains-douches* in the city proper were located in or near neighborhoods with large North African populations.

Yet a 1946 propaganda film about Muslim life in Paris that took the Mosquée as its central site lavished attention on the very aspects of the Mosquée complex that did not seem to weather this period of crisis well. *In the Shadow of the Mosquée*—the very title implies that North African life in the French capital revolved entirely around the Mosquée—was made in cooperation with the Ministries of Foreign Affairs and Information.[51] Film had become an integral element in state propaganda during the Second World War, right alongside magazines, newspapers, and the radio. The Vichy regime, however, used other tools as well to valorize the colonies as essential to France's prestige and image. Fairs, expositions, and parades took place in both occupied and free France under the guidance of the Agence economique des colonies.[52] The film was designed to portray Paris, the very incarnation of France, as a welcoming and tolerant city to Muslim visitors and residents. The eighteen-minute film is remarkable for the fact that it reproduces images and discourse about the Mosquée de Paris as an embodiment of republican *Islam français* from the World War I years, even as religious programming was designed to distinguish carefully between "authentic" religious practices observed by Muslims and the display of Muslim holidays to a public French audience. The film's exoticization of the Mosquée's architecture and décor and simultaneous emphasis on its presence in the Latin Quarter does not reflect the more ambiguous *Islam français* of the World War II years and the decade that followed. The film opens with a series of views of the Mosquée's different areas, with close-ups of the woodwork, mosaics, and so on, all to "oriental" music. The narrator's opening could have been taken from any of the speeches made at the Mosquée's inauguration:

> Under the sign of the minaret, from where the muezzin lances his call to prayer morning and night, is a beautiful mosque. Carefully tended gardens, svelte columns, walls covered in Arab proverbs or polychrome mosaics, a hundred testimonies of the Muslim faith form a strictly oriental décor. There, every time the Quran commands, the faithful can turn their faces towards the tomb of the Prophet and piously fulfill the duties of their religion. This oasis of peace and contemplation, however, is not in Cairo, Damascus or Quarayin. We are in the heart of Paris, between Notre Dame and the Pantheon, just steps away from the

> Museum. In this Paris where races rub elbows, where all civilizations meet, all philosophies and all beliefs tolerate each other.

Such references to the strictly religious character of the Mosquée and its compatibility with French civilization is notable because of its absence from the French administration's discourse about the Mosquée during World War II and the decade that followed, which suggests that the film was directed at an Algerian audience in an attempt to portray France as a society of equals.

The film also emphasizes the tourist potential of the Mosquée's cafe and *hammam* in a way that makes clear to its audience that although non-Muslim Parisians should take advantage of these sites, they are so authentic that Muslim North Africans also use them. The restaurant, the film's narrator emphasized, is a place where "the believer can invite his friends to take nourishment other than spiritual" in "a scrupulously reconstituted ambiance" reminiscent of palaces in Marrakesh, Fez, or Meknes. As he describes the quality of the restaurant's couscous, the camera pans over images of a presumably North African man dressed in a suit serving pastries to his two European female companions. At other tables, Arab men smoke chichas, or water pipes. From the restaurant, the film then takes us to the *hammam,* and the narrator tells his audience that "if your day has been tiring, the luxuriously appointed *hammam* will let you ease your body at the same time as your mind. You need only abandon yourself to the beneficial warmth and the talented hands of the masseurs. Then, on your mattress, you can taste the welcome drowsiness as the minutes pass smoothly." The *hammam,* unlike the restaurant, does not seem to have attracted any Europeans. The camera moves slowly around the room, focusing longest on the darkest-skinned men, especially dark-skinned men massaging or soaping lighter-skinned men. This is merely the most explicit visual cue to indicate an obsession with the racialized bodies of North African men, but throughout the film the contrast between darker-skinned immigrants and white French people, particularly women, is emphasized.

The attempt by Si Kaddour and his staff as well as the French administration to underscore the importance of the Mosquée complex as the physical embodiment of *Islam français* and as the center of Muslim Paris in the years immediately following World War II demonstrates a continuity with earlier rhetoric. As restaurants, cabarets, and stores featuring North African–inspired foods, music, and home décor began to dot Paris's landscape, the Mosquée's leaders vaunted its tourist potential while simultaneously emphasizing its religious authenticity. Unlike the many restaurants that lined the small streets around Saint-Michel, bearing names like "El Djézair," "El Djenna," and

"L'Oasis tunisien," which promised their customers "oriental ambiance," "attractions," "Arab dance," and "oriental music," the Mosquée's restaurant was also the site of post-prayer lunches and teas, which differentiated it from the other North African cafés used for political meetings, fundraisers, and other activities. Although the discourse about the importance of the physical space of the Mosquée did not change during this period, the kind of Islam it stood for was no longer clear. This only serves to underscore the crucial role played by the built environment in defining different visions of Islam in the metropole: the space of the Mosquée, and other Muslim sites, could be used to signify different and even competing visions.

The Mosquée de Paris and the Provinces: Islam in France or *Islam français*?

The expansion of the Mosquée de Paris's religious authority into the provinces was part of a wider government program in the 1940s that attempted to consolidate an Islam in France that was not the *Islam français* of the Mosquée's first decade. The administrations in metropole and the colonies also made some small gestures toward inclusiveness in geographic and empire-wide terms: although the Mosquée de Paris as well as the provincial mosques continued to be perceived as North African (that is, Algerian or Moroccan) in the imaginations of the site's leaders and the French state as revealed by their internal documents,[53] they occasionally argued that the sites were in fact intended to serve all Muslims, including those from Western Africa. These arguments were often made in the context of propaganda or fundraising, such as when the Ministry of Foreign Affairs reminded the Ministry of Information that it would need to modify the script of *In the Shadow of the Mosquée.* The site, the Ministry's report read, "was created for all Muslims in French territories, and not only Moroccans as seems to emerge from the screenplay." However, it is implicit that the ministry was only considering North African Muslims in its expansiveness, since other comments included the suggestion to replace references to Moroccans with "Algerians, Tunisians, and Moroccans" or to replace an Arab word used in the Middle East with one used in North Africa.[54] Likewise, the minister of foreign affairs asked the minister of overseas territories to increase the financial contribution of the AOF to match those of the North African colonies. He argued that "Frenchmen of West African origin are coming [in increasing numbers] to seek spiritual assistance at the Mosquée and to make contact with their coreligionists from North Africa."[55] Both the letter's aim and its phrasing nod to the ways in which the Muslim referent for France was North Africa and that West Africa could only hope to participate in something that had been framed as a Maghrébin project.

One engagement that was explicitly designed to address the particular legal issues faced by Algerian Muslims after the reforms of 1947 changed their status, the idea to create a *mahakma*[56] in Paris with authority over the metropole, was nevertheless supposed to give the impression that it was intended to serve all Muslims living in France. As Conseiller de l'Union Française Jean Scelles explained in a letter to the minister of foreign affairs, "the presence of many hundreds of Muslims in France, most of them of Algerian origin," necessitated the creation of a Muslim tribunal under the authority of the Mosquée to regulate questions of marriage contracts, inheritance, and other issues stemming from Muslim personal law.[57] Scelles echoed the opinion of the Union Française's Juridical Committee when he said that "in order for [the *mahakma*] to enjoy its full moral authority and efficacy, it must not be an Algerian creation under the authority of the Ministry of the Interior, but of the entire Government."[58] Scelles argued that it was vital to find someone who would be acceptable to the Algerian administration but also to Morocco, with its "special touchiness" as far as the Mosquée was concerned. The Ministry of Foreign Affairs appreciated the attempt to establish a legal body on French soil capable of administering Muslim justice for immigrants from all over the French empire but ultimately decided that it would be too dangerous a proposition given the current political climate and that no matter who was chosen as *qadi*, or Muslim religious judge, the *mahakma* would become a center for anti-French political activity. The refusal to confront the challenge posed to *laïcité* by an engagement with Muslim religious law in the metropole stands in marked contrast to the excessive attention the French administration gave to the far less dangerous question of providing Muslims with "ritual" foods during holidays.

Less threatening to French national interests than the specter of Algerians having recourse to Muslim law in France was the construction of small-scale, local prayer sites in provincial cities and towns. These sites were created in acknowledgment of the presence of Muslim workers on French soil and in response to demands for Muslim religious sites in the metropole. Unlike earlier decades, in which it is difficult to know whether Muslims appreciated the metropolitan administration's gestures, letters from Muslims explicitly demanding such spaces from the government make it clear that in many cases these prayer sites were neither imposed on a working-class Muslim population nor built for the education of non-Muslim French.[59] What is most important about these provincial sites, which were supposed to be placed under the authority of the Mosquée de Paris, is that those that eventually were built embodied an Islam *in* France that was neither secular nor constructed in relation to French republicanism. Those sites that were *not* built embodied the original vision of *Islam français* that fell out of currency in the Mosquée itself during this period. In other words, certain sites (Vichy, Nice) were conceived almost entirely on the model of the site in Paris: they were to be visually lavish "North African" built environments to be used by an international Muslim elite whose Islam was strongly inflected with French principles. Others (Saint-Etienne, Marseille) were more modest, built for local proletarian populations whose Muslim practices were foreign but were becoming "French" in the sense that observant Muslims were beginning to adjust their practices to the reality of their permanent presence in France. The one exception to this pattern, the large mosque intended for Marseille that was never built, reflected the tension between Islam *in* France and *Islam français*: throughout the debates over its construction, no references were made to secularism, republican values, or the compatibility of Islam with democracy, the hallmarks of French Islam. Yet the site, with its central placement and monumental architecture, was also explicitly intended to serve as an embodiment of France's relationship with the North African residents and Muslims in its colonial empire.

It is instructive to consider the spaces and places of these new provincial centers in light of Jewish ecclesiastical construction during the interwar years. In many ways, the architectural questions that were debated in reference to synagogue construction would be rehearsed again in planning for the creation of new Muslim sites during and immediately following the Vichy years. In provincial centers with new waves of Jewish immigration, for example, smaller-scale oratories were built, rather than "cathedral" synagogues. French architectural historian Dominique Jarrassé explains this as the result not only of a lack of funds but also of Jewish populations too small to support larger sites. New immigrant communities that did have the means to do so, however, constructed synagogues that replicated the monumental style of "traditional" French synagogues. In Paris, on the other hand, well-established Jewish communities built new synagogues and enlarged the existing ones.[60] The interwar years, he argues, saw the creation of two competing models for Jewish religious architecture: the "traditional" model of a religious site and the "modernist" model based in new architectural aesthetic norms that emphasized function over form. Jarrassé notes that the "modernist" model in fact conformed to earlier conceptions of synagogue space in which meaning was given to the space by the gathering of Jews for religious purposes, not by a particular aesthetic or decor signaling Jewish religious space.[61]

While several monumental "cathedral" synagogues were built in Paris during the nineteenth century, as early as 1928, two years after the Mosquée's inauguration, a project for a resolutely modernist religious site was launched. The new synagogue would be built in the northeastern Parisian neighborhood of Belleville, home to a large immigrant Jewish community. The Belleville synagogue featured the temple itself, which was flanked on either side by conference rooms, which could be used to seat overflow worshippers for major holidays or used as oratories during the week; two large classrooms; and spaces for recreation. Jarrassé writes that the Belleville site was "first conceived to be functional and to respond to religious and cultural needs" by creating a "community center" space that would come to serve as the model for postwar synagogues. This resolutely "modernist" solution was nevertheless inspired in part by Eastern European community center traditions. The building's design reflected a contemporary art deco aesthetic. The simple lines of the concrete exterior were reproduced in the sober and geometric forms of the synagogue's interior. No "traditional" motifs were used to decorate the Belleville synagogue. As Baron Rothschild noted at the synagogue's inauguration in 1930, Parisian Jewish religious architecture had come a long way from the historicist "cathedral" synagogue on rue de la Victoire (1874).[62]

The Muslim provincial religious sites built with the support of national and local administrations (and occasionally with the financial support of local Muslim communities) during and immediately after World War II followed a similar logic to the construction of Jewish religious sites twenty years earlier. Unlike the cathedral synagogues of the late nineteenth century or the cathedral mosque of the 1920s, provincial sites were not designed to serve as monuments or representations. Rather, they were intended to serve as multipurpose community centers, serving both religious and socio-cultural needs. They featured spaces like storage rooms and kitchens, absent in the Mosquée de Paris but vital to a center to be used for things other than prayer. In the Saint-Etienne *salle de prière,* for example, the "functional" rooms were on the ground level while the actual prayer room was on the second floor, accessible by a flight of stairs. The difference between the spatial layout of this site and that of the Mosquée de Paris, in which the *salle de prières* is visible on the ground floor, is striking. While the Mosquée de Paris was also supposed to serve as a community center of sorts, its design lent itself to representation and not merely function. Furthermore, like the Belleville synagogue, provincial Muslim religious sites were usually located in neighborhoods with large immigrant populations, rather than being centrally located and thus visible to a larger audience.

As early as August 1943, the Ministry of the Interior assured Si Kaddour that it "proposed to establish a *salle de prières* for the Muslims of St-Etienne" as "a new manifestation of the Government's solicitude for the Metropole's North African *indigènes*."[63] A series of decisions taken in 1943 and 1944 allocated 125,000, 50,000, and 27,900 francs in addition to the 1.2 million francs originally inscribed in the ministry's budget for the construction of a mosque in Saint-Etienne. The remaining funds came from the Service Central des Affaires Nord-Africaines, the minister of labor, Amitiés Africaines, the Comité des Houillières, the Département de la Loire, and the Ville de Saint-Etienne.[64] As we shall see, the site was conceived as a modest space with a simple floor plan (see figures 4 and 5). Its center was the *salle de prières,* and few other rooms were featured in the building's design (though one room was of course devoted to ablutions). Unlike the Mosquée's multi-domed roof, Saint-Etienne's mosque had a simple angled roof whose only visual flair was the tiles on the façade. The more glaring absence from the site's roof is of course the minaret. Even if the Mosquée's minaret was silent, the key visual symbol of the mosque present from West Africa to China was still physically present in the site's roof and immediately visible when looking at its façade. It is not clear from any of the letters exchanged about the construction of the site in Saint-Etienne why a minaret was not included in the architectural plans. The building's façade, in fact, echoed some of the aesthetic elements of the Mosquée de Paris (rather than any particular North African mosque), with its large window flanked by two smaller ones, but on a more modest scale. In the Parisian site, however, such a wall could be found inside the complex's walls, rather than serving as the first aesthetic element that greeted the visitor.

Aside from these major aesthetic differences in the site's external elements, the Saint-Etienne site's structural elements raise questions about the kinds of activities its creators imagined would take place there. Unlike the Mosquée de Paris, there was no café or restaurant imagined for tourists who, it was hoped, would visit the site in large numbers. Yet the site includes a kitchen and not one but two bathrooms (which were separate from the ablution rooms), none of which are usually part of the floor plan of a North African mosque and which suggest a conscious decision to adapt to local architectural norms. The creation of two halls (one of which is labeled "Mosquée hall") as well as the storage room suggest a flexibility of functions for the site's spaces, including community gatherings and activities that were not strictly religious.

In Marseille, where a "cathedral" mosque was planned but never executed, a Muslim *carré*, or corner, in the municipal cemetery came to serve as

FIGURE 4. Plans for the Mosquée de Saint Etienne, exterior. Reprinted courtesy of the Archives nationales d'outre-mer, 81F 832.

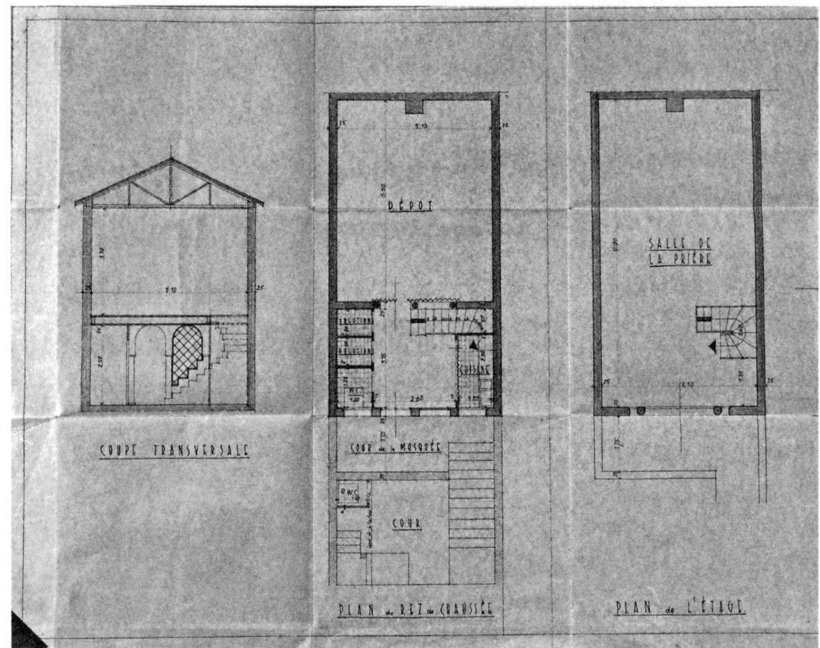

FIGURE 5. Plans for the Mosquée de Saint Etienne, interior. Reprinted courtesy of the Archives nationales d'outre-mer, 81F 832.

the city's Muslim principal religious site. The city donated a piece of land, large enough to contain a thousand bodies, for a period of five years. The *carré*'s white *kouba*, or dome, was built with funding from the Ministry of the Interior and the General Government in Algiers. The argument made locally in favor of a special section for Muslims in St Pierre was that in 1943, a funeral cortege of "Europeans" cut through a Muslim cortege lined up in prayer and caused an altercation "because of European ignorance about the rigors of the Muslim religion."[65] So the idea that Islam was a religion whose requirements were far stricter than those of any other faith, an idea that inspired the proponents of the Mosquée, was also instrumental in the rhetoric surrounding the creation of this site in Marseille. The initial enthusiastic support for this project from the préfets of Marseille was apparently echoed in the city's Muslim population when they learned of the planned Muslim *carré*. This realization "modified the mood of our North African subjects to the extent that their primitive thought, which would have been to consider this land as a relay before the transportation of their compatriots' bodies to their countries of origin, has been transformed, for certain people, to the point of planning to leave the mortal remains forever in this corner of

FIGURE 6. Kouba, Muslim quarter of Marseille's St-Pierre Cemetery, 15 November 1945. Reprinted courtesy of the Archives nationales d'outre-mer, 81F 834.

France which many of them have begun to love," according to the interim chief of Algerian Services of the *prefecture* of Marseille.[66] For the local political officials in charge of the cemetery's creation, this change of heart was due, in no small measure, to the addition of the *kouba*.

Muslims unhappy with the derelict corner allotted to them grew "attached" to the cemetery once the addition of an "all-white Kouba, with a gold crescent, surrounded by cypresses" had been made: this gesture transformed the *carré musulman* into a "place of eternal rest [with] all the ambiance of our Muslim cemeteries in North Africa."[67] Yet this modest visual symbol of North Africa in fact became a sign of Islam's permanence in France, for it meant that people's final resting place would now be Marseille rather than their own village, town, or city on the other side of the Mediterranean. The success of this small-scale religious site, as opposed to the grandiose and central Mosquée de Marseille, also demonstrates what kinds of sites and Muslim practice officials were willing to support. That it was the cemetery that eventually garnered the state's financial support rather than the mosque suggests that the model used in Saint Etienne was ultimately a more comfortable one for local and colonial officials alike.

In Nice, on the other hand, the impetus to construct a Muslim religious site came from a motley crew of former colonial administrators in Algeria, an Algerian businessman installed in southern France after leaving Algeria under suspicious circumstances, and the mayor of Nice. The first person to propose building a mosque in Nice was apparently a retired colonel, whose idea was then taken up by Mayor Médecin, in collaboration with Si El Madani, otherwise known as Mekki el Madani of Laghouat, Algeria. Si El Madani explained to the governor-general of Algeria that such an edifice would be financed through a partnership between the city of Nice and the *département* of Alpes-Maritimes, even though the site had both national and local importance.[68] As he imagined it, it would consist of a mosque and an institute, somewhat along the lines of the Mosquée and Institut Musulman, although the comparison with the Parisian complex was never explicit. The participation of the Ministry of the Interior and the Algerian administration was essential to the project, thus Ibnou Zekri, president of the *culte musulman* in Algiers, was to be sent to Nice to take stock of the situation and make recommendations for the institution's final plans. Ultimately, Si Mekki hoped that the Algerian administration would take charge of the institution so that "generations of young Algerians" would be able to be educated at the site, making it unnecessary for them to "go looking East and West for a foreign education which can only hurt the good harmony and frank, loyal collaboration which should define the relationship between France and its oldest daughter, Algeria."[69] However, Mekki emphasized the importance of including Morocco and Tunisia as partners in the venture, since "mosques are the houses of God and thus open to all, [so] our neighbors would not understand their absence" in such a project. "They could," he warned, "accuse us of egoism," though the presence of Moroccan and Tunisian delegates in the planning committee was likely to ward off that possibility.

The governor-general, while voicing no objections to such a plan "in principle," raised several important potential problems with the construction of a mosque/institute complex in Nice. His first concern was that it "does not seem possible, under current legislation . . . to make public funds pay, even partially, for expenses related to the construction of a building whose nature is exclusively religious."[70] The only way to resolve this would be to create "a Franco-Muslim institute or a social services center for Muslims." A more serious concern was the potential Muslim reaction to the construction of a mosque in Nice rather than Marseille. "In reality," the governor-general pointed out, "it is the city of Marseille where North African Muslims pass through or settle," not Nice. Muslims from the Maghreb would be "justified" in being upset by the decision, especially since the Muslim community of Nice that supported the project was "composed of individuals belonging to a very wealthy elite from different countries, especially Egypt." Although he was willing to send Ibnou Zekri to investigate the situation on the ground, the governor said it was imperative to plan for the construction of a Muslim religious site to serve Marseille's eight thousand Muslims. This sentiment was echoed by the Algerian administration's directeur des affaires musulmanes, who voiced his concerns far more bluntly:

> The Muslim colony of Nice, far smaller than those of Marseille, Lyon, Saint-Etienne, Alès, etc., is mostly comprised of Orientals, most of them very rich (the entourage of the ex-Sultan of Turkey Abdulmadjid, of the ex-Khédive of Egypt Abbas Hilmi, of the representative of the Hedjaz, Fouad Hamza, etc), and it is certain that some of them are no strangers to M. Jean Médecin, the Mayor of Nice, and M. Madani El Mekki's decision to continue work on the Godchot project.
>
> North African Muslims and in particular Algerian Muslims will not miss the opportunity to criticize this project, and to accuse France of favoring foreigners, if a mosque is not built first in Marseille, with its population of 8,000 North African Muslims, of whom 7,000–7,500 are Algerian, and which is also the door to North Africa and the Orient. . . .
>
> If the Government is nevertheless in favor of the construction of a mosque and Institut Musulman in Nice, procedures need to be put in place to make sure that the foreign Muslims who participate financially in the construction, and who will be almost the only ones who will benefit from it given the eccentric situation in Nice, do not play a preponderant role in the designation of personnel, in the administration, and the functioning of this Mosque and Institut and that these creations do not thus escape French influence.[71]

The directeur added that it would be especially inappropriate to open a fund-raising campaign across North Africa, as had been done for the construction of the Mosquée de Paris, which would only inflame matters further.

Unlike the projects considered in Saint-Etienne, Marseille, and Nice, the question of a Mosquée for Vichy emerged after World War II. The city's Conseil Municipal officially voted to construct a mosque in Vichy on 13 October 1947, though the first glimmerings of such a project had emerged twenty years earlier. An unnamed Tunisian businessman attempted to convince the Compagnie fermière des Eaux Minérales de Vichy to establish a mosque in the city, which at the time was home to the former Moroccan sultan, Moulay Hafid, and many members of the Middle Eastern Muslim elite. This plan was soundly rejected by Algerian colonial officials and Si Kaddour; the colonial politicians feared that such a site would become a center for political agitation, while the leader of the Mosquée saw a potential competitor for the preeminent role in the French Muslim landscape played by his Parisian institution. This opposition was enough to stop the site's planning in its earliest stages, but after the war a group of Muslims led by the former président du conseil of Egypt asked Vichy's mayor for a gift of free land on which they could finance the construction of a mosque. They argued that "one of the only religious faiths not to have a cultural edifice in the city of Vichy is Islam" and suggested to the mayor that building a mosque would serve "France's national interest and Islam's interest at once."[72] Both the préfet de l'Allier and Si Kaddour continued to oppose the project, but this time the Ministry of the Interior's Algeria division voiced strong support, which created conflict with the local administration.[73] Si Kaddour, when pressed, said he would not oppose the creation of a Muslim oratory dependent on the Mosquée de Paris, as was standard in other French cities.[74] The negotiations continued, and in 1948, the minister of the interior was still asking the préfet de l'Allier for specific information, such as whether the Vichy mosque's proponents saw it as dependent on the Mosquée de Paris, which for the ministry was non-negotiable; and what juridical structure they envisioned for the building's creation, given the restrictions posed by the law of 1905.[75]

The Mosquée, which had begun to be imagined as early as 1937, was still merely a set of blueprints a full decade later.[76] This was partially a result of wartime realities but also of Si Kaddour's opposition to the creation of a southern mosque to rival his own.[77] In March 1942, the préfet régional of Marseille informed the governor-general of Algeria that, based on their conversations as well as discussions with the minister of the interior, he had already commissioned studies for the building's construction and arranged for the city to donate the land for the project. The governor-general, however, was less interested in a site that fit into a local Marseillais response to the presence of Muslim immigrants in the context of the city's own development, but rather in a micro-managed Algerian institution located in Marseille. In his mind, the mosque "should be particularly tied to Algeria, the prolongation of the Metropole" and should thus be staffed exclusively by Algerian *ministres du culte*. He proposed that the architect charged with designing the building travel to Algeria to prepare his plans.[78]

Nevertheless, it was in Marseille more than any other provincial center that the plans to build a mosque were most firmly anchored in the city's needs, even while clearly evolving in a trans-Mediterranean colonial reality. The needs that the Muslim religious building was intended to meet were not merely those of local and North African Muslims but also those of a city struggling to rebuild itself at war's end and to redesign areas marked by urban blight. National and empire-wide concerns definitely informed discussions of creating such an institution. It is clear from the Municipal Delegation's meeting on 19 December 1944 that Marseille was positioning itself as a city equal to Paris in its ability to determine the tenor of metropolitan-colonial relations. The rhetoric used to advocate for the construction of a Muslim religious site could have been taken almost word for word from arguments made in favor of the construction of the Mosquée de Paris. The committee argued that the mosque would be "proof of the Government's solicitude to its North African subjects" and would also be "the expression of French gratitude to North Africa and more generally the Muslim religion for their ceaseless efforts since 1940 and their participation in the country's . . . liberation."[79] The trope of mosque as war memorial is of course familiar from the discussions surrounding the creation of the Parisian site. Yet Marseille's local authorities also echoed the national and Parisian politicians who claimed that the capital needed a mosque because of its importance as the center of the French Muslim world. The delegation explained that the construction of a mosque would "affirm the primordial role that our Cité must play in French-North African relations."[80]

Yet though Marseillaise politicians paid due service to the exigencies of empire during the dangerous years of increased North African nationalist activity, the mosque they envisioned was also going to be a source of renewal for a battered city. This particular trope, that of the mosque as urban patrimony in the metropole and engine for economic and spatial transformation, was almost entirely absent from discussions of the Mosquée de Paris. The aesthetics of the planned building were less vital to its proponents than its urban placement, whereas for the Parisian site they were of equal importance, as the two elements worked together to articulate the vision of *Islam français* the Mosquée embodied. Here is how the municipal leaders described the land they intended to donate for the mosque's construction:

> After a fairly laborious search, a location was picked, neighboring the Boulevard des Dames and limited by that boulevard, rue du Trou d'Airain, rue des Grands Carmes and rue du Terras. This location, [made up of] mostly empty or housing dilapidated buildings of little value, would offer the advantage of being in a region that Muslims often passed through, and of being in immediate proximity to the ports and the train station. Finally, the management and extension plans for the city include the complete renovation of the Carmes neighborhood, thus the construction of the Mosquée would be the seed.[81]

The Mosquée was thus not only a Muslim religious site, but part of a much larger program for the renovation of an entire neighborhood. It is not chance that led the committee to note first that "the realization of such an architectural ensemble would enrich the City's artistic patrimony" and only later that it would serve the French *politique musulmane* well.

The Mosquée's architect, André Devin, went even further than the city's officials in his plans to make the Muslim religious edifice part of Marseille's renewal. Unlike the Mosquée de Paris, his building was to be inspired by North African architecture, but "sober" and modern, fitting into a renovated and extended cityscape of which it would be the center. The map below shows the place the Mosquée would occupy in a new Marseille (it is the darkened site adjacent to the Place Maréchal Galliéni, in figure 7).

In his description of the site's placement he refers first to the appropriateness of locating it in a Muslim neighborhood and only then to the felicitous coincidence of the terrain also being in the middle of those areas slated for renewal. Devin rejoiced over the fact that

> the Boulevard des Dames, where the Mosquée's main entrance would be, is the principal artery directly linking Gare Saint Charles [the train station] to the seaport. . . . It is halfway between these two essential spots that the proposed terrain is located. The width of the arteries as they are or as they will be when widened gives rise to interesting perspectives, and it's not superfluous to emphasize that the minaret was placed . . . so that a traveler arriving by Gare Saint Charles discovers its silhouette in the intersection of rue Bernard Dubois. By the same token . . . the building is visible from the beginning of the bd des Dames, in other words, from the busy center of the grand maritime arrival and departure zone. . . . At 90 meters from the Place du Maréchal Galliéni, almost upon it, the Mosquée will be *integrated,* so to speak, and will participate note only in its architectural layout but also to its movement.
>
> The insalubrious neighborhood of butte aux Carmes is slated to disappear, and will give way to vast gardens bordered by the southern façade of the Mosquée while the main façade will border the bd des Dames on the north. The progressive demolition of the insalubrious buildings of the Carmes neighborhood, kicked off by the construction of the Mosquée, will provide for the green spaces, desirable to all, which are called for by the project.[82]

Devin's choice of the word *integrated* when describing the relationship of his site to its city highlights the striking difference between his plan and that of

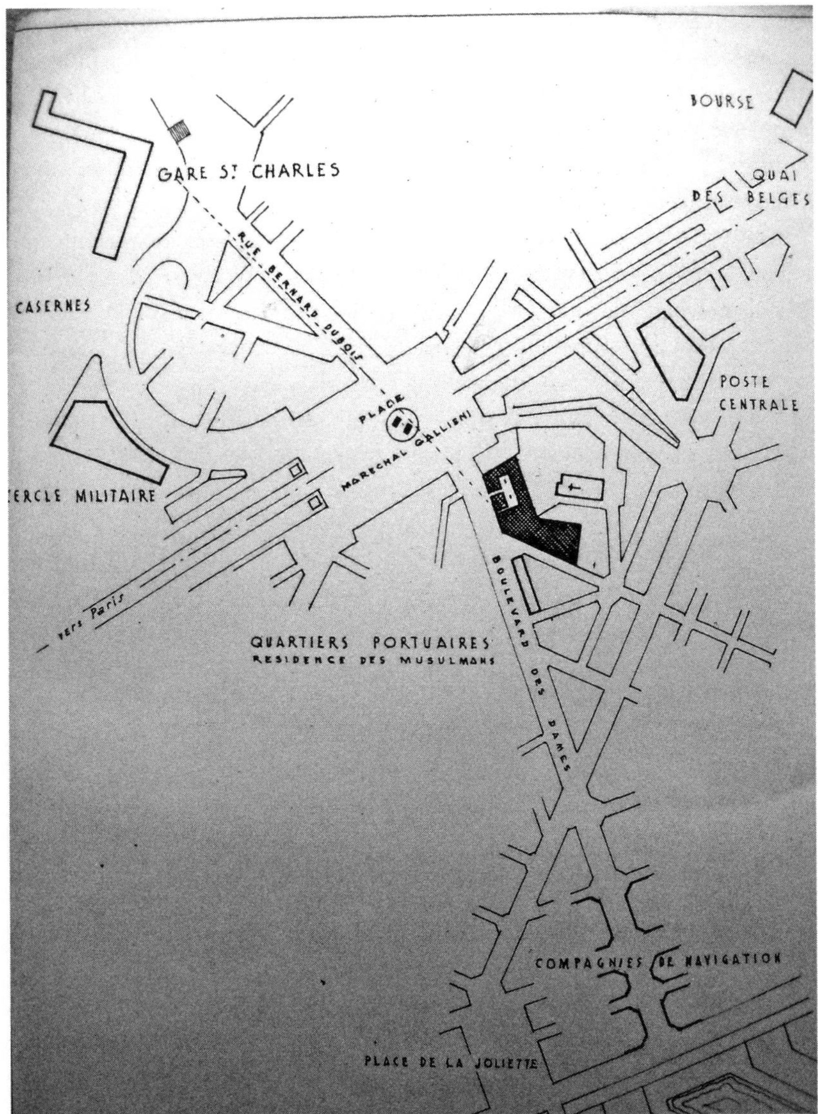

FIGURE 7. André Devin, Plan de Situation, Mosquée de Marseille. Reprinted courtesy of the Archives des Affaires étrangères et européennes, Afrique/Levant/Généralités 1944–1952/48.

the Mosquée de Paris's architects. The Parisian site was designed expressly not to be integrated into its surroundings and was placed in the Quartier Latin not to be accessible to Muslims but to exist in the heart of French republican and *laïc* civilization. Although the Parisian site needed to adjust to some modern conveniences, it was supposed to replicate its Fez-inspired model as closely as possible, not be part of a program of active urban renewal. Devin's description refers to a site in motion, at the heart of a pulsating urban center: a mosque that would embody an Islam in France as lived by people coming and going across the Mediterranean and setting down roots in France's southern capital, rather than the Mosquée de Paris' museumified *Islam français.*

However, when we examine Devin's vision of the site's architecture and décor rather than the space it would occupy in a new Marseille, it becomes less clear what Marseille's local officials had in mind in terms of Muslim religious practice in their city.

As this drawing shows, the Mosquée de Marseille's minaret immediately indicates a Muslim religious site in a way that the Saint-Etienne mosque did not. The large scale of this site also echoes the Mosquée de Paris rather than a provincial *salle de prières.* Devin wrote that his plans were "inspired" by Moroccan designs but that some aspects were more commonly used in Algeria. The word he uses most often to describe his mosque is sober, such as the sculptures that would decorate the arcades leading to the *salle de prières,* the walls of the room itself, and the complex's exterior walls (which are "extremely and voluntarily sober"). Devin sought a "modern tendency"

FIGURE 8. André Devin, Drawing of Mosquée de Marseille. Reprinted courtesy of the Archives des Affaires étrangères et européennes, Afrique/Levant/Généralités 1944–1952/48.

while respecting "Muslim ambiance," but he found it necessary to break up "the monotony of the tradition forest of columns" by creating a series of vaults that made hallways appear taller and gave the impression of columns. He argued, likewise, that the atmosphere necessary for the *salle de prières* could better be cultivated by decorating less rather than more. He did see room for ceramics and sculptures done by North African artisans, but this was not foregrounded in his plans, as it was in those for the Mosquée de Paris. Devin's mosque included, like the Parisian site, several courtyards, an ablutions room, the *salle de prières,* offices, a library, and residences for the site's staff. The blueprints and more particularly the illustrations that accompany his text, however, undercut the image of the sober, modern mosque he describes.

The architectural plans show a site whose composition is still very much based in French conceptions of North African architecture, though it is expressed in the language of modernist architecture rather than that of the orientalizing Beaux-Arts style that defined the Mosquée de Paris. His illustrations of the interior courts, inhabited by *indigènes* in "traditional" North African clothing sitting under what may be palm or date trees, look more like postcards from an *exposition coloniale* than drawings of a modern site integrated into a changing city (see figures 9a, 9b, 10a, and 10b). It is nevertheless striking that he did in fact include human figures in his drawings of the planned site: none of the images of the Mosquée incorporated actual people, whether Muslim or not, dressed in "Arab" or "European" clothing. Whether this inclusion was intended to make the site more authentic or to indicate the hope that it would actually be used by Muslim worshippers—or both—is unclear.

The contrast between Devin's verbal description of a modern site and his illustrations showing classic French imaginings of Moroccan aesthetics is puzzling. Yet in the end, his ambitious plan for a modern site serving local Muslims, Marseillaise politicians, and French interests and moving between an Islam *in* France and *Islam français* was never completed, making it impossible to see how the site would have been used.

These religious edifices, representing both an Islam in France (Saint-Etienne, Marseille) and the *Islam français* of the Mosquée's early years (Vichy, Nice), represented a fissure in the monolithic character of the vision of Islam sponsored by the French state. In the meantime, independent sites continuously offered Muslims living in Paris alternative spaces for worship and sociability. The novelty of this period was that it represented the first time that the state had financed several Muslim religious sites whose Islam did not correspond neither to the Mosquée's original vision nor to the Islam practiced there during this time.

FIGURE 9a. Interior views, courtyard, and *salle de prière*. Mosquée de Marseille, Reprinted courtesy of the Archives des Affaires étrangères et européennes, Afrique/Levant/Généralités 1944–1952/48.

Social Assistance or Religious Guidance: What Role for Muslim Leadership in the Metropole?

One of Si Kaddour's major distinctions between the Mosquée de Paris and the provincial religious sites during this period was the relative importance to the Mosquée's social assistance work, whereas the regional mosques and *salles de prières* were represented as almost exclusively religious. In his accounts of the Mosquée's activities during this period, he emphasized this aspect of the institution's programs to the extent that its religious vocation seemed

FIGURE 9b. Interior views, courtyard, and *salle de prière*. Mosquée de Marseille, Reprinted courtesy of the Archives des Affaires étrangères et européennes, Afrique/Levant/Généralités 1944–1952/48.

negligible. The occasions when Si Kaddour emphasized the Mosquée's social work almost exclusively usually coincided with those when he sought financial support from metropolitan and colonial administrations. It was very simple to document the financial burden these programs put on the institution: social assistance expenditures rose from 10,270 francs in 1939 to 47,937.40

FIGURE 10a. Drawings to accompany the plan for the Mosquée de Marseille. Reprinted courtesy of the Archives des Affaires étrangères et européennes, Afrique/Levant/Généralités 1944–1952/48.

FIGURE 10b. Drawings to accompany the plan for the Mosquée de Marseille. Reprinted courtesy of the Archives des Affaires étrangères et européennes, Afrique/Levant/Généralités 1944–1952/48.

in 1944, while religious ones for the same years increased from 5,530 to 8553.30 francs. One suggestive explanation for this emphasis is that during a period when the French state seemed to have lost interest in the "Frenchness" of *Islam français,* Si Kaddour sought to reinscribe the Mosquée's mission within the framework of *laïcité.* In this vision, the Mosquée was certainly a religious site and was responsible for the spiritual health of France's Muslims, but like many other organizations it was also a thoroughly modern, public institution engaged in the difficult business of postwar social assistance.

While Si Kaddour described the role of imams in the provinces as "purely religious," the Mosquée's staff, in addition to its "purely religious work in Paris," had the "mission to assist *Musulmans français,* citizens, subjects or protégés living in France, which entails visiting the sick in hospitals, distributing food to the poor, paying for the funerals of indigent Muslims, furnishing shrouds" and other tasks. Si Kaddour made it clear that the Mosquée did not have the same mission to serve as a social assistance center when it was created in 1926, but his description of its works after the war indicates that these programs were its only priority.[83] At a meeting of the Société des Habous in Rabat in January 1946, Si Kaddour explained the Mosquée's activities in 1945 as follows:

> During the year 1945, the Mosquée furnished free shrouds for 400 of the 460 Muslims who passed away. Of those 400, at least half, all indigents, were taken to their final resting place at the Mosquée's cost. . . .
>
> Thanks to the facilities that the Service de Ravitaillement has given us . . . we have been able to help provide food to more than 100 families on the occasion of their children's circumcisions. In addition, poor families receive food at the Mosquée on Fridays.
>
> The Imams often visit patients' sickbeds in hospitals, sanatoriums, or even in prisons, to bring them material and spiritual aid.
>
> I should also note that over the last year the Mosquée's Imams performed 22 marriages between Muslims . . . many of them, of course, receiving financial help from our Foundation.[84]

This mixture of social and religious services provided by the Mosquée to Paris's Muslim community stands in marked contrast to the institution's other mission, the oversight of provincial sites charged with "permitting Muslim workers in the metropole to practice their religion."[85]

The Mosquée, in its role of provider of social services to the Muslim population, and the Ministry of Labor, providing financial support for Muslim religious practice, both filled in the cracks in the division of labor in a *laïc* state, one whose *laïcité* had been compromised by the legacy of Vichy, faced with serving foreign populations. We need only look to the 1940s to see that contemporary debates about the wisdom of using Muslim religious sites and personnel as intermediaries between the republic and "immigrant" populations were not new. As a critic of the Mosquée put it in 1943, "Does Cardinal Suhard bother himself with the worldly questions faced by his flock?

No, right? Then what is Si Kaddour ben Ghabrit doing mixing himself up in these stories of [food distribution]?"[86] In a *laïc* state in which all religions occupied the same space, of course, Si Kaddour and the Mosquée would no more be responsible for social welfare than would the Catholic Church, but the metropole's *laïcité* put Islam in a liminal space. On the one hand, other religious groups *were* actively involved in social assistance (particularly during the war); on the other hand, the state did not use those associations as intermediaries to manage particular groups of people.

"You Should Go to the Mosquée More Often": Alternative Expressions of Islam in the Paris Region

The Mosquée, however, did not have a monopoly on social welfare programs mixed with religious activities destined for Paris's North African population. Parallel celebrations of all the major holidays took place at sites all over the city and suburbs. These observances often involved meals or food distributions as well. While in previous decades both the Mosquée's leadership and metropolitan and colonial observers scorned Muslim practices outside of the Mosquée as pagan and the Mosquée's imams rarely ventured out of the city center, during this period there was considerable overlap between attendance at the Mosquée and other religious and social centers. Algerian businessmen moved easily between gatherings at the Mosquée and suburban sites, and the institution's imams occasionally traveled outside Paris to participate in these observances.

At Dar es Sultan, the center in Gennevilliers owned by the Oeuvre Marocaine de bienfaisance, Moroccans celebrated the "orthodox" holidays observed at the Mosquée as well as a range of Moroccan holidays in honor of local saints, such as Moulay Yacoub and Moulay Youssef. Dar es Sultan's programs combined religious observances, political meetings, food distribution programs for the poor, and fundraising drives among the city's Muslim business class. The celebration of Moulay Yacoub in August 1952, for example, drew two thousand people for a gathering that lasted until 2 a.m. (more than attended either Aïd service at the Mosquée) and took place over four days (though attendance decreased every day). Surprisingly, attendees included Si Kaddour himself and Si Abdelaziz, the mufti of the Mosquée, in addition to the Oeuvre Marocaine de bienfaisance's leadership and members of the Moroccan nationalist Istiqlal Party, all of whom also appeared at the Mosquée's services. The participation of members of the Mosquée's leadership at an event in which the main speaker gave a rousing speech in Berber about "chasing the *roumis* out of Morocco and obtaining victory for the Islamic faith" was surprising, to say the least. Yet Si Abdelaziz, after "exhorting the attendees to come in greater numbers to mosques, especially" the Mosquée, concluded his remarks by begging his listeners to "unite as Muslims and not differentiate between citizens of the three brother countries of North Africa, since . . . the problem of independence is the same . . . as is the cause, Islam."[87] This pronouncement in favor of Moroccan independence by a Mosquée staff member is particularly shocking, as it was made in the company of Si Kaddour, who apparently did not respond. It also raises questions about the political and religious commitments of other members of the Mosquée's leadership, since the archival records reflect Si Kaddour's positions exclusively.

Nonreligious events also marked the holidays, such as the Union des Travailleurs Nord-Africains of the Front Social du Travail's "artistic matinée" at the Salle d'Iéna, where "several North African recording and radio stars" gave a live performance to celebrate Aïd es Séghir. Tickets for the event cost from 20 to 40 francs.[88] The Association Marocaine de Bienfaisance also organized many such events as fundraisers for its programs, including an "artistic program" to celebrate Aïd es Séghir in 1950.[89] Political parties organized concerts and shows to celebrate the holidays, as the nationalist Mouvement pour le Triomphe des Libertés Démocratiques (MTLD) did for the "Nuit du destin" (the twenty-seventh night of Ramadan) in 1951.[90] Unlike the nationalists who, decades earlier, had attacked the Mosquée as an insult to Islam, the people who organized and attended these alternative religious celebrations moved easily between the world of the Mosquée and their own peripheral positions.

Finally, there were those who did not celebrate the holidays in Paris at all but returned to Algeria. As the governor-general explained to the minister of the interior, the number of returns was much higher than the number of departures from May until July for two reasons: first, because many peasants returned during the summer months to harvest their land or to participate in local religious festivals; and second, because many workers went home to spend Ramadan with their families.[91] For many Muslims living in France, then, both *Islam français* and the Islam *in* France of the provincial mosques were largely creations of the French state that did not shape their religious lives. In attending services and social events at alternative Muslim religious sites rather than the Mosquée, choosing to return across the Mediterranean to celebrate holidays and life cycle events at home, or simply ignoring Muslim religious practices and holidays, these immigrants demonstrated that the state's *Islam Français* was far less influential than its proponents would have hoped.

Demographic Changes, Changing Neighborhoods?

Was the decidedly nonsecular character of *Islam français* during this period only a result of the Vichy regime's orientation and its postwar legacy? Another factor may have been that this particular vision of Islam was not one that was meant to coexist with an ever-increasing North African proletarian population taking up residence in the metropole. The period immediately following the war was a difficult one for Paris's residents, including North African and other immigrant workers. The Parisian police observed that one effect of the rampant unemployment that plagued the region's North African manual laborers was that "many North African barmen and restauranteurs no longer want to offer credit to their coreligionists, since they themselves are having a hard time meeting their own obligations." Maghrébin men formed long lines at the employment offices of factories in Paris and its suburbs, but "the number of North African layabouts increase[d] constantly."[92] The "community" of Algerians, Moroccans, and Tunisians, however, was certainly not monolithic, as even the police acknowledged in their discussion of the North African "populations" of the Paris region: in 1945, immediately after the war's end, they counted 60,000 North Africans (50,000 Kabyles, 5,000 to 6,000 Chleuhs from southern Morocco, Algerian Arabs, and a small number of Tunisians). Of this group, there were few doctors, lawyers, or intellectuals, and fewer students than during the interwar years. The police contended that there was a considerable population of North African *nouveaux riches* whose "huge fortunes" were built on doing business with Germans during the war; stocking coffee, sugar, soap, and other black market items; looting abandoned homes after the exodus from Paris in 1940; or establishing prostitution networks. Finally, they spoke of the large group of "courageous and handy manual laborers" and the "fairly numerous" unemployed.[93]

In spite of an increase in the North African immigrant population in the postwar years, it is difficult to establish with any certainty precisely where the different North African immigrant social classes lived in Paris and the suburbs, making it impossible to argue that certain neighborhoods became "Maghrébin" virtually overnight.[94] The statistics on which these calculations are made are not entirely reliable and are mere police estimates. Police figures from 1948 and 1952 show how the population of Algerians, Moroccans, and Tunisians was spread across neighborhoods in various *arrondissements* and Paris banlieues, or suburbs. Their admittedly imprecise estimates were based on ration cards and employment figures, which they used to determine where North African workers actually lived.[95]

Police figures indicate that the net increase of the North African population in the city and its surrounding suburbs was not necessarily accompanied by a marked increase in their presence in particular neighborhoods. For example, the 1948 figures report 400 Algerians, 50 Tunisians, and no Moroccans in the 1st *arrondissement.* The 1952 figures refer to a total North African population of between 120 and 150 people for the same area. Similarly, the 2nd *arrondissement's* population shrank from 400 Algerians, 50 Tunisians, and no Moroccans to 180 people total. On the other hand, the Algerian "fief" of the Goutte d'Or neighborhood[96] in the 18th *arrondissement,* which was one of the neighborhoods perceived to have been the most altered by this immigration, appears to have had a population of 5,720 North Africans in 1948, while in 1952, there were anywhere from 5,500 to 6,400 people there. Thus there were potentially *fewer* North Africans living in the neighborhoods of the northern working-class *arrondissements* over a four-year period rather than a marked increase. The 19th *arrondissement,* on the other hand, shows an increase of between a thousand and three thousand people.

It seems clear that the French sensation of an explosion of the region's North African population is not explained by real demographic changes. A more likely cause was perceived changes to the "physiognomy of neighborhoods," even though police records show that certain neighborhoods of the 18th, 19th, and 20th *arrondissements* had long boasted a North African, particularly Algerian, presence.[97] In the 19th *arrondissement,* for example, the police reported as early as 1918 that the area around Stalingrad/Jaurès had a high concentration of North African bars and cafés, most of which, they claimed, were also gambling dens. Several were located within blocks of each other on the Boulevard de la Villette.[98] The novelty of postwar Maghrébin immigration for Parisian observers was the way migrants appeared to dominate the neighborhoods in which they established themselves. As a report on the "structures of Algerian Migration" produced by the police in the early 1950s explained:

> Contrary to popular opinion, Algerian migration is not anarchic. To a large extent, it is organized.
>
> It proceeds by groups from the same village or *douar.*
>
> All the individuals from the same *douar* or village maintain close contacts with each other and make up a sort of defensive community against competition from other *douars,* whether to monopolize the jobs in a given factory or profession, or to monopolize available space in a hotel, sometimes even the street [itself].
>
> The cell achieves its perfect organization when it has gained possession of a base establishment, a café, hotel, or furnished room.

> This fixed point henceforth constitutes the gate through which all emigrants from the *douar* or village pass.
>
> The cell acts in such a way that one can quickly know who is part of it, its allies, its competitors . . . its enemies.
>
> The process . . . is a process of conquest, or colonization, conquest of a profession, of jobs, of places to live.
>
> When the concentration reaches a certain saturation point, the community explodes and finds secondary points of implantation which maintain close ties with the principal point.[99]

The process described above, of course, could easily describe any immigrant group's struggle to establish itself in a new country or city. Paris, before and after the war, was certainly home to many other immigrant groups who carved out niches for themselves in particular trades and specific neighborhoods, or even streets within a given neighborhood. Furthermore, as Colette Pétonnet argues in her discussion of space in the *banlieue,* "There is never a complete takeover of space by any exclusive group." She argues further that perceptions that label a given street or neighborhood as exclusively Portuguese or Jewish are both true and inexact: "We cannot deny the presence of synagogues and kosher butchers" on the rue de Rosiers, in Paris, but neither can we deny the non-Jewish elements on the same street.[100] Demographic statistics cannot adequately explain the French perception that the capital was overwhelmed with migrants from the other side of the Mediterranean. The perception that North Africans were invading the capital, however unfounded in demographic realities, was nevertheless a possible factor in the transformation of *Islam français* during this period. An increased concern about the space Muslim immigrants were seen to be occupying, as well as the changes that said occupation supposedly produced, could have led to a vision of Islam in which bodily practices, the use of space, and particular foods and smells were given far greater importance than in the early years of the Mosquée's existence.

North African Muslim immigrants were not embraced with open arms by mainstream French society, nor by the metropolitan administration, during the Vichy years or in the decade that followed. Yet they did not bear the brunt of Vichy racism, as did Jews. The shift in the state's attitude towards *Islam français,* in the evacuation of its *laïc* content, is also a reflection of the racialization of society that took place under Vichy. As political tensions mounted in North Africa, the idea that Algerian Muslims were invading France and transforming familiar neighborhoods into strange new places gained currency in the popular press and in the police discourse as well.

During the Occupation, then, the re-Catholicized French state continued to use Islam as the means to manage its colonial population, yet Vichy's Islam was purely about religious practice, specifically bodily practices, and had nothing to do with French republicanism or secularism. This continued in the decade that followed the war, which saw the construction of provincial prayer sites. The Islam of these sites was not the original *Islam français* of the Mosquée, but it was an Islam *in* France that tended to reflect the practices of those Muslims who used them.

How did Muslims themselves think about their beliefs and practices during and after the horrors of the Second World War, particularly the genocide of one of France's other religious minorities? The sources are not rich enough to allow a thorough consideration of the ways in which the racialization, deportation, and murder of French Jews during the Second World War might have changed the self-perceptions of Muslim residents of France during a period in which their cultural/religious difference was overemphasized by the French administrators responsible for managing Muslim life in the metropole. Those who emigrated from Algeria came from a society in which, unlike them, Jews were considered equal French citizens thanks to the Crémieux Decree. The French citizenship of Jews, of course, was revoked under Vichy by the law of 7 October 1940 (but was not, on the other hand, extended to Algerian Muslims). The first of the anti-Semitic laws, that of 3 October 1940, defined a Jew as "any person with three grandparents of the Jewish race, or of two grandparents of the race if his spouse is Jewish."[101] French Jews, whom the law had regarded as full citizens of the Republic since the Emancipation, became racial subjects with no rights as Frenchmen. Their cultural and religious differences were crystallized in racial otherness. Many of those who survived the war and returned to France changed their names and raised children who received little Jewish education and often were not even aware of their Jewishness.[102] How did Muslims in France, witnessing this process, think about their place in France as racial and religious others?

CHAPTER 5

Islam français, Islam algérien: Islam and the Algerian War in Paris

The Algerian War (1954–1962) brought about profound changes in the lives of Algerian and French people on both sides of the Mediterranean. The impact of the war on people's daily lives was perhaps more immediately obvious in Algeria, but those living in France, particularly Paris, were also touched by the violence of the conflict. The press stoked the fears of an apprehensive Parisian public by warning repeatedly that the Arab hotels, cafés, and bars, which were "changing the physiognomy" of the capital, held a new menace: they shielded those working for the Fédération Française du Front de Libération National (FFFLN, the metropolitan branch of the Algerian Front de libération nationale). In this metropolitan battleground of a war being fought on both sides of the Mediterranean, the minister of the interior warned the Parisian police force that every hotel or café owned and patronized by North Africans was a potential "meeting place, mailbox, or refuge" for the FLN and its supporters.[1] Algerian residents of the capital had to make sure not to run afoul of the Parisian police or the FFFLN. Unlike their metropolitan French neighbors, colleagues, and employers, Parisian Algerians had to structure their daily lives in response to the very real threat of arrest or expulsion by the police and of harassment, extortion, and violence by the FFFLN.

It is important to keep this climate of profound fear and insecurity in mind when we seek to understand the way both the FFFLN and French authorities mobilized different visions of Islam in an effort to structure Muslim life in Paris and thus, ultimately, maintain political as well as moral authority over the capital's North African population. I argue in this chapter that in the midst of the radical dislocations produced by the war, both the FLN and the French state (through the Mosquée de Paris) continued to maintain that Islam should be used as a tool to define and manage the metropole's Algerian community. The brief tenure of Si Ahmed Ben Ghabrit as *recteur* of the Mosquée (1954–1956) challenged this strategy, and the Ministry of the Interior replaced him with a more suitable candidate in their eyes, Si Hamza Boubakeur (1957–1982).

During and immediately after the Algerian War, the question of how to distinguish between "French" and "Algerian" was paramount.[2] The FLN and the French state did their utmost to maintain Algerian Muslims as a distinct and separate group. *Islam français* and *Islam algérien* were both used to define and maintain this population, and it is my contention that the immutable association between North Africans and Islam in the context of the French empire was strong enough to survive the war, which heralded the official end of the French colonial era. Notably, it was during the Algerian War that "Muslim" and "Algerian" became almost completely synonymous, to the exclusion of other Muslim North Africans. Furthermore, the FLN's attempt to define Algerians living in Paris exclusively as Muslims is highly suggestive of the power of the association between Islam and "Algerian-ness" on both sides of the Mediterranean. Although the FLN used different discursive voices to articulate its struggle when addressing different audiences, the organization relied heavily on Islam in its interactions with Algerian immigrants in the metropole. The FLN's *Islam algérien* emerged for different reasons, but it was in many ways the mirror image of *Islam francais.*

Defining these different visions of Islam necessitated work on two levels: that of high politics and administration and that of the politics of everyday life. While the FLN instructed its metropolitan branch on how formally to structure and to enforce its authority in North African neighborhoods, the Ministry of the Interior replaced a leader of the Mosquée deemed too favorable to the Algerian cause with another whose loyalty to France was unquestioned. Both the FFFLN and the French government were also interested in intervening in the life practices, both quotidian and exceptional, of Algerians. One issue of particular concern was marriage and the ceremony that consecrated it. Yet the French state had the financial and political resources to articulate *Islam français* through the medium of the Mosquée de Paris, while the FFFLN had no physical embodiment of *Islam algérien* to testify to its power to define Islam for Algerians living in the capital. Maintaining control over the Mosquée, particularly under the aegis of its new *recteur,* allowed the French state to project a particular image of Islam and Muslims to non-Muslim Parisians as well.

The Algerian War and the Possibility of Change

The conflict known in Algeria as "the Revolution" and in France as "operations to maintain order" began with the FLN-led uprising of 1 November 1954 and ended with the signing of the Evian Accords on 18 March 1962.[3] Although groups seeking to act on behalf of the Algerian people were many and diverse, including Ferhat Abbas's reformist Union Démocratique du Manifeste Algérien (UDMA), Ben Badis's Muslim-based Ouléma, and Messali Hadj's separatist Parti du Peuple Algérien (PPA) whose legal, political wing was known as the Mouvement pour le Triomphe des Libertés Démocratique (MTLD), it was ultimately the Front de Libération Nationale that assumed the leadership of the armed struggle. The FLN, which emerged out of the Comité Révolutionnaire pour l'Union et l'Action (CRUA) in 1954, sought to bring together different currents of the nationalist struggle into one unified group in order to overcome sectarian divisions. Disappointed by the failure of political reform, the moderate nationalist Abbas joined the FLN in 1955, and Badis's Oulema "would eventually be forced to accept the role of subordinate members" of an FLN whose methods were very different from their movement's own.[4] Messali Hadj, whose Etoile Nord Africaine had long been outlawed and had transformed into the PPA, originally aligned his movement with Abbas's Amis du Manifeste de la Liberté (AML) but would later refuse to see his movement fall under the umbrella leadership of the FLN.[5] Messali Hadj contested the FLN's presumption to lead the Algerian people's revolution exclusively, and in the early years of the war, he called for round tables and meetings among leaders from all revolutionary tendencies and French officials, to negotiate a cease-fire and to put an Algerian Assembly in place that would negotiate Algeria's future status. The FLN feared Messali Hadj's working-class support base, which had been consolidated over the previous twenty years, and labeled his Mouvement National Algérien (MNA) a terrorist organization. The consequences of the terrible struggle for legitimacy between the MNA and the FLN would engender scores of political assassinations, leaving the FLN as the sole voice of the Algerian Revolution.[6]

The FLN's 31 October 1954 call to arms exhorted Algerians to fight for national independence under two conditions: "the restoration of the sovereign, democratic, and social Algerian state within the framework of Islamic principles" and "respect of basic liberties without distinction as to race or religion."[7] To members of Algeria's non-Arab and non-Muslim communities, these two principles seemed incompatible. Many Kabyles, whose prominence in Algerian nationalist movements was especially notable in France, rejected the Ouléma's slogan of "Islam is my religion; Algeria is my nation; and Arabic is my language," which was eventually taken up by the socialist FLN. Algerian novelist Kateb Yacine refers evocatively to this motto when he writes of "an errant people, who nevertheless always gathered together around the passionate prison which they called Islam, Nation, Front, or Revolution, as if none of the words alone had enough salt."[8] Kabyle nationalist militants like Ali Yahia Rashid argued instead for an "Algerian Algeria," imagining a future independent state as secular and multicultural and rejecting the elision of "Algerian" and "Arab." As early as 1949, these dissident voices within the nationalist fold began to be excluded in what became known as the "Berberist crisis."[9]

Algerian Jews felt equally threatened by the vision of Algerian identity proposed by the FLN: they were neither Arab nor Muslim, and many of them no longer used Arabic as their primary language, having largely become Francophone. The FLN asked Algerian Jews to demonstrate their "belonging to the Algerian nation" as early as 1956, as such a gesture would "extirpate the germs of hatred maintained by French colonialism."[10] By phrasing their call for support this way, the FLN made clear that the onus was on the Jewish community, which was of course far from monolithic, to take sides with Algerian Muslims against the *pieds noirs* and metropolitan state. While Algerian Jews had access to French citizenship since the passage of the Crémieux Decree—with the important exception of the Vichy period—the FLN nevertheless urged them to commit themselves to a new Algerian citizenship:

> It is because the FLN considers Algerian Jews as sons of our country that we hope the leaders of the Jewish community will have the wisdom to contribute to the construction of a free and truly fraternal Algeria. The FLN is convinced that leaders will understand that it is the duty and of course in the interest of the entire Jewish community not to remain "above the fray," to condemn without fail the dying French colonial regime, and to proclaim their choice of Algerian nationality.[11]

In spite of the participation of some members of the Jewish community in the struggle for Algerian independence, it quickly became clear that it was increasingly unlikely that a truly "fraternal" Algeria was possible. Whether there was really no room for Jews in an independent Algeria, or whether Jews were unwilling to negotiate their place in a new Arabo-Muslim state, most of them ultimately cast their lot with the *pieds noirs* who left Algeria behind and moved to France in 1962, if not sooner.

The FLN's program to restitute an authentic and unique "Algerian-ness" was predicated on a valorization of Arab identity, the Arabic language, and Islam, which excluded those of Kabyle, Jewish, and European origin from membership in a new Algerian community. This three-part agenda was enshrined in both the Tripoli Program, unanimously adopted by Algerian leadership in May 1962 and the Algiers Charter of April 1964. The Tripoli Program was supposed to create a clearly defined Algerian culture, largely through the medium of education. Its first two goals were "the restoration of national culture and the progressive Arabization of education on a scientific basis" and "the preservation of the national patrimony of popular culture," with other items relating to the expansion and Arabization of nationalized mass education at all levels.[12] The Algiers text, which formed the basis for the constitution, made it explicit that the newly independent country was to be "Arabo-Muslim." This definition of Algeria's national culture did not necessarily mean that there was no room for non-Arabs and non-Muslims in the new state, but it did raise questions about how they might fit into Algerian society.

The need to create something that could be proclaimed Algerian was a response both to the French assertion that Algeria, unlike neighboring Morocco and Tunisia, had never been an independent country and had been entirely fashioned through its encounter with French colonialism and to a generalized North African and Middle Eastern devalorization of Algerian history and culture. In other words, as Lyautey believed, unlike Moroccans, Algerian Muslims existed only in a "pan-Islamic" Ottoman universe with Constantinople and Mecca as its centers, not as a unique nation with its own history and identity, as discussed in chapter 1.[13] By denying Algerian Muslims an Algerian identity, French historian Jacques Frémeaux argues, generations of French politicians were able to define "Algerian" as people of European origin living in the colony, while indigenous residents were referred to by ethnic denominations such as Arab or Kabyle.[14] The FLN's exclusive pairing of "Algerian" with "Muslim" thus responded directly to the French colonial discursive de-linking of Islam and Algeria during the nineteenth century. Yet at the same time, it also replicated the French rhetorical move that viewed Algerians exclusively as Muslims and managed them as such.

The FLN's characterization of Algerians as Algerian, Muslim, and Arab was but one of its rhetorical strategies. The organization used different discursive registers to describe Algeria's revolutionary struggle, turning sometimes to religion and other times to the language of anticolonial progress.

These different discourses were not only strategic, they were also reflective of the many different nationalist currents that contributed to the FLN's legitimacy, including the support of the Oulléma.[15] For as Franco-Tunisian sociologist Mounira Charrad explains, some of the postwar difficulties of the FLN stemmed in part from its heterogeneity. Its many factions, she argued, were united only inasmuch as they all supported Algerian independence.[16] As American historian Matthew Connelly argues, the FLN "used Islamic names and symbols" to appeal to rural Algerians' religiosity by referring to the war as a "jihad" against the "infidels." Yet the party newspaper, *El Moudjahid*,[17] repeatedly argued that their struggle was nationalist, anticolonial, and progressive, *not* religious, and Algerian leaders always downplayed Muslim elements when speaking to international diplomats.[18] In speaking to an Algerian audience, whether in Algeria, in France, or elsewhere, however, the FLN spoke almost exclusively in the language of Islam. French sociologist Monique Gadant argues that not only did this reliance on Islam help to distinguish Algeria from France and give it a distinct identity and construct an ahistorical sense of unity that ignored non-Muslim and non-Arab Algerians, it also allowed the FLN to use Marxist discourse without being accused of bending to "foreign influences." Speaking in terms of Muslim sentiment and morality let FLN leadership present socialism as the means to an end, that of a just Muslim society, rather than an end in itself.[19]

The question of whether and how an independent Algeria would be constituted was not merely a discursive one. It was debated not only with words but also with guns, bombs, knives, and torture devices. The violence of the conflict and its effect on villages, towns, streets, and homes, on both sides of the Mediterranean, cannot be underestimated in considering the long afterlife of the war and the population shifts it engendered. The creation of a new Algeria and the failed attempt to hold on to *Algérie française* were born out of immense physical and emotional violence. During the war itself, Algerian men, women, and children were often uprooted and relocated collectively or individually, in both Algeria and the metropole. In Algeria, the French army began creating detention camps as early as March 1956, in which rural or nomadic populations were forced to reside in particular zones that could be secured by the military. By 1961, more than two million people had been resettled in these camps. The consequences were disastrous: abandoned villages were destroyed, agricultural production was irrevocably disrupted, and the population suffered from tuberculosis, high infant mortality, and severe psychological distress.[20] In France, Algerian men suspected of FLN membership were routinely detained in retention centers all over France for unlimited amounts of time. As of 1959, approximately one thousand Algerians were arrested every month, and by 1960 there were almost ten thousand Algerians detained in camps.[21] "Algerian" neighborhoods in metropolitan urban centers and Muslim neighborhoods in Algeria were subject to curfews and searches, creating a level of daily tension that was difficult to manage. One example of military interference in the space of daily life was the French army's breaking of the general strike during the Battle of Algiers, which began on 30 September 1956: shops and businesses were forcibly opened, Algerians were loaded onto trucks and forced to go to work, curfews were enforced, and neighborhoods were isolated from each other.[22]

The violence committed against spaces and homes, of course, was happening as grievous violence was being committed against Algerian and French bodies. Although historians and members of associations continue to dispute the number of deaths due to the war, some estimates suggest that 141,000 soldiers of the Armée Nationale de Libération (ALN, the FLN army) were killed alongside 27,500 French soldiers, of which 3,500 were *harkis,* Algerian Muslims engaged in the French army, although it is estimated that as many as 100,000 *harkis* were killed in Algeria after the cease-fire in 1962.[23] The Algerian government gives the figure of 300,000 Algerian Muslim dead during the course of the war, in addition to 4,000 people who died in France.[24] Many deaths were the results of horrific attacks by both the French army and the ALN on Algerian villages, whose images were burned into public consciousness by newspaper photographs. Others were the results of FLN and OAS bombs on both sides of the Mediterranean. The French state also responded violently to nonviolent political mobilizations, most famously in the police's repression of a peaceful demonstration in favor of Algerian independence, which took place in Paris on 17 October 1961.[25] There is still no definitive figure for the number of victims of this attack. A French leftist demonstration against the OAS on 8 February 1962 was also violently repressed by the police, resulting in eight deaths at the Charonne metro station. The violence of the war on Paris's streets was visible not only in police attacks on nonviolent demonstrators but also in "invisible" everyday police brutality. The FFFLN was responsible for violent attacks on French targets as well as internal political assassinations within the Algerian community. FLN operatives organized actions against the Parisian police all over the city, from the 5th *arrondissement* to the 18th, from the eastern suburbs of Lilas and Vincennes to the southern suburb of Ivry.[26] Paris and its suburbs were thus the stages for French and Algerian violence throughout the course of the war. Finally, for a France whose memories of World War II were still painfully fresh, it was the widespread use of torture by the French army that would finally throw the war into question.[27] Commander in Chief Raoul

Salan and General Jacques Massu were responsible for institutionalizing the use of torture during the interrogations related to the Battle of Algiers. Historian Raphaëlle Branche has argued forcefully against the idea that torture was a necessary evil that was used to save lives, suggesting instead that it was a technique to impose French domination at a moment when French authority was on the wane.[28]

The reverberations of the violence and divisions engendered by the eight long years of war lasted far beyond the signing of the Evian Accords. When Algeria became independent, almost all remaining 800,000 members of the country's *pied noir* population, including Algerian Jews, left their homes for the metropole. In addition to these "*rapatriés*" (many of whom, of course, were not of French origin, nor had ever resided in France), a smaller number of Algerian Muslims (approximately 49,000) also migrated to France: the *harkis,* Algerians who had fought for France during the war. The *pieds noirs,* of French, Spanish, Italian, Maltese, German, or Swiss origin[29], had begun to leave Algeria over the course of the war as it became increasingly apparent that *Algérie française* would not survive much longer. Yet it was in the summer and fall of 1962 that the final departures took place, with boats carrying men, women, and children arriving in French ports. Although the quality of life of the *rapatriés* was often 15% to 20% lower than that of their metropolitan fellow citizens,[30] the French state nevertheless enacted a series of laws designed to ease their social and economic insertion into French life. Even before the war's end, the law of 26 December 1961 called for a program for the welcome and reinstallation of *Français d'outre-mer* who had been forced to leave "a territory where they had been established and which was formerly under the sovereignty, protection, or guardianship of France." The law assured them of temporary subsistence loans, housing allocations or subsidized public housing, help with professional and educational insertion, social benefits, and other loans.[31] Later legislation spelled out more clearly what would be provided to repatriated *pieds noirs,* such as free transportation to France by boat, a moving and departure allowance, and a week's free lodging upon arrival in the metropole as well as a monthly food allowance.[32] Laws were also passed to give *pieds noirs* first priority for jobs in industrial or commercial companies of at least fifty employees.[33] The social safety net provided for this population could not, of course, compensate for the hostility with which many of them were greeted on their arrival in a country in which they had never lived, nor for the loss of the only country many of them had ever known.[34]

Of the *pieds noirs* who arrived in France in 1962, 100,000 were Jews.[35] The very inclusion of Jews in the category "*pied noir*" is telling, for as Todd Shepard has pointed out, at the war's beginning there was not necessarily an established "Jewish" position on the war or its aftermath, and anti-Semitism had long been a hallmark of right-wing French colonial politics. Yet in the last two years of the war, both the OAS and French officials stopped referring to Jews as a separate and distinct group within the larger European community of Algeria, and these French men and women would chose overwhelmingly to be "repatriated" to France in spite of Israeli efforts to encourage their mass immigration to Israel. Shepard argues that this "shared exodus" of Europeans and Jews in 1962 showed that Frenchness could accommodate *some* differences, such as Jewish difference, but not *all* differences, such as Muslimness.[36] The inclusion of Algerian Jews within the boundaries of Frenchness in 1962 serves to emphasize how pervasive the exclusion of Muslims would continue to be during the postcolonial era.

As French citizens, whether of European origin or not, Algerian Jews benefited from the same financial, social, and administrative services that the state provided to the rest of the *pied noir* community.[37] Like the *pied noir* community, some Jews left during the course of the war, but most left in 1962. Algerian Jews arrived after an initial wave of Moroccan and Tunisian Jewish immigration in 1955–56 as those two countries gained their independence, which meant that French Jewish organizations had already begun to organize a response to this sudden influx of migrants. Jewish associations actively sought out the new arrivals and programmed religious, cultural, and educational activities for them. Like other *rapatriés,* however, in spite of eventual social and financial success, many Algerian Jews lived their arrival in the metropole as an exile. A Jewish resident of a formerly shared Muslim-Jewish residence in Sétif whose Jewish families had slowly trickled away over the war years described the ache of these progressive departures: "From the day they started to leave, there was no more light, not only was it dark, we couldn't see anything, but it was lugubrious! We were the last to go. And at that moment, it was over, I was itching to go."[38]

Perhaps the most difficult migration of the years immediately following the war was that of the *harkis,* the Algerian Muslims who had been forcibly or voluntarily conscripted into the French army.[39] Essentially abandoned by the French army and Europeans fleeing Algeria, many *harkis* and their families were killed by the victorious ALN. Some army officers disobeyed official orders and took personal responsibility for bringing their soldiers to the metropole, though by the end of the summer of 1962 the French navy commissioned ships to transport the *harkis* to Marseille, from where they would be sent to transit camps in Larzac, Bourg-Lastic, Rivesaltes, and Saint-Maurice-l'Ardoise-Lascours.[40] They did not receive the same kinds of financial and administrative assistance as did the European *rapatriés*. In addition to being at a socioeconomic disadvantage upon their arrival in the metropole, the *harkis* were regarded as traitors by many Algerian immigrants as well as many French. Tensions were high between Algerians who had lived through the war in France or in Algeria, whether they had actively supported independence or not, and the newly arrived *harkis*. Under Si Hamza's leadership, the Mosquée tried to reconcile a divided North African, particularly Algerian, community in the 1960s. The size of the Algerian population in France wavered in the immediate aftermath of the war, when many Algerians who had been living in France returned home, but they and many new emigrants quickly crossed the Mediterranean again. From September to November 1962 alone, France's Algerian population increased by 46,000 people.[41] Promoting unity through a common Muslim identity, however, would not be enough to integrate the *harkis* into the rest of the Algerian community living in the metropole.

The creation of an independent Algeria and a postcolonial France was violently new. A redefined Islam and "Algerian" culture, not to mention the Arabic language, played a crucial role in the elaboration of Algerian nationalism and in the independence struggle. Muslims, Jews, and Christians who had lived through the terrors of the war in Algeria and arrived on French shores afterwards into the uncertainty of a new life, as well as those who had lived through the "war without a name" in the metropole, all bore the scars of eight years of violence and rupture.[42] The collapsing of space between the metropole and colony through the war's violence on both sides of the sea made conceptualizing the place of Islam and Muslims in France that much more complicated for both the FLN and the French government.

Islam and Nationalism at the Mosquée: The Brief Reign of Si Ahmed Ben Ghabrit

The brief period during which the temporary leader of the Mosquée, Si Ahmed Ben Ghabrit, allowed speakers to advocate Algerian independence from the institution's very prayer room was perceived as a serious threat by the metropolitan administration. In rejecting the site's *Islam français* and using an Islam aligned neither with France nor with the FLN as an integral element in the independence struggle, Si Ahmed opened up the possibility of a radically new way of being Muslim in France. Under his leadership, the Mosquée continued its program of two-tiered holiday celebrations (a "private" celebration for Muslims with a "public" one to which French officials were invited) but Si Ahmed seemed to be more invested in the Muslim religious ceremonies than the French "receptions" at which his predecessor and successor excelled. During his brief tenure, the promotion of *Islam français* through the pedagogic display of Muslim religious practices was challenged, but more importantly for the French state, the transparency and accessibility of Islam was threatened for the first time in the very site designed to ensure these two things. Si Ahmed's replacement by Si Hamza Boubakeur, whose *Islam français* conformed with the Mosquée's original vision, demonstrates the French state's unwillingness to conceptualize a different relationship among Muslims, Islam, and the republic.

Si Kaddour, who had singlehandedly run the Mosquée since its creation, died in June 1954, only five months before the Algerian War began. The institution's first and only *recteur* had reigned for almost thirty years, in a sometimes contentious but always close collaboration with the metropolitan, colonial, and local Parisian administrations. Si Kaddour's death, at such a difficult moment, threw the Mosquée and the French state into a period of crisis. The defunct *recteur*'s nephew, Si Ahmed Ben Ghabrit, was given temporary authority over the site by the minister of foreign affairs, since he "was up to date about all [the Mosquée's] business and presented all guarantees [of loyalty]."[43] The minister of the interior, on the other hand, supported the candidacy of the elderly Si Mohamed Mammeri.[44] Si Mammeri, like Si Kaddour, was an Algerian serving in the Moroccan sultan's court. He too was a "*français musulman d'Algérie* whose loyalty to France has never been at fault." Perhaps of greater importance was the fact that Si Mammeri "represents a happy synthesis between Muslim Culture and French culture, and the perfect dignity of his personal life allows him to assume the religious functions which behoove the Director of the Mosquée before the Muslim community."[45] This candidate, it seems, was the perfect incarnation of *Islam français,* and the archival evidence does not make clear why the Ministry of the Interior did not succeed in enshrining its candidate in the position of *recteur* and avoiding the troubles caused by Si Ahmed's tenure. Not only was Si Mammeri identified as a living incarnation of *Islam français,* but he was a North African rather than a Parisian like Si Ahmed. Although provincial prayer sites were increasingly staffed with "locals" rather than religious figures imported from North Africa, the decision to allow a Parisian Muslim to assume the helm of the Mosquée was a potentially risky one. I suspect that Si Ahmed's appointment had more to do with expediency and the desire to have someone occupy the position immediately in an increasingly tense climate than with a decision *not* to give the post to Si Mammeri. Many French officials were probably convinced that Si Ahmed would simply continue the work of his uncle, without making any waves.

In addition to questions involving the institution's leadership, including whether the Mosquée's *recteur* should be Moroccan or Algerian, its judicial status was also unclear. Not only did the Société des Habous' statutes make no mention of the procedures to be followed in the event of the death of its president (Si Kaddour), but the association technically ceased to exist upon the deaths of its founding members (Si Kaddour had been the last surviving member of the group). The Société des Habous' character as a 1901 association was a "*fiction juridique*"[46] lacking formal guidelines, French officials argued. As the Section for Moroccan Affairs of the Quai d'Orsay explained, following the nonexistent "procedures" to designate a new *recteur* would be especially dangerous "in present circumstances" for it would "remove all French public power's prerogatives on the Mosquée."[47] Rather than allowing the Société des Habous to designate the Mosquée's new leader, the Quai d'Orsay proposed naming someone by a joint ministerial decision. In order to justify taking direct control of the administrative functioning of the Mosquée, the ministry proposed that the French state take over almost all of the institution's financial costs so that it could "conserve the right to watch over the Mosquée."[48]

The metropolitan and colonial administrations alike were deeply concerned about the Mosquée's status as the political situation across North Africa became increasingly tense. As a note from the Moroccan section of the minister of foreign affairs explained:

> We are thus . . . in the delicate situation in which a Muslim religious establishment, right in the heart of Paris, has no defined judicial status and gives no reassuring guarantees to Public Authorities, especially given the current circumstances; headed by a temporary figure whose authority comes only from the justified confidence the Department [of Moroccan Affairs at the MAE] has placed in him. It is doubtless important to take care of the situation now to avoid running the risk of seeing the Mosquée escape all governmental control and becoming a Muslim anti-French center in the middle of Paris.[49]

The fear evoked by the officials at the Quai d'Orsay—that a site in Paris's very core would become the center of anti-French activity—reflects not only the fact that it was anticolonial nationalist activity that was at stake but also the fact that this activity could be embodied in and nurtured by a site ostensibly given to Muslims by the French state located in the heart of the Hexagon's capital. The spatial occupation of Paris by Algerian immigrants had been a preoccupation of metropolitan officials since the earliest days of their arrival in the metropole. As we have seen, the police kept detailed records of their lodgings, cafes, places of leisure, and so on, while other agencies noted their religious practices. The outbreak of the Algerian War only increased French anxieties about mapping the Algerian presence in the capital and identifying sites of concentrated populations or activities. Finally, Guy Mollet, the président du conseil, acting on the advice of Robert Lacoste, ministre résident en Algérie, named Si Hamza director of the Institut Musulman and the Mosquée de Paris on 17 May 1957.[50] According to Si Ahmed's nephew, Hassan Benghabrit, police officers from the Commissariat of the 5th *arrondissement* helped Si Hamza's family to move into their new apartments in the Mosquée and forcibly removed Si Ahmed's family.[51]

Si Ahmed himself does not appear to have been the *éminence grise* behind the expressions of support for the Algerian Revolution that were uttered within the Mosquée's walls, but his decision to allow others to use the *interior* of the site as a politicized and contestatory space for the first time stood in marked contrast to the behavior of his uncle Si Kaddour. The Mosquée had long been used as a site to protest French colonialism, but these protests had taken place *outside* its walls, by nationalists who contested the site itself as part of the colonial project. During the war, the police also believed that implicit protests were staged by strategic absences: not observing Muslim holidays at the Mosquée was interpreted, rightly or wrongly, as opposition to either the site's vision of Islam or to French colonialism. This particular view, however, gave too much power to the site in defining Muslim religious practice in Paris and, as we shall see, also gave too much power to the FFFLN's authority to regulate Algerians' religious observance.

While it is difficult to know what, if anything, Muslims hoped to signal by not observing holidays at the Mosquée, the French state's interest in charting attendance was based in its belief that presence and absence could have only political causes. In 1954, Aïd el Kébir fell in the beginning of August, three months before the beginning of the Algerian War. Many of Paris's Moroccan and Algerian leaders (though apparently not the Tunisians) appeared to use the holiday to express their beliefs about political developments in their respective countries. A report from the Ministry of the Interior's section on Algerian affairs notes that the holiday would "not be celebrated by the members of the Paris region's Moroccan colony, as a sign of protest against the deposing and exile of Morocco's ex-Sultan." The report adds that the refusal to observe the holiday was in accordance with Moroccan nationalist groups' directives, issued to Paris's Moroccans from across the Mediterranean.[52] However, Paris's Moroccans did not follow the call for a general strike from 9–20 August that was also issued by nationalist leaders, maintaining their businesses open as usual. Their apparent willingness to observe the religious "strike" while refusing to comply with the labor strike is suggestive: would those whom the Ministry of the Interior saw as consciously boycotting the Mosquée with their absence on this particular Aïd el Kébir have worshipped there at other times? Chances are that they would not have attended services at the Mosquée, and that if they chose to celebrate Aïd in a large public setting, they would have done so at Dar es Sultan in Gennevilliers. The ministry's figures do, in fact, report that approximately three hundred Moroccans were present at Dar es Sultan from 10 to 11 a.m., the same time the ceremony took place at the Parisian site.[53] The Moroccans' perceived compliance with the religious but not the commercial strike suggested to the author of this report that their religious sentiments were not as important to them as their commercial success, but an alternative interpretation could be that Parisian Moroccans were observing neither the religious nor the business strike and were acting on their own rather than following the directives of Moroccan nationalists.

The Algerians of Paris were also asked to participate in their own political mobilization on the day of Aïd el Kébir. The MTLD hoped to use the holiday as a "day of action in favor of the liberation" of its leader Messali Hadj, with meetings in public spaces such as "factory gates, bus stops, metro exits, cafés, markets."[54] Yet the Ministry of the Interior reported that although no Moroccans were present, since they were protesting the sultan's fate, of the five hundred people present, the worshippers were almost entirely Algerian, aside from diplomats from the Muslim world. A Syrian imam made a short speech in which he alluded to the principle of jihad and reminded those in attendance that "liberty required sacrifices."[55] Of Si Ahmed's role in the holiday's observance, the ministry's observer reported only that he "received the faithful and conversed with different Muslim notables of Paris." But even if Si Ahmed did not pronounce vaguely nationalist words, as did the unnamed Syrian imam, he allowed such sentiments to be expressed in the temple of *Islam français*. It is important to note, however, that Si Kaddour died in June 1954 and that the "official reception" that always took place at the Mosquée for French and Muslim dignitaries was cancelled for that reason.[56] It was perhaps easier for Si Ahmed to tolerate the expression of such views given that aside from the usual surveillance by French officials, there were fewer French observers present than there otherwise would have been.

In May 1955, however, well after the November 1954 uprising that marked the beginning of the Algerian War, the usual two-part celebration was set in place for the observance of Aïd es Séghir, and thus French officials were present at the Mosquée in the evening after a morning of significant nationalist activity at the site. Ministry of the Interior observers estimated the attendance at 2,500 people at the morning's religious service, including members of Moroccan nationalist groups and of the Oulêma, in addition to the usual array of ambassadors from Muslim countries. Si Ahmed does not appear to have led any portion of the morning's prayers or speeches, but an imam named Ben Achour concluded his sermon by "calling for unity to achieve independence." An unnamed Muslim, speaking in Arabic, told the assembled crowd that Nasser's Egypt was ready and willing to help North African Muslims in their fight. At the threshold that physically separated the Mosquée and its activities from those of Muslim associations, Messaliste MNA activists stood at the exit and collected donations from worshippers leaving the site.[57] Hours later, at the evening "official reception at the Muslim holiday of 'Aïd Es Seghir,' which crowns the end of 'Ramadan,'" Si Ahmed welcomed 150 guests, including French officials and some of the elite Muslims who had been present at the morning's prayers. Although "many photographers and journalists" were present, no allusions were made to the political situation.[58] Si Ahmed's Mosquée was thus a politicized space only during the "religious" morning services and not during the evening "receptions." The strategy of bringing political concerns into the walls of the Parisian site during the more "authentically" Muslim activities in the morning but maintaining the traditionally apolitical display of Islam to a French audience in the evening made the Mosquée's activities both unknowable and dangerous for the first time. Of course, French observers were still present at the morning ceremonies to keep watch over the activities of the Mosquée's personnel and those who came to worship: but the speeches they heard were no longer audible to the larger audience who assembled in the evening. The public privacy of the Mosquée's religious observances, in which there was perfect symmetry between the Muslim morning and French evening activities, had been disrupted by Si Ahmed's allowing the morning ceremonies to be used to express nationalist sentiments. The upsetting of the equilibrium between public and private displays of Muslim practice also signaled that Si Ahmed's Islam was not *Islam français*: although he did not halt the practice of the gatherings of French officials, that the morning ceremonies went "off message" meant that he allowed for the possibility that Islam could occupy a different space in Parisian Muslims' lives, whether they attended to the Mosquée's celebrations or not.

The celebration of Aïd el Kébir in July 1955 further revealed the extent to which the Mosquée under Si Ahmed's leadership had become a troubling site for the French administration. Paris's Moroccans were urged to come "in great numbers" to the morning service to show their presence at "a prayer said in memory of the victims of the recent demonstrations which took place all over the Cherifian Empire."[59] But while Moroccans were invited to use the site to implicitly protest the violence occasioned by French colonialism in their country, Algerian nationalist leaders "told their faithful not to attend the service and not to join in any festivities." Ministry officials counted a mere 600 people at the morning ceremony (mostly Moroccans and West Africans), including the usual array of ambassadors from Muslim countries. The low attendance was apparently a source of shock and consternation to those who were present. No speeches were made, though the prayers themselves were both played on loudspeakers mounted outside the Mosquée and recorded by Radiodiffusion française.[60] Unlike every other year, pastries were sold outside the Mosquée after the ceremony rather than distributed freely within—perhaps a particular association was selling them as a fundraiser for nationalist activity. Cakes and mint tea were once again served to the French and Muslim dignitaries who gathered for the evening reception, which seems consistent with the notion that their not being distributed in the morning was not because of a sudden budgetary cut but was rather a conscious decision to allow an unidentified group or individuals to use the occasion to raise money.[61] It is not clear from archival evidence who was responsible for organizing the Mosquée's celebration of the holiday in this way.

The politics of the morning's activities do not lend themselves to easy interpretation. Mosquée leaders knew that Algerians would most likely not attend services and that the FLN may have planned to organize fundraising drives on the holiday. It could be argued that Si Ahmed hoped that in explicitly showing sympathy for the Moroccan independence struggle, which was in its final stages—Moroccan independence was inevitable at that point—he was also implicitly showing support for the newer Algerian anticolonial battle, even though Algerian militants would have identified his institution as collaborationist. What is more intriguing is that the call to prayer was, for once, replayed outside the Mosquée as well as diffused over the radio, since one of the perennial problems with the site's "traditional" functioning had always been that the muezzin was inaudible outside its walls. The intrigue stems from the fact that this would have required the approval, not to say cooperation, of the Ministry of the Interior and probably also the Parisian police. I suspect that what was at work in the state's decision to tacitly support the Mosquée's endorsement of Moroccan nationalism was that broadcasting the call to prayer into French public space allowed it to accomplish more important work. By making the increasingly private Muslim practices that seemed to be escaping French authority publicly audible, the state reinforced its ultimate control over Islam in the metropole through authorizing the diffusion of prayers. Even if support for Moroccan independence fell far outside of the contours of *Islam français,* the rendering public of Muslim religious practices was an integral element of that vision of Islam.[62]

Unfortunately, archival records do not allow us to see how Si Ahmed's last year as the leader of the Mosquée unfolded during the two major holidays of the Muslim year celebrated at the site. The state's decision to replace him, however, makes clear that his political inclinations remained problematic, so we can presume that gestures in favor of Algerian independence continued to be made at or around the Mosquée with his approval. The brief and exceptional tenure of Si Ahmed and the French administration's reaction to it reveals the state's investment in maintaining the original version of *Islam français.* An Islam not conflated with culture, race, or nationality, one that made no arguments about the relationship of Muslims to the French state, was intensely troubling for an administration trying to hold on to the formula it had used for decades to manage France's North African immigrants. But a vision of Islam that precluded Muslim participation in French civic society was not the sole property of the state. The FLN's strategy of organizing both special holiday observances as well as restructuring daily life relied on a different and competing Islam, one I call *Islam algérien,* which conflated Algerian-ness and Muslimness as did the French state.[63]

Islam, Nationalism, and the FFFLN: Making Muslim Everyday Life, Making Everyday Life Muslim

The FLN's program of isolating Algerians from French society through the organization of everyday life around Muslim practices, intended to create a firm barrier between their movement and French society, in fact did the same work as that of the French state. It marked Algerians as others defined by their "Muslimness." As the direct agent of the FLN in France, the FFFLN used policies and discourse taken from the movement in Algeria rather than adapting them to local circumstances.[64] One of the FLN's major tasks in organizing France's Algerian community was "thwarting the Préfecture de Police's Social Commission's programs and isolating Algerian Muslims from French society."[65] This strategy was clearly understood by the Ministry of the Interior, which reminded departmental préfets that providing Algerians with the necessary social services was even more important than usual since the "nationalists" were trying to isolate Muslim Algerians. French local administrations were warned that "the battle against the terrorists is tightly linked to the efficiency of social services."[66] As a clandestine organization waging a war on metropolitan soil, the FLN kept tight control over its militants as well as the rest of the Algerian and in fact Muslim community. Benjamin Stora has argued that "the heavy hand of the [FLN] . . . regulated the private and professional lives" of Algerians in France. Some of these restrictions included not being able to leave one's neighborhood without permission, not being able to change jobs, needing to get authorization to go to the movies, and not being able to have sexual relationships with other militants in the same FLN network without special permission.[67] Clearly it was not possible for FFFLN local leaders to ensure total enforcement of their regulations, but accounts of the internal workings of the FLN in France suggest that they were in fact fairly successful at keeping track of militants' actions.[68] In addition to establishing its authority over the Algerian population through restrictions on movement and personal freedom, the FLN created the Comités d'hygiène et d'aide sociale which were designed to replace local and national French state social service agencies whenever possible and to help Algerians negotiate their interactions with these agencies when it was unavoidable. The four-member committee, familiar with the laws concerning hygiene, unemployment offices, assistance to families, and commercial law, was to help "those brothers who had troubles with the French state."[69]

In addition to everyday life and life cycle events, Algerian nationalist groups also sought to shape the celebration of holidays. Before Ramadan began in 1957, leaders in Paris and its surrounding suburbs spread the word that all Algerians were to observe the fast and that they were prepared to enforce these orders.[70] The FFFLN made a special target of the Algerian cafés and bars in the 18th *arrondissement,* warning owners that there would be retaliations against those who opened their doors during the daylight hours or served alcoholic drinks.[71] According to observers from the Ministry of the Interior, however, "In spite of the FLN's orders to close, more than half of the bars run by North Africans are open during the day and closed at night."[72] Such estimates must be taken with a grain of salt, since the Ministry of the Interior was hardly an impartial observer when it came to reporting on the organization's effectiveness in managing the city's Algerian population. Yet the very fact that FLN militants regularly made rounds to intimidate bar owners and did, on occasion, carry out their threats, suggests that it is likely that many owners refused to obey orders—had they all complied, the level of surveillance would not have been so elevated. Their grounds for refusal are harder to uncover, and it is not clear whether such refusals to close were protests against the FLN's leadership, economic decisions made by businessman, both, or neither.

On both Aïd el Kébir and Aïd es Séghir of 1957, the FLN used the holiday as an occasion to champion their cause. Although the MNA urged their followers to observe Aïd es Séghir at the Mosquée, it appears that those who did choose to attend the Mosquée's services under the leadership of Si Hamza were mostly the usual Muslim elites, as well as a few West Africans.[73] After the official service ended and the imam left (having given a completely apolitical sermon), a member of the FLN took the floor to denounce French colonialism. After his speech, Muslims leaving the Mosquée were greeted by an Algerian flag, political pamphlets, and requests for donations for FLN "combatants," while French policemen stood by maintaining order. It is telling that the last line of the Ministry of the Interior's report on the interruption of the Mosquée's normal observance by the unidentified member of the FLN was, "By 11:45, the grounds of the Mosquée had reverted to their usual physiognomy."[74] The presence of FLN activists within the confines of the Mosquée and immediately outside its walls was not only disruptive to the site's functioning on a political level, it also shifted the Mosquée's very appearance and turned its space into something quite different. Since the site was the physical embodiment of *Islam français* and loyalty to the French government, Si Ahmed and his tolerance for nationalist activity notwithstanding, the claiming of its space for a radically different use was that much more jarring.

"The Sacred Precepts of Our Religion": Muslim Marriage, Civil Marriage

The use of Muslim public spaces was important to the FFFLN's struggle, but one of the most important battlegrounds on which the FFFLN tried to impose a religious order on France's Algerian population was in the realm of the family: marriage. The question of marriage was particularly contentious in the context of the Algerian War, as the French government had identified the "emancipation" of Algerian women from their status in Muslim society as one of the goals of France's continued presence in Algeria. As Judith Surkis has argued, the place assigned to women in Muslim religious law had been the subject of French debate since the nineteenth century and "reified differences between French and Muslim marriage law became the principal ground on which categorical distinctions between citizens and colonial subjects were made in Algeria."[75] The different programs designed to "emancipate" Algerian women, such as public "unveiling" ceremonies, women's suffrage, and girls' education, have been covered exhaustively elsewhere, but what concerns us here is the debate around marriage and personal status of 1958–59 and the consequences of that debate for the metropole.[76] The existing legislation governing marriages in Algeria was not uniform, and Arab and Kabyle communities applied different religious laws to govern their communities in this regard. Generally speaking, however, the issues that the French government found most objectionable included the fact that marriages (including those of prepubescent girls) were arranged by fathers or legal guardians; that men had the right to contract additional marriages and also unilaterally repudiate wives; that men had no financial or legal obligations to repudiated or divorced women (yet could maintain guardianship over any children). In late 1958, newly elected president Charles de Gaulle directed his administration to undertake a reform of the status of Muslim women, and a commission of French and Algerian Muslim experts on Muslim law was quickly assembled to begin debating the question. Those French politicians intimately involved in Algerian issues were extremely circumspect about the extent of these reforms. The general secretary for Algerian affairs informed the minister of justice that the government must not try to help Muslim women by taking any "unsuitable measures" in a "domain marked by the presence of custom and religious tradition" and that it should instead examine the possibilities of "modifying the existing rules governing personal status (notably as concerns . . . marriage, polygamy, and especially repudiation)."[77] As Neil MacMaster has demonstrated, in spite of serious objections from both Algerian Muslim and French administrator members of the Algiers Commission, brought together to evaluate the proposed reforms, de Gaulle created a new commission in Paris to draft the ordinance without acknowledging the criticisms from Algeria. The reform of 1959 was met with outrage by many influential Algerian Muslim members of the French colonial administration as well as shock and concern on the part of French administrators in the colony. It called for a minimum age for marriage (15 and 18 years for men and women, respectively); required the free consent of both spouses, both of whom had to appear in person in front of a religious or civil authority; and the marriage had to be registered and the couple given a marriage certificate. Only a judge could decide on whether or not to accord a divorce, which could be requested by the husband or wife, and the judge was additionally urged to push the couple to reconcile. If divorce was the only solution, the judge would decree how much and what kind of support was owed to the woman and children. The ordinance was not retroactive and applied only to marriages contracted after its passing.[78]

The Algerian Muslim members of the Algiers Commission who objected so strongly to this ordinance were drawn from different regions, but were all senior religious authorities, including muftis, *qadis,* and imams who supported the French administration. One of the most vocal critics of reform was none other than Hamza Boubakeur, Si Ahmed's replacement as *recteur* at the Mosquée since 1957, but also a deputy from the Oasis *département.*

Boubakeur had already made clear his opposition to reforms of marriage law during earlier debates on the same subject.[79] During the initial committee meeting in December 1958, Boubakeur expressed "shock" at the speed with which the French government was seeking to push through a reform that would have "immediate and profound effects on family structures, the orientation of society and the emancipation of women."[80] For him, the problem was that "whether we like it or not, Muslim marriage is religious marriage," which he opposed to "legal" French marriage.[81] In his own written report to the commission, Boubakeur made clear that the issue of Muslim religiosity extended well beyond the confines of the marriage debates. "The religious factor," he wrote, "is primordial in a deeply faithful society attached to its customs."[82] Any attempts to force reform, he warned, would be resented by an Algerian people "fiercely attached to its customary-juridical system, anarchist by atavism, subject to the wildest impulses when religion—inseparable from jurisdiction—is challenged, ready and willing to participate in disorder, to provoke discontent which would aggravate the current perturbations."[83] For Boubakeur, the crucial problem was that the marriage reform project did not take into account the fundamental difference between "Muslim" and French society. The Mosquée's *recteur* described French "morals and sensibility" as "half-Christian, half-*laïques*" and thus profoundly incomparable with Muslims' deeply religious sociability. What Boubakeur objected to was the notion that French laws could turn Algerian Muslims into secular subjects overnight, with no consequences for Algerian Muslim society. His opposition to the project, in spite of de Gaulle's insistence on its importance, represented a firm commitment to *Islam français*. In arguing that Quranic verses about repudiation, however distasteful to a French audience, were legitimate and crucial to Muslim notions of morality and custom, Boubakeur was agreeing that Islam was not compatible with Frenchness and that it was the French state's responsibility to *protect* Islam rather than try to *reform* it.

Paul Delouvrier, de Gaulle's personally appointed head of the Algerian administration, voiced a more strategic version of Boubakeur's concerns, warning that Muslim elites would see these reforms as an incursion of French power into the realm of Muslim religious authority and that the FLN would use the reform as highly effective propaganda to rally Algerians against the French.[84] Fearing that Delouvrier's predictions would come true, French administrators launched a propaganda campaign in favor of the reforms, including the publication of many interviews with the children of repudiated women describing their lives as well as rumor campaigns that spread the idea that Muslim religious authorities opposed the reforms because of what it would mean to their livelihood through a loss of "business." In reality, while both the French government and the FLN accorded great importance to the Ordinance of 1959, it was rarely applied on the ground in Algeria because there was simply no bureaucratic apparatus that would have made it possible.[85]

In France, however, both the French state and the FFFLN used Muslim marriages as a weapon in the struggle for French Algeria and for independence. Unlike the FLN, who urged their supporters to marry religiously before going through French bureaucratic procedures for legal reasons, the Mosquée required Muslims to contract a *laïc* marriage in the space of a French institution before having a religious ceremony consecrated on the grounds of the Mosquée. The institution of marriage is a useful one to explore the conflicts and paradoxes of a "reinforced" Algerian Islam as imagined by the FLN, the secular Islam of the Mosquée, and the *laïc* rituals of republican France. What was at play during the 1950s and early 1960s was on the one hand a struggle to achieve religio-cultural dominance over a colonizing power and on the other to assert the compatibility of Muslim ritual with *laïc* ritual while explicitly acknowledging republican faith and the state's authority as paramount. By requiring North Africans to perform civil marriages and recognizing only the symbolic importance of marriages performed at the Mosquée, the French state placed Muslims squarely into the same juridical space occupied by non-Muslim French citizens. In this particular case, however, this exceptional attitude toward Muslims can be explained by the administration's need to respond directly to the FFFLN's attempt to establish judicial authority over Algerians by recognizing Muslim marriages as binding and to be seen to be promoting gender equality.

The institution of civil marriage in France dates from 1792, when the law of 20 September decreed that the only legally recognized form of marriage was one performed at the *mairie*. This broke with the *ancien régime* tradition which recognized only religious marriages. Not only must the civil marriage precede any form of religious marriage, but the performance of a religious wedding before going to the *mairie* is a criminal act. Marriage, which organized everyday political, economic, and social life, was one of the major sites where the new French republic made clear that the state might not have outlawed religious practice, but it did certainly rob it of its power to structure the lives of French citizens. Although civil marriages displaced religious ones, they were as elaborately choreographed and laden with symbolism as any church or synagogue wedding. The ceremony required a special space, the *mairie*'s *salle de mariages,* in which a statue of Marianne was often placed to symbolize the Republic. The doors of the room in which marriages were officiated had to remain open at all times since the act being performed within was a public one. To this end, civil marriages also required at least one adult witness for each spouse and as many as four witnesses in total. Marriages could only be performed by the mayor or an adjunct, who was required to wear a sash reflecting the solemnity of his role as the state's representative. The couple being married had to dress appropriately and in such a way that the officer performing the ceremony could be sure of their identities.

The civil marriage also had its own liturgy, for the person officiating read the articles of the Civil Code pertaining to marriage aloud to the couple, their witnesses, and any people in attendance. These articles included injunctions such as "the spouses owe each other fidelity, aid, and assistance"; "the spouses are responsible together for the family's moral and material direction. They oversee their children's education and prepare their future"; and "the spouses are obliged to share their lives." After this recitation, the officer obtains each spouse's consent to the marriage, then celebrates the union, and establishes and signs the marriage declaration. Aside from the absence of reference to a deity or religious faith, there is not much that separates this ceremony (complete with the statue of Marianne to symbolize the republic, its sacralized public space, its sartorial requirements and its liturgy) from the Catholic, Protestant, Jewish, and eventually Muslim ceremonies that could be performed following, and in addition to, the civil marriage.

Catholics and Protestants, whose marriage rites and laws differed, had similarly different attitudes toward the institution of civil marriage in France, as did Jews. The Catholic Church, with its canonical law governing marriage, did not recognize unions performed exclusively at the *mairie*: only a Church marriage, one of the seven sacraments, was considered legitimate. The Protestant Church, on the other hand, considers marriages performed according to civil law to be valid, and a ceremony in the church itself is optional. Unlike the Catholic rite, it is not a sacrament but merely a blessing of the couple.[86] With the acquisition of French citizenship in the late nineteenth century, Algerian Jews lost their Jewish religious status, and thus Jewish religious marriages were no longer legally recognized. While republican metropolitan Jewish leaders urged their Algerian coreligionists to accept civic marriages as binding and valid, Algerian Jewish religious leaders lived the transition from Jewish religious law to French civil law as a catastrophe. As one Algerian rabbi explained, French colonialism robbed Algerian Judaism of its "religiosity" by systematically replacing Jewish religious authority, such as courts, with French civil authority. For him, that "we had to wait until a marriage was done at the *mairie* for the rabbi to be able to bless the new couple" was one of the most glaring signs of the overturning of the normal order of things.[87] The Algerian Jewish establishment's position was thus closer to the Catholic one, while metropolitan Jewish leaders seemed to share the Protestant position.

The Ministry of the Interior, fully aware of the challenge to French legal authority the FLN's Muslim marriages represented, made clear that they had absolutely no juridical status before the state.[88] In a pamphlet entitled "Regulations concerning Marriage according to Muslim Law," the FFFLN advised its "compatriots living in France" of the proper procedures to follow concerning marriages, "since we are Muslims and we believe in respecting the sacred precepts of our religion."[89] The FFFLN framed its discussion of marriage by assuming that Muslims living in France were sometimes reluctant to marry for lack of resources, but also "from fear of not being able to respect the religious obligations of the Muslim [Law] Code." To this end, the pamphlet's authors "think it useful to turn to Muslim Law, with its foundation, the Quran."[90]

The document's subsequent exclusive focus on the religious requirements for marriage evacuates the question of the socioeconomic issues, raised by its own authors, that may have prevented Muslims from marrying and establishing households in the metropole. Additionally, ideological constraints dictated that the FLN repress knowledge of what was obvious to everyone, including French legal authorities: Algerian men, and to a far lesser extent Algerian women, were living in unmarried partnerships or in civil marriages with other Algerians and French. The document's authors did not address these two issues and proceeded to explain the norms of Muslim religious marriage in order to encourage people to contract religious marriages before entering civil unions. The FFFLN explained that before even considering the formalities of a marriage, it was essential to ensure that "the union was based on affection, and decided in common and complete agreement between the two fiancés, with their reciprocal consent." The joint consent for the marriage needed to be approved by the FFFLN's justice committee and if it was "persuaded of the sincerity of the two fiancés," the ceremony could then take place. Unlike the marriage ceremonies at the Mosquée, those of the FFFLN were spartan in their simplicity. They took place "in the presence of [the couple's] parents or guardians . . . as well as witnesses for both parties." The president of the committee asked each partner if he or she accepted the other as spouse, and then, along with everyone present, recited the "'Fatiha'[91] pronounced according to Muslim rites." According to *Les Cahiers Nord-Africains,* a publication devoted to issues facing North African immigrants, this version of a Muslim marriage ceremony was a fairly faithful reproduction of contemporaneous Algerian practices. On the other side of the Mediterranean, marriages were performed in one of two ways: either as a simple legal document prepared by the *qadi* (a religious judge) or in a blessing recited before friends and family.[92] The FFFLN explained that having performed this religious ceremony, the couple could then proceed to "validate their marriage legally" at the Algerian consulate or the *mairie* to avoid potential bureaucratic or legal difficulties. The FFFLN's Muslim religious wedding was not to be celebrated with much fanfare: they discouraged both the giving of gifts and the traditional dowry, limiting the latter to 5,000 francs.

Marriages at the Mosquée, unlike those of the FLN, needed to straddle Muslim and French exigencies. Weddings performed at the site were supposed to protect Muslims' Muslim personal legal status while at the same time keeping them firmly within the legal boundaries of the French state. Such marriages had only symbolic, not legal, value, as a certain *français musulman* who had been living in Tunisia before moving to Paris found out. In the middle of the Algerian War, the complicated personal life of Hadji Khalifa Bouezza was made even more difficult by his dependence on a myriad of different metropolitan and colonial administrative agencies in order to regularize his marital situation. Bouezza, a former soldier in the French army living in the Parisian suburb of Sarcelles, wrote to de Gaulle to solicit his help in recognizing his Mosquée-consecrated marriage as legal. When his wife refused to leave Tunisia to join him in France with six of their ten children, he eventually decided to get a divorce since he could not take care of his many children alone, especially with his low-paying work as a hospital aide. After divorcing his wife, he remarried in November 1959. "The marriage," he explained to President de Gaulle, "was performed by the Imam of the Mosquée de Paris, Abd-el-Kader, who lives at the Muslim Cemetery of Bobigny, according to the rites of the Muslim religion." Yet Bouezza was unable to get a document recognizing his marriage from the Algerian Office, the Ministry of Foreign Affairs, the Mairie of the 20th *arrondissement,* the Préfecture de Police, or the Mosquée de Paris.[93] The government officials from the Ministry of the Interior's Algerian Office who looked over his dossier agreed that Bouezza's marriage was not legally valid since it had not been performed by a French official and thus had only religious significance for him.[94]

Si Hamza explained to officials from the Ministry of the Interior's Bureau of Muslim Affairs that prior to his arrival, "fairly irregular procedures were followed and officially tolerated by [his] predecessor for various opportunistic reasons."[95] He characterized the French government's attitude toward Algerians living on French soil as irregular as well: Si Hamza explains that since France "was then the world's greatest Muslim power," the state guaranteed its Muslims living in France (whether *musulmans français* from Algeria or protégés from Morocco and Tunisia) their Muslim personal status, as would have been the case had they lived in North Africa. Yet at the same time, it denied the legitimacy of marriages performed under Muslim law. Given this situation, he noted, "the Institut Musulman of the Mosquée de Paris was solicited" to perform Quranic marriages and divorces. Si Hamza described the confusion that this legal grey area engendered by emphasizing that the recourse to the Mosquée's authority did not derive from any judicial text or written authorization from any governmental agency. To this end, the *recteur* requested a written document rather than vague verbal recommendations from the government so that he could understand precisely how and when Muslim law was to be applied.[96]

By 1965, after the war ended, the Mosquée's position on Muslim marriages was clear. Si Hamza stated that in accordance with the Ministry of Justice's decisions, the Mosquée does not "celebrate, judge, or establish, but religiously consecrates Muslim marriages."[97] The religious consecration, furthermore, could only be completed under the following conditions: for *français musulmans,* the couple had to produce proof of a civil marriage delivered by a French official; for foreign Muslims, the couple was required to show proof of a marriage performed by diplomatic or consular officials in Paris; for Moroccan or Tunisian "refugees" living in France after the two protectorates had gained their independence, the couple needed to formulate the request via the Ministry of Foreign Affairs. Ultimately, the Mosquée counted religious marriages as a central feature of a Muslim everyday but specifically an *Islam français* everyday. Weddings at the Parisian site gestured toward the importance of maintaining Muslim religious practices, but in a context in which those practices were only symbolically significant. Had the FFFLN not used marriage as an essential element of defining *Islam algérien,* it is worth speculating how concerned the French administration would have been about the legality of Muslim marriages in the metropole and whether it would not, on the contrary, have preferred that Muslims living in France marry only under Muslim law and thus remain outside of the rights and responsibilities of French civil society.

The Mosquée and the Muslim Everyday

The Mosquée was supposed to perform the complicated work of bridging the French state and its Muslim residents, while Si Hamza hoped at the same time to maintain the site's attraction as a destination for Parisians and Muslim visitors in spite of the political upheaval of the war. In opposition to the FLN and its Muslim programs, the Mosquée sought to inscribe itself in Muslim everyday life in the Paris region, according to the precepts of *Islam français* rather than "pure" Algerian Islam. It continued to provide (or attempt to provide) the social services for which the Mosquée had become known during the World War II years. Thus, like the FLN, it continued to use Islam as a way to manage the city's Muslim population. Of course, the Mosquée's funding for social programming, unlike the FLN's, came from different ministries of the French state as well as the Algerian colonial administration. In essence, the Mosquée was supposed to continue to play the same role in Muslim Paris, and Si Hamza was to take Si Kaddour as his model. As a delicately worded letter from the minister of justice to Si Hamza reminded him, "I see only advantages in your continuing to persevere in the path you have traced out and pursue the work begun in 1926 by your predecessor Si Kaddour Ben Ghabrit. Your great religious and moral authority, in and of itself, permits you to persuade spirits and convince hearts. You can thus assure Muslim families living in the metropole the enjoyment of the status that is their due."[98]

Yet Si Hamza assumed leadership of the Mosquée during a very different era than that of Si Kaddour. A much larger population of Algerians and Moroccans lived in the Paris area, including many politically active nationalists. Some of these immigrants had come to the metropole recently, while others had been living there for years. The police believed that there was a distinct shift in Parisian Muslim religious practice after the war's end, with the dissolution of the FFFLN. In a report from June 1965, the police stated that "of Muslim faith, the Algerian workers of Paris are unevenly pious. Half of them neglect their most elementary canonical duties, 40% content themselves with limited observance, and only 10% respect the 'legal' prescriptions."[99] Police observers explained the decline in religious practices with several factors: "contact with the materialist West, distance from their native country and the weight of traditions, working conditions that don't easily lend themselves to the exercise of a demanding religion": all of these elements had led to an abandonment of Muslim rituals. The authors of the report claimed that some practices were more widespread than others, such as the celebration of major holidays with "collective rejoicing," but that few Muslims fasted during Ramadan and almost no one completed the pilgrimage to Mecca. There did indeed appear to be a decline in some forms of Muslim religious practice among male immigrant laborers in the Paris region, and the pattern of men returning to Algeria for the entire month of Ramadan or for other holidays had mostly faded away. However, it is difficult to even speak of a "decline" in Muslim religiosity given that the sources we have to describe it in past and contemporary moments are almost exclusively produced by the French state, whose observers only validated certain expressions of religious sentiment, observers who did not even have access to many practices performed by North Africans living in the metropole.

French authorities, however, were interested not only in the external manifestations of religious faith but also in the impact of Islam on people's self-consciousness and self-identity, as evident in the attention paid to life cycle events in the private sphere. The same report noted that "the decline of faith has had very little effect on the daily life of Muslim workers, whose thinking and behavior is marked by the contribution of generations of islamicized [ancestors]." Thus children's births were still celebrated by "the special religious ceremonies particular to the event," and circumcisions continued to be performed. Marriages were celebrated at the Algerian Consulate "and gave rise to traditional festivities." Of course, all of the practices to which the report's authors refer (the celebration of holidays, fasting, the pilgrimage, marriages, birth celebrations, and circumcisions) are at once public and private. Although the police were happy to be able to report that "applying the directives of the Algerian government, the *Amicale des Algériens en France*"[100] had distanced itself from the "religious militancy" of the FFFLN, they also recognized that even if people had chosen to neglect certain "public" celebrations or private rituals that, during the war, would have been encouraged by the FFFLN, the rhythm of their everyday lives was still informed by Islam to a large extent.

The Mosquée, in addition to trying to provide its own version of a Muslim framework for daily life in Paris, continued to combine social and religious services to Muslims living in the metropole. French authorities and Mosquée staff referred to those served by these programs as "Muslims" and "North Africans" or "Algerians" interchangeably, thus continuing to conflate national and religious identities and to maintain them as a separate and distinct population. In September 1957, the Mosquée was put under the authority of the Ministry of the Interior, which not only was responsible for "the administrative control and management of the Mosquée de Paris and Institut Musulman" but was also "in cooperation with the other ministries concerned [with Muslim issues]," responsible for subsidizing "social and educational action in favor of French people of Algerian origin living on metropolitan territory."[101] The site had formerly been managed by the Ministry of Foreign Affairs, and this transition from one ministerial portfolio to another was quite significant, for the Ministry of the Interior with its Bureau des cultes was responsible for all religious institutions in France. Thus the Mosquée's new status conformed somewhat to that of Catholic, Protestant, and Jewish sites, yet the collaboration between the Ministry of the Interior and other ministries and agencies concerned with Muslim affairs made clear that it was still a distinct case that could not be assimilated into the normal administration of France's other religions. The insistence on social welfare was unique to the Mosquée. Local and national French authorities referred social workers to the assistance programs offered by the religious site when informing them of the resources available to their North African clients. It is worth noting that the Mosquée was listed in these sourcebooks as both a social service and religious resource for Paris's Muslim communities. One official listing distributed by the Ministry of the Interior entitled "Social Action in Favor of North Africans in the Paris region" described the Mosquée's offerings this way:

> Its principal activity is religious services (daily prayers and the Friday sermon, funeral arrangements, religious consecration of Muslim marriages, conversions to Islam, moral assistance). It is also devoted to the following activities, among others, for Muslims in the metropole:
>
> (a) Social Services: Muslim family questions; assistance and aid to disinherited Muslims; visits to prisons, hospitals, and sanatoriums; a soon-to-be-opened clinic; assistance to students.
>
> (b) Cultural Services: Teaching of North African colloquial Arabic, Classical Arabic, and Advanced courses in Muslim theology, law and literature (in Arabic); introductory French courses for Muslim women; bookstore devoted to works on Islam and the Muslim world; visits and initiation to Muslim art.[102]

Another brochure from the same period destined for employers with large numbers of Muslim employees provided information about the services available to Maghrébin workers and also explained the Muslim religious calendar and the different ritual celebrations that accompanied each holiday, including a note that the Ramadan fast was the "most observed" Muslim religious obligation. The Mosquée was listed as the source for further information and to confirm the dates for each holiday.[103]

Si Hamza, much like his predecessor, emphasized both the religious and social aims of the Mosquée when seeking financial support from the French state. He focused especially on the medical and emergency care his site offered Paris's Muslims. As he argued in his budget for 1961, "The Mosquée de Paris is considered a social assistance center by the metropole's North African Muslim community."[104] He described those seeking urgent help as refugees from all over the world who, for political reasons, cannot seek aid from their embassies; "beggars and invalids . . . who take refuge at the

Mosquée as near a wall of lamentations"; as well as formerly wealthy North African families who were forced to emigrate to France and who "refuse out of self-respect to go to the numerous social centers created by the Département de la Seine." He also argued that it was important for the defunct clinic to be reopened. The site's medical facilities were not large enough to be declared a "social hygiene clinic" by the Ministry of Health and Population, so the Ministry of the Interior urged Si Hamza to seek recognition of the Mosquée's clinic as a "medico-social center," which would allow it to be subsidized by the Social Security administration and thus reimburse patients from 80 to 100 percent of their costs.[105]

Islam français and Using the Mosquée

Yet the bulk of the funds Si Hamza sought were directed toward activities that upheld the Mosquée's role as the embodiment of *Islam français* for Muslim and French visitors alike. Perhaps the most salient example of this was his desire to increase the holdings of the fictive Institut Musulman's nevertheless real library. In pleading for additional funds, Si Hamza argued that "we know the attraction the riches of such a library would hold for the intellectual elites of the entire world, especially specialists in Muslim questions of the modern Middle East and Africa. In this respect, an enriched . . . library could have a great cultural mission and serve as a crossroads for the exchange of ideas and for scientific collaboration between elites."[106] This plea echoes the rhetoric of the Mosquée's earliest proponents who rejoiced that the site would be built in the Latin Quarter, providing an unprecedented opportunity for the classics of Muslim and French thought, which were fundamentally similar, to come into contact through scholarly exchanges.

However, most of Si Hamza's work to make the site a center for the experiential display of Islam as in past decades was concentrated squarely on its less esoteric pleasures. His quest to ensure the Mosquée's profitability as a tourist destination was particularly complicated in light of the new place "North African" culture occupied in metropolitan French space and imagination. Algerian, Moroccan, and Tunisian foods, smells, and decorations had never been so intimately familiar to so many people living in France: *pieds noirs,* Jews, *harkis,* and metropolitan soldiers returned from tours of duty in Algeria all had greater or lesser exposure to some of the sensory experiences that the Mosquée was supposed to evoke. These new residents of Paris may have missed the mint teas or couscous whose smells reminded them of home, but whether a *pied noir* would choose to consume these nostalgic foods in a mosque in Paris is somewhat questionable. It seems even more unlikely that

Algerian, Moroccan, or Tunisian Jews, in spite of feeling their exile particularly sharply, would eat at a café that was part of a Muslim religious complex. North African Jews were more religiously observant than their Ashkenazi French counterparts. In 1961, there was only one certified kosher restaurant in Paris; ten years later there were only three more.[107] Because North African Jewish immigrants arrived in families, rather than as groups of single men, and because there were almost no kosher restaurants, North African or not, we may perhaps assume that familiar foods were being prepared and consumed in the home rather than outside. Finally, although North African Jews arrived under very different circumstances than many Muslim North African immigrants, they too tended to settle in peripheral neighborhoods within city limits and, more often, in Parisian suburbs. Thus for them, too, the Mosquée was a geographically inaccessible place. Non-Jewish *rapatriés,* on the other hand, were more likely to settle in southern France and in other regional centers than in Paris, so they would not have been a strong potential base for Mosquée tourism.

For French people with no personal knowledge of or associations with the Maghreb, did the Mosquée represent a reminder of Algeria's humiliating victory over the once powerful French empire? Or was its "mysterious African charm" still attractive in new or similar ways? One intriguing piece of anecdotal evidence suggests that even during the war, the site evinced a certain curiosity that made it attractive to non-Muslim Parisians. On 25 May 1961, there was an armed attack on the Mosquée by unidentified assailants. An Algerian man who was not a member of the site's staff was wounded by the gunfire. Among the people questioned by the police were three young French women who had been inside the Mosquée at the time of the attack. None of the women, all students in their early twenties, was from Paris: two were born and still lived in the suburbs, and one was from Haute-Loire but was staying with relatives in the capital. All three claimed to have been invited by a male Lebanese classmate to go to the Mosquée to see the Aïd celebration. The youngest of the three women confided to the police that "curiosity" had inspired her to venture into the Mosquée during the holiday.[108]

The rest of Si Hamza's requests, however, concerned the aspects of the Mosquée that were devoted to displays of North African "tradition," which were also, of course, part and parcel of the founders' visions for the site. In formulating certain requests, he spoke explicitly of the need for the Mosquée to maintain a certain aesthetic in order to attract visitors; other times this was left implicit. Thus Si Hamza's desire for a larger budget for "dinners, tea, Oriental pastries" and other items considered essential for receptions at the Mosquée was justified because:

> The establishment's influence exerts an increasingly strong attraction towards the Mosquée de Paris on officials and French and foreign notables, Ministers, Diplomats, Intellectuals, Foreign Aristocracy, politicians, men of science or religion, legal scholars, travelers, tourists all honor the establishment with their visit, which, according to the tradition of Islam, is never exempt from [the duty to provide] receptions . . . the slightest contact requires the observance of this tradition.[109]

This description of the Mosquée's receptions confirms that the elitism of its founders had not dissipated over the decades that followed its initial construction, nor had the Mosquée's vocation to serve as a display of Moroccan hospitality changed. The "traditional" rituals for which the Mosquée was known were important enough to require additional funding, and they were listed before any of the requests for funding strictly religious activities. Of course, the enacting of North African hospitality had to take place in a very particular aesthetic space, and to this end Si Hamza also noted the financial needs related to the building's decoration and maintenance. The receptions he described above, for example, required a certain ambiance to be successful, one that was lacking in the Mosquée of 1961: "During every reception, the problem of hiding the holes and tears in the dyed textiles which decorate the Cour d'Honneur is raised. These [fabrics] in the hispano-mauresque artistic style, which have not been replaced since 1926, are rare in Morocco and impossible to find in Paris." Having the right kind of fabric, which necessitated buying them from a specialist in Fez, as well as replacing all the curtains in the hallways and classrooms, was integral to the experience of being at the Mosquée. Likewise, many of the rugs and *objets d'art* that adorned the *salle de prières* also needed to be replaced, as did the "old pieces of furniture in the Arab style" in the entry hall.[110]

A visit to the Mosquée, which could be commemorated by buying postcards (both color and black-and-white) or booklets "for tourists," involved both the site itself and its personnel in the attempt to bathe visitors in North African culture. The staff who were more likely to interact with non-Muslim tourists on a daily basis (such as the tour guides and security guards) needed "Arab" suits, headwear, and shoes, while those who were more likely to come into contact with French officials or transnational Muslim elites (chauffeurs and interpreters, for example) needed new "European-style" suits, caps, and shoes. The personnel involved in both the morning prayers and evening receptions were all dressed in "traditional" North African clothes, which means that the vestimentary division between Arab and European styles depending on one's job was not hard and fast. Nevertheless, the line item for clothing suggests that staff who participated in the display of North African embodied Muslim traditions had to be dressed in clothing that evoked the atmosphere they were trying to create, while those who were supposed to participate in meetings to bridge Muslim and French worlds dressed in the European clothing that their French counterparts would be wearing.

The Mosquée's offerings that he believed should have been most intriguing to visitors, the restaurant and café, continued to suffer, and Si Hamza sought significant funding to try to maintain their viability. He explained the difficulties faced by the restaurant:

> The restaurant and *café maure* . . . have been confided since 1926 to the management of Hamouda Bassoum, a Tunisian, a faithful friend of France . . . the establishment had a period of prosperity and high-class clientele. One used to need to reserve several days in advance to get a table. Its decline began with the events in North Africa. As a French *foyer*, whose moral action and commentary on current events, it cannot, of course, gain the sympathy of the fanatics and intolerant people who denounce it as a "colonialist center."
>
> In addition, several similar establishments have been created in Paris and have gradually spirited away a good portion of the Mosquée's restaurant's tourist clientele because they serve wine with meals, which is out of the question in religious establishments.
>
> If the Mosquée's café is still holding up fairly well because of its elegant setting and the traditional dress worn by its staff, the restaurant . . . is traversing a crisis so severe that it is necessary and urgent to either finance it or close it.[111]

This short description of the problems facing the restaurant reveals several important things about the uses of the Mosquée's space during the Algerian War. Si Hamza explicitly acknowledges the Mosquée's allegiance to the French state in identifying the restaurant's manager as "a friend of France" but more importantly in acknowledging the institution's position on the question of Algerian independence. The space itself, in Si Hamza's description, was imagined for the pleasure of elites who could afford to dine at a place where one needed to reserve a table. The café's waiters, clad in "traditional" dress, like some of the Mosquée's other staff who also worked with tourists, were supposed to contribute to the authenticity of one's meal or tea and pastries. Si Hamza's remark about the increase in North African restaurants and cafés for Parisian tourists that served alcohol robbing the Mosquée of its customers is telling. It fits well in the tradition of Si Kaddour's *Islam français,* in which restrictions related to food were given heightened importance so as to preserve an element of undiluted tradition in the mixture of Muslim and French civilizations. On the other hand, it suggests the possibility that non-Muslim Parisians and perhaps also Muslim tourists and even Parisians were not interested in "authenticity" at any cost: they did want to eat couscous and *cornes de gazelle,* but they wanted to be able to consume these Moroccan foods in the space of a French meal, of which wine was an integral part.

The religious activities that took place at the Mosquée and in its provincial satellites seemed to be Si Hamza's lowest priority. The activities for which he did request funding were for the most part linked to the site's social assistance programs, such as imams' visits to prisons and hospital and funeral expenses for indigent Muslims. Other requests included funds to pay for provincial imams' trips and lodgings for the site's annual conference before the beginning of Ramadan; the production of Muslim calendars showing holidays and prayer times; a voice-recorder to record "quranic melodies and rhythmic recitations of the classical liturgy which tend to disappear with the old religious staff"; and, of course, the salaries of all the religious personnel at the Mosquée, the Institut Musulman, and the provincial religious sites. One request he made in terms of support for religious programs concerned a reorganization of the Mosquée's space to cope with new demands. Si Hamza explained that "in all mosques . . . there is a special room [a *maksoura*] where imams receive the faithful in reference to personal matters or questions of conscience." The Parisian sites' imams had previously managed with one office for this use, but it was now being used as a legal office to cope with the new demand for advice on legal matters. Si Hamza thus sought funding to reorganize one of the rooms next to the *salle de prières* as a new *maksoura.* This request illustrated the tension between the Mosquée's religious and social assistance roles: the legal quagmires in which many Algerians found themselves during the war displaced any religious questions they may have had.

In looking at his prioritization of the Mosquée's activities, it is clear that Si Hamza was interested in bringing the site back in line with the aesthetic, the programs, and the rhetoric of its earliest years, while still attending to its social service calling, which emerged most strongly during World War II. This decision, taken immediately after his appointment in the middle of the Algerian War, set the stage for the rest of his tenure. Si Hamza's vision of Islam was *Islam français* in the 1920s sense of the term with an updated 1960s twist. Thus, North Africans were first and foremost Muslims and required separate social assistance programs, but the general decline in religious practices meant that the public display of Islam was a less important element of this elaboration of Islam than it had been in earlier decades. Instead, Si

Hamza focused his attention on "cultural" displays of Islam, trying desperately to compete with alternative Parisian sites offering tourists a "North African" experience. Yet the most important element of Si Hamza's modified *Islam français*, in some ways the mirror image of the FFFLN's *Islam algérien*, was that it continued to equate Algerians with Islam, which had important reverberations for his attempt to create a Muslim "community" out of Algerians, Moroccans, Tunisians, and West Africans.

Si Hamza's politics had been clear to members of Paris's Muslim communities from the beginning of his tenure as *recteur* in 1957: he was firmly aligned with the metropolitan and colonial authorities. Si Hamza, who had served as a member of parliament for southern Algeria before the war, sought reelection during the war, which merited death threats from the FLN as a "traitor" who "collaborated with the colonialists."[112] As soon as the war was over, the newly established government of independent Algeria tried to remove Si Hamza from his position as the Mosquée's leader. Because of Si Hamza's own political and personal orientations, many of the people he chose to surround himself with at the Mosquée were, like him, *français musulmans,* Algerian Muslims who had opted for French citizenship.[113] Most of the imams whom he appointed in the set of provincial mosques built in the 1940s and 1950s were Algerians who had become French. This gesture did nothing to increase his popularity among Algerian Muslims who retained their Algerian citizenship.

Si Hamza's attempt at inclusiveness was not sufficient to create a Muslim community in the capital because *Islam français* could not bring together people who had little in common other than their religion. From its inception, the Mosquée was designed as a tool to project the French republic's vision of its relationships with *North African* Muslims, not with all of the Muslims of the French empire. France's West African colonial administrators were expected to contribute financially to the site's construction, but they recognized that "their" Muslims were not considered by the metropolitan administration as potential beneficiaries of the Mosquée's programs. The Algerian War, a moment of profound rupture, paradoxically served as a moment of reaffirmation of the vision of *Islam français* that conflated Muslimness with Algerian-ness, in which Algerians could not and should not be French. This particular elaboration of the relationship between the French Republic and Algerian Muslims was also supported by the FFFLN's *Islam algérien,* which made the same argument from a different political position. Both of these visions precluded any other potential identities for Algerians living in the metropole, and they also precluded the possibility that other Muslims even entered into the picture. Thus the potential opportunity to rethink what it meant to be a Muslim in France offered by the Algerian War was foreclosed before it even began. The continued conflation of "Muslim" with "North African" would become even more problematic in the 1970s, as North and West Africans struggled for authority over religious sites in workers' hostels in the Paris area.

Chapter 6

"Culture" and "Religion": Immigration, Islams, and Race in 1970s Paris

Changes in immigration policy during the 1970s meant that for the first time in French history Algerian and other North and West African immigrants began to take seriously the possibility that they would live their lives in France and not return to their home countries.[1] This represented an important shift from preceding decades, in which it was tacitly assumed that temporary labor immigrants would eventually find their way back across the Mediterranean. Increasingly, immigrants were no longer single men gathered with fellow countrymen, but families, with women and children, negotiating life in a new country. Questions of "Muslim" identity were weighed differently than they had been in previous generations, and the complicated overlaps of race, culture, and religion were increasingly visible.

In order to respond to changed demographic realities in a climate of economic insecurity and violent anti-Arab racism, the French state developed a new apparatus of national and local administrative agencies designed to address the needs of potentially permanent immigrants. Officials worked to create a new cultural politics designed to reflect the possibility of sedentarization. One such authority was the Secrétariat d'état aux travailleurs immigrés, whose director, Paul Dijoud, explained that the recent "events" in Algeria had created a sense of heightened tension around the "profoundly uprooted" rural immigrants from North Africa. People arriving from West Africa, he went on, had "analogous problems [to the North Africans]" in attempting to succeed in France, but on a much larger scale.[2]

For the French administration as well as many local associations working with immigrant groups, the most significant factor leading to this sentiment of "uprootedness" was their removal from a Muslim milieu. While the vast majority of new immigrants from former French colonies were at least nominally Muslim, and while it would in fact be West African Muslims who would be at the forefront of certain demands for Muslim religious sites, the French state conflated North African-ness with Islam while defining West Africans more frequently simply as "black." Maghrébins suffered from the transition to French society, immigration specialists argued, in large part because of "the rupture of spiritual ties, which, in Islamic countries, play an essential role in collective and individual equilibrium."[3] At the heart of the state's cultural politics of immigration was the identification of Islam as the central aspect of these immigrants' lives and as an important area for intervention. Indeed, some voices from within the increasingly diverse Muslim communities in Paris did demand that the state provide them with religious sites or that employers provide prayer rooms in their factories. Still others organized and funded their own sites or made arrangements with local church and neighborhood association leaders to use existing spaces for Muslim worship.

In this new mix of immigrants, the universalist character of Islam (rather like French republicanism's claims of universalism) was challenged by the ways in which race and Islam worked in both Muslim and non-Muslim French opinion. Although it was widely agreed that West Africans were more "religious" than North Africans, for reasons having to do with not only their more recent arrival in France but also their perceived "primitiveness," neither Maghrébins nor French considered them to be "real" Muslims in the way that North Africans were assumed to be. The case of West Africans not being considered Muslim represents a refracted mirror image of the ways in which Maghrébin immigrants could be *only* Muslim and shows the extent to which Islam was so profoundly characterized as North African (and more particularly, Algerian).

The paradox this chapter will explore is why, in a climate where "traditional" Muslim practices such as daily prayer were said to be on the wane by both Muslims and non-Muslim French observers, did the state continue to use the funding and creation of Muslim religious sites as the centerpiece of its cultural politics for managing North and West African immigrant populations? And if Muslim religious practices were truly on the decline, how do we explain the real demands for Muslim places of worship? To put it another way, when working-class Muslim associations or unions demanded that the state and employers provide spaces to be used for prayer, what were they asking for, exactly? French policy makers, the Mosquée leadership, and North African associations all recognized that the Mosquée's authority was more eroded than ever: for the first time, the state began to invest financial resources in other religious sites beyond the purview of the Mosquée de Paris. Thus while the model of the Mosquée de Paris seemed to fall out of favor, or at least to be viewed more realistically, the choice of the mosque itself as the ideal vehicle for interaction with the "Muslim community" continued to drive policy. The conflation of Muslim religious sites with racial, national, and cultural identities during a period where observance was said to be on the wane, I argue, demonstrates the deep-seatedness of the French belief in the fundamental inability of certain Muslim immigrants to be anything other than Muslim subjects. It also represents a deployment of that same argument by some Muslim individuals and associations as a strategy to achieve particular goals. Islam was the terrain for negotiating issues that had as much to do with virulent racism, inadequate housing, unemployment, and legal status as they did with religion.

Changing Immigration Politics and Changed Cultural Politics

In the years after France's former African colonies gained independence, a series of different legal regimes regulated North and West Africans' position with regard to their access to the French labor market and to French citizenship. A multilateral accord signed in June 1960 guaranteed that citizens of Madagascar, Senegal, and Mali had complete freedom of movement to and within France with their national identity cards. Once on French territory, they had the same rights as French citizens when it came to employment. This initial agreement was eventually extended to all of France's former West African colonies.[4] Immigrants from Algeria were subject to a different series of regulations, which nevertheless resembled the policy on West African immigration. The Evian Accords of 1962 enshrined the freedom of movement between France and Algeria. Algerians living in the metropole were considered foreigners and were treated as such, though they could opt for French nationality at any moment until the end of an initial five-year transition period.[5]

The government of newly independent Algeria halted emigration to France in 1973, officially to protest one in a series of racist incidents targeting North African immigrants in the metropole.[6] This wave of anti-Maghrébin violence began in the spring of 1969, with attacks on Moroccan- and Algerian-owned cafes in the Paris region by racist groups claiming to defend "the pure race."[7] One particularly savage "*ratonnade*" in Marseille in 1973 left eight North Africans dead.[8] The December attack served as a catalyst for the Algerian decision to halt emigration was a direct assault on the Algerian Consulate in Marseille, killing four people and injuring twelve.[9] The abrupt change in policy was also linked to diplomatic tensions between France and Algeria over the nationalization of Algeria's oil production as well as Algerian internal economic and industrial issues. This decision was followed by France's 1974 suspension of new working-class immigration.[10] In the panic that ensued over whether or not families would be able to reunite given the potentially long-term moratorium on movement across the Mediterranean, many North and West African families chose to join relatives already established in France.[11]

Given that these "temporary" workers and their families would now likely be permanent residents of France, the government began to consider a new direction in its cultural politics of immigration.[12] In May 1974, before the suspension of immigration on 3 July, the government created a new position within the Ministry of Labor: the Secretary of State for Foreign Workers (Secrétaire d'état aux travailleurs immigrés). This post, designed to accompany "the birth of a new all-encompassing policy in favor of immigrants," came into being "in the context of the economic crisis of 1974–1975" and the belief that immigration needed to be controlled so as not to add to the large numbers of unemployed.[13] This new policy's twenty-five elements were adopted by the Conseil des ministres on 9 October 1974. Most of them were dedicated to providing immigrants with the same liberties their French counterparts enjoyed. The Conseil's conception of immigrants' "liberty" was twofold: it referred to the freedom to remain in France or to return to their country of origin, but more importantly, it meant the freedom to preserve one's linguistic, religious, and cultural identity. The right to "cultural identity," it was argued, allowed the immigrant to remain close to his country in spite of his geographical distance.[14]

The new government agencies concerned with immigrant workers believed that the immigrant was first and foremost a "*déraciné,*"[15] someone whose fundamental self had been altered in potentially crippling ways upon arrival in France. The concept of *déracinement,* or uprootedness, in the social sciences was not novel in the 1970s. As early as 1937, French sociologist Georges Mauco investigated the psychological effects of immigration on isolated Polish workers who had been responsible for acts of violence. The classic work on the subject of "urban pathology" by the Chicago School was done in the 1950s, when sociologists argued that the effects of a passage from one kind of society to another can be devastating and that the rootlessness born of immigration is one of the causes of urban problems. Most importantly, Pierre Bourdieu and Abdelmalek Sayad's famous 1964 study, *Le déracinement,* examined the impact of forced relocations on Algerian peasants during the Algerian War. Their conclusions informed the thinking of metropolitan French officials debating how to manage Algerian immigrants, many of whom had been uprooted in their own country and would be uprooted once again upon arrival in France.[16] French fears about the potential traumas that could result from ruptures produced by immigration coincided with a profound ambivalence about new immigrants, of European and North African origin, arriving from postwar Algeria. The link sociologists had drawn between violence and uprootedness was particularly ominous for French officials as they considered how to manage immigrants from a country whose war of independence had recently heralded the end of the French empire.[17]

The portrait of the generic immigrant, "shared, torn between two universes, two civilizations," generated by the Secrétariat d'état aux travailleurs immigrés and inspired by the work of social scientists is one marked by sympathy. It is, nevertheless, one with no nuances and no room for more complicated experiences. In this vision, the immigrant's "country of origin represents his deepest attachments, his memories," and the absence of "sun, religious customs, and the habits of everyday life," which "in those countries constitute a knot of very close ties," provokes "a painful lack."[18] In order to "evoke their lost light," the officials argued, immigrants "build decors which tend to resemble their countries: oriental pastries, cluttered dens, sunlit music" in their neighborhoods. This "glittering façade" is a form of "pride and dignity and seeks to dissimulate the misery of the housing."[19] To characterize French and non-French universes and civilizations as polar opposites, magnets dragging helpless immigrants between them, is problematic not least because French and other cultures and civilizations had been in contact with one another for more than a century in some colonies. That North Africans in particular had resided in France in smaller and then larger numbers since the 1920s also meant that there were already established neighborhoods with shops and services catering to those populations; "exotic" and upscale restaurants and shops in "North African" styles also catered to a French audience. Not only were French and non-French "civilizations" presented as polar opposites, but immigration was also identified as a purely negative experience of loss. In attending only to the element of loss and lack, the state effectively made it difficult for immigrants to decide to build new identities that might draw on some aspects of both their old "universes" and their new ones. Finally, the ingredients that constituted an immigrant neighborhood in this definition—oriental pastries, excess, and cheerful music—signal an exoticized North African neighborhood but not necessarily any other immigrant space. This image of what constitutes "immigrant" culture is significant because it shows the extent to which the state's discourse was elaborated using a North African model, and, as we will see, how the equation of Islam with immigrant culture meant that Islam, North Africans, and immigrants were forever linked in French official discourse.

In order to facilitate the cultural exchanges which were supposed to help immigrants retain their identities, the National Office for the Cultural Promotion of Immigrants (Office national pour la promotion culturelle des immigrés), created in May 1975, began its work in November 1975. The ONPCI was at once a "privileged instrument" for the administration and a "tool for popular culture," which would be responsive to the "preoccupations of the entire immigrant population."[20] The ONPCI's work was decentralized across France's *départements,* and local officials were charged with coordinating between the *département*'s immigrant associations, city halls, *foyer* associations, business groups, and anyone else who could potentially help orchestrate demonstrations of immigrant cultures or expose immigrants to "French" culture. In concrete terms, these initiatives included programs like sports activities and vacation camps for immigrant children; libraries with works in both French and various immigrant languages; the diffusion of foreign radio, TV, and movies; performances and tours of cultural groups from immigrants' home countries; and exhibits on art, folk art, and artisanship from those same home countries.[21]

The ONPCI's active members included government employees "directly concerned with cultural action," while its associate members included representatives from the major working-class immigrant associations. Additionally, the ambassadors of the countries that supplied France with the highest numbers of immigrant workers (Algeria, Spain, Italy, Mali, Morocco, Mauritania, Portugal, Senegal, Tunisia, Turkey, and Yugoslavia) also served as honorary members.[22] Seven of the eleven countries were majority-Muslim lands, and Yugoslavia also had a Muslim population. Yet the "Muslimness" of these partners in this government agency did not shape the agency's belief that culture and Islam were virtual synonyms, for the ONPCI's program had been oriented in that way from its inception.

While it would be an overstatement to suggest that the ONCPI was designed with the exclusive intention of managing a Muslim immigrant population, the agency often emphasized Islam as the most important element of "culture" or identity of working-class immigrants. In 1978, the Centre d'Information et d'Études sur les Migrations Méditerannénnes (CIEMM) published a short document surveying the French Muslim landscape, inspired by the ONCPI's emphasis on the importance of Islam. The study both echoed and explained Dijoud's team's own conclusions:

> What importance does Islam have in the lives of Muslims to push a secular state like France to take the Islamic religion into account and to decide to help in the construction of religious sites?
>
> Man, according to Islam, is a Man who has submitted to God, who is present throughout his life. He is also a communitarian man. . . . The personal and community status of a Muslim . . . is eminently religious and informs every aspect of public and private life for the faithful.[23]

The CIEMM's justification of the secular state's political and financial participation in the construction of Muslim religious sites rests on several important assumptions: first, that North African's identities were first and foremost, if not exclusively, religious. Second, that North African immigrants' allegiance was to their fellow Muslims—the possibility that they might have other communities made up of their colleagues, neighbors, political or leisure association members, or otherwise, seemed remote. Finally, and most classically, that Muslims were incapable of separating their public and private spheres, rendering their participation in secular French public life difficult, if not impossible, and necessitating the creation of separate structures for their use. These separate structures would continue to blur the constantly shifting boundaries between "cultural" and "religious" identities.

Given the continued belief that the "cultural" lives of Muslims were entirely driven by their religious identities and that the state was supposed to preserve the "cultural" lives of immigrants, the construction of communal religious sites was a significant element of a *circulaire* from 2 September 1976 on "cultural action in favor of immigrants."[24] The "Religious Sites" program of the 1976 policy defined two levels of action:

> Aid for the creation of religious sites:
>
> *Objective*: Since cultural life has traditionally been inseparable from the respect of religious prescriptions for Muslims, it is necessary to put spaces reserved for religion at the disposal of the faithful in neighborhoods with high Muslim populations, particularly in Immigrant Worker Hostels.
>
> Aid for existing Mosques and prayer rooms:

> *Objective*: To respond to the material religious cultural needs of the Muslim population which makes use of existing mosques and prayer rooms.[25]

The language of providing services necessary to and desired by the Muslim population is similar to that of earlier arguments made in favor of the construction of mosques.

While restating the idea that Muslims do not separate the religious elements of their lives from the rest of their existence (a claim which is made even more explicit elsewhere in the new policy), the bureaucrats who produced the "Religious Sites" program were not as invested in the creation of a particular kind of space for these Muslims to use as the Mosquée's founders were. Although they were less concerned about the space of Islam, the place of Islam was vitally important to 1970s administrators. The major difference in this program was that these new religious sites should be constructed where Muslims lived, not in parts of the city visible to tourists, as in Paris, or slated for urban renewal, as in Marseille. I suggest that the new program's emphasis on the geographic location of Muslim religious sites reflects one of the important shifts *Islam français* underwent during this decade. These sites were private spaces designed for religious subjects, not public places designed for public display. The notion that Muslim embodied practices could be performed in different kinds of spaces broke with decades of *Islam français* rhetoric. French observers did not believe that these practices were any less physical or any less central to the lives of Muslims, but they no longer argued that they had to be performed in a particular aesthetic setting.

What is also remarkable about the new religious-cultural politics of the 1970s was the acknowledgement that a mosque is not a church is not a synagogue. This was a major shift in itself, but French officials also acknowledged that the mosque's meanings are in fact multiple and may signify different things for different members of the Muslim community. An attempt was made to distinguish among different types of Muslim sites, which had overlapping functions. Dijoud's collaborators defined the mosque, or the "official religious site," as a space where "the community of believers meets for regular prayer (the Friday prayer and the entire duration of Ramadan) or for occasional ceremonies (marriage, burial, circumcision, departure for Mecca)."[26] The mosque is not the same as the *salle de prière,* which is not the same as the "family habitat," in which a simple prayer rug suffices to delineate the space for family religious observance. Administrators reported that there were three kinds of public religious spaces in the Paris region: mosques, *salles de prière,* and socio-cultural centers. The mosque, which was described above as a physical space that allowed believers to gather collectively for prayer and to celebrate special religious occasions, is, however "not exclusively a place for prayer." It is "essentially a community meeting place for all the questions which concern [the community]," be those questions cultural, social, or political.[27] The reference to the mosque as a politicized public space is new, for the question of the potential politicization of the Mosquée de Paris or any other Muslim religious sites was always a source of profound fear for the metropolitan and colonial officials, who did all in their power to de-politicize Muslim religious sites. If mosques were to have any political valence, it was to be as the embodiment of a particular kind of relationship connecting metropole, colony, and Muslim subjects, and that orientation was to be controlled by the administrations rather than members of the "community." Other than the mosque, the other kinds of Muslim sites described were the *salle de prière,* which is a site reserved exclusively for prayer; and the socio-cultural center, which, "in certain neighborhoods with a high North African or Turkish population, has put rooms at the disposition of the Muslim community for prayer and meetings."[28]

However, the construction of Muslim religious sites in the 1970s brought the problems of Islam's "late" arrival to the metropole to the foreground. One policy report remarked that "the Mosquée de Paris, created immediately after World War I in memory of the Muslims who died for France, was the only meeting place for Muslims (and Muslims do not all recognize it)." They emphasized the Mosquée's lack of overarching authority repeatedly, even going so far as to refer to it as "the structure which is *supposed* to represent Islam" but does not speak in the name of the "majority" of French Muslims.[29] The "representativeness" that French officials would have hoped for from a Muslim interlocuteur was made difficult by the fact that Islam was not organized along the same channels as France's other religions. French immigration theoreticians were troubled by Islam's lack of "a hierarchical organization compatible with French public life" and a "sizeable cultural apparatus" with respected notable figures and a firm understanding of the way French society works. These lacunae deprived Muslims of "the means to ensure the continuity of their religious and national identity in the country of immigration."[30] For the French state, Islam's different structure was "lacking" rather than simply organized along alternative lines than Catholicism and France's older minority religions, Protestantism and Judaism. Furthermore, French immigration policy makers continued to conflate "religious" and "national" identities in ways reminiscent of the Mosquée's founders.

While there were certainly some important shifts from earlier policies and discourses, the French state had viewed Islam as the best medium for interacting with subaltern Muslim populations since the creation of the Mosquée and the Hôpital Franco-Musulman, if not earlier. The Ministries of War and Labor in particular had been at the forefront of efforts to provide Muslim soldiers and workers with their version of the means to perform Muslim religious practices since World War I. Individual companies and factories had also made accommodations for Muslim workers, with concessions such as work schedules that allowed laborers to return to North Africa for the entire month of Ramadan. There is a distinction to be made between providing religious Muslims with prayer sites that would have otherwise been unavailable to them and using Islam as a medium to interact with Muslims in France. Yet the French state's policy of providing religious sites according to the logic of *Islam français,* in which Muslims could only ever be Muslim, did both at once. The French state's long history of maintaining its relationship with the Muslim working class resident in France through the medium of Islam belies French political scientist Gilles Kepel's assessment of the SONACOTRA strikes, which I discuss below, and the creation of the *salle de prière* at the Renault factory in Billancourt as a major shift in French policy.[31]

Foyers and Factories: Religion, Labor, and the Cultural Space of Home

From 1975 to 1980, a series of strikes emerged in state-funded SONACOTRA[32] workers' hostels in cities and suburbs all over France. It began in January, with the residents of the Romain-Rolland hostel in Saint-Denis refusing to pay the rent increase SONACOTRA had instituted for February 1975.[33] The system of workers' hostels, founded in 1957 to house single male workers responding to the needs of the French labor market, housed Algerians almost exclusively until 1962 but then opened its doors to immigrants from the rest of North and West Africa as well as Europe. In 1975, in the Paris region, the most represented immigrant group in SONACOTRA *foyers* was actually the Portuguese (27.6% of all foreigners), while Algerians made up 21 percent, Moroccans 7.1 percent, Tunisians 4.9 percent and Africans 3.4 percent (the remaining 11% were Spaniards).[34] Thus in Ile-de-France, the *foyers* were not overwhelmingly populated by residents from majority Muslim countries: this population made up about a third of a whole whose other two thirds were nominally Catholic or Christian.

Almost all of the *foyers* were run by former colonial officials chosen for their experience with managing colonial populations, even though North and West Africans did not always represent a majority of the resident population.[35] A study commissioned by SONACOTRA itself found that its directors treated residents differently depending on their nationality, salary, and professional situation, reserving the worst discrimination for North Africans.[36] Of 155 directors in the Paris region, 144 were also former military men having fought in at least one if not more of France's colonial wars.[37] Because of their supposed knowledge of the "native mind," many *foyer* directors devoted space for a *salle de prière,* believing it was important to maintaining a well-run institution.[38] The exact layout and features of each *foyer* differed, but all of them featured a combination of the following: individual or occasionally collective bedrooms (ranging from 72 to 512 rooms, with an average of 280 rooms) and shared spaces such as bathrooms and showers and kitchens with individual lockers on each floor. Shared spaces for the entire *foyer* included the bar, the TV room, and sometimes a room or rooms that could be used for classes, cultural associations, or *salles de prière.*[39]

Many residents were unhappy not only with what they saw as the high cost of a fairly wretched existence but also with the administration of the *foyers* and their own lack of representation in the decision-making process about regulating daily life in the residencies. The strikers' demands ranged from the economic (a 50% reduction in rents) to the hygienic (more frequent laundering of linens) to the social (the freedom to have visitors of both sexes twenty-four hours a day, forbidding staff from entering residents' rooms without permission; no expulsions without agreement from the residents' committee; transparency in rental procedures; and the replacement of directors with concierges) to the political (the freedom of assembly and speech).[40] In some individual *foyers*, residents also demanded *salles de prière* and sometimes also a halt to the selling of alcohol at the bar.[41] But the strike was about more than just changes in the management of the workers' *foyers.* As the bilingual newspaper *La Voix des Travailleurs Algériens* explained, the fight was against the exploitation of the immigrant working class, not just about SONACOTRA. For them, the strike was "against the organized theft of immigrant workers by the French state," and their demands included full family support payments even if a worker's family remained in Algeria, full pension payments, an end to all programs for immigrants' cultural integration, and *foyer* and neighborhood cultural activities run by residents themselves, not the state's cultural agencies.[42] The strikes also drew French student activists and members of the far left into the fray, who saw the immigrants' struggle as an ideal site for intervention. The Arab Workers' Movement (Mouvement des Travailleurs Arabes, MTA) was one of the groups at the organizational center of the strike, and their demands did not focus on recognition as Muslims or demands for Muslim religious sites.[43] Organized French labor as well as the Algerian-state-run Amicale proved powerless to negotiate in the name of the striking workers.[44]

It was certainly easier to provide residents with a room to use for religious purposes than it was to address their other demands, and in one system of *foyers*, the management did so quickly, even before the SONACOTRA strikes began. The ADEF (Association pour le Développement des Foyers du Bâtiment et des Métaux) *foyers*, which were privately owned by construction companies employing largely immigrant workers, had a "religious policy" that already provided for Christian religious observances as soon as they opened in 1955. When waves of Muslim workers began arriving in the 1970s, the management realized that not only were they refusing to eat the *foyer*'s restaurant's food, they were also creating their own makeshift spaces for prayer in halls and bedrooms. The directors of the ADEF *foyers* quickly gave Muslim workers access to rooms that had been used as games or television spaces, sometimes going so far as to provide two different rooms to allow North Africans and Turks to pray separately.[45] In the case of the SONACOTRA *foyers*, on the other hand, things happened more slowly: by 1973, there were *salles de prière* in only a handful of *foyers*, including Bobigny and Nanterre. However, some SONACOTRA directors claimed that they tried to make sure Muslim residents were able to perform their religious obligations. As one director said, "I respect their holidays very much. Ramadan, though, that's something else. I have to explain to the Portuguese . . . that for a whole month, the Arabs are going to be up all night. The classroom is turned into a lotto room, and they play until 4 or 5 a.m. The others accept it very well. At the end of Ramadan, we bring in an orchestra, and it's another celebration."[46]

French ethnographer Jacques Barou, who conducted interviews with *foyer* residents active in the strike as it was happening, argued that "the leftist and Marxist language used by the coordinating committee contributed to occult the Islamic aspect of this conflict."[47] Barou wrote that demands for Muslim religious sites were so ubiquitous that SONACOTRA management began to move one step ahead of the strikers by budgeting for the construction of *salles de prière* in *foyers* that did not yet have one, thus removing one of the rationales for the strike. In his analysis, the Marxist tinge of the strikes did not represent the real orientation of *foyer* residents, to the extent that even some of the French far-left associations and the Marxist immigrant groups also adopted the language of Muslim practice in order to participate in the struggle. The Marxist MTA, for example, whose demands focused on social and economic justice for all immigrant workers, nevertheless invited workers to celebrate all the major Muslim holidays. I would not suggest that the "Marxist" or "Muslim" elements of the SONACOTRA struggles need to be put into competition or that one needs to be seen to be "genuine" while the other was merely "strategic." Different people were moved to strike for different reasons, and what concerns us here is not the overlaps between religious and labor demands but that Islam was invoked at all.

Similar demands were made in factories at the same time as the demands for Muslim spaces in *foyers* were being voiced. In examining the case of the *salle de prière* at the Renault factory in Billancourt in conjunction with the experiences of the SONACOTRA strikers, I will explore the question of the demands for Muslim religious spaces during a period when French observers perceived a decline in religious practice in tandem with the issue of racial difference and the tensions between North and West Africans. As in the *foyers*, Islam had been present in Renault's Billancourt factory before the 1970s: the cafeteria had long offered menus without alcohol or pork; in the 1960s, the Comité d'entreprise began to sponsor celebrations of Muslim holidays while work schedules were also finessed to allow workers to observe Ramadan.[48] From these existing arrangements in favor of practicing Muslim employees, the move to create a *salle de prière* was hardly a revolutionary proposition. It was officially opened in October 1976, during Ramadan, as a response to a petition launched by a group of Senegalese Renault employees that gathered more than eight hundred signatures the afternoon it was circulated. The petition came at a time when no major conflicts between labor and management had arisen in the previous two years, and the general atmosphere at the factory was calm.[49] Jacques Barou (who had also interviewed the SONACOTRA strikers), Moustapha Diop, and Subhi Toma argue that unlike the case of the rent strike, the creation of the *salle de prière* took place very peacefully. The only groups to express ambivalence about supporting the effort were the unions, but Renault management was well aware that many Muslim workers were already in the habit of praying in the factory and thus pragmatically decided to create prayer sites as an attempt to regulate what was already everyday practice.[50] For Barou, Diop, and Toma, the way in which the demands emanated also showed that the desire for Muslim religious space in the factory was totally autonomous, not the result of outside interference or pressure.

A year later, another *salle de prière* would open in a different workshop in the same factory, in a larger space that could accommodate up to 150 people. Its imam was apparently more popular among Renault employees and also had a tendency to encourage Muslim workers to keep their own company and not participate in any other aspects of factory life.[51] The imam of the second *salle de prière* launched a series of attempts to create a truly distinct sacred space in the workshop. The practices he encouraged were those associated with North Africa, such as the distribution of mint tea after Friday services and the creation of a community fund to purchase North African–style white djellabahs (which were also laundered on a regular basis) so that workers could put them on over their clothes and enter the *salle de prière* even if they did not have time to wash themselves fully or change their clothes.[52]

"Second-Class Muslims"

The white djellabahs that distinguished between the pure space of the *salle de prières* and the impure space of the factory also marked the religious site as North African.[53] Yet many scholars have argued that it is not coincidental that the workers who pushed for the creation of a Muslim religious site at the Renault factory were Senegalese. West African Muslims, who had arrived more recently than their North African colleagues, also had to affirm their Muslim identity in ways that North Africans did not because neither French nor North Africans took them seriously as Muslims. This hierarchization within France's Muslim community was visible to non-Muslims, and those who were concerned by the status of West African immigrants had to overcome their own prejudices in order to accept them as equals. As one Catholic involved in inter-religious dialogue explained:

> The Subsaharan African Muslim is not a second-class Muslim, even if he does not resemble the North African Muslim. Of course, his Arabic is very limited, and he is not always a scrupulous observer of the religion's pillars. But even there we cannot generalize: some peoples have been Muslim for a very long time, for example, those along the Senegal River since the 11th century, while others are very recent neophytes.
>
> Islam in Africa, like everywhere else, is not static. There are *marabouts* who are excellent masters of doctrine and spirituality, who introduce others to knowledge of the Quran. Believers travel, such as going on the pilgrimage to Mecca, or going to study in Morocco, Tunisia or Egypt. For many years, they have created educational and cultural associations for a more enlightened faith. Reformist or modernist currents exist in cities. If there have been delays in this evolution, the responsibility lies with the colonial policy repressing the development of a religious culture deemed too Arab, out of fear of pan-Islamism which would be hostile to it.
>
> In brief, if we are first taken aback by African-style Islam, upon a closer look, we can recognize the Black Muslim as the Arab Muslim's brother.[54]

This outreach worker, while declaring that African Muslims were just as Muslim as Maghrébin Muslims, undermines himself by effectively arguing not that Muslims on both sides of the Sahara are equal but that West African Muslims can be taken seriously *if* their *marabouts* have formal training, *if* they have traveled and opened themselves to Arab Islam, and *if* they belong to a modernizing or reformist urban Muslim movement. The Muslimness of West Africans was thus evolutionary and conditional, not taken for granted as was that of Arab immigrants (whether they were observant or themselves identified as Muslim or not). In other words, "Arab" Islam was the standard to which West Africans Muslims should aspire.

Journals from Muslim associations whose vision of Islam emphasized its universalism reveals that even groups that sought to overcome national, ethnic, and racial divisions still reflected those same cleavages in their own discourse. The association Musulmans en Europe, for example, explained to its members in an article entitled "Why Pray Only in Arabic?" that one of the reasons for Arabic prayer is that "if Islam were only a regional, racial, or national religion, one would certainly have used the language spoken in that region, by that race, or by that nation. But the demands of a universal religion are entirely different, one whose faithful speak hundreds of regional languages."[55] Praying in Arabic was not, according to them, an exclusive practice designed to maintain Arab superiority but rather a lingua franca to unify an increasingly "cosmopolitan"[56] Muslim *umma*. However, in spite of this language of universalism, the advertisements and the articles in *France-Islam* concerned North African immigrants and, more particularly, Algerian immigrants, rather than a diverse and inclusive Muslim community. Ads for Air Algérie and cargo services took up all available ad space, and while any articles on topics other than Muslim religious texts, thinkers, or history concerned only the experiences of North African immigrants in France. By the late 1970s, most of the journal was printed in Arabic, effectively rendering it an Arab publication: even if non-arabophone Muslims were familiar with the Arabic liturgy or had studied the Quran, many of them would not have been capable of reading a journal in Arabic. Likewise, the MTA's materials reflected a tension between their desire to identify as members of the North African working class fighting for the rights of all immigrant workers regardless of their origin and their cultural and religious specificities. While they proposed teach-in style programs or education plays about racial discrimination and exploitation, which were advertised in French to make them accessible to the largest number of people, they also organized celebrations of Muslim holidays or concerts featuring different styles of North African music, dance, and theater.

Testimony from West African Muslim workers and *foyer* residents confirms the existence of tensions between "Arab" and "African" Muslims, which in fact seemed to stem less from "Arab" disdain for "African" Islam than from social conflicts around everyday life practices in the *foyers*, ranging from table manners to attempts to subvert the legal procedures for room attribution in favor of compatriots. Manara Kamitenga, a Zairean resident of a SONACOTRA *foyer* in the Paris suburb of Saint-Ouen, addresses this issue in his short memoir describing life in his *foyer* in the late 1970s. In addition to his vivid depictions of the serious material problems facing residents (filthy kitchens, unsanitary bathrooms, and so on), he also wrote about the relations between the different racial groups. One of the major sites of conflict, he explained, was the dining hall: "It's rare to see Arabs and Blacks at the same table. Theoretically, the tables are all shared, but in reality they're separated. . . . The Arabs think of themselves as more 'clean' than the Blacks and tend to segregate themselves by monopolizing certain tables." Issues of cleanliness surface again and again in explanations of the tensions between North and Sub-Saharan African residents. Kamitenga writes that "our *foyer* is a melting pot where the races represented should melt together. But we can't talk about 'race' without thinking of the cultures they represent and without which the darkness or lightness of one's skin can't distinguish between men. Isn't what distinguishes the Arab from the White and the two of them from the Black their respective customs and traditions? The way of seeing the world, of feeling, of reacting, are different depending on whether one is Arab, White, or Black." Kamitenga distinguishes between the "biological" aspects of race and the cultural characteristics associated with different races. Ultimately, however, he falls back on the French model and conflates the two, arguing that each "race" has particular customs and traditions that define it.[57]

Although the historiography tends to suggest that an important distinction among the diverse members of Paris's Muslim community is that West Africans were more observant than North Africans, this was not necessarily the case. In interviews conducted in the late 1970s in both Paris and Dakar, most West Africans, while identifying "everyone" as Muslim when asked "how many people are Muslim," also said that only 50 to 60 percent of them were practicing Muslims.[58] Almost all those interviewed affirmed that "all the old people are observant" while few of the younger generation prayed or fasted; however, everyone practiced to a lesser extent in France than they did in Senegal. The reasons these workers gave to explain this situation centered on the effects of their migration to France. Their new industrial-time work schedules made it difficult to maintain the prayer schedule, which was more easily accommodated by the rhythms of work in their home countries. In addition, their new living spaces did not always give them access to spaces for collective prayer. As one person said, "There is no collective prayer: we don't have the space for it," or, as another remarked, "Even those who are the most observant don't necessarily go to the mosque (or the common *salle de prière*). In the *foyer*, there are problems with collective prayer because the *salle de prière* is the same as the TV room."[59]

West Africans may not have been *more* observant than North Africans, but they were *differently* observant. Their religious activities were often centered around *marabouts* from their home communities. The Quranic-trained *marabout*'s responsibilities included serving as the teacher and religious leader of the group as well as making *gris-gris,* or talismans, for community members.[60] *Marabouts* sometimes lived in individual apartments, but more often they lived in the *foyers* among people from their regions. Those who did live in the *foyers* were said to be "the hard core of the observant [Muslims], often the rigorous censurers of young people's non-Muslim behavior."[61] Their making of *gris-gris,* however, and the importance that many West African workers accorded these objects presented their Muslim practice in a light at odds with "orthodox," or North African, Islam. Workers said that they sought out *gris-gris* for many reasons: for help with getting a job, to maintain a good relationship with one's employer, to move up the social ladder, for help with naturalization paperwork, and to protect against ill wishes. In fact, the richest of the *marabouts* (through their sales of *gris-gris*) were those with connections to factory hiring managers and police and other administrators: they used their personal connections to ensure positive results for their talismans.[62] Practices like these were used by members of the North African Muslim community to denigrate the "Muslimness" of West Africans. The way people who were all nominally Muslims conjugated racial difference and Muslimness was reflected and refracted in both similar and different ways among non-Muslim French.

Nationality, Race, and Islam: "Racing" Islam from Without and Within

An 1971 article entitled "Hatred of the Emigrant," published in the FLN's newspaper, *El Moudjahid,* explained the Algerian perspective on the wave of violence committed against North African, especially Algerian, immigrants in the metropole:

> More than ever, the Algerian in France is prey to this evil form of human relations. More and more, he constitutes the expression of an

> ethnicity whose "biological properties" leave much to be desired, and it is true that one attributes extremely vulgar qualifications to Algerians, whose "linguistic simplicity" has a psychological effect which could not possibly be more effective [in shaping] public opinion. . . .
>
> Prejudices, stereotypes, insults and many other manifestations make the Algerian worker into an artificial being invented piecemeal by the racist.[63]

In this article, the author explains the racism that Algerians experienced in the metropole as a function of their nationality and perhaps implicitly of their socioeconomic status as members of the working class. Their identity as Muslims was not part of the rationale for the hostility they faced, according to this analysis. In fact, the state newspaper's official stance on the attacks on Algerian immigrants held that they were the victims of France's anger at the independent state's decision to naturalize their oil industry. As another article explained:

> Even before the decisions of February 24, taken by the Revolutionary Power in the hydrocarbants domain, a vast press campaign had been prepared and unleashed in France against Algeria in general and our emigration in particular. But since these historic measures, the campaign has reached a veritable frenzy and become an exacerbated racism whose outrages our emigrant brothers suffer every day.[64]

In this editorial introduction to a special issue devoted to the "daily drama" and "hell" of Algerians' lives in France, it is clear that the Algerian government and state press saw the racism that was literally attacking their emigrants to be based in political concerns.

On the other hand, groups like the Mouvement des travailleurs arabes tended to speak less of "Algerians," choosing instead to use explicitly racial language ("Arabes," "Noirs").[65] Furthermore, the MTA did not confine its struggle to the rights of "Arabs"; it was concerned with the problems faced by all immigrants, including those from Sub-Saharan Africa. In a poster advertising a two-day conference against racism, the MTA scorned the creation of the new Secrétaire d'état aux travailleurs immigrés as proof of the government's intention to end discrimination. "Because one is Arab or Black, is it fair that one has almost no chance of finding decent housing? Is it fair that one be the victim of intolerance and mistrust? . . . Is it fair not to have all the rights of French workers?"[66] In this formulation, race and class are the central elements that define the second-class existence of the North or West African worker, rather than their national, "ethnic," or religious identities.

Yet another perspective was offered by the Amicale des Musulmans en Europe, a pan-European association with aspirations to speak in the name of all Muslims, regardless of national origin.[67] French racism was absent from its analysis of the problems facing Muslims in France, as were questions of discrimination, unequal access to resources, economic injustice, and other issues. For the Amicale des Musulmans, the real danger France presented to Muslims was that increased exposure to the de-Christianized, materialistic society in which they found themselves would cause them to lose their identities. Too much exposure to life in France could potentially allow Muslims "to envisage a secularized Muslim society, more or less in the image of contemporary Western societies."[68] The real enemy in this vision is not the racist or the capitalist exploiter but the "Muslim countries" that have done little to help their emigrants in France, since they are preoccupied by their own internal politics. This third conception of the identity of "Muslim" immigrants is thus entirely religious, one in which race and nationality play no role whatsoever.

Si Hamza, speaking in the name of the Mosquée, made statements about immigrants that tended to conflate these three visions in ways that many elements of France's Muslim communities found profoundly disturbing. The Mosquée's *recteur* took a very public stance on the issue of anti–North African racism in an article in *Le Monde* dated 22 September 1973. The catalyst for Si Hamza's article, "On the Anti-Racist Demonstration," was the MTA's organization of a demonstration against racism held on 14 September, which gathered about a thousand immigrant workers outside the Mosquée. In his article, Si Hamza wrote that the demonstration's organizers did not contact him before moving ahead with their plans and then offered his own analysis on the question of racism, which differed significantly from that of the MTA and many other organizations. He argued that North Africans arriving in France felt as though they were in a "hostile milieu" and that the effect of this sentiment was a deterioration of their "psychic state" to the point of feeling like persecuted pariahs. The Maghrébin immigrant learns to dread learning of a crime committed by one of his fellows, because he knows that in the French imagination "individual responsibility" is transformed into "collective responsibility." In this vision, then, Si Hamza seemed to be suggesting that North Africans are not, in fact, pariahs, they only feel themselves to be so, and that they bear much of the responsibility for their predicament because of their own thoughts and sentiments. He went on, however, to put forth even more questionable propositions. While condemning "hurtful speech," Si Hamza nevertheless argued that he did not believe that words could be transformed into "aggressive action."[69] The problem, as the *recteur* saw it, was not that the French were racist toward "North Africans or any other ethnic group" but that they "rose up against the abuses, the excesses, and everything that 'disturbed' their habits," especially when it was a question of North Africans doing things in France "that they would not do at home." Si Hamza's solution to the problems of North African immigrants was a simple one: he urged his fellow Maghrébins, "who benefit from [French] hospitality," to strive toward "friendliness, forgetting knives, respecting women, polite manners, [and] proper language" as paths to improve the situation.[70]

In Si Hamza's account of the problems facing North African immigrants, there is no mention of their religious identities; "North African" is a sign for a particular ethno-cultural identity with social practices (violence, misogyny, vulgarity) that are unacceptable in French society. Coming from the caretaker of the temple to *Islam français,* this is an especially interesting analysis because it departs in a key way from the French state's vision of North African immigrants in which their Muslimness is the most important element of their identities and ethnic/cultural/racial particularities are all signaled under the category of Islam. Furthermore, although Si Hamza was instrumental in trying to unlink Islam from national, political, and ethno-cultural identities in the late 1960s by reaching out to West African Muslims and to the *harkis,* his stance on the issue of racism seems to suggest that only North Africans are concerned (and not West Africans, for example).

By speaking almost exclusively about the particular experience of immigrants of North African origin while claiming to be the representative of all Muslims in France, Si Hamza threw into question the extent to which his universalist vision of Islam in which race and nationality were immaterial was a true reflection of his own thought or of the reality of Muslim existence in France. I argue that Si Hamza's definition of North Africans as an ethno-cultural community rather than a national or religious one reflects an internalization of the ways in which the French state's discourse on North African immigrants emphasized embodied religious practices to talk about the innate nature of Muslim identity along ethno-racial lines. The Mosquée's *recteur* brought this discourse to previously unseen heights by dispensing with the Muslim label and speaking directly about ethnicity and culture. Si Hamza's evacuation of the religious content of North African immigrants' identities in his commentaries on their place in French society signaled a new stage in the development of *Islam français* in the 1970s: while the French state and factory owners created new mechanisms to manage immigrant populations through "cultural" programs that quite often were projects designed to facilitate Muslim religious practices, the leader of France's premier "Muslim" site had paradoxically made the opposite move and dispensed with Islam as a code for speaking about North African immigrants in France. As we will see, Si Hamza's responses to the violent (verbal and physical) opposition he faced from different elements within France's Muslim communities on religious and political grounds were almost always free of religious grounding. While I do not contest the authenticity of certain Muslims' attacks on the *recteur* and the Mosquée on religious grounds, I do argue that Si Hamza understood that far more was at stake in the fights over Islam in the 1970s than interpretations of religious practice. His direct recourse to political arguments in his rebuttals of these critiques demonstrates the ways in which the decades-old model of using Islam to negotiate cultural and political realities was being strained beyond recognition.

"Unbearable Tyranny": Claiming and Owning Muslim Religious Space in Paris

Representatives from almost all of France's diverse Muslim communities responded vehemently to Si Hamza's arguments, agreeing that he was blaming the victims for their own suffering. But the attacks were made in different discursive registers: opposition to Si Hamza's statements was couched in the language of Islam, of nationality, and of class solidarity, with some groups drawing on more than one of these themes in their counterarguments. The strong opposition to Si Hamza's presence in the Mosquée's leadership, especially after 1974, was often voiced in and around the site itself: Muslims seemed, for the first time, to be laying claim to the space of the Parisian site while rejecting its leadership. In other words, by voicing strong criticisms of Si Hamza during prayers or at holiday services, many Muslims in Paris were trying to separate the institution, which they wanted to salvage for their own "proper" Muslim use, from its leadership, which was described as corrupt both religiously and morally. In a truly interesting turn, some Muslim groups called on the French state to "save" the Mosquée from its leader and restore it to its rightful owners, France's Muslims. Thus secular France, for some Muslims, became the best guarantor of Muslim religious freedom.

Trying to parse the critiques of Si Hamza made on religious grounds from those made on the basis of his politics is difficult, as few attacks were formulated exclusively in one way or the other. However, opposition to the Mosquée's *recteur* can be divided into those who primarily doubted his religious and moral capacities to lead a Muslim institution and those who found fault with his positions on the place of immigrants in French society or with his relationship with the French and Algerian states. The Amicale des musulmans en Europe was one of the groups that led the charge in attacking Si Hamza's leadership on religious and moral grounds; it was also this group that made explicit demands of the French state, as the guarantor of religious freedom, to remove Si Hamza from power. The group's critiques ranged from comments on specific events to more wide-ranging attacks on the *recteur*'s management of the institution. One frequent complaint was that Si Hamza used the Mosquée not as a shrine to Muslim religious values and practices but as a personal money-making venture in ways that were counter to the basic principles of Islam. An example of this kind of situation is cited in an article by an opponent of the Mosquée, describing a "savage attack" by Si Hamza and Mosquée staff on a "perfectly behaved Muslim student" who had been distributing free pamphlets listing the hours for Ramadan prayers after Friday's service. "Do we really need to explain that all employees of the Mosquée de Paris, without exception, must be the zealous servants of Islam, and of the community, not its nobility? Naturally, they are free to cede this honor, to those who are better qualified, conscious of their duty and not interested in disputing the ownership of this place of prayer."[71] The subtext of this particular incident was that the student was distributing free pamphlets, whereas the Mosquée's schedules were sold rather than distributed. "Soon the Mosquée's administration will charge the faithful for the air they breathe," wrote the author who described this particular incident, deploring the un-Islamic way in which the Mosquée "never tires" of making money from Muslims and "our non-Muslim brother visitors." Si Hamza was also criticized for allowing the Mosquée's *salle de prières* to be used in an advertisement for oriental rugs and for trying to set up his own *halal* butcher shop in the Mosquée's complex (with non-*halal* meat imported from Ireland still bearing the export stamps).[72]

The thornier issue in these critiques of Si Hamza on religious grounds, however, was who was distributing what kind of Muslim information within or around the Mosquée, not simply whether the Mosquée's financial practices were in keeping with Muslim ethics. What was at stake for the Amicale and other groups was the question of who had the right to use the site's space to spread what message.[73] In addition to the "attack" described above, a series of incidents in which Si Hamza or members of his staff either forcibly ejected men trying to distribute tracts, lead study sessions, or give classes or otherwise made it impossible for them to use the Mosquée's space for their religious practices, suggested to certain members in the Muslim community that Si Hamza's Islam was quite exclusive. One such event took place on 16 April 1970 when three "foreign" sheikhs came to Paris "to remind their brothers of God's teachings" were "chased out of the Capital's mosque, probably to allow tourists who paid an entry fee to admire the architecture of an empty room where the rugs moan under the weight of sand and dust."[74] The point about the Mosquée as a tourist destination echoes the critiques made by groups like the ENA in the 1920s. These critiques, however, were more urgent in the 1970s, when the emptiness of the mosque-museum was contrasted with the desire of a large Muslim community to use the space for Muslim religious practices. In this case, the men and those who had remained in the *salle de prière* after the Friday prayers to study with them were "rudely chased" out of the room when Mosquée staff overwhelmed their conversation "with a deafening loudspeaker playing a Quranic recording."[75]

From other critiques made by the Amicale on religious grounds, such as their disdain for Si Hamza's French translation of the Quran,[76] as well as their turn to a more "rigorous" form of Islam during the course of the 1970s, it seems that the Mosquée's attempts to silence their members or to keep them from having access to the site's space grew out of a desire to maintain the institution as a temple to *Islam français*. One particularly evocative illustration of the conflict between the French Islam that the Mosquée was supposed to embody and the Islam of increasingly vocal Muslim associations in France is the conflict around Si Hamza's response to the French orientalist Maxime Rodinson's book on the Prophet Mohammed. A diffuse group of Muslims calling themselves "Les Associations religieuses Islamiques de France" were scandalized by Si Hamza's refusal to condemn the "*laïc*" Rodinson's work, as well as that of another French scholar whose book contained "defamatory propositions" about the Prophet.[77] Worse than this, the group argued, the *recteur* had "allowed Rodinson to speak in the heart of the Mosquée" after the publication of his work on Mohammed.[78] The work was a historical materialist account of the origins of Islam as well as a consideration of the Prophet's life in its socioeconomic context. Si Hamza's invitation to Rodinson to speak at the Mosquée was very much in keeping with the site's founders' vision of the institution as a place for encounters between French scientific thought and Muslim "civilization," and it was this vision that was rejected in the "Les Associations religieuses Islamiques de France's" condemnation of Si Hamza's perceived relationship with Rodinson.

Muslims who made these kinds of critiques also turned to the French state as a potential arbiter and protector of religious freedoms. The long-established collaboration between the Mosquée, the embodiment of the government's vision of secular Islam, and local and national politicians no longer seemed to matter to those who criticized Si Hamza primarily on religious grounds. In other words, Muslims whose vision of Islam had little to do with "traditional" *Islam français* sought the assistance of the secular state to guarantee their right *not* to be secular and to promote their own vision of Islam within the Mosquée's walls. The Amicale made one of the most explicit calls on the French state to help their cause:

> The Muslims of Paris call on the French Authorities to deliver them from the unbearable tyranny of the direction of the Mosquée de Paris which has been imposed on them for many years.
>
> They would be infinitely grateful for their willingness to put an end to the undignified behavior of these scandal makers at the Mosquée de Paris, thus ridding Islamic community of an administration far too interested in the shameless exploitation of the faithful, all the while humiliating them.
>
> The faithful want to choose themselves an Islamic Direction in the service of God and the community.
>
> They have adopted France as their second homeland to live there freely, far from any dictatorship.
>
> They are determined to be worthy of their adopted homeland.
>
> This is why the Mosquée de Paris needs to be a real Islamic Institute where human fraternity is cultivated, and not the de facto property of an individual or a family.[79]

This appeal to the French authorities willfully ignores the fact that it was the French government that replaced Si Ahmed with Si Hamza because his politics were less threatening to French authority in the midst of the Algerian War. More important, however, is the discourse of loyalty to the "adopted homeland" of France: the trope of loyalty and sacrifice was the rallying cry of the Mosquée's French Islam, but now it was being used to contest it. The Muslims making this plea did not claim to be secular, and were not interested in being *laïc* subjects: they wanted to serve God and their community, not the French republic, even though they did promise their loyalty to France. But the contemporary political climate and the new cultural politics of immigration suggested to this group that the French state was their best hope for creating the space for their Muslim religious practice within the walls of the Mosquée de Paris.

The critiques of Si Hamza on political grounds reflected a similar rupture in the old and established equation between the French state's *politique musulmane* and the capital's Muslim institution: the Mosquée's *recteur* was being attacked not for his close relationship with the French state, as Si Kaddour had been, but for his difficult relations with Algiers and with the Muslim community itself. The accusations of complacency if not complicity in the racist attacks on North Africans were one element that explained Si Hamza's poor relations with many members of the Muslim immigrant community.

The *recteur* was also attacked for his perceived openness to Jews, Judaism and Zionism.[80] These criticisms certainly did not ignore Islam, but in this context it was less a question of particular interpretations of Muslim practice and belief than of Islam as a symbol of immigrant integrity and autonomy to be defended and championed. Islam was also conflated with race and national identity in many of the more politically oriented critiques. These charges indicated an important shift in the relationship between the state and the Mosquée, between Muslims in France and the French state, and between the Mosquée and the increasingly large and diverse Muslim communities in France.

One of the most widely publicized attacks on Si Hamza's leadership was a tract distributed at the Mosquée after a protest staged by "several hundred Muslim faithful" during the service for Aid es-Séghir on 3 January 1974.[81] The demonstration itself targeted Si Hamza's "mercantile spirit" as well as behavior that showed him to be "much more of an ally of the exploiters of Muslim workers than the spiritual protector of the Muslim community." A pamphlet distributed by various Paris-area Muslim associations[82] would later be reprinted in both the immigrant and French press. "Of all the religious communities living in France," the authors of the tract argued, "the people of the Muslim community have paid the heaviest tribute to racial intolerance." This text's identification of Muslims as a *religious* community that had been *racially* targeted is illustrative of the complex intersections between race and religion in France. While representatives of French Jewish groups might have contested the claim that Muslims were the French religious group to have suffered the most from racialized violence, the question of competing victimhood is less important here than the implicit self-identification of "Muslims" as a racial group. The document's authors accused Si Hamza of confusing the executioner and the victim and asked rhetorically, "Whom does he represent? Whom does he defend?" They responded to this question by "denying the right of the *recteur* to intervene in the name of Muslims and to preach an Islam which he perverts." The authors give Islam a strong social justice and class inflection; Si Hamza is said to have perverted Islam's principles of charity, tolerance, and justice. "There is a chasm of difference between the exploited Muslim worker and the aristocratic life of this emulator of pashas," they claimed.[83] This critique of Si Hamza echoes the class-based arguments of the Étoile nord-africaine from the 1920s and 1930s, yet the Mosquée leadership is here criticized as a representative of Islam, not as the mouthpiece of the colonial (or neocolonial) state.

The Algerian ruling party's newspaper's own position was slightly different from that voiced by the Parisian Muslim associations. For *El Moudjahid*'s editors, Si Hamza's actions were traitorous to the Algerian nation itself, and his betrayal of both "true" Islam and the immigrant working class were merely symptoms of his "mad desire" to harm Algerian interests.[84] The newspaper of course also accused Si Hamza on class grounds (also labeling him an "emulator of pachas" and "ally of the exploiters of Muslim workers") and on the grounds that his leadership had transformed the Mosquée into a ridiculous tourist trap. As they saw it, "under the reign of this '*recteur,*' [the Mosquée de Paris] has become a shopping center with a cafe, hammam, etc. . . . a miniature casbah for tourists in need of sun!"[85] But Si Hamza's worst betrayal, in the eyes of the FLN, was of the independent Algerian state: describing him as a man who ran away "the day after independence to make a place in the sun for himself elsewhere," *El Moudjahid* accused him of "having harmed the Maghreb, in the most vile manner possible" and then "usurping the role of spiritual head of the Maghrébin community and of all the Muslims in France."[86]

Unlike the Amicale des musulmans en Europe, *El Moudjahid* did not call on the French state to save the Mosquée from Si Hamza—rather, it accused the *recteur* of perpetuating the colonial relationship between metropole and colonies through the medium of the Mosquée. Si Hamza, "emphasizing himself his exclusive allegiance to the French administration," as the journalist put it, "was merely persevering in his behavior of constantly positioning himself against Algerians, against North Africans, against Muslims, in the camp of colonialists of all stripes, of renegades and traitors."[87] His crimes against Islam were the least of the Algerian's state's concerns: for Algiers, Si Hamza's real faults were political ones targeting the country during its struggle for independence and in the years following its victory. Algiers accused Si Hamza not merely having served as a *député* during the colonial era, but also of being an agent for the French secret services and being paid for services rendered with the gift of the Mosquée. The subtext to this entire discussion, of course, was Si Hamza's determination to maintain the Parisian site as a French, rather than North African, possession, "even though it was built with the money of Maghrébins!"[88]

Another variation of the politically oriented attack on Si Hamza was one in which he was accused of Zionist sympathies and of being in league with French Jews and Israelis. This particular critique was often part of a larger one in which he was accused of being a traitor to the Algerian people and the Algerian state, but added an element that made his treason even worse in the context of the recent 1973 war. A tract distributed at the Mosquée begins a recounting of the Mosquée's leader's many betrayals with the earliest sign of his perfidy: "It appears that he was breastfed by a Jew."[89] As though he had imbibed his affinity for the Jewish community with his wet nurse's milk, critics accused Si Hamza of more serious actions, all the worse for being conscious acts: one example was his membership in the Association of Abrahamic Brotherhood (Association de Fraternité Abrahamique); another was the fact that he hosted one of the group's meetings (in cooperation with the Chief Rabbi of France and Church representatives) at the Mosquée on the eve of the 1973 war. Si Hamza's participation in fundraising events for LICRA, such as a gala performance with Johnny Hallyday, Enrico Macias, and the Kol Aviv Jewish folk ensemble,[90] was also used as proof of his objectionable alliances by his Muslim and North African critics. Those who accused Si Hamza for his willingness to engage in inter-religious dialogues and to participate in the fight against anti-Semitism (particularly while seeming less concerned about anti-Arab racism) did so on political grounds, not religious ones. Tensions between the Jewish and Muslim communities in France began to rise towards the end of the 1960s and spiked at moments of conflict in the Middle East, and the criticisms of Si Hamza reflect that situation.[91]

Si Hamza's decision to mount his explicit public defense on political grounds, that is to say, against the charges of treason to the Algerian nation and people, rather than on the basis of his religious authority or his ability to speak in the name of Muslim immigrant workers is revealing of the way he saw the issues involved in the attacks on his role as *recteur.* He perceived the real threat to the Mosquée (and to his own power) as coming from Algiers and the FLN, who sought to gain control over the Parisian site. The question of alternative expressions of Muslim religious belief and practices was not unimportant to Si Hamza, as is evident from his censoring or outright removal of Muslims using the Mosquée to give voice to their own perceptions of Islam. But his responses to the threat posed by a multiplicity of visions of Islam were contained within the confines of the Mosquée and its surroundings, within the confines of the Muslim community. The rendering public of Si Hamza's response to other Muslim practices was done by the groups or individuals who felt targeted by his actions, not by the *recteur* himself. On the other hand, Si Hamza responded to the charges of treason, made in *El Moudjahid*'s pages and in tracts distributed to Muslim worshippers with letters to the Algerian president; the ministers of justice, the interior, and national defense; the general procurer, and to the French press. Si Hamza stated that he had never "betrayed his country, for which [he had] known torture and prisons." He declared himself ready to appear before any Algerian judicial authority, civil or military, at a moment's notice to refute the charges made against him.[92] The Amicale des Imams de France (led by the grand mufti, Cheikh Ameur, of the Mosquée de Paris) issued a press release to voice their support for Si Hamza, whose subtext revealed a similar perception that the attacks on his authority were political more than anything else. The document congratulated the *recteur* for "maintaining this international institution safe from base intrigues and all from any political control incompatible with its mission and with the dogma of Islam."[93]

In interviews with the French press, Si Hamza's tongue was considerably looser than in his letter to Algiers. In one interview in particular, he gives an account in (relatively) *longue durée* terms of why the mid-1970s attacks on him were really political attacks that stemmed from the immediate aftermath of the Algerian Revolution. The Mosquée's *recteur* saw the attacks on his person as part of a larger strategy of the Algerian government to organize Islam in Algeria and France in the service of the FLN. As Si Hamza explained:

> Everything began in December 1962. . . . Ben Bella, in power, sent his friend Chami as an ambassador, with a letter offering me the post of ambassador of the new Algerian Republic to Austria.
>
> It was obviously a trap. In virtue of the principle that all which is Muslim in France legally belonged to them, the Algerian leaders wanted to get their hands on the Hôpital Franco-Musulman de Bobigny, among others, and, most especially, on the Mosquée de Paris.
>
> In their vision, the splendid and vast construction that is the Mosquée would become a super-embassy for Algeria in the heart of Paris. They would also install party[94] officials there. They would control the faithful. Religion would serve political ends.
>
> This is what would happen all over Algeria. Mosques there have become political cells. Qualified and independent imams have been replaced with completely servile FLN bureaucrats. They don't even preach, they content themselves with reading printed Marxist texts sent by the Ministry. Religion is annexed to partisan ends, so as to better indoctrinate the masses.
>
> I could predict all of this by 1962. Thus my response to Ben Bella was negative.
>
> Sorry, I told him, but the Mosquée de Paris of which I was elected *recteur* for life does not belong to me. It is not an Algerian mosque, it is a French creation.
>
> And it's true. The Arab countries did not contribute to it. It is in hommage to the Muslims who fell for France that the Chamber of Deputies and the Senate voted unanimously, on August 19, 1920, on Edouard Herriot's report, the decision to construct the Mosquée

> de Paris. The stunning architectural ensemble cost . . . more than 150 million francs. The principal funder was the city of Paris itself, which donated the land and offered an enormous subvention.
>
> And hardly born, the Algerian state wanted to put its hands on the Mosquée? I refused as *recteur,* but also as the Frenchman I have never stopped being, a veteran and a former deputy of the Oasis. Finally and above all, the Muslim I am could never accept this takeover. The Mosquée de Paris is open to all sects . . . all the universes of Islam, without any discrimination. . . . I would not accept obedience, intolerance, exclusivities.[95]

The account of the Mosquée's origins Si Hamza gives his interviewer is a highly selective one that elides the financial and political contributions of all three North African territories, not to mention the West African colonies, to the construction of the Mosquée de Paris. The donations given by Muslims from beyond the boundaries of the French empire are also erased from this story. The absence of France's former colonies in Si Hamza's version of the founding of the Mosquée is an essential tool in the elaboration of his argument that he was being attacked on political grounds for his defense of (legitimate) French interests against (spurious) Algerian ones. His accusation that the FLN was using Islam for political ends with political appointees serving as imams was not untrue[96] but is also somewhat disingenuous coming from someone who was himself a politically appointed *recteur,* parachuted in to replace someone whose politics were problematic.

"The Crypt of the Ménilmontant Church Hosts Belleville's Neighborhood Mosque": Finding Other Muslim Space in the Capital

Si Hamza's belief that the biggest challenge to his authority came from Algiers rather than from different movements in the Muslim communities of Ile-de-France was an indication both of his lack of regard for other Muslim leaders in France and his underestimation of the authority enjoyed by new Muslim sites among many Muslims in the capital. In addition to the prayer spaces in factories and *foyers, salles de prière* and mosques began to inhabit church basements and abandoned warehouses in neighborhoods with large Muslim immigrant populations. The visions of Islam enshrined in these spaces were distinct from those of the Mosquée's leadership.

Local church leaders were among the strongest proponents of attributing spaces for Muslims to use as religious sites. Breaking with decades of French discourse on the particularities of mosque architecture and aesthetics, they argued that finding and providing such spaces would be relatively easy given that "religious practice is not tied to an edifice" in Islam.[97] Considering that the Church's social welfare and outreach programs brought clergy and lay people into contact with immigrants, it was not unusual for Muslims to seek their assistance in locating appropriate spaces for prayer after being rejected by municipal authorities. A Parisian priest wrote that a particular Muslim man asked him each time they met to find the neighborhood's Muslims a room they could use for prayers and for Arabic and Quran lessons for children. "Why did he ask me? Because we often talked about our faith, and he must have thought that I would better understand his need for a *salle de prière.*"[98] In the case of "Monsieur R," the priest's attempts to secure a space through City Hall and the Préfecture met with failure. Ultimately, their church's chaplain found an available room for them in a neighboring parish. Muslims were right to suspect that the church, both Catholic and Protestant, would help where the state was unwilling to step in: across the country, many clergy sympathetic to the plight of Muslim immigrants allowed them to use spaces within their churches or sold them church lands or buildings at very low prices. For Christians concerned with social issues, the lack of access to religious spaces was a symptom of all the problems facing Muslim immigrants:

> For the average migrant, the home, which is normally the place for prayer, is too cluttered, too crowded to allow for reflection. The incredible overpopulation impedes normal life. The HLM apartments are the biggest, but are not made for families with more than eight children. Or for family groups of 12 or 15, which are not rare. Where, then, can they gather?
>
> The city is witnessing the opening, almost everywhere, of prayer sites: cramped spaces where Muslims can gather together after their working day. But these asylums born of private initiatives are few and far between. It seems only fair, in this country of welcome, where depending on one's political leanings, one prides oneself on fraternity or charity, that facilities be made which would make possible the legitimate expression of a secular and non-subversive faith.[99]

The paucity of Muslim religious sites was merely one of many things lacking in the everyday lives of immigrant workers, Christian social workers realized. In addition to the problems in access to housing, of course, was the fact that the housing which was available was inadequate for large immigrant families. Although as this author emphasized, Muslim religious practice does not require a particular kind of space for its proper observance, the locales available to immigrants, whether sacred or profane, were simply not spacious enough to allow for their inhabitants' everyday activities. Yet on the other hand, Christians who independently provided Muslims with spaces for prayer and community gatherings also believed that the secular French state should do the same to help a "secular and non-subversive" faith. In other words, Christians called on the *laïc* state to provide religious sites for a *laïc* religion like their own.

The "secular and non-subversive" Islam so staunchly defended by those members of the church concerned with immigrant welfare and inter-religious dialogue in fact resembled the *Islam français* of the 1920s Mosquée. In their perception, it was still attached to its traditions (in a way they feared Christians no longer were), yet those traditions were in fact in perfect harmony with French republican principles.[100] As the Catholic organizer of an association called All Sons of Abraham (Tous fils d'Abraham) designed to promote encounters between Christians and Muslims explained, the "Muslim knows, better than the Christian of our century, that God is also part of the everyday. He shows it in a way which mixes sovereign God and the most ordinary occupations, with a natural air that can easily disconcert those of us in a secularized society."[101] Misogynist or patriarchal behaviors, they argued, were mere perversions of "real" Islam. Thus the Church was in fact hoping to aid the practice of the kind of Islam the Mosquée was supposed to embody, though the Mosquée was of course highly opposed to the creation of these independent sites that escaped its authority.

One such site was what would become known as the Mosquée de Belleville, under the guardianship of the Association culturelle islamique (more commonly known as the Association islamique de Belleville). The association, founded in 1969 by a French citizen of Algerian origin, was made up primarily of Algerians and Pakistani members of the Jama'at al Tabligh (known in French as Foi et pratique, or Faith and Practice, founded in France in 1972).[102] The group established its mosque in an old and fairly decrepit two-story building owned by a Muslim immigrant in the midst of Belleville, with its large population of Muslim (as well as Jewish) North African immigrants. A Catholic visitor to the original home of the mosque was surprised by the building's small size, observing that it

> does not correspond to our image of such a place. There is no minaret or arabesques, rather a kind of spruced up hangar. . . . On the ground floor of this almost dilapidated two-story house, an orange wall-to-wall carpet extended by two worn oriental rugs takes away a bit of the

> sadness. At the back, a big sink (where several running faucets leak) allow the faithful to perform their ablutions before prayers. A wooden stairwell leads to the first floor, to the *salle de prière.* Here too a big carpet covers the floor . . . a stepladder covered with a rug acts as the pulpit. Seated on top of it, the muezzin launches the call to prayer on his microphone . . . the faithful will soon be more than 400 in this cramped space.[103]

The aesthetic contrast between the opulence of the state-sponsored Mosquée de Paris and the independently financed and organized Mosquée de Belleville is glaring, as is the fact of their respective locations in the center of Paris and in the middle of a lower-class immigrant neighborhood. Church sympathizers noted that the Mosquée did not welcome this independent upstart, an "independent reality" with no connection to Boubakeur's institution.[104] The difference was only accentuated by an accident in which the weight of the faithful in the *salle de prière* brought the floor crashing down into the ground level.

The founders of the Belleville Mosque, seeking a new home, met with rejections from tenant associations when they tried to buy spaces in existing buildings. Seeking help from the Catholic Church, they were pleased to learn that the *curé* of Notre-Dame de la Croix de Ménilmontant Church, Père Loubier, was sympathetic to their cause and often lent available space to community groups. At the same time as they pleaded their case to Loubier, they alerted the ONCPI of their problems finding an appropriate home. As a priest involved in negotiating their temporary placement in the Ménilmonant church explained, the agency "attached great importance to the Muslim community of Belleville" and followed the issue with interest given Paul Dijoud's policy of support for Muslim religious space.[105] Loubier sought his parishioners' approval for his idea to offer the church's crypt to Muslims, and while there were some negative reactions, almost everyone supported allowing Muslims to use the crypt (which was already a space to be rented out for meetings, parties, theater productions, and other activities).[106] The Muslims of the Belleville Mosque covered the crypt's decorations, which featured human or animal forms, and began to attend in large numbers.[107] A few years later, in 1981, the Association islamique de Belleville was able to purchase an old fabric warehouse on rue Tanger, in the 19th *arrondissement,* which was large enough to accommodate up to four thousand people. This new site was formally known as the Mosquée Ad'dawa, and it is still an important player in Parisian Muslim life.

Finally, it is important once again to emphasize that while the 1970s saw the growth of many new prayer sites and the most serious challenges to the

Mosquée's authority, much of Muslim religious and cultural life continued to take place outside of the framework of any of these religious sites. Many of the markers of Muslim everyday life, such as Ramadan celebrations, occurred in the home or in the neighborhood. In North African neighborhoods such as Barbès, the rhythms of daily life adjusted to the holiday:

> Sunday afternoon, all the food stores are open. The butchers who sell the meat of the sheep which have been sacrificed according to Muslim tradition are literally invaded by dozens of Algerian clients sometimes coming from neighboring suburbs. It is the same in the grocery stores, where one is sure to find all the ingredients necessary for a good "shorba," [soup] while the outdoor display cases of pastry shops are piled with mountains of "zlabia" [fried honey pastries] and all the Algerian, Tunisian and Moroccan specialties. The restaurants busy themselves, knowing that around 5:30, there will be huge crowds.[108]

In one Paris suburb, a small group of young Muslims tired of celebrating the communal holiday of Ramadan exclusively with families in the home. They decided to produce a brochure in French and Arabic explaining the meaning of the holiday and distributed it to all their neighbors. Initial confusion and reluctance from non-Muslim neighbors turned to interest and curiosity, and that year Ramadan was celebrated communally, with children ferrying meals back and forth between neighbors.[109] Another communal event was the welcoming of pilgrims returning from the *hajj,* which began at Orly airport: in 1976, for example, about four thousand friends and relatives gathered to wait for four hundred people flying home from Mecca. The pilgrims themselves invited all their friends and relatives to their homes upon their return. During these gatherings, which often featured musicians chanting verses of the Quran, the *hajj* would anoint his guests with perfume and then serve them dates and water from the desert well from which the Prophet had drunk.[110] There were additional venues for the expression of Muslim religious or cultural practices, such as gatherings organized by politically oriented groups like the MTA or the Amicale des Algériens. Thus the growth of new prayer and community sites in the city and suburbs, in factories and *foyers*; the support (in some cases) accorded to these spaces by the French state and the Catholic Church; and the further erosion of the Mosquée's authority in the wake of these newly established institutions should not, however, create the impression that all Muslim life revolved around these centers. In particular, the new mosques and *salles de prière* were very specifically gendered and did not offer much room to immigrant women for their own expressions of belief. These spaces were very welcoming of children and often offered

Arabic and Quran classes. Yet that female members of the Muslim community did not use these religious sites as the primary loci for their own practice reminds us that these sites did not exclusively define Muslim religious life in Paris during this period.

Si Hamza's response to the growth of autonomous religious sites and, more importantly, to the French state's groundbreaking recognition of alternative Muslim authorities in Paris was more often than not to issue ultimatums and threats in the hopes of consolidating his power. When he realized that it would be difficult to restore the Mosquée to its former prominence in Muslim France, Si Hamza took the paradoxical step of transferring authority over the site to Algiers. The *recteur,* reviled and accused of treason in the Algerian and North African press in France, ultimately decided to cast his lot and that of the Mosquée with the FLN government rather than the new and, to his mind, uncooperative Socialist government in France. Si Hamza's decision did not emerge from a sudden sense of nationalist pride or a desire to "return" what began as a colonial institution to the masters of the independent former colony. On the contrary, the *recteur* had no desire whatsoever to see Algiers take over leadership of what he saw as his institution. Rather, I suggest that it was a response to the French state's abandonment of its commitment to the original vision of *Islam français* through its support for alternative sites of Muslim religious authority over the course of the 1970s. In raising the specter of Algerian ownership, Si Hamza hoped to recall the French state to its duties as the defender of *Islam français.*

Both the national administration and the city of Paris refused to increase their subsidies of the Mosquée in spite of Si Hamza's repeated requests, so as early as 1977 he began threatening to make whatever decisions he felt necessary and warning that "the Mosquée would no longer be French."[111] In fact, Si Hamza's campaign to ensure his authority over the Mosquée began much earlier, in 1958, when he pushed through an amendment to the Société de Habous' statutes giving the president greater powers and an unlimited tenure. Having assured his power, he then formally transferred the Société de Habous' headquarters from Algiers to Paris almost immediately after Algerian independence in 1962. This action greatly angered the Algerian authorities, who, along with the Moroccan and Tunisian authorities, declared that they no longer recognized Si Hamza as *recteur* and named an Algerian, Abdelkader Boutaleb, in his place. However, Si Hamza's authority was preserved by a legal decision that confirmed his position as the Mosquée's recteur and rejected the North African attempt to take over the institution.[112] Throughout the 1970s, Si Hamza proceeded to make gestures to both Algerian and Moroccan authorities, naming each of them in turn the primary beneficiary of all of the Mosquée's patrimony should the Société de Habous be dissolved, in the hopes of forcing the French authorities to increase their own contributions to the Mosquée's budget. He finally made good on his threats when the Société des Habous decided the legal transfer of all the patrimony of the Institut Musulman and Mosquée de Paris to Algeria during its 4 August 1982 meeting.[113] Shortly thereafter,[114] Si Hamza also presented his demission as *recteur* to the Société de Habous. The Algerian government designated Cheikh Abbas Ben Cheikh el Hocine, a member of the Ouléma who had served as an FLN representative in Cairo during the War, as Si Hamza's successor and also expressed the hope that French authorities would cooperate with the Société des Habous decision. However, it was not until January 1983 that Si Hamza told the minister of the interior of the decisions taken internally at the Société de Habous' General Assembly, well after Algiers had begun to plan its administration of the Parisian site. The French state refused to recognize the agreement between Si Hamza and Algiers, and the Moroccan government, along with other Muslim states, formally protested the decision. Legal wrangling among Algeria, France, Morocco and Tunisia over the possession of the Mosquée continued until 1987, when Algiers formally declared the site's new organization with the Préfecture de Police.

In 1989, the Algerian minister of religion declared, "We are at home here: this mosque is an Algerian mosque, and if the *Français musulmans* want their own, the French state can build them one."[115] His use of the colonial-era term "*Français musulman*" rather than "*Musulman français*," or French Muslim, is a reference to those Algerian Muslims who took French citizenship in exchange for their Muslim personal status. The political implications of his comment are clear. Yet in spite of the radical rupture a remark like this seems to signal that little had actually changed in the day-to-day administration of the Mosquée de Paris with the transition to Algerian stewardship and a new *recteur.* Cheikh Abbas held the position from 1982 through 1989 and was followed by Dr. Tedjini Haddam from 1989 to 1992; Haddam was an Algerian surgeon who, like Cheikh Abbas, had served the FLN in Cairo during the war. Both of these Algerian *recteurs,* however, would spend their years as *recteur* defending *Islam français* during a decade in which the Salman Rushdie affair electrified the world, the infamous headscarf debates erupted on a national scale in France, and the "Muslim" landscape in France continued to change and evolve. The demographic shifts of the 1960s and 1970s continued during the 1980s and 1990s, and although the majority of Muslims in France continued to be immigrants or their descendants from North Africa, the Muslim populations of France were not homogenous. Immigrants from

France's former colonies, including those from the Indian Ocean territories of Reunion and Mayotte, were joined during the 1970s by immigrants from Turkey as well as later waves of immigrants from the Middle East and South Asia who sometimes came to France as refugees, bringing greater diversity to France's Muslim communities.[116] Yet throughout the 1980s and 1990s, in spite of France's Muslim diversity and the global concerns about Islamic fundamentalism, "Muslim" continued to be a synonym for "Arab" in France.[117]

Conclusion

"We Want to Contribute to the Secularization of Islam": *Islam français* in the Twenty-First Century

Does *Islam français* still exist at the moment I write these words, in the summer of 2011? Several developments of the last two decades suggest that it does not: the law banning headscarves in schools suggests that, contrary to its original promise of openness, it is now legally impossible to practice both "Muslimness" and "Frenchness." At the same time, the creation of the official consultative body the Conseil français du culte musulman (French Council of Muslim Religion, or CFCM) gives the impression that *Islam français* no longer exists because Islam has been normalized to the extent that it now fits comfortably alongside Catholicism and Judaism as a major French religion, fully compatible with French secularism. Finally, in 2013, almost a century after the ceremony marking the beginning of the Mosquée's construction, the mayor of Paris, presumably in the company of Muslim religious and community leaders, as well as politicians, intellectuals, and artists, will inaugurate the Institut des cultures d'Islam (ICI) in the 18th *arrondissement.*[1]

The ICI is intended to mark a new kind of state support for Islam and Muslims. Occupying two separate lots, the four thousand square meters of the ICI will be located in the Goutte d'Or, a working-class neighborhood in northeastern Paris that has long been home to successive waves of immigration. The Institut has three "distinct activities," which the project's mission statement describes as "a university center for education, research and documentation," "social and cultural activities and animations," and "religious activity."[2] As for the choice of neighborhood, the ICI planning committee explains that "Goutte d'Or . . . emblematic of a Muslim presence inscribed in the long history of Paris, appears the ideal place to anchor this institute."[3] Is the ICI not the "anti-Mosquée," a sign of how much things have changed since the stones of the Mosquée de Paris were laid in 1922?

I conclude my exploration of development of *Islam français* over the course of the twentieth century by arguing that the superficial differences between the Mosquée de Paris and the Institut des cultures d'Islam, the ambiguity of the CFCM's role as both religious and ethno-cultural arbiter, and the slippage during the headscarf debates between practice and essence in fact mask the ways they continue to embody French Islam. *Islam français* did not disappear in 1982 when the Mosquée de Paris ceased being a French institution—on the contrary, it is alive and well. An examination of the headscarf laws, the creation of the CFCM, and the planning for the ICI tends to underline three points I have made throughout this book. First, the controversies of the turn of the twenty-first century do not represent a "new Muslim problem" in France. All of the issues at stake in these debates have animated French Muslim policy since the First World War. Second, all three of these institutional sites (a law, a representative council, a building) demonstrate that "Islam" and "Muslims" are not intrinsically incapable of separating their religious and public spheres and thus becoming secular; rather, it is the French state that continues to blur the boundaries between racialized essence and religion. In the end, *laïcité,* or secularism, is not the most useful way to think about the place of Islam and Muslims in metropolitan France.

The Islamization of France: The Headscarf Debates

1989, the bicentennial year of the French Revolution, represented a turning point in debates about French national identity and sovereignty in the face of immigration, globalization, and European integration as well as fears of political Islamism.[4] "Islam" seemed to be everywhere, from the Ayatollah Khomeini's fatwa against Salman Rushdie after the publication of *The Satanic Verses* to the beginning of the Algerian Civil War of the 1990s with the rise to power of the Front islamique du salut (Islamic Salvation Front). It was in this climate that three adolescent girls (one of Tunisian origin and two sisters of Moroccan origin) showed up to their Paris-region middle school wearing headscarves on 3 October 1989 and were promptly expelled by their principal. Shortly thereafter, national politicians and public intellectuals began to intervene in what had until then remained a local affair. The school's principal, Eugène Chenière, argued that he was trying to preserve *laïcité,* an argument voiced by many on the left who publicly urged the minister of education, Lionel Jospin, to ban headscarves as well as other signs of religious affiliation, such as Jewish skull caps. The far-right, xenophobic National Front staged protests against the "Islamization of France," but the mainstream media outlets also ran stories with titles like "Fanaticism: The Religious Menace," featuring photographs of girls in full-length black chadors.[5] At the same time, Muslim groups sponsored demonstrations during October in support of the right to wear a headscarf in French public schools, prompting Tedjini Haddam, the Mosquée's *recteur,* to "call for de-dramatizing [the conflict] and for dialogue," saying that the march was "regrettable" because in spite of the indignation of the "Muslim community," the heart of the headscarf controversy was ignorance, not racism, and that only constructive dialogue could resolve it.[6] The *recteur*'s reluctance to countenance the possibility of racist motivations in the anti-headscarf camp provides an interesting echo of Si Hamza's refusal to characterize anti–North African violence as racist in the 1970s.

The 1989 debates came to a close with the Conseil d'État's ruling that girls had the right to wear scarves in class because of the freedom of religious expression, so long as they were not trying to proselytize or disrupt school proceedings. They were reopened, however, five years later, when Chenière, now a parliamentary deputy for a center-right party, publicly announced that *laïcité* was threatened by girls wearing headscarves in schools and Minister of Education François Bayrou decreed in September 1994 that all "ostentatious" signs of religious affiliation in public schools be banned. About a hundred girls were subsequently expelled. Again, the Conseil d'État ruled against Bayrou's decree, upholding its 1989 decision, holding that girls could be expelled only for failing to attend classes or otherwise disrupting school activities, not for wearing headscarves. As in 1989, however, the legal decision taken in 1994 did not represent the end of the headscarf wars. They erupted again in 2003, when Minister of the Interior Nicolas Sarkozy mandated that women and men appear bareheaded in national identity cards, including Muslim women. Although he did not say anything about schools, Sarkozy's decision launched a new round of debates about the subject, this time resulting in parliamentary discussions and the proposition of a bill to ban headscarves from schools, which had wide support on the right and left. President Jacques Chirac appointed a commission in 2003, known as the Stasi Commission, which was charged with reflecting on the state of *laïcité* in France. The issues to be considered by the commission ranged from poverty to labor discrimination, whose connection to the principle of *laïcité* was tenuous at best, but it was clear to all involved that the real issue was headscarves. The group's work resulted in the signing of the law of 2004 that banned all "ostentatious" signs of religious affiliation, including veils but also yarmulkes and Sikh turbans.[7] In the face of the public opposition to the law voiced by some Muslim associations, the Mosquée's *recteur,* Dalil Boubakeur, declared, "Personally, I will not take to the streets . . . and I don't advise my brothers to scare the bourgeoisie two months before the regional elections," arguing that "the priority for girls is education at the secular, obligatory, free public school."[8] While echoing his predecessor's opposition to demonstrations, he also voiced his support more forcefully for the school as a secular space.[9]

The attempt to eliminate signs of Muslim religious affiliation from the public sphere beginning in 1989 and (perhaps) ending in 2010 with the law banning the "*voile intégral*" demonstrates the perceived incompatibility of "Islam" with French republicanism, of "Muslims" with "Frenchness," for many French people across the political spectrum.[10] The headscarf controversies threw into relief all of the contradictions of *Islam français*: girls and women who sought to observe what they believed to be a Muslim religious requirement were told that they could not do so and remain French. But at the same time, the "Muslimness" of those same women and girls was innate, and the wearing of headscarves was but the visible sign of their essential Muslimness on their bodies. This last point was especially evident in the commission's impassioned defense of girls and young women who "courageously" chose not to wear the veil. Without explicitly qualifying these unveiled girls and young women as "Muslim," the commission's members explained that in the inner cities, "young women find themselves victims of a resurgence of sexism which translates into different pressures and acts of violence, whether verbal, psychological or physical. Young men impose asexual or all-covering outfits on them, or force them to lower their eyes at the sight of a man; if they don't conform, they are stigmatized as 'whores.'"[11] The lack of any qualifying adjectives to describe the alleged victims of these pressures as Muslim, Arab, or African is shocking in its absence, for it is of course to these young women to which the commission was referring. Yet this same absence underscores that for the men and women who made up the commission, not only was there so much slippage between ethnic and racial identities and a "Muslim" identity as to render any qualification unnecessary, but it was also to be taken for granted that "Muslim" women and girls could be identified as such to others, whether or not they wore ostensible signs of religious affiliation. Finally, of course, the paradoxical figure of the veiled girl who is at once religious agent and female victim was complicated by the fact that many French observers doubted the sincerity of the girls and women who professed to cover their heads out of religious obligation, arguing instead that they did so either because they were forced to do so by authoritarian and fundamentalist male family members or that they chose to wear the veil in an act of political provocation.[12] The headscarf debates and law demonstrate the French state's continued blurring of the boundaries between racialized essence and religious practices when it comes to "Muslims" and its refusal to allow for the possibility of being both French and a practicing Muslim.

A Muslim *Consistoire*? From CORIF to CFCM

Yet while the wearing of the veil was being defined as incompatible with secular Frenchness, a simultaneous institutionalization of Islam in postcolonial twenty-first-century France was unfolding. At the same time that the visible signs of Islam were to be erased from French public schools, "Islam" was to be organized in an official, institutional body in which elected "Muslim" representatives would act as partners with the French state to see to the proper administration of Muslim affairs in France. This process began just as the first headscarf debates erupted: in the fall of 1989, Socialist Minister of the Interior Pierre Joxe brought together fifteen Muslim leaders in what he called the Council for Reflection on Islam in France (CORIF). CORIF had no legal status; its role was to advise Joxe on Muslim issues (such as Muslim areas in cemeteries, *halal* slaughterhouses, the dates for Ramadan, and so on) and to think about a future Muslim representative body. According to French scholar of Islam Franck Frégosi, CORIF included members drawn from France's many diverse Muslim communities in order to signal that the Mosquée's role as the "window" of Islam in France had come to end.[13] Muslim associations that contested the Mosquée's authority to speak in the name of all French Muslims included the Fédération française des Associations islamiques d'Afrique, des Comores et des Antilles (the French Federation of Islamic Associations of Africa, the Comores, and the Antilles, or FFAIACA, which tries to protect the interests of Muslims of Sub-Saharan origin, who are largely ignored in the other Muslim associations); the Fédération nationale des musulmans de France, which is funded primarily by Morocco and represents a conservative Islam (National Federation of Muslims of France, or FNMF); the Union des organizations islamiques de France (the Union of Islamic Organizations of France, or UOIF, the largest Muslim organization and one not associated with any ethnicity or nationality, which and gained prominence for supporting the girls expelled from schools during the headscarf controversy of 1989); and finally, Millî Görü , a Turkish Muslim organization close in ideology to the UOIF. But the possibility that CORIF might represent an alternative to the monopoly on "Muslim" authority of the Mosquée de Paris was foreclosed not only by the internal disagreements among its members but also the 1993 legislative elections that brought the Minister of the Interior Charles Pasqua of the right-wing RPR Party into office. Pasqua, unlike Joxe, preferred to rely on the Mosquée as the government's privileged partner for the administration of Islam, which meant that once again, the *recteur* would represent *Islam français*. Perhaps no one was better suited to this task than Dalil Boubakeur, Hamza Boubakeur's son, who was chosen for the post when Tedjini Haddam was forced to abandon it after accepting a position in the Algerian government.

After several years of tension during Pasqua's tenure, the 1997 election that brought Minister of the Interior Jean-Pierre Chevènement into office provided an occasion to rethink the question of a Muslim representative body, a process he called "*Al Istîchara*" ("consultation" in Arabic), in which he invited members from the major Muslim federations and the major mosques, as well as experts on Muslim affairs, to "sit at the Republic's table" to determine a concrete charter for "the relations between public powers and the Muslim religion."[14] In December of 2002, the discussions resulted in a formal agreement to create the CFCM. The presidency of the body was awarded to the Mosquée de Paris, with the vice presidencies going to the UOIF and FNMF. Delegates were elected through a complex formula that was based on the size of each mosque that participated.[15] Neither Boubakeur nor the leaders of the federations were pleased with this arrangement, for the federations objected to the Mosquée being so clearly favored by the French state, while the Mosquée's leadership feared the implications of a voting mechanism that allowed smaller mosques to contest its authority through sheer numbers.[16] Only those Muslims who were part of a particular mosque community would have representatives who would vote, on behalf of that mosque, in the CFCM elections. Since not all mosques in France agreed to participate in the CFCM, members of such communities did not have a voice in elections (nor did people who identified as Muslims but did not attend a mosque).[17] John Bowen, among others, suggests that one way to think about the CFCM is to compare it to two Jewish institutions that are supposed to somehow represent French Jews: the Consistoire, discussed in chapter 1, and the Conseil representatif des institutions juives de France (Representative Council of Jewish Institutions of France, or CRIF). The Consistoire, as we have seen, is composed of rabbis who are supposed to work with the French state to coordinate Jewish religious questions (such as kosher slaughterhouses, the dates of holidays, and so on), whereas the CRIF, composed of scholars and community activists, is meant to speak in the voice of France's Jews on matters it believes affect them. As Bowen points out, the CFCM is neither one nor the other: the CFCM is regularly called upon to speak for "Muslims" (often on controversial political and social issues) *and* to provide theological guidance on religious matters.[18] Because it is construed as a religious authority, the CFCM cannot possibly "represent" all of France's "Muslims"; that its leaders were appointed by the French state (most significantly, its Mosquée de Paris president) has discredited it in the eyes of many. I suggest that the CFCM is sign of the longevity of *Islam français*: while the council could be argued to embody Islam's normalization and acceptance and its equivalence with Catholicism and Judaism, it in fact shows that even in the twenty-first century, the French Ministry of the Interior continues to try to identify certain French citizens who may or may not be religiously observant as Muslims and to govern them through the intermediary of a semi-appointed, semi-elected body that blurs religious and cultural roles. While the headscarf law and the creation of the CFCM demonstrate the continuity in French Muslim politics, the Parisian government is preparing to unveil a site to physically embody France's commitment to *Islam français*.

Embodying *Islam Français* in Postcolonial France: The Institut des cultures d'Islam (ICI)

In a 2002 magazine interview, Hamou Bouakkaz, Mayor of Paris Bertrand Delanoë's advisor for Muslim issues, was asked whether the city's contribution of approximately 10 million euros toward the ICI's construction was not "a disguised way of financing a religious site in the name of cultural activities" in violation of the law of 1905. Bouakkaz replied, "No. We are subsidizing culture. Not religion." But he followed this firm assertion with a far more ambiguous response, saying:

> We cannot give Parisian Muslims the choice between receiving suspicious foreign funds and praying in basements. That is creating boils and then sending in the police to lance them. . . . We hope to contribute to the secularization of Islam already en route in rendering the Muslim presence in Paris—about 200,000 people *intra muros*—banal. To do this, we are making the most of this law, while taking into account the evolutions of our century. That is what it means to be modern, progressive, and fully *laïc*.[19]

After categorically denying that the city was funding a religious site, Bouakkaz makes an argument that combines the ideology of then–Minister of the Interior Sarkozy with the implicit logic used by Senator Herriot in the 1920s debates about the Mosquée's financing.[20] Given the choice between building a twenty-first-century temple to *Islam français* and allowing Sarkozy's nightmare of autonomous community prayer sites to develop, Bouakkaz suggests that the only true solution is to subsidize a new Muslim religious site. By his logic, the very construction of the ICI will *further* the state's project of secularizing Islam.

The creation of the ICI shows how much and how little has changed in *Islam français* over the course of the last hundred years. The fine line separating *culte* and *culture,* religion and culture, that characterized the Mosquée is still evident in the ICI, and the same arguments about the compatibility of the law of 1905 and the funding of a religious and cultural center were invoked to justify the construction of both sites. These arguments, however, are now being made in a climate in which funding Muslim institutions is far more controversial than it was in the 1920s, not least because a demand for such sites actually exists at the beginning of the twenty-first century. Islam is France's second religion, and Muslims are now French citizens: Islam occupies a far different place in France than it did almost a century ago.

The ICI falls under the authority of the city administration's Cultural Affairs and Patrimony and Architecture departments, whose representatives oversee the site. However, "due to the novel nature of this project," the city thought it important to create two advisory committees to help in developing the ICI. The Scientific Council, made up of academics, cultural programmers, association leaders, and Goutte d'Or neighborhood representatives, is charged with providing background information to the steering committee made up of municipal officials, while the Expert Committee, a smaller group within the Scientific Council, is made up of scholars responsible for creating partnerships with universities and cultural institutions and associations. Unlike the planning of the Mosquée, then, the ICI is being designed in part by local actors: there is no national government involvement, and does not depend on contributions (financial or otherwise) from majority-Muslim states.

The Parisian religious and cultural site is described in its mission statement as a project designed with a resolutely twenty-first-century vision of *laïcité* as *vivre-ensemble,* or respect for the practices of others, including their religious principles:

> The initial objective of the operation is to ameliorate the conditions of the exercise of the Muslim religion in offering its faithful dignified and relatively vast *salles de prière.* Such an initiative is based in the realization that many Parisian Muslims, especially in the 18th *arrondisse-*

> *ment*, are often obliged to practice their religion in difficult conditions, because space is lacking, cramped, or situated in inappropriate places. This desire is inscribed in respect for the principle of *laïcité,* conceived as recognition of all religious sensibilities in accord with the values of the Republic.
>
> The city of Paris wants to create an establishment which will also offer the tools necessary for the knowledge and comprehension of the ensemble of Muslim cultures present in Paris, and more particularly in the Goutte d'Or neighborhood.
>
> It is thus a question not only of ameliorating the conditions for Muslim religious practice, but also of offering all Parisians ways to familiarize themselves or deepen their relation with Islam, its religious content and its diverse cultural expressions, avoiding all oversimplifications and reductionist conceptions. The Institute of Muslim Cultures will thus favor "*vivre-ensemble*" and dialogue between citizens.[21]

This definition of *laïcité* is quite distinct from that of the Mosquée's founders. Unlike early *Islam français,* the Islams of the ICI exist in a secular public sphere that respects all religions in their "original" forms. Yet the ICI faithfully builds on the Mosquée's pedagogic project. Helping all Parisians understand the religious and cultural elements of Islam, according to the ICI's creators, will create better French subjects whose sense of *vivre-ensemble* is a true reflection of the spirit of *laïcité* and republicanism.

The rhetoric surrounding the rationale for the creation of the ICI evokes earlier formulations used to lobby for the Mosquée. Again, the French state (in this case, at the local level) is *giving* Muslims a site that they can use to express their religious beliefs, thereby implicitly defining what kind(s) of Islam and Muslim practices are legitimate and acceptable within the site's walls. Again, the city's administration is convinced that the best way to maintain a peaceful relationship with the many diverse immigrant communities from North and West Africa is through the medium of Islam—in this case, through the construction of the ICI. The language of recognition is highly evocative: although in the case of the ICI, the Muslims who will ostensibly benefit from this site did not sacrifice their lives for France during World War I (as did those who were recognized with the Mosquée de Paris), the project's mission statement is full of the language of recognition of Islam and Muslims.[22] What is being recognized explicitly is the lack of material resources available to practicing Muslims to enable to them to perform their religious obligations. As a more recent brochure distributed at the temporary informational center designed to present the ICI to the public explains, there are simply not enough religious sites to meet Muslim demands. This is especially true in the neighborhood of the Goutte d'Or, the ICI's leadership claims, where "Muslim residents are numerous and the prayer sites crowded. Every Friday, the faithful of Northern Paris crowd around two mosques . . . until they occupy public spaces and pray in the very streets, in terrible conditions. The problems for the neighborhood are clear, as concerns traffic circulation and the neighbors, whether residents or shop owners."[23] This rhetoric marks an important shift from the language of recognition that characterized the creation of the Mosquée and that also played a role in the creation of the ICI: here, the creation of a religious site is both a gesture toward a disadvantaged population and the solution to a larger problem of urban development.

The services the ICI will offer residents and other Parisians, as already mentioned, are centered on three axes: research programs, social and cultural programs, and religious programs. The university center, divided among education, research, and documentation, will offer degrees through a series of conferences and continuing education courses. Although the ICI's planners make clear that it is *not* a theological institute for the training of imams, they suggest that "it could propose [such a program] based in republican and *laïc* values, in addition to an openness to other religions practiced in France."[24] Its essential goal is to bring together different methodological and disciplinary approaches to the study of Islam. The research pole will focus exclusively on the study of Islam in France, especially Paris, which is another reason why its location in the Goutte d'Or is so essential. The documentation center will house the archives of Muslim associations and other sources. The social and cultural programming axis is supposed to be a place for exchanges involving neighborhood residents, Parisians, and local and international artists. It will include exhibits, films, theater productions, and concerts that focus in some way on Islam. Finally, the religious axis will be divided into different spaces: some rooms will be permanently dedicated to religious observance; others will be used for religious purposes on holidays where crowds are to be expected.

The choice to situate the ICI in the Goutte d'Or is as essential to its conception as the Mosquée's location near the Jardin des Plantes was. As the report states,

> The poverty-stricken image often associated [with the Goutte d'Or neighborhood] should not make us forget the constant renewal of its residents, of its traditions of hospitality and tolerance and its highly attractive neighborhood life which enriches the economic and social life of the entire *arrondissement*. The ICI will thus also expose the diversity

> of the religious and cultural practices of the Goutte d'Or on a citywide scale, indeed beyond, by associating its activities with exterior partners (universities, cultural centers and associations).[25]

The reference to the Goutte d'Or as the site of a long history of Muslims in Paris and the coded references to its "authenticity" as a Muslim neighborhood (lower class, traditions of hospitality, vibrant streets) are intended to make clear that the city of Paris' twenty-first-century mosque will be built for Muslims on their own territory, not like the Mosquée de Paris in its inaccessible city center.

The site's location and aesthetic/architectural character are essential to its function. The complex, which will total approximately 4,000 square meters, will be divided into two buildings—one (on rue Polonceau) is 950 square meters, the other (rue Stephenson) is 535 square meters. Its creators argue that the division into two sites, which are not adjacent, will not keep the site from "assuming a total coherence in its cultural programming by optimizing the complementarity" of the spaces.[26] The three poles of activity proposed by the ICI will "be clearly identifiable on the spatial level so as to conserve the technical specificities of each and more importantly to distinguish between the sacred spaces reserved exclusively for Muslims and 'profane' spaces open to all. At the same time, it is important to make the most of the decompartmentalizing of these different activities present in the same institution by supporting their encounters and in building bridges between them."[27]

The longstanding question of which aspects of Muslim experience are secular, and thus public, and which are religious, and thus private, is raised again in this discussion of the division of space at the ICI. Though these sacred and profane spaces will exist in both sites, the Polonceau site will be more "*grand public*" because of its larger size and its closeness to boulevard Barbès, the main artery of the neighborhood. Each site will have a lobby area, an area that can be converted into rooms for religious programming, and spaces dedicated exclusively to religious programs. The Polonceau site also offers a café and spaces for cultural programs as well as the university center. The Stephenson site, on the other hand, will offer visitors a *hammam*. It will be interesting to see who patronizes the ICI's café and *hammam*, which will almost assuredly be more expensive than the many cafés and *hammams* located in the immediate surroundings.

While the description of the programs its founders envision for the ICI in many ways echoes those of the Mosquée de Paris, the architectural vision for the new site marks an important difference:

> The plurality of Muslim cultures must be legible in the building's architectural identity. Far from being an orientalist conception, it will not be conceived as a simple transposition of Islamic architecture (a mosque with its minaret) in a Western context but will be exemplary of an "intercultural" architecture certainly drawing some elements of its construction in the architectural of Muslim (not only Arab) countries, but above all taking into account its insertion in the city of Paris, and more precisely in the renovation of the Goutte d'Or neighborhood. . . . This establishment is not conceived as a foreign cultural center but rather like the architectural transcription of this religious element, an integral part of French culture and identity.[28]

The professed refusal to make ICI into an "orientalist" version of Muslim architecture indicates the desire to mark a strong contrast to the Mosquée de Paris as well as an attempt to dispense with the strong association between "Arab" and "Islam" in France. Yet what this description does call to mind is the never-built mosque of Marseille: André Devin, that site's architect, also rejected orientalist architecture and argued for a modern site that would play an essential role in renovating a dilapidated neighborhood in the center of the city while also making an important gesture to the city's Muslims.[29] As with the Marseille mosque, we need also to consider developments in French architecture when examining the plans for the ICI: the modernism of the 1940s meant that it would have been difficult for Devin to sell, or even to conceive of, a mosque built along the *hispano-mauresque* lines of the Mosquée de Paris. Likewise, twenty-first-century postcolonial and postmodern styles make it impossible to build a pseudo-Moroccan mosque that resembles Paris's first Muslim religious site. While architectural styles change, however, what remains constant is the expression of a particular vision of Islam (in this case, multi-ethnic and French) through the aesthetics deemed appropriate by French government authorities.

From the Mosquée de Paris to the Institut des cultures d'Islam: A Hope for the Future?

The Mosquée's current *recteur* Dalil Boubakeur said in a 2003 interview that "there is no more a French Islam than there is a Patagonian Islam" and that the only possible "hope for the future" was to begin talking about Islam *in* France.[30] He is evasive about what exactly he thinks such an Islam would look like and how it would develop but believes that his institution, along with the CFCM, is implicated in that process. Yet if the history of *Islam français* as embodied in the Mosquée de Paris has shown us anything, it is that a religious system conceived by the state in cooperation with other elite actors and designed to serve as a tool to mediate between them and a subaltern immigrant population is doomed as a spiritual project. In the case of Islam in France, it is also safe to say that while the idea of using religion as a strategy for interactions with "Muslim" populations is still used by Paris City Hall, it has not proven to be especially productive for the state as a political project either. The Mosquée de Paris enjoys little support among the city's mosque-attending Muslims and hangs on to its presidency of the CFCM only because of the council's organizational charter. "Muslim" citizens of France, particularly women, are conscious of the ways their skin color and national origins are conflated with a religious identity to which they may not even ascribe, and some of them refuse to have any relationship with the government other than that of republican individual, not racialized Muslim subject.[31]

Islam français did not remain static from the creation of the Mosquée to the planning for the proposed ICI; it underwent several important shifts, especially in terms of its relationship to changing visions of *laïcité* and the divisions between the public and private worlds of Muslim subjects. In its purest discursive form, *Islam français,* as embodied by the Mosquée, in fact offered the promise of openness to Muslims and the compatibility of Islam and republicanism. In other words, one could perfectly well be both an enlightened, religiously observant Muslim and a modern secular French republican. Yet this vision was immediately undermined by the way Islam was defined in this equation. In the French imagination, Islam's invasive nature and its collapsing of the public and private spheres made it impossible to truly be anything other than Muslim. The state's emphasis on Muslim embodied practices in its social assistance and policing programs in the 1920s laid the groundwork for the characterization of Muslimness as an innate quality. During the Vichy years, the secular and republican content of *Islam français* was evacuated, and the "archaic" aspects of Muslim religious observance were emphasized to an even greater extent. The legacy of this period shaped the kinds of provincial Muslim sites that were built in the immediate postwar period, sites whose Islam was an Islam *in* France that was in no way defined in reference to French principles. During the Algerian War, *Islam français* defined itself as resolutely French in the fierce competition with the French branch of the FLN to gain authority over the metropole's Muslims. Once again, it emphasized Islam's compatibility with secularism and the need for a relationship with the French state. Yet by the 1970s, with waves of colonial immigration beginning to settle in the metropole permanently, the French state introduced a new politics for immigrant workers that effectively separated "Muslim" immigrants from French society.

As I have argued throughout this book, it has sometimes been the identification of secularism as the most French of values that has justified the exclusion of Islam and Muslims from the French republic. In other words, it is because Muslims cannot relegate their religious identities to the realm of the private sphere that they cannot be republican subjects. As political theorist Cécile Laborde explains, French republicanism

> seems to incorporate central liberal intuitions, such as commitment to the impartiality of the state, the universal and egalitarian status of citizenship, the separation between private and public spheres, preference for individual over collective rights, commitment to individual autonomy, and a civic not ethnic mode of national identity. But it also appears communitarian in its advocacy of a strong public identity transcending private preferences and identities, its emphasis on the good of popular self-government, social solidarity, and cultural assimilation, and its commitment to the unitary nation-state as the chief site of citizenship.[32]

It is the latter half of this equation, of course, that has historically made it difficult for individuals with "private" identities that could not or would not be kept private to be considered part of the French nation. Religious identity has been singled out in recent years as the most formidable opposition to integration, far outstripping all other "communitarian" identities as the most problematic. Publicly visible religious affiliation, the headscarf in particular, is seen as a threat to *laïcité,* which has increasingly been argued to be synonymous with republicanism. Like Joan W. Scott, I am troubled by "the elevation of *laïcité* as the unquestioned and immutable truth of French republicanism," which she places in a very particular moment, namely, fears about national unity during the 1980s and 1990s as "communitarian" groups like women, immigrants, homosexuals, and others demanded recognition both legally and socially.[33] In her definition, *laïcité* is in fact a tool for exclusion and a closing of republican openness.

Laïcité continues to be held up as a stumbling block for Muslim entry into full French citizenship and belonging, though some public intellectuals argue that while *laïcité* may have been a problem historically, it no longer is. In an interview published at his request on 14 July 2011, the French national holiday, French historian and demographer Emmanuel Todd forcefully rejected the public recuperation of some of his ideas by National Front candidate Marine Le Pen's presidential campaign. Todd explained that unlike Le Pen and his sympathizers, he believed immigrants, particularly Muslims, were a fundamental part of France's national community. He emphasized his conclusions that demonstrate the "low [levels] of religious practice of French Muslims, which brings them closer to Catholics" in order to "underline the fact that, precisely because they act like Catholics and have become profoundly *laïcisé,* French Muslims are ordinary French people."[34] In other words, for Todd, the problem of national belonging no longer exists "precisely because" the majority of French Muslims have become "Catholic," which is to say, they have abandoned those distinctive religious practices that made it impossible for them to accommodate themselves to French secular society. In seeking to distance himself from the racist, xenophobic and Islamophobic positions adopted by Le Pen and the National Front, Todd perhaps inadvertently echoes the logic of early twentieth-century *islamologues* who debated Muslims' capacity to abandon religious practices in order to become French.

Yet in fact, *laïcité* is not the sole explanation for the Muslim "problem," and it is essential that we begin to move beyond the analytical category of secularism and secularization to think about Islam in France. Debates about Islam's supposed incompatibility with *laïcité* occurred in tandem with a more insidious process through which "Muslim" became a racialized identity over the course of the twentieth century. In this conclusion, I have singled out three recent developments of the turn of the twenty-first century to demonstrate the continued importance this racialized identity plays in contemporary France. The headscarf law was not about religious practice but about the visibility of a racialized religious essence. The CFCM did not represent a "normalization" of Islam within the secular state's framework for managing minority religions but a continued blurring of the religious/cultural boundaries of France's nominally Muslim communities with the support of the French state. The ICI may be located in an immigrant neighborhood and its design may reflect a greater diversity of "Muslim" aesthetics, but it reproduces perfectly all of the tensions between rite and culture, public and private, that characterized the original temple to *Islam français.* I have argued throughout this book that focusing only on secularism as the site of exclusionary practices and attitudes directed at France's Muslim populations ignores the ways in which Islam functioned as a marker of essentialized difference. In other words, Muslims in France could only ever be Muslim not because they refused to accept the relegation of religious practice to their intimate spaces of personal and community life but because their Muslimness was inscribed on their very bodies. The "secularization" of Islam to which the Mosquée de Paris and the ICI hoped to contribute will not erase that distinction.

Notes

Introduction

1. Jacky Durand, "'Parler d'islam radical et montrer des gens en train de faire la prière, c'est dramatique.' Entretien avec Abdelhak Eddouk." *Libération,* 1 November 2005.

2. There has been much important recent work by social scientists on the question of what "French Islam" or "Islam in France" might mean in the late twentieth and early twenty-first centuries. See, for example, Mayanthi Fernando, "Reconfiguring Freedom: Muslim Piety and the Limits of Secular Law and Public Discourse in France," *American Ethnologist* 37, no. 1 (2010): 19–35; and "Exceptional Citizens: Secular Muslim Women and the Politics of Difference in France," *Social Anthropology/Anthropologie Sociale* 17, no. 3 (2009): 379–92; John Bowen, *Can Islam Be French? Pluralism and Pragmatism in a Secularist State* (Princeton: Princeton University Press, 2010); Jocelyne Cesari, *Musulmans et républicains: les jeunes, l'Islam et la France* (Brussels: Editions Complexe, 1998); and Franck Frégosi, *Penser l'islam dans la laïcité* (Paris: Fayard, 2008). This literature analyzes how residents of France (whether citizens or not) who identify themselves as Muslim imagine Islam in France and how they construct themselves and their religious practices. Some work focuses explicitly on struggles to reconcile daily personal practices with French law and society, other research looks at Muslim associations or Muslim institutions designed to interact with the state. My analysis differs from this body of research in that I focus on the attempt of the French state to define a vision of Islam for the metropole. The participation of a transnational Muslim elite in this process, as well as the variety of responses to *Islam français* from members of France's diverse Muslim communities, are certainly essential elements in this book. Nevertheless, it is important to emphasize that the French Islam at the heart of this story is quite distinct from the Islam in France that has been the subject of much recent research.

3. See Joan Wallach Scott, *Only Paradoxes to Offer: French Feminists and the Rights of Man* (Cambridge, MA: Harvard University Press, 1996) and *Parité: Sexual Equality and the Crisis of French Universalism* (Chicago: University of Chicago Press, 2005); and Gary Wilder, *The French Imperial Nation-State: Negritude and Colonial Humanism between the Two World Wars* (Chicago: University of Chicago Press, 2005). See also Elisa Camiscioli, *Reproducing the French Race: Immigration, Intimacy and Embodiment in the Early Twentieth Century* (Durham, NC: Duke University Press, 2009).

4. Wendy Brown, "Tolerance and/or Equality? The 'Jewish Question' and the 'Woman Question.'" *Differences* 152 (2004): 1–31, 12. See also *Regulating Aversion: Tolerance in the Age of Identity and Empire* (Princeton: Princeton University Press, 2008).

5. Brown, "Tolerance and/or Equality?" 13.

6. On the "scientific" elaboration of racial categories in Algeria, see Patricia M. E. Lorcin, *Imperial Identities: Stereotyping, Prejudice, and Race in Colonial Algeria* (London: I. B. Tauris, 1995); and Richard Keller, *Colonial Madness: Psychiatry in French North Africa* (Chicago: University of Chicago Press, 2007).

7. For a discussion of this moment in French racial thinking, see Tzvetan Todorov, *Nous et les autres: La réflexion française sur la diversité humaine* (Paris: Seuil, 1989).

8. Pierre-André Taguieff, "Les métamorphoses idéologiques du racisme et la crise de l'anti-racisme," in *Face au racisme, Tome II: Analyses, hypothèses, perspectives,* ed. Pierre-André Taguieff (Paris: La Découverte, 1991), 35–36.

9. "Traditional" is of course often a synonym for "primitive," and much of the French characterization of popular Islam was done in the language of primitivism.

10. Adam B. Seligman et al., *Ritual and its Consequences: An Essay on the Limits of Sincerity* (Oxford: Oxford University Press, 2008).

11. One example of this would be the fact that meat was not served in public school cafeterias on Fridays in accordance with Catholic religious practice.

12. See, for example, Jacques Le Goff and René Remond, eds., *Histoire de la France religieuse: Tome IV: Société sécularisée et renouveaux religieux* (Paris: Seuil, 1992).

13. See Paula Hyman, *The Jews of Modern France* (Berkeley: University of California Press, 1998); Dominique Jarrassé, *Une histoire des synagogues françaises entre Occident et Orient* (Arles: Actes Sud, 1997); Joëlle Bahloul, *La maison de mémoire: Ethnologie d'une demeure judéo-arabe en Algérie (1937–1961)* (Paris: Métailié, 1992); and Benjamin Stora, *Les trois exils, Juifs d'Algérie* (Paris: Stock, 2006).

14. Steven Kruger, *The Spectral Jew: Conversion and Embodiment in Medieval Europe* (Minneapolis: University of Minnesota Press, 2006), xxi.

15. Ibid., xxiv.

16. Brown, "Tolerance and/or Equality?" 6–7. Anthropologist Kimberly Arkin's work on the racial imaginary of Sephardi Jewish adolescents in contemporary Paris provides a fascinating account of the ways in which the idea of unassimilable Jewishness is articulated by some Jews today. See Arkin, "Rhinestone Aesthetics and Religious Essence: Looking Jewish in Paris," *American Ethnologist* 36, no. 4 (2009): 722–34.

17. For a survey of different theories of the built environment, see Denise L. Lawrence and Setha M. Low, "The Built Environment and the Spatial Form," *Annual Review of Anthropology* 19 (1990): 453–505.

18. Georges and William Marçais, who together studied Muslim law, literature, architecture, and art in Paris, eventually became the director of Institute for Oriental Studies at the University of Algiers and director of the École practique de hautes études, respectively. The Marçais brothers held particular authority in the realm of Muslim, particularly Algerian, architecture.

19. See André Raymond, "Islamic City, Arab City: Orientalist Myths and Recent Views," *British Journal of Middle Eastern Studies* 21, no. 1 (1994): 3–18.

20. See, for example, Janet Abu-Lughod, *Rabat: Urban Apartheid in Morocco* (Princeton: Princeton University Press, 1980); Jean-Louis Cohen, "Architectural

History and the Colonial Question: Casablanca, Algiers, and Beyond," *Architectural History* 49 (2006): 349–68, Gwendolyn Wright, *The Politics of Design in French Colonial Urbanism* (Chicago: University of Chicago Press, 1991); Paul Rabinow, *French Modern: Norms and Forms of the Social Environment* (Cambridge, MA: MIT Press, 1989); and Zeynep Çelik, *Empire, Architecture, and the City: French Ottoman Encounters, 1830–1914* (Seattle: University of Washington Press, 2008).

21. These proponents, for the most part members of colonial lobbying groups, will be discussed in greater detail in chapter 1.

22. The site's original plans were created by Maurice Tranchant de Lunel, the inspector-general of the Beaux-Arts department under Lyautey's government in Morocco. The trio of Mantout, Heubès (who replaced Henri Eustache after his death), and Fournez completed the construction.

23. Maurice Merleau-Ponty, *Phénoménologie de la perception* (Paris: Gallimard, 1945), 271, 230.

24. For an especially clear articulation of the "problem" of Morocco for French colonialism, see David Robinson, *Paths of Accommodation: Muslim Societies and French Colonial Authorities in Senegal and Mauritania, 1880–1920* (Athens: Ohio University Press, 2000), 76.

25. Ibid., 94–95.

26. French West Africa, or Afrique Occidentale Française (AOF), brought together eight of France's African colonies into a federation in 1895. AOF was made up of Mauritania, Senegal, the French Sudan (present-day Mali), Guinea, the Ivory Coast, Niger, Upper Volta (present-day Burkina Faso), and Dahomey (present-day Benin).

27. Tunisia became a French protectorate in 1881, and Morocco followed in 1912. Their status as protectorates rather than colonies meant that their existing governments remained in place and maintained a small measure of autonomy within the French administration.

28. As David Prochaska argues, settlers constitute a "third group" between the temporary residents of the colonies (administrators, soldiers, and so on) and the indigenous peoples. Their presence complicates the colonial situation as they make demands on peoples, places, and resources in the colonies as well as political claims on the state. See *Making Algeria French: Colonialism in Bône, 1870–1920* (Cambridge, U.K.: Cambridge University Press, 1990), 9.

29. Unique among France's colonies, Algeria was divided into three *départements* (Oran, Alger, and Constantine) in 1848, giving it the same legal status as a metropolitan *département.*

30. On the brutality of the conquest of Algeria, see Olivier Le Cour Grandmaison, *Coloniser, exterminer: Sur la guerre et l'état colonial* (Paris: Fayard, 2005). The technique of asphyxiating the populations of entire villages in caves was not only accepted by military leaders, but soldiers were also given instructions on how to do it properly. Assia Djebar's novel *L'amour, la Fantasia* relies in large measure on the images of these "*enfumades*" and links the early violence of the conquest to the brutality of colonial rule.

31. Jacques Frémeaux, "Les ambiguïtés de l'idéologie coloniale," in *Histoire de l'islam et des musulmans en France du Moyen Age à nos jours,* ed. Mohamed Arkoun (Paris: Albin Michel, 2006), 533.

32. In addition to the work of Richard Keller, Gwendolyn Wright, and David Prochaska, see also Michael J. Heffernan, "The Parisian Poor and the Colonization of Algeria under the Second Republic," *French History* 3, no. 4 (1989): 377–403.

33. The French also created a hierarchically organized system of Muslim clergymen for a religion in which such a structure does not exist. The administration authorized the payment of muftis and imams as well as lower-ranking officials such as Quranic teachers. See Charles-Robert Ageron, *Les Algériens musulmans et la France* (Paris: Presses Universitaires de France, 1968), 892.

34. As Todd Shepard points out, the reliance on assimilationist logic in Algeria continued into the 1950s, in spite of the turn to "associationist" models in France's other overseas territories. See *The Invention of Decolonization: The Algerian War and the Remaking of France* (Ithaca: Cornell University Press, 2006), 22–23.

35. It is worth noting that the bey of Tunisia was referred to as "His Highness" and put forth decrees, while the sultan of Morocco was referred to as "His Majesty" and put forth *dahirs,* so as to maintain a more "traditional" character in the protectorate. See Daniel Rivet, *Le Maghreb à l'épreuve de la colonisation* (Paris: Hachette, 2002), 214.

36. After the establishment of the French protectorate in 1912 with the signing of the treaty of Fez, Lyautey became Morocco's first resident-general. His administration of Morocco was interrupted by a short-lived position as minister of war in 1916, but he then returned to Rabat and continued to head the colonial administration until 1925. Before serving as resident-general in Morocco, Lyautey had also held various positions in the colonial administration in Algeria, Indochina, and Madagascar. His interest in promoting France's empire continued after his return to the metropole in 1925, leading him to devote himself to projects such as Paris's Exposition coloniale of 1931.

37. Cited in Charles-Robert Ageron, *France coloniale ou parti colonial?* (Paris: PUF, 1978), 201. For a discussion of the assimilation and association trends in French colonial thought, see Raymond Betts, *Assimilation and Association in French Colonial Theory: 1890–1914* (New York: Columbia University Press, 1961). Betts argues that assimilation held sway in French colonial theory from 1890 until 1914, when new ideologies led to the rejection of assimilation and the move to association. He softens this position by saying the break was never made completely and that there was often a wide gap between theory and practice because the French always had a strong moral leaning toward assimilation. Betts defines assimilation as an ideology growing out of the universalist principles from the Revolution, which acted as the governing principle for much of nineteenth-century French colonialism. The *mission civilisatrice* derives from this source. In the late nineteenth century, however, Betts writes that many forces conspired to convince the French that assimilation was no longer tenable. One influence was the self-comparison with the immensely successful British empire, which had adopted a decentralized administration that could be adapted in different colonies to suit local needs. Scientific ideas about race and Nietszchean ideas about force also led French colonial theorists to conclude that not all races were equal, that peoples should develop on their own trajectories, and that imperialism was the natural result of some of those peoples' need to expand. From these new ideas evolved the policy of associationism, which came to replace assimilationism. Associationism emphasized a varied colonial practice that took local particulars into account when determining policy and left sufficiently developed native institutions intact.

38. On Lyautey's architectural politics in Morocco, see Wright, *Politics of Design*; Rabinow, *French Modern*; and Abu-Lughod, *Rabat.*

39. On the Banania *tirailleur,* see Leora Auslander and Thomas C. Holt, "Sambo in Paris: Race and Racism in the Iconography of the Everyday," in *The Color of Liberty: Histories of Race in France,* ed. Sue Peabody and Tyler Stovall (Durham, NC: Duke University Press, 2003), especially 168–69. See also Pap Ndiaye, *La condition noire: Essai sur une minorité française* (Paris: Calmann-Lévy, 2008).

40. On the *tirailleurs algériens,* see Gilbert Meynier, *L'Algérie révelée. La guerre de 1914–1918 et le premier quart du XXè siècle* (Geneva: Droz, 1981).

41. On the aesthetic fetishization of the "primitive" in Sub-Saharan African culture, see Benoît de l'Estoile, *Le goût des autres: de l'Exposition coloniale aux arts premiers* (Paris: Flammarion, 2007); Herman Lebovics, *True France: The Wars over Cultural Identity, 1900–1945* (Ithaca: Cornell University Press, 1992); James Clifford, *The Predicament of Culture: Twentieth-Century Ethnography, Literature, and Art* (Cambridge, MA: Harvard University Press, 1988); and Patricia Morton, *Hybrid Modernities: Architecture and Representation at the 1931 Colonial Exposition* (Cambridge, MA: MIT Press, 2000).

42. Wilder, *French Imperial Nation-State,* 6.

43. In addition to previously cited texts, see, for example, Tyler Stovall, "The Color Line behind the Lines: Racial Violence in France during the Great War," *American Historical Review* 103, no. 3 (June 1998): 737–69; Richard Fogarty, *Race and War in France: Colonial Subjects in the French Army 1914–1918* (Baltimore: Johns Hopkins University Press, 2008); Elsa Dorlin, *La matrice de la race: Généalogie sexuelle et colonial de la Nation française* (Paris: Découverte, 2006); and Didier Fassin and Éric Fassin, eds., *De la question sociale à la question raciale?* (Paris: Découverte, 2006). See also Emmanuelle Saada, *Les enfants de la colonie: les métis de l'empire français entre sujétion et citoyenneté* (Paris: Découverte, 2007); and Laurent Dubois, *A Colony of Citizens: Revolution and Slave Emancipation in the French Caribbean, 1787–1804* (Chapel Hill: University of North Carolina Press, 2004) for further explorations of race in colonial settings other than North and West Africa.

44. On gender, see Scott, *Only Paradoxes to Offer*; on colonialism and race, see Wilder, *French Imperial Nation-State.*

45. Shepard, *Invention of Decolonization,* 33.

46. See Raberh Achi, "La séparation des Églises et de l'État à l'épreuve de la situation coloniale. Les usages de la dérogation dans l'administration du culte musulman en Algérie (1905–1959)," *Politix* 17, no. 66 (September 2004): 81–106; and James McDougall, "The Secular State's Islamic Empire: Muslim Spaces and Subjects of Jurisdiction in Paris and Algiers, 1905–1957," *Comparative Studies in Society and History* 52, no. 3 (2010): 553–80.

47. Franck Frégosi, in *Penser l'islam dans la laïcité,* attempts to do this. See also Olivier Roy, *La laïcité face à l'islam* (Paris: Stock, 2005).

Chapter 1

1. Paul Bourdarie, "L'Institut musulman et la Mosquée de Paris," *La Revue Indigène* (October–November 1919): 5, emphasis in original.

2. See Pascal Le Pautremat, *La Politique musulmane de la France au XXe siècle: De l'Hexagone aux terres d'Islam, Espoirs, réussites, échecs* (Paris: Maisonneuve and Larose,

2003), 42–43; and Henry Laurens, *Orientales II: La Troisième République et l'Islam* (Paris: CNRS, 2004), 219.

3. It should also be pointed out that Lyautey scorned the CIAM, along with the Sous-Secrétariat d'Etat aux Affaires musulmanes, and angrily informed Paris that "I have only retained my hold on Morocco by my own *politique musulmane*. I am sure mine is the right way and I demand instantly that no one come to mess up my game." Cited in Daniel Rivet, *Lyautey et l'Institution du protectorat français au Maroc 1912–1925 Tome II* (Paris: L'Harmattan, 1988), 122.

4. Henry Laurens, "La Politique Musulmane de la France," in *Orientales II,* 57–60.

5. Louis Massignon, *Situation de l'Islam* (Paris: Geuthner, 1939), 35.

6. In contemplating the creation of the Mosquée, Lyautey invoked his fears that Morocco's "brilliant past" and "former splendor" as a center of Muslim learning could be compromised by attempts to introduce Muslims to French civilization. See Lyautey's letter to the Minister of Foreign Affairs, 24 May 1922, AMAEE Série Afrique 1918–1940/Affaires musulmanes/11.

7. On French fears of Islam as a tool for anticolonial mobilization during the nineteenth and twentieth centuries, see, for example, Julia Clancy-Smith, *Rebel and Saint: Muslim Notables, Populist Protest, Colonial Encounters (Algeria and Tunisia, 1800–1904)* (Berkeley: University of California Press, 1997); George R. Trumbull IV, *An Empire of Facts: Colonial Knowledge, Cultural Power, and Islam (Algeria, 1871–1914)* (Oxford: Oxford University Press, 2009); and Gregory Mann and Baz Lecocq, "Between Empire, *Umma*, and the Muslim Third World: The French Union and African Pilgrims to Mecca, 1946–1958," *Comparative Studies of South Asia, Africa, and the Middle East,* 27, no. 2 (2007): 367–83.

8. The proliferation of university chairs on the Muslim world at the turn of the century, which included the Univeristé de Paris's chair in colonial geography (1893); the Université de Paris's law faculty's chair in Muslim law (1895); and the Collège de France's chair of Muslim sociology (1902), among others, was the result of political pressure and ran counter to the desires of the academic community. The pressure exerted by those interested in France's mission in Morocco was particularly strong and resulted in political/academic partnerships that produced the Mission scientifique au Maroc, the Institut des hautes études marocaines, and the influential *Revue du monde musulman*. See Laurens, "La Politique musulmane," 58.

9. Ibid., 219.

10. Sadek Sellam, *La France et ses musulmans* (Paris: Fayard, 2006), 29.

11. Ibid., 42.

12. "Le régime de l'Algérie au début du XXe siècle," *La Revue des deux mondes,* 1 April 1903. It is interesting to note the move from "Western religions" to "Christianity," thus excluding Judaism from this rapprochement, especially given Judaism's similar ritual practices.

13. Arnold Van Gennep, *En Algérie* (Paris: Mercure de France, 1914), 154. On Van Gennep's Algerian ethnographies, see Emmanuelle Sibeud, "Un ethnographe face à la colonisation: Arnold Van Gennep en Algérie (1911–1912)," *Revue d'Histoire des Sciences Humaines* 10 (2004): 79–103.

14. "Du douar à l'usine: La religion musulmane," *Cahiers Nord-Africains* 11 (1956): 6. *CNA* was the journal produced by Assistance Morale Aux Nord Africains

(AMANA), an association founded after World War II to help immigrants from the Maghreb assimilate to French society.

15. See Tomoko Masuzawa, *The Invention of World Religions* (Chicago: University of Chicago Press, 2005), 197.

16. Edgar Quinet, *Du Génie des religions* (Paris: Charpentier, 1842).

17. See Paul Powers, "Interiors, Intentions, and the 'Spirituality' of Islamic Ritual Practice." *Journal of the American Academy of Religion* 72, no. 2 (June 2004): 425–59.

18. Saba Mahmood, *Politics of Piety: The Islamic Revival and the Feminist Subject* (Princeton: Princeton University Press, 2005), 137.

19. Mohamed Hocine Benkheira, *Islâm et interdits alimentaires: juguler l'animalité* (Paris: PUF, 2000), 29.

20. Robert de Caix, a member of the Parti colonial and later secretary general of the High Commission in Beirut under the French Mandate, wrote in 1900 that a certain measure of "philosophy" was necessary to be able to imagine Algeria as three French *départements* rather than "a piece of that Orient, where race is so tenacious, where traditions are so strongly resistant, that groups of people cohabit almost indefinitely without losing their originality in an alloy that mixes them together." Robert de Caix, *L'Afrique française,* November 1900.

21. Alexis de Tocqueville, "Lettre sur l'Algérie," in *Sur l'Algérie* (Paris: Flammarion, 2003), 57–58. Or, as Thomas-Robert Bugeaud, one of the leaders of the Algerian conquest and then governor-general of Algeria, explained in 1844, "We have made the Algerian tribes feel our force and our power, now we need to make them know our goodness and our justice . . . thus we can hope to first make them accept our domination . . . and, in the long term, for them to identify with us, in such a way as to form one same people under the paternal government of the King of the French." See Maréchal Bugeaud, *Circulaire du Gouverneur Général à MM les officiers généraux et colonels commandant les divisions, subdivisions et cercles, et à MM les officiers chargés des affaires arabes, renfermant des instructions generals sur le gouvernement et l'administration des populations indigenes* (17 September 1844), in *Par l'épée et par la charrue, écrits et discours de Bugeaud* (Paris: PUF, 1948), cited in Jean-Loup Amselle, *Vers un multiculturalisme français: l'empire de la coutume* (Paris: Flammarion, 2001), 94.

22. Louis Massignon, *Opera Minora: Textes recueillis, classés et présentés avec une bibliographie* (Paris: PUF, 1969), 286.

23. Charles-Robert Ageron, *Les Algériens musulmans et la France* (Paris: Presses Universitaires de France, 1968) 906.

24. Clifford Geertz, *Islam Observed* (New Haven: Yale University Press, 1968), 9.

25. Ageron, *Les Algériens musulmans,* 907.

26. Ibid., 908.

27. Edmond Doutté, *Magie et religion dans l'Afrique du Nord* (Paris: Maisonneuve, 1984), 21. Doutté's study was originally published in 1908.

28. Ibid., 15.

29. Geertz, *Islam Observed,* 33. He correctly points out that is difficult to approximate a translation of *Baraka.* See also Jean-Noël Ferré, *La religion de la vie quotidienne chez les marocains musulmans* (Paris: Karthala, 2004).

30. Edmond Doutté, *L'Islam algérien en l'an 1900* (Algiers: Girault, 1900), 40.

31. Alfred Le Châtelier, *L'Islam dans l'Afrique occidentale* (Paris: Steinheil, 1899), 312–13.

32. Christopher Harrison, *France and Islam in West Africa, 1860–1960* (Cambridge, U.K.: Cambridge University Press, 1988), 51.

33. Jean-Louis Triaud, "Politiques musulmanes de la France en Afrique," in *Le choc colonial et l'Islam: les politiques religieuses des puissances coloniales en terres d'Islam,* ed. Jean-Pierre Luizard (Paris: La Découverte, 2006), 274.

34. Hélène Grandhomme, "Connaissance de l'islam et pouvoir colonial: L'exemple de la France au Sénégal, 1936–1957," *French Colonial History* 10 (2009): 171–88.

35. Fanny Colonna, *Les versets de l'invincibilité: Permanence et changements dans l'Algérie contemporaine* (Paris: Presses de Sciences Po, 1995), 332.

36. See, for example, James McDougall, *History and the Culture of Nationalism in Algeria* (Cambridge: Cambridge University Press, 2006) and also his article "The Secular State's Islamic Empire: Muslim Spaces and Subjects of Jurisdiction in Paris and Algiers, 1905–1957," *Comparative Studies in Society and History* 52 no. 3 (2010): 553–80.

37. Colonna, *Les versets de l'invincibilité,* 333, emphasis added.

38. Ali Merad, *Le réformisme musulman en Algérie de 1925 à 1940* (Paris: Mouton, 1967), 33.

39. A *zarda* was "a public distribution of food to the poor, celebrated as a two-day festival of social solidarity and religious community, on a sacred site—the city's cemetery—which symbolically connected the living and the dead of all social ranks in the sharing of bread, meat and the word of God." McDougall, *History and the Culture of Algerian Nationalism,* 130.

40. Ben Badis's letter, from the *Dépêche de Constantine,* dated 10 October 1936, is quoted in McDougall, *History and the Culture of Algerian Nationalism,* 134.

41. *Rissala d'Ibnou Zekri* (Algiers, 1903), 318, translated and reprinted in Kamel Chachoua, *L'islam kabyle: religion, état et société en Algérie* (Paris: Maisonneuve and Larose, 2001), quotation marks in original.

42. McDougall, "Secular State's Islamic Empire," 575.

43. James McDougall provides a helpful discussion of the different interpretations of the Oulféma's significance (primarily in Algerian historiographical debates) in the introduction to his *History and the Culture of Nationalism in Algeria.*

44. Doutté, *L'Islam algérien en l'an 1900,* 11, emphasis added.

45. Ibid.

46. Rapport du Lt-Colonel Justinard sur les travailleurs marocains dans la banlieue parisienne, 26 November 1930, AMAEE K Afrique/Questions générales 1918–1940/Emploi de la main d'oeuvre indigène dans la Métropole 1929–1931.

47. "L'Islam en Afrique noire." *Croissance de l'Eglise* 34 (April 1975): 13. For a discussion of the history of twentieth-century French perceptions of *Islam noir,* as it was known, see Rudolph Ware III's description in "*Njàngaan*: The Daily Regime of Qu'ranic Students in Twentieth-Century Senegal," *International Journal of African Historical Studies* 37, no. 3 (2004): 515–38.

48. In addition to the Four Communes, residents of the "old colonies" of Martinique, Guadeloupe, Guyane, and la Réunion were also made citizens in 1848.

49. See Isabelle Merle, "De la 'légalisation' de la violence en contexte colonial. Le régime de l'indigénat en question." *Politix* 17, no. 66 (2004): 137–62.

50. For a full discussion of Algerian Jewry's path from subject to citizen and the arguments made to distinguish between Jews' and Muslims' worthiness for republican citizenship, see Joshua Schreier, *Arabs of the Jewish Faith: The Civilizing Mission in Colonial Algeria* (New Brunswick, NJ: Rutgers University Press, 2010).

51. The actual text of the law is as follows: "Article I: The Muslim native is French, nevertheless he will continue to be subject to Muslim law. He may be allowed to serve in the army and navy. He can be called to civic posts in Algeria. Upon his demand, he may be allowed to enjoy the rights of French citizenship; in this case, he is subject to French civic law." Should the Muslim Algerian request French citizenship, it could only be conferred by an Imperial Decree made in the Conseil d'Etat. See Mohand Khellil, *L'intégration des Maghrébins en France* (Paris: Presses Universitaires Françaises, 1991), 133–34.

52. See Pascal Le Pautrement, *La Politique musulmane de la France au XXe siècle: De l'Hexagone aux terres d'Islam, Espoirs, réussites, échecs* (Paris: Maisonneuve and Larose, 2003), 231.

53. On the religious dimension of this exclusion, see Paul Silverstein, *Algeria in France: Transpolitics, Race, and Nation* (Bloomington: Indiana University Press, 2004), 51.

54. The conditions of the 1919 law stipulated that only people who met the following conditions could be eligible for consideration for French citizenship: aged twenty-five or higher; monogamous or single; no record of any criminal activity; no hostile acts committed against French sovereignty; no religious or political affiliations that could be a threat to public security; at least two years' residency in the same locale; service in the army with a good disciplinary record; ability to read and write in French; owner of rural or urban property; service in public office; and several others. Even for candidates who met all these conditions, the governor-general could still reject anyone he chose. See Khellil, *L'intégration des Maghrébins en France,* 134.

55. Ageron, *Les Algériens musulmans,* 1218.

56. Ibid., 1220–24.

57. Benjamin Stora, *Histoire de l'Algérie coloniale 1830–1954* (Paris: La Découverte, 2004), 42.

58. Khellil, *L'intégration des Maghrébins en France,* 137.

59. Westernized Moroccan Jews resented the refusal to consider Morocco's Jewish community as French. See Daniel J. Schroeter and Joseph Chetrit, "Emancipation and its Discontents: Jews at the Formative Period of Colonial Rule in Morocco," *Jewish Social Studies: History, Culture, and Society* 13, no. 1 (Fall 2006): 170–206.

60. Khellil, *L'intégration des Maghrébins en France,* 137, Pautrement, *La Politique musulmane de la France au XXe siècle,* 241.

61. Wilder, *French Imperial Nation-State,* 129. In spite of this legislation, the local colonial administration put many restrictions in place that curtailed the rights of those citizens of the communes who were legal French citizens. Such restrictions included stripping them of their rights if they left the communes and making access to French law courts extremely difficult.

62. Conklin, *Mission to Civilize,* 87–97.

63. Wilder, *French Imperial Nation-State,* 130–31.

64. A recent spate of historiography has added to the strong work on citizenship and nationality; it focuses on the panoply of administrative practices put into place in

twentieth-century France to manage foreign and colonial populations. Alexis Spire's sociology of the bureaucrats charged with deciding whether or not to attribute residency and work permits or naturalization from 1945 to 1975 is an important contribution to our understanding of how immigration law functioned and how much of its practice depended on individual agents. Clifford Rosenberg's work on interwar immigration control in Paris sheds light on the way social assistance programs were tied to policing activities, especially in the case of North African immigrants. These recent studies go a long way to uncovering the mechanics and everyday practices of the management of subaltern immigrant populations in France; what I hope to contribute to this discussion is an exploration of how and why Islam was an integral part of this mechanism. See Alexis Spire, *Étrangers à la carte: L'administration de l'immigration en France* (Paris: Grasset, 2005); and Clifford Rosenberg, *Policing Paris: The Origins of Modern Immigration Control between the Wars* (Ithaca: Cornell University Press, 2006). See also Mary D. Lewis, *The Boundaries of the Republic: Migrant Rights and the Limits of Universalism in France, 1918–1940* (Stanford: Stanford University Press, 2007); Patrick Weil, *Qu'est-ce qu'un français: Histoire de la nationalité française depuis la Révolution* (Paris: Grasset, 2002); Rogers Brubaker, *Citizenship and Nationhood in France and Germany* (Cambridge: Harvard University Press, 1992); Laure Blévis, "Sociologie d'un droit colonial. Citoyenneté et nationalité en Algérie (1865–1947): une exception républicaine?" Ph.D. dissertation, Institut d'Études Politiques, d'Aix-en-Provence, 2004; and Amelia Lyons, "Invisible Immigrants: Algerian Families and the French Welfare State in the Era of Decolonization (1947–1974)," Ph.D. dissertation, University of California at Irvine, 2004.

65. Far fewer Moroccans and Tunisians immigrated to France than did Algerians from the beginning of the twentieth-century migration. On the first, smaller, wave of Muslim immigrants at the turn of the nineteenth century, see Ian Coller, *Arab France: Islam and the Making of Modern Europe, 1789–1831* (Berkeley: University of California Press, 2010).

66. By the war's end in 1918, there were approximately thirty thousand Algerians who had come to France independently, and only five thousand who had come via the Ministry of War recruitment program. See Claude Collot, *Les Institutions de l'Algérie durant la période colonial (1830–1962)* (Paris: CNRS, 1987), 203.

67. The Algerians were accompanied by approximately 35,500 Moroccans and 18,300 Tunisians, according to some estimates. See Charles-Robert Ageron, "L'immigration maghrébine en France: Un survol historique," *Vingtième siècle* 7 (July–September 1985): 59–70. There were also 49,000 Indochinese, 37,000 Chinese, and 4,500 Malagasy workers brought to France as part of the SOTC's program. See Gérard Noiriel, *Immigration, antisémitisme et racisme en France (XIXe–XXe siècles): Discours publics, humiliations privées* (Paris: Fayard, 2007), 293.

68. On Algerian immigration statistics, see also Neil MacMaster, *Colonial Migrants and Racism: Algerian Migrants in France, 1900–1962* (London: McMillan, 1997); and Jacques Simon, *L'immigration algérienne en France des origines à l'indépendence* (Paris: Editions Paris-Méditerranée, 2000).

69. At the same time, there were approximately one hundred thousand Moroccan immigrants in France. See Noiriel, *Immigration, antisémitisme et racisme en France,* 313.

70. As Joan Wallach Scott rightly points out, "It is part of the mythology of the specialness and superiority of French republicanism—that same mythology which

paradoxically offers French universalism as different from all others—to insist that laïcité can only be used in its original tongue." See Scott, *Politics of the Veil,* 15.

71. This is relevant for Algeria, though not for Tunisia (which was a protectorate and not a colony) and Morocco (which had not yet come under French power and would eventually become a protectorate rather than a colony).

72. Jean Baubérot, *Vers une nouvelle pacte laïque?* (Paris: Seuil, 1990), 33.

73. Rabbis, unlike Christian clergy, were not recognized and paid until 1831. See Rita Hermon-Belot, "La genèse du système des cultes reconnus: aux origines de la notion française de reconnaissance." *Archives de sciences sociales des religions* 129 (January–March 2005), 25.

74. The Revolutionary and Napoleonic reforms of the legal status of Jews and Judaism, of course, were made against the backdrop of Catholicism. As historian Simon Schwarzfuchs explains, French Jews "doubtless realized quickly that even if their religion was authorized, recognized, and in theory placed on equal footing with the other religions, [they] must have reminded themselves that the Christian religion remained dominant and that even Protestantism didn't enjoy the same benefits as Catholicism. Jews knew that their life was framed resolutely by Christianity, that the seventh day of the week was Sunday and not Saturday, and that holidays were those of the Christian calendar." See *Du juif à l'israélite: Histoire d'une mutation, 1770–1870* (Paris: Fayard, 1989), 281. For members of France's Jewish communities, "*israélite*" provided an alternative to "*juif*" for assimilated bourgeois Jews who sought to distinguish themselves from more recent immigrants from Central and Eastern Europe. See Dominique Schnapper, *Juifs et israeélites* (Paris: Gallimard, 1980), 190.

75. Baubérot, *Vers une nouvelle pacte laïque?* 46.

76. A law of 1942 allowed the *communes* to allocate funding to religious associations that would undertake the renovations of post-1905 religious sites, whether or not the sites were classified as historical monuments.

77. They were not to exceed 1800 francs and could only be maintained for a period of ten years.

78. See Raberh Achi, "La séparation des Eglises et de l'Etat à l'épreuve de la situation coloniale. Les usages de la dérogation dans l'administration du culte musulman en Algérie (1905–1959)." *Politix* 17, no. 66 (September 2004): 81–106.

79. The administration's attempts to control the activities of these "official" Muslim religious leaders were more or less active in different regions and at different moments, but during the 1930s French officials instituted a series of policies designed to curtail the independence of Muslim actors. The *circulaire Michel,* a regulation passed in March 1933, suspended the publication of certain Muslim newspapers, closed some independent Muslim schools, and required that imams be authorized to preach in Mosques.

80. McDougall, "Secular State's Islamic Empire," 553–80, 563–64, 570.

81. See Raberh Achi, "'L'Islam authentique appartient à Dieu, "L'Islam algérien" à César': La mobilisation de l'association des oulémas d'Algérie pour la separation du culte musulman et de l'État (1931–1956)," *Genèses* 69, no. 4 (2007): 49–69.

82. Achi, "La séparation des Eglises et de l'Etat à l'épreuve de la situation coloniale," 1–2.

83. Elisa Camiscioli, *Reproducing the French Race: Immigration, Intimacy, and Embodiment in the Early Twentieth Century* (Durham, NC: Duke University Press, 2009), 15.

84. Marcel Paon, *L'Immigration en France* (Paris: Payot, 1926), 126.

85. See Patrick Weil, *How to Be French: Nationality in the Making since 1789* (Durham, NC: Duke University Press, 2008), especially chapter 3, on naturalization policy and questions of demography from 1889 to 1940. See also Pierre-André Taguieff, "Face à l'immigration: Mixophobie, Xénophobie ou Sélection: Un Débat Français dans l'Entre-Deux-Guerres," *Vingtième Siècle* 47 (July–September 1995): 117.

86. Elisa Camiscioli, "Producing Citizens, Reproducing the 'French Race': Immigration, Demography, and Pronatalism in Early Twentieth-Century France," *Gender and History* 13, no. 3 (November 2001): 605.

87. René Martial, *L'Immigration continental et transcontinentale* (Paris: Baillière, 1933), 29.

88. Ralph Schor, "Le facteur religieux et l'intégration des étrangers en France (1919–1939), *Vingtième Siècle* 7 (July–September 1985): 106–7.

Chapter 2

1. "Une Mosquée à Paris," Ministère des Affaires Etrangères, Direction des Affaires Politiques et commerciales, 22 September 1916, SHAT 7N 2104, Divers 1916–1917. This text, particularly the above citation, is drawn from Paul Bourdarie's "L'Institut Musulman et la Mosquée de Paris," *La Revue Indigène* (October–November 1919).

2. For the most wide-ranging account of the role of colonial soldiers in World War I, see Richard S. Fogarty, *Race and War in France: Colonial Subjects in the French Army, 1914–1918* (Baltimore: Johns Hopkins University Press, 2008). See also Michel Renard, "Gratitude, contrôle, accompagnement: le traitement du religieux Islamique en métropole, 1914–1950," *Cahiers de IHTP* 83 (June 2004): 54–69.

3. Prior to 1914, the French state was not enthusiastic about the use of colonial troops in the event of a war on European soil, yet by 1915, it was clear that more soldiers would be necessary for the war effort. Soldiers were conscripted in Algeria, Senegal, and Tunisia; soldiers from Morocco, Indochina, Madagascar, French Equatorial Africa (AEF), and the Pacific served as volunteers. By the war's end, the colonies had furnished the French war effort with between 535,000 and 607,000 soldiers, which constituted 7% to 8% of all French soldiers mobilized during World War I. Of those soldiers, between 66,000 and 71,000 lost their lives, which was proportionate to the losses experienced by metropolitan soldiers.

4. Most West African mosques bear almost no physical resemblance to the different styles of Mosque architecture found across North Africa. For a contemporary description of West African Muslim religious architecture, see Alfred Le Châtelier, *Islam en Afrique occidentale* (Paris: Steinheil, 1899).

5. Meynier, *L'Algérie révelée,* 416.

6. Tyler Stovall, "The Color Line behind the Lines: Racial Violence in France during the Great War," *American Historical Review* 103, no. 3 (June 1998): 737–69.

7. Meynier, *L'Algérie révelée,* 103.

8. Letter from Ministre des Affaires Etrangères to Ministre de la Guerre, 3 December 1915, SHAT 7N 2104/Politique musulmane 1916.

9. This exchange of letters from December 1915 can be found in SHAT 7N 2104/Politique musulmane 1916.

10. Letter from M. de Saint Aulaire, Délégué à la Résidence Général to the Minister of Foreign Affairs, 7 January 1916, AN Fonds Lyautey 475AP/95: Lettres au département 1916.

11. Compte-rendu de la séance de la CIAM du 17 juin 1920, ANOM AOF 19G20: Affaires musulmanes.

12. Michel Renard has emphasized that the CIAM should not receive credit for an idea that was independently generated by other actors.

13. Bourdarie, "L'Institut Musulman et la Mosquée de Paris," 4.

14. Emir Abdelkader, whose resistance against the French invasion in 1830 lasted fifteen years, is still revered as a nationalist and anticolonialist leader in Algerian historiography.

15. On Herriot's sympathy for the *Jeunes algériens,* see Charles-Robert Ageron, "Enquête sur les origines du nationalisme algérien. L'émir Khaled, petit-fils d'Abd El-Kader, fut-il le premier nationaliste algérien?" *Revue de l'Occident musulman et de la Méditerranée* 2 (1966): 9–49. Shortly after these meetings took place during the war, Emir Khaled's Young Algerian faction would defeat that of Dr. Benthami in the Algiers municipal elections of 1919, arguing against Benthami's platform of gradual assimilation. See James McDougall, *History and the Culture of Nationalism in Algeria* (Cambridge: Cambridge University Press, 2006), 93.

16. Bourdarie, "L'Institut Musulman et la Mosquée de Paris," 6–7.

17. It is interesting to note that in debates over *laïcité,* the question of the Mosquée as a sort of war memorial seems not to have mattered. In Daniel Sherman's discussion of war memorials following World War I, he pays close attention to conflicts over the place of religious symbols in monuments in light of the law of 1905. He writes that although most communes sought consensus between religious and anticlerical residents, some mayors reminded townspeople that monuments could be topped with a cross if they were located in a cemetery rather than in front of city hall. See *The Construction of Memory in Interwar France* (Chicago: University of Chicago Press, 1999), 236–42.

18. "Coup de pioche sur les lois intangibles," *Bulletin religieux du diocèse de Bayonne,* 12 November 1922.

19. Procès-Verbal, "Adoption d'un projet de loi relatif à la construction d'un institut musulman à Paris," Sénat, 31 July 1920.

20. Imprecisely, the senator here voices grudging acceptance of the fact that because there are Muslims in French protectorates, there is no conflict over state funding for mosques. In fact, it was only Algeria that was formally part of the French Republic, and it was there that the law of 1905 was applied only under a full regime of exceptions, which pertained to Islam.

21. *Journal Officiel,* 1 July 1920.

22. When the Société des Habous was first created, it was clear in the minds of Algeria's governor-general Lutaud and Si Kaddour that it would be registered under Muslim law as an Algerian association. See Lutaud to Briand, 8 February 1917, SHAT 7N 2140/Organisation du pèlerinage à la Mecque, 1917.

23. Bourdarie, "L'Institut Musulman et la Mosquée de Paris," 11.

24. The préfet de la Seine asked the minister of foreign affairs to have the Mosquée declared to have "*utilité publique,*" which would allow the city to recuperate some of the 175,000 francs it had also implicitly donated in agreeing to assume the

costs of transferring the land to the Société des Habous. See letter dated 12 December 1921, AMAEE Afrique/Affaires Musulmanes/11.

25. Si Kaddour was wary of opening the field to donations from all over the Muslim world, fearing that this would give the Mosquée a pan-Islamic character that would be dangerous for French authority. It was for this reason primarily that he insisted that the donations come from Muslims in North and West Africa. He also called for donations within France, as Mahieddine Bachetarzi explains: "He developed an intense propaganda [campaign], in which he had me participate by having me sing classical Arab songs on the air at Radio-Paris." See Bachetarzi, *Mémoires 1919–1939* (Algiers: SNED, 1968), 54.

26. This article, entitled "Création à Paris d'un Institut Musulman" and published in the Moroccan newspaper *Es Saada* (1 September 1920) is anonymous, but the accompanying note from the Ministry of Foreign Affairs identifies it as having been written by Si Kaddour himself.

27. Letter from Si Kaddour to Briand, 10 January 1922, AMAEE Afrique 1918–1940/Affaires Musulmanes/11.

28. The letters from the Ministry of Foreign Affairs directed to the North African colonial administrators began by reporting how much the other colonies and protectorates had donated to the Mosquée before asking to be informed of the amount the administrator in question was prepared to set aside. The responses often began in the same vein, thanking the minister for the information about the contributions from other colonies, the resident or governor would offer his own amount. See also a letter from Lyautey to the Minister of Foreign Affairs, 11 January 1921, AMAEE Afrique 1918–1940/Affaires musulmanes/11.

29. Letter from Sarrault, Minister of Colonies, to the Gouverneur Général, AOF, 17 April 1921, ANOM AOF 19G20: Affaires musulmanes.

30. Letter from Gouverneur Général to the Direction des Affaires Politiques et Administratives, 10 May 1921. The total amount he donated was 50,000 francs, to be broken down as follows: Mauritania, 5000; Senegal, 8000; Guinea, 6000; Ivory Coast, 2000; Dahomey, 2000; Sudan, 7000; general budget, 20,000. Negotiations also took place at the level of the individual territories. The lieutenant governor of Mauritania informed the governor of AOF that it would be necessary to be "very prudent" in organizing the collection of donations that were perceived by Mauritanians to be forced contributions to the French treasury (letter dated 26 October 1922).

31. Letter from Lyautey to Minister of Foreign Affairs, 24 May 1922, AMAEE Afrique 1918–1940/Affaires Musulmanes/11.

32. Ibid.

33. Oleg Grabar, "Symbols and Signs in Islamic Architecture," in *Architecture and Community: Building in the Islamic World Today,* ed. Renata Holod (Millerton, NY: Aperture, 1983).

34. See Barbara Daly Metcalf's introduction to her edited volume, *Making Muslim Space in North America and Europe* (Berkeley: University of California Press, 1996).

35. Sherman, *Construction of Memory,* 216.

36. Dominique Jarrassé, *Une histoire des synagogues françaises: Entre Occident et Orient* (Arles: Actes Sud, 1997), 15.

37. Ibid., 16.

38. René Weiss, *Réception à l'Hôtel de Ville de Sa Majesté Moulay Youssuf, Sultan du Maroc, Inauguration de l'Institut Musulman et de la Mosquée de Paris* (Paris: Imprimerie Nationale, 1927), 2, xxv.

39. Ibid., 36. President Doumergue would also celebrate the friendship between "the Muslim elite and the French elite" in his speech. At no point in the creation of the Mosquée were non-elite Muslims on either side of the Mediterranean taken into account, other than that they were solicited for donations. As we will see, this would be one of the reasons the Mosquée was critiqued by nationalist leaders.

40. Si Kaddour's speech at the Mosquée's groundbreaking ceremony, cited in Weiss, *Réception à l'Hôtel de Ville de Sa Majesté Moulay Youssef, Sultan du Maroc, Inauguration de l'Institut Musulman et de la Mosquée de Paris,* 49.

41. Doumergue's speech at the groundbreaking ceremony, cited in ibid., 70.

42. This decision did not go uncontested. Paul Fleurot, who represented the neighborhood of the Jardin des Plantes at the Conseil Municipal de Paris, remarked in his speech at the Mosquée's orientation ceremony that "in ceding the land formerly occupied by the Hôpital de la Pitié, I had to abandon certain projects I had hoped to bring about; but I made this sacrifice gladly, once I realized the grandeur that this project represented and its national importance." Cited in Weiss, *Réception à l'Hôtel de Ville de Sa Majesté Moulay Youssuf, Sultan du Maroc, Inauguration de l'Institut Musulman et de la Mosquée de Paris,* 37. The projects he would have liked to bring to fruition included the use of that land to build low-income housing to deal with the housing crisis in the city. See the Procès-Verbal, 15 July 1921, *Bulletin municipal officiel.*

43. See Pierre Justinard, "La Mosquée de Paris." Mémoire à l'Ecole Nationale de la France d'Outre-Mer, 1944, 25–26.

44. Weiss, *Réception à l'Hôtel de Ville de Sa Majesté Moulay Youssuf, Sultan du Maroc, Inauguration de l'Institut Musulman et de la Mosquée de Paris,* 37; Bourdarie, "L'Institut Musulman et la Mosquée de Paris," 8.

45. Speech given by the préfet de la Seine at the Mosquée's orientation ceremony, cited in Weiss, *Réception à l'Hôtel de Ville de Sa Majesté Moulay Youssuf, Sultan du Maroc, Inauguration de l'Institut Musulman et de la Mosquée de Paris,* 45.

46. Emile Dermengham, "Musulmans de Paris," *La Grande Revue* 799 (December 1934): 15–21.

47. Ibid., 44.

48. Résumé des déclarations des M. Morand, Doyen de la Faculté de Droit d'Alger, 28 October 1919, AMAEE Afrique 1918–1940/Affaires Musulmanes/11.

49. Letter from Saint Aulaire to Ministre des Affaires Etrangères, 7 January 1916, AN Fonds Lyautey 475AP/95/Lettres au département 1916. See also Commissariat Général à l'Information et à la Propagande. "Projet de loi relatif à l'édification à Paris d'un Institut Musulman" (undated), AMAEE Afrique 1918–1940/Affaires musulmanes/11.

50. The Mosquée's original plans were drawn by the former director of the Service, Maurice Tranchant de Lunel, and another member, Maurice Mantout, would be part of the team whose design was ultimately used.

51. Henri Descamps, *L'Architecture moderne au Maroc* (Paris: Librairie de la Construction moderne, 1931), 1.

52. Letter from Si Kaddour to Leygues, 6 October 1920, AMAEE Afrique 1918–1940/Affaires musulmanes/11.

53. Didier Madras and Boris Maslow, *Fès, Capitale artistique de l'Islam* (Casablanca, Morocco: Editions Paul Bory, 1948), 134–35.

54. Letter from Si Kaddour to Leygues, 27 December 1920, AMAEE Afrique 1918–1940/Affaires musulmanes/11. One of the Mosquée's architects, Mantout, would also write to Leygues to tell him that the Mosquée was inspired by "one of the most beautiful specimens of Moroccan architecture." See, in the same box, Maurice Mantout, "Note descriptive de la Mosquée et de ses dépendences," 12 August 1922.

55. Antony Goissaud, "L'Institut musulman et la Mosquée de Paris," *La Construction moderne* 3 (2 November 1924): 50–55, 52.

56. Gwendolyn Wright, *The Politics of Design in French Colonial Urbanism* (Chicago: University of Chicago Press, 1991), 134.

57. As Justinard put it in his thesis on the Mosquée, "Isn't it . . . paradoxical that it's easier for a Christian who wants to see a Muslim religious building to penetrate a mosque in Paris than in North Africa, where most mosques are closed to non-Muslims?" Here an analogy is made between the situation in Morocco (where under Lyautey's protectorate mosques were "protected" from visits by non-Muslims) and that of the rest of the territory. The refusal to allow non-Muslims to enter mosques is not a feature of Islam and was not even applied uniformly in the French empire. However, it is instructive that Justinard made this remark, for many of the tourists who visited the Mosquée may well have been disappointed by their inability to do so in Morocco and hoped to see "the same thing" back home. Justinard, "La Mosquée de Paris," 57.

58. This is the only reference that situates the Mosquée so specifically in Paris's geography.

59. The archival evidence is not clear as to why this was the case. Mantout wrote to the préfet de la Seine requesting permission (which was granted) to construct the entries on rue Geoffroy Saint-Hilaire as they appeared in the drawing in spite of the fact that they were slightly too large for the city's building code. He argued that this was unavoidable to keep with "the general composition" of the site and the other façades. There is little information in the file at the Archives de Paris on the Mosquée's construction, so it is difficult to say why construction of these entries did not proceed as planned. See letter from Mantout to the préfet de la Seine, 24 March 1923, AP VO[11] 1365.

60. Mantout defines these as the "Director" and "Priest," respectively, which do not correspond to the roles played by the men who occupy these two positions. The mufti is responsible for making juridical decisions, and the imam is the person who leads communal prayer. In no way, however, is he equivalent to a Catholic priest, for he does not occupy a hierarchical position of power and does not act as an intermediary between the divine and the believer. The *recteur* of the Mosquée, Si Kaddour, also bore a title that has no equivalent in Islam. It is, however, revealing that the title devised for him by the French proponents of the Mosquée referred to the university system, thus underscoring the intellectual and secular nature of the Institut.

61. It was also mentioned in their verbal descriptions. As one critic wrote, "The place du Puits-de-l'Ermite bordering the rue Quatrefages . . . will allow . . . for a

larger recession, the better to admire the minaret." Goissaud, "L'Institut musulman et la Mosquée de Paris," 52.

62. For example, it is only in Northern Morocco that the square minaret was preponderant. See Boris Maslow, *Les Mosquées de Fès et du Nord du Maroc* (Paris: Les Editions d'Art et d'Histoire, 1937), 3.

63. Maslow explains that Fez's minarets were intentionally constructed with vastly varying dimensions so that from the top of each one the muezzin could see the Quarayin's minaret, which would announce the call to prayer to be taken up by all the other mosques. In Paris, of course, construction of the minaret did not need to take this into account. This small detail is just another indication of the difference between the copy and the Moroccan institution. See Maslow, *Les Mosquées de Fès et du Nord du Maroc,* 4.

64. Although Mantout accords the *salle d'ablution* relatively little importance, it is in fact one of the most important components of a large mosque complex in Moroccan religious architecture. In the biggest ones, the room is actually placed outside the mosque itself, though in most cases it is contained within it (though in those cases it often has its own entrance). The Mosquée's blueprints, on the other hand, featured a small room that was neither separated nor with its own entrance.

65. While care was taken to ensure that the *salle de prières* was oriented towards Mecca, it is interesting to note that only one synagogue in Paris (rue Buffault) is correctly oriented so that the ark is facing towards Jerusalem. Dominique Jarrassé explains that in the capital, the land given by or purchased from the municipality did not usually allow the sites to be constructed with the proper orientation. According to him, rabbis accepted this, recognizing that in contemporary architectural style it was inconceivable that the arch not be placed in the middle of a wall or along the main line of symmetry. Thus rather than the building itself being oriented properly, it was left to the faithful to orient their own bodies eastward. See Jarrassé, *Une histoire des synagogues françaises,* 75.

66. As we will see in the final section, the decision to wear "traditional" North African clothing was one that was associated with members of the Muslim elite. Working-class Muslims, it seems, took pains to dress like their French colleagues.

67. All of these citations are drawn from the "Note descriptive de la Mosquée et de ses dépendances dressée par M. MANTOUT, Architecte de la Société des Habous des Lieux Saints de l'Islam" [undated, but presumably from 1922], AMAEE Afrique 1918–1940/Affaires musulmanes/11.

68. Georges Buchet, "La Mosquée de Paris," *En Terre d'Islam* 34 (January 1930): 28–32, 30.

69. Additional mosaics were required, and Si Kaddour organized for them to be transported from Morocco. In addition, he successfully argued that it was necessary to bring Moroccan artisans to Paris to complete the decoration of the site. See letter from Si Kaddour Ben Ghabrit to Poincaré, 13 March 1923, AMAEE Afrique/Affaires musulmanes/12.

70. *Le Petit Journal,* 25 February 1922.

71. "Un décor d'Orient sous le Ciel de Paris." *L'Illustration* (26 November 1926): 582.

72. Rapport Général [sur l'Exposition Coloniale Internationale et des Pays d'Outre-Mer Paris, 1931] Présenté par le Gouverneur Général Olivier, Rapporteur

Général, T. II: Construction, p. 102, ANOM FM ECI/7/Inauguration et fermeture de l'exposition.

73. Ibid., 127.

74. Bachetarzi, *Mémoires 1919–1939,* 133.

75. Note from 26 June 1930, APP E^b 125/Aït el Kébir.

76. Paul Marty, "Mission d'étudiants marocains, août 1923" and "Voyage en France des Etudiants Marocains 1925," AN Fonds Lyautey 475 AP 171/13: Voyages des Marocains civils en France, juillet 1922.

77. "Séjour du sultan du Maroc" APP Da 457: Fêtes Nationales de 14 juillet 1921–1926/1926.

78. See his chapter on "Consumerism, Spectacle and Leisure," in *Paris: Capital of Modernity* (New York: Routledge, 2003).

79. Bachetarzi, *Mémoires 1919–1939,* 62.

80. *Réception à l'Hôtel de Ville de Paris de Son Altesse Mohamed EL Habib Pacha Bey, Possesseur du Royaume de Tunis, 13 juillet 1923* (Paris: Imprimerie Lapine, 1923).

81. "Note sur la participation de Paris aux manifestations du Centenaire de l'Algérie et sur les dispositions prises par la Commission du centenaire pour assurer cette participation conformément aux déliberations du Conseil Municipal des 11 juillet et 31 décembre 1929, présentée par Pierre GODIN, Conseiller Municipal, Président de la Commission Municipale du Centenaire de l'Algérie." Rapports et documents du Conseil Municipal de Paris, 20 March 1930.

82. Wilder, *French Imperial Nation-State,* 28.

Chapter 3

1. In 1923, the North African population of Paris was somewhere between 10,000 and 20,000 people. By the following year, however, there were slightly more than 50,000 immigrants of North African origin. This number would dip slightly and then rise as high as 60,000 in 1928 and 70,000 in 1930. In the war years and immediately after, this immigration was made up almost entirely of young men working in the Paris region's factories. They lived primarily in the city's peripheral *arrondissements* and the north and northwest suburbs, far from the city center, where the Mosquée was located. For further demographic information, see Stora, *Ils venaient d'Algérie*; and Simon, *L'immigration algérienne en France des origines à l'indépendance.*

2. Mary Dewhurst Lewis has argued convincingly that immigration policies during the interwar years were not always applied in the same ways across metropolitan France, and in fact their application could change drastically depending on when and where they were being applied to whom. She has also emphasized the need to distinguish between the structures designed to track immigrants in the capital and the methods used in provincial cities. Lewis's reminder that French immigration policy was highly contingent is important to bear in mind when examining the histories of "Muslim" immigrants. Yet at the same time, evidence suggests that when it came to programs put in place for colonial subjects from North Africa, practice tended to fol-

low policy more closely than general immigration policies seemed to in Lewis's study. This difference suggests that Islam and Muslim subjects were indeed considered to be a different kind of immigrant than those coming to France under other labor regimes. See Mary Dewhurst Lewis, *The Boundaries of the Republic: Migrant Rights and the Limits of Universalism in France, 1918–1940* (Stanford: Stanford University Press, 2007).

3. Clifford Rosenberg, *Policing Paris: The Origins of Modern Immigration Control between the Wars* (Ithaca: Cornell University Press, 2006), 123.

4. Noiriel, *Le creuset français,* 119–20.

5. Ibid.

6. Ibid., 121.

7. Esther Benbassa, *Histoire des Juifs de France de l'Antiquité à nos jours* (Paris: Seuil, 1997), 231.

8. This was finally rectified by law in 1942. See Le Pautremat, *La Politique musulmane de la France au XXe siècle,* 293.

9. Weil, *Qu'est-ce qu'un français,* 82.

10. Ibid., 86.

11. Ibid., 89.

12. Benbassa, *Histoire des Juifs de France de l'Antiquité à nos jours,* 235–36.

13. On the Kabyle myth, see Patricia Lorcin, *Imperial Identities: Stereotyping, Prejudice, and Race in Colonial Algeria* (London: I. B. Tauris, 1995).

14. Rosenberg, *Policing Paris,* 145.

15. "Note sur le Docteur BEN THAMI, Médecin aide-majeur de 2ème classe de reserve" Ministère de la Guerre, Etat-Majeur de l'Armée, Section d'Afrique, 4 January 1915, SHAT 5 N 132/Documents divers reçus au Cabinet du Ministère de la Guerre, Janvier–Juin 1915.

16. Lettre du Président du Conseil Ministre de la Guerre à M. le Commandant du Dépôt des Travailleurs Coloniaux-Marseille et à Messieurs les Commandements de Groupements de Travailleurs Nord-Africains, 9 June 1918, AMAEE K Afrique 1918–1940/Questions générales/30: Emploi de la main d'oeuvre indigène dans la métropole, juin 1918–1921.

17. French historian Belkacem Recham writes that military cooks who were found to have distributed food containing pork to Muslim soldiers were punished by their commanding officers. The army went so far as to publish and distribute an Algerian cookbook to chefs assigned to North African companies. See Recham, "Les musulmans dans l'armée française, 1900–1945," in *Histoire de l'Islam et les Musulmans en France*, ed. Mohamed Arkoun (Paris: Albin Michel, 2006) 758.

18. These guidelines were cited in *Les Amitiés musulmanes* 2 (15 January 1916) and are cited in Michel Renard, "Gratitude, contrôle, accompagnement: le traitement de religion islamique en métropole, 1914–1950." *Cahiers de l'IHTP* (June 2004): 54–69.

19. Captain Sylvain Halff, "Jewish Participation in the Great War." *American Jewish Yearbook* 21 (1919–1920): 94.

20. See "Soldats," *Les Archives israélites,* 25 March 1915; and "Nos illustrations," *Univers israélite,* 4 April 1916.

21. P. Haguenauer, "Lettre d'un aumônier," *Archives israélites,* 19 October 1916. I am grateful to Ethan Katz for providing me with the above references to Jewish religious practices in the French army during World War I.

22. Gilbert Meynier, *L'Algérie révélée. La guerre de 1914–1918 et le premier quart du XXè siècle* (Geneva: Droz, 1981), 455.

23. Ibid.

24. Ibid., 102.

25. In 1920, the Minister of the Interior wrote to the Minister of Foreign Affairs about the "interest there is in assisting the numerous North African *indigènes* still living in Paris and in the Département de la Seine, many of whom served as soldiers or workers during the war. To this effect, an Iman [*sic*] has been designated to:

1. Visit *indigènes* in civil and military hospitals.
2. Preside over burials, according to Muslim rites, for those who have just died.
3. Make contact with the many *indigènes* who desire his services."

The minister notes that because most of these men are Algerians, the gouverneur général of Algeria has agreed to take charge of paying the imam's 600-franc monthly salary. He adds that since this salary would be insufficient for all the traveling the imam would be required to do, and since Moroccans and Tunisians would also benefit from his services, the Résidences générales of the two protectorates should each contribute 150 francs a month for his travels, which subsequent letters reveal they agreed to do. Letter from Minister of the Interior to Minister of Foreign Affairs, 2 November 1920, AMAEE Afrique 1918–1920/Affaires Musulmanes/11.

26. See Benjamin Stora, "Locate, Isolate, Place under Surveillance: Algerian Migration to France in the 1930s," in *Franco-Arab Encounters: Studies in Memory of David C. Gordon,* ed. L. Carl Brown and Matthew S. Gordon (Beirut: American University of Beirut, 1996).

27. See Rosenberg, *Policing Paris,* 155–57. He also points out that in spite of Godin's desire to forge a team of former colonial officials with expertise in the management of North African Muslims, the council member's criteria were met by few of Rue Lecomte's officers, including the requirement that at least 40% of the force speak Arabic and Kabyle.

28. "Proposition tendant à créer à la Préfecture de Police une section d'affaires indigènes nord-africaines qui s'occupera de la situation matérielle et morale et de la police des indigènes nord-africains, résidant ou de passage à Paris. Déposée par MM. Pierre GODIN, BESOMBES, et Emile MASSARD, Conseillers Municipaux," Proposition no. 178, 20 December 1923. *Conseil Municipal de Paris, Rapports et Documents* 1923, Nos. 151–91.

29. The proposal to establish a hotel for North African workers in Gennevilliers in 1924, for example, met with violent objection from neighborhood residents. As the Comité de Défense explained in one of their posters:

> The inhabitants of the Neighborhood of Grésillons (Asnières and Gennevilliers) protest to the Public Authorities against the installation of a camp for Algerians and Moroccan in the heart of the area . . . opposite a clinic, a nursery and the Departmental Medical Office, and situated in the midst of the Grésillons market.
>
> Considering that the installation of a Colony of Africans is contrary to our habits, to our security, and to our morality, as well as a danger

> to PUBLIC HEALTH, and constitutes a very clear depreciation of our City, we demand the installation of these camps outside all agglomerations.

The Communist Party of Asnières-Gennevilliers responded to the Comité's protest with a poster of their own:

> Behind the hypocritical pretext of "morality," a local battle has just begun for the expulsion of North Africans.
>
> Certain Bourgeois are beginning to worry about those whom they consider slaves. They fear a devaluation of their property and want to chase out the Moroccans and Algerians who are, however, men like any others.
>
> During the war, they were side by side with French workers in the trenches, and we made them countless promises in return for their lives. What happened to the Bourgeois' promises? . . .
>
> The North Africans did not ask to come to France. It was the French Capitalists who stole their land and ripped them away from their country, where they were happy before the advent of European "civilization." . . .

Both posters are located in ANOM FM 81 F 1030.

30. "Proposition tendant à créer à la Préfecture de Police une section d'affaires indigènes nord-africaines qui s'occupera de la situation matérielle et morale et de la police des indigènes nord-africains, résidant ou de passage à Paris. Déposée par MM. Pierre GODIN, BESOMBES, et Emile MASSARD, Conseillers Municipaux," Proposition no. 178, 20 December 1923. *Conseil Municipal de Paris, Rapports et Documents* 1923, Nos. 151–91.

31. Rue Lecomte's staff had a reputation as not only incompetent but also corrupt. Made up of retired police officers, "native" informants, the force did not conform to the stipulation that at least two out of every five officers should speak either Arabic or Kabyle. See Rosenberg, *Policing Paris,* 158.

32. Lieutenant-Colonel Justinard, Rapport sur sa mission en France, November 1930, AMAEE K Afrique/Questions Générales 1918–1940/32: Emploi de la main d'oeuvre indigène dans la Métropole, 1926–1928.

33. See Max Hulman, "L'Hôpital Franco-Musulman de Paris et du département de la Seine," *La Presse Médicale* 74 (14 September 1935): 1443–45.

34. Justinard, "Rapport." Medical professionals also supported the establishment of segregated North African workers' hostels as a means to fight against the slum-living and alcoholism of "*déracinés.*" See Hulman, "L'Hôpital Franco-Musulman de Paris et du département de la Seine."

35. Rosenberg, *Policing Paris,* 171.

36. Justinard, "Rapport."

37. Josiane Chevillard-Vabre comments on this close relationship. She claims that "the many soirées organized at the Mosquée were much sought-after. They provided a meeting ground for members of the municipal, prefectoral and military administrations. Many of *tout Paris'* personalities made appearances. The Director of the Hospital and its doctors were courteously invited to these receptions. Si Kad-

dour Ben Ghabrit was interested in the Hôpital Franco-Musulman and talked it up to Moulay Youssuf." See her thesis, "Histoire de l'Hôpital Franco-Musulman," MD Dissertation, Faculté de Médecine Saint-Antoine Paris, 1982.

38. Clifford Rosenberg argues that all of the medical and funeral services created for North Africans in Paris were largely the work of Godin. His Algerian career started in 1896 when he served as a clerk for the General Government; he was later promoted to a role in the police force. See Rosenberg, *Policing Paris,* 641.

39. Rapport de la CIAM, séance du 10 février 1927. ANOM 81F 834.

40. In fact, the question of how and where to bury Muslims had been raised almost a full decade earlier. In 1923, plans to build a small Muslim corner in Père Lachaise, including a room for the ritual preparation for burial, was abandoned "considering that a great mosque [was] currently in construction in the Jardin des Plantes neighborhood." The proposed construction in Paris's eastern cemetery was to have been financed by Algeria, Morocco, Tunisia, and AOF's annual budgets. See the exchange of letters between the minister of foreign affairs and the minister of the interior, 18 December 1923, ANOM FM 81F 834.

41. The law of 14 November 1881 formally put an end to article 15 of the Décret of 23 prairial an XII in which all religious communities in a given commune had the right to have separate cemeteries.

42. This letter, dated 9 December 1930, is cited by M. Augustin Bernard at the CIAM's meeting on 27 February 1931. See Procès-Verbal de la CIAM, 27 February 1931, Question 2: Demande de création d'un cimetière pour les Musulmans de Paris et de la région parisienne. ANOM FM 81F 834: Cimetières musulmans.

43. Letter from Préfet de la Seine to the minister of the interior in response to Si Kaddour's letter. Cited in the PV de la CIAM, 27 February 1931.

44. Article I of the text of the décret (23 February 1937) allowing the creation of this cemetery reads as follows: "May be buried in the cemetery created in execution [of this décret], other than those persons who died in the Hôpital Franco-Musulman de Paris et du département de la Seine, those whose burial will be specially authorized by the Préfet de la Seine on the proposition of the Director of the above-mentioned hospital or the director of the Institut Musulman and Mosquée de Paris." Article II assigns the responsibility for executing the décret to the Minister of the Interior.

45. Letter from Henri Gaillard to Aristide Briand, 21 March 1927. ANOM 81F 834.

46. According to a journalist's account of the ceremony, Si Kaddour presided over the ceremony with the assistance of the Mosquée's secretary general, Robert Reynaud. The official guests included Godin, "who is interested in all Muslim programs," Paul Fleurot, whose point of view on the Mosquée's placement in the fifth *arrondissement* has been discussed; Gérolami of the Bureau de la rue Lecomte; and several female nurses from rue Lecomte's dispensary. The afternoon's activities included a tour of "the operating room and the sterilizing room," both of which were "perfectly organized" and concluded with a "glass of mint tea at Si Brahim's *café maure.*" "A l'Institut musulman," *Les Annales coloniales,* 10 January 1928.

47. For a discussion of the peripheral placement of this hospital, see Neil MacMaster, "Imperial Façades: Muslim Institutions and Propaganda in Interwar Paris," in *Promoting the Colonial Idea: Propaganda and Visions of Empire in France,* ed. Tony Chafer and Amanda Sackur (New York: Palgrave, 2002).

48. It was only in 1941 that the system of public hospitals was opened to the general public.

49. For example, in 1925, foreigners made up 10% of Paris' population but only 8% of its hospitalized patients in the month of December. See Rosenberg, *Policing Paris,* 172–75.

50. Max Hulman, "L'Hôpital Franco-Musulman de Paris et du département de la Seine," *La Presse Médicale* 74 (14 September 1935): 1443–45.

51. "L'Hôpital Franco-Musulman," *Revue Médico-Sociale* 4 (April 1935): 134–35.

52. Hulman, "L'Hôpital Franco-Musulman de Paris et du département de la Seine," 1444.

53. Statuts de l'hôpital franco-musulman. Conseil général de la Seine, 9 July 1930.

54. The hospital's policy of enforcing the observance of the Ramadan fast is actually counter to Muslim practice. As in Judaism, religious fasting is proscribed when someone is ill; the patient is not only excused from the fast but also required to eat to aid recovery. This is merely another example of French policy makers' overemphasis on religious practices that concern the Muslim body.

55. Speech given by Augustin Beaud, Président du Conseil Général de la Seine.

56. See "L'Action charitable de la Ville de Paris et du Département de la Seine," *Le Plus Grand Paris* 1 (February 1938).

57. See Rosenberg, *Policing Paris,* 661–62. He writes that the bulk of the hospital's patients arrived in police vans, after having sought treatment at other Paris hospitals and having been "invited" by the police to go instead to Bobigny.

58. Rapport, Commission d'études du Haut Comité Méditerranéen, 16 June 1937.

59. Conseil Général de la Seine, JO 1938.

60. Bourdarie, "L'Institut musulman et la Mosquée de Paris," 7.

61. It is interesting to note that Dalil Boubakeur declared in 1999 that "today the Mosquée de Paris jealously preserves the symbolism of its creation. A Temple of Memory, a Monument to the Dead, it preaches, as its glorious founders decided, an Islam of Tolerance, Peace and above all indestructible Friendship with France in inscribing on a daily basis its message for the defense of the republican values of civicism and the recall of the glorious hours of France as an overseas Muslim power." Dalil Boubakeur, "Les valeurs d'un symbôle," *As-Salam* 7 (March 1999): 3–8, 8. Thus Boubakeur characterizes the institution first and foremost as a war memorial rather than as a living center for daily religious practices, as did its proponents in 1916. He also echoes the description of an Islam whose principles are fundamentally linked with French republicanism.

62. "Rapport du Lieutenant-Colonel Justinard, Chef de la Section sociologique de la Direction Générale des Affaires Indigènes, sur sa mission en France," 23 October 1930, AMAEE Afrique/Questions générales 1918–1949/33: Emploi de la main d'oeuvre indigène dans la métropole. Justinard notes that this report was prepared with the cooperation of the Quai d'Orsay, the 2ème bureau de l'Etat-Major de l'Armée, the Section d'Afrique of the Ministry of War, the Moroccan Office of Paris, and the Service de la rue Lecomte. The report was prepared for the Moroccan Direction Générale des Affaires Indigènes, but copies were sent to the interested parties at the Quai d'Orsay.

63. The Souss region is in southern Morocco, it comprises the area around Agadir. Many Soussis emigrated either to the north of Morocco or to France looking for work during this period.

64. The qualification of these organizations as "spontaneous" and "curious" (note that the networks of mutual aid were also described as "spontaneous") probably says more about either Justinard's inability to correctly interpret the way Moroccans organized these meetings or his informants' refusal to explain to him how they worked.

65. The *zaouïa* so derided by Justinard seems to have been taken seriously by the police, whose notes on the confrèries of the Paris region contend that there are "three Algerian and Moroccan *confréries* . . . their members' activities are purely religious. The oldest appears to be the *confrérie* known as Alaouite, whose members, who number 100, venerate Cheikh ben Aliaoua, deceased. It is led by a certain Djafrani Hassen, the brother of the Cheikh of the Confrérie of Algeria. The Moroccans in Gennevilliers have a fairly important *confrérie* under the patronage of Si Ahmed Tidjani. In the same area there is another *confrérie* which venerates Sidi Amara Boussena. It has forty members, mostly Algerians." *Groupements politiques musulmans: leur rôle et celui des Partis de la région parisienne dans l'Afrique du Nord,* 2 February 1937. APP H[a] 25: Activités des Nord-Africains à Paris 1937–1956.

66. See Soheib Bencheikh, *Marianne et le Prophète: L'Islam dans la France laïque* (Paris: Grasset, 1998); and Charles-Robert Ageron, *Les Algériens musulmans et la France, 1871–1919* (Paris: PUF, 1968).

67. Letter from Préfet de la Seine to Ministre des Affaires Etrangères, 13 October 1926, AMAEE K Afrique/Questions Générales 1918–1940/32: Emploi de la main d'oeuvre indigène dans la Métropole, 1926–1928.

68. Rapport du Lt-Colonel Justinard sur les travailleurs marocains dans la banlieue parisienne, 26 November 1930, AMAEE K Afrique/Questions Générales 1918–1940/Emploi de la main d'oeuvre indigène dans la Métropole 1929–1931.

69. "Note au Sujet de tournées de Ziaras faites par des Chefs indigènes en France pendant l'année 1938 par Lt. Huot," 10 October 1938, AMAEE Afrique/Questions Générales 1918–1940/36: Emploi de la main d'oeuvre indigène dans la Métropole.

70. The speech by Shaykh Faudel al-Wartilani is cited in McDougall, "Secular State's Islamic Empire," 575.

71. Bachetarzi, *Mémoires 1919–1939,* 54, 104.

72. Ibid., 84–85.

73. Ibid., 88.

74. Ibid.

75. A critique of one of El Moutribia's concerts in a hall owned by *Le Petit Journal* (in August 1934) by a French observer is very revealing of French impressions of Algerian culture and the Algerians who consume it:

> All the Arabs of the capital and suburbs, from Gobelins to Billancourt, went up to rue Cadet to applaud their compatriots. Scheduled for 8:30, the first of these "artistic" representations did not start until half past nine. For a longtime, a horrible concert of strident whistles and shoes stamped in cadence

> scandalized the ushers. This anger turned spontaneously into enthusiasm as soon as the velvet curtain finally consented to open. Then all the *sidis* [a racist term for North Africans] in caps, all the Algerians . . . in aggressive ties, all the enormous women who still had a semblance of beauty hidden by the fat from abusing bonbons and pastries . . . all began to undulate in their chairs to the accents of the guitars and violins (article by George Stuart in *Vendémiaire*, quoted in Bachetarzi 202).

The offensive nature of this description (which goes on to describe the music in equally unpleasant terms) confirms the impression that many French had of North Africans as vulgar, bestial, and uncivilized.

76. Georges Buchet, "Les Musulmans en France, Enquête. Gennevilliers: La Cité Arabe," *En Terre d'Islam* 33 (December 1929): 336–48, 347. Although it is beyond the scope of this book, it is interesting to note that this priest, like his colleagues, wished that Paris' North African immigrant community would make more use of the Mosquée and/or go back to their religious practices: this was seen as the best defense against the politicization of Paris' Muslim proletariat.

77. "Note au sujet de l'Aïd el Kébir 1934," 27 March 1934, AMAEE K Afrique/Questions générales 1918–1940/34: Emploi de la main d'oeuvre indigène dans la métropole, 1932–34.

78. As we shall see, the official implantation of "Islam" in factories in and around Paris began in the 1970s. In the case of the Renault factory in particular, the *salle de prière* in Sector 74 opened during Ramadan in 1976. This is not to say, however, that Islam was entirely absent from the factory in earlier decades. For example, an imam was brought to pronounce the prayer over the dead after an accident killed an Algerian worker in 1933. It also seems that the canteen offered alternatives for Muslims observing dietary laws for many years before the opening of the *salle de prières*. See Jacques Barou, Moustapha Diop, and Subhi Toma, "Des Musulmans dans l'Usine," In *Ouvriers spécialisés à Billancourt: Les derniers témoins,* ed. Renaud Sainsaulieu and Ahsène Zehraoui (Paris: L'Harmattan, 1995).

79. Ibid. Mouloud is the celebration of the Prophet's birthday. It is interesting to note the language in which this "wish" is formulated: the official refers to factories employing "North African" workers and then suggests that they give their "Muslim" workers time off. Did he intend to imply that not all North African workers identified themselves as Muslim, or were "North African" and "Muslim" equal and interchangeable for him?

80. Ibid.

81. Paul Quatre, "L'Orient à Paris: Ce matin gala d'allégresse et de deuil à la Mosquée: On y célèbre 'l'Aïd-el-Seghir' et les obsèques de l'ancien Shah de Perse," *Paris Soir,* 3 March 1930.

82. Ibid.

83. "Les Musulmans en France: Nanterre, Puteaux." *En Terre d'Islam* 34 (January 1930): 22–27. The term "Apache" here refers to groups of young men and women in Belle Époque Paris's working-class neighborhoods, whose particular style of dress and behavior marked them as a distinct social group. See Michelle Perrot, "Les 'Apaches', premières bandes de jeunes." *Les marginaux et les exclus dans l'histoire, Cahiers Jussieu* 5 (1979).

84. Letter from Si Kaddour to M. Doynel de Saint Quentin, Sous-Director de l'Afrique et du Levant, Ministère des Affaires Etrangères. 28 February 1935, APP E[b] 125.

85. For example, Belkacem Radef, an important nationalist figure, and Mohamed Bansak were arrested before they were able to enter the Mosquée on 17 January 1934 on Aïd el Séghir and taken directly to the police station. The police report on the incident notes that unfortunately, in spite of their rapid response the two were still able to sell about forty copies of their journal *El Ouma* and possibly spread their propaganda among their "comrades." Note du 18 janvier 1934, APP B[a] 2170.

86. As Messali Hadj explained in his memoirs, the ENA was unusual compared to other Algerian nationalist groups, for none of its leaders were religious leaders or notables. Before the ENA, he writes, "There had never existed, neither in France nor in Algeria, an organization like ours. . . . Our compatriots were very pleased, but also a bit wary because we were not well known. At home, none of us were municipal council members or *caïds*, not even monitors in the native schools. Between us and the Emir Khaled, for example, the difference was night and day. My comrades worked in factories and myself, I was a salesclerk in a clothing store." Renaud de Rochebrune, ed., *Les mémoires de Messali Hadj 1898–1938* (Paris: Editions J.-C. Lattès, 1982), 151. Unlike the Ouléma, the ENA sought independence from France rather than sharing the Ouléma's interwar position demanding that Algeria be fully integrated into France and that Algerians be represented in French parliament (as enunciated at the Algerian Muslim Congress held in Paris on 18 July 1936).

87. Messali Hadj believed that "there [was] something remarkable, if not divine [in the coincidence]. . . . It was as if the ENA had been created to take up the combat of Emir Abdelkader and Emir Abdelkrim." Ibid., 153. The Rif War (1920–1926) was a struggle between Moroccan Berbers (led by Abdelkrim) and Spanish authorities seeking to expand beyond the territory granted Spain in the Treaty of Fez in 1912. French forces joined the Spanish side in 1925, and the combined European armies defeated Abdelkrim's attempt to create a Rif republic independent of both Spain and Morocco.

88. The ENA's first meeting and Abdelkrim's last battle both took place on 26 June 1926, and the Mosquée was inaugurated less than a month later, on 16 July.

89. Cited in Pascal Blanchard et al., *Le Paris arabe* (Paris: La Découverte, 2003), 132. In his memoirs, Messali Hadj wonders "[how] exactly can they build a mosque in Paris while at the same time sending North African soldiers to Syria to fight their brothers?" *Les memoires de Messali Hadj 1898–1936,* 159.

90. "Elle est bénie!" *El Amel* 14 (June 1933): 3.

91. Rosenberg, *Policing Paris,* 198.

Chapter 4

1. Eric Jennings has argued that Pétain's fetishization of "authenticity," "tradition," and "folklore" led colonial administrations in Madagascar, Guadeloupe, and Indochina to blend Vichy ideology with "native" practices and to valorize indigenous activities that promoted traditional hierarchies and a respect for the past. Although Jennings's study does not address the question of Islam in the North African colonies, nor in the metropole, the Pétainist celebration of "tradition" in certain

colonial contexts seems to have been replicated in the management of metropolitan Islam. See Eric Jennings, *Vichy in the Tropics: Pétain's National Revolution in Madagascar, Guadaloupe and Indochina, 1940–1944* (Stanford: Stanford University Press, 2001).

2. For a discussion of Jews and Muslims in Vichy France, see Ethan Katz, "Secular French Nationhood and its Discontents: Jews, Muslims, and Public Religion and Ethnicity in Occupied France." Unpublished paper.

3. "Note au sujet des Fêtes de l'Aïd es Séghir," 18 August 1947, ANOM 81F/833.

4. Jacques Cantier, *L'Algérie sous le régime de Vichy* (Paris: Odile Jacob, 2002), 257.

5. Jacques Berque, "La Société musulmane algérienne en 1945," 29 June 1945. AN F^{1a} 3293, VI-B: Algérie.

6. Ferhat Abbas, among others, was inspired by the language of the Atlantic Charter and its condemnation of governments imposed by force. See Samya El Machat, *Les États-Unis et l'Algérie: De la méconnaissance à la reconnaissance. 1945–1962* (Paris: L'Harmattan, 1996).

7. Note relative à l'emploi d'aumôniers musulmans auprès des unités indigènes Nord-Africains. Prepared by Le Colonel Sous-Chef de l'Etat-Major de l'Armée, 30 October 1939, ANOM ALG/GGA 8 CAB 19.

8. The law of 8 July 1880 governed the military chaplaincy and guaranteed that soldiers at any kind of army encampment would benefit from ministers of the Catholic, Protestant, and Jewish religions. This legislation came out of the Concordat period and thus did not make provisions for Muslim chaplains. The law of 1905 did not apply to army chaplains, since soldiers were not free to perform their religious duties elsewhere (the same logic applied to continued state funding for chaplains in prisons and other closed spaces). The Catholic, Protestant, and Jewish head chaplains were named by the minister of war and had authority over all of their respective chaplains. Certain of these religious figures had full-time contracts with the army, others worked part-time, and still others were volunteers and had no formal contract at all. During World War II, however, they were provided with uniforms, unlike the imams, even though most of them did not have a formal military rank. It was only in 2005 that the Ministry of Defense began to prepare the ground for the creation of a Muslim head chaplain: in June 2006 Abdelkader Arbi became France's first Muslim head chaplain in the history of the French army.

9. See "Décret portant création d'un Service d'Assistance religieuse pour les militaires musulmans," 14 May 1940.

10. Note pour M. le Directeur du Cabinet de M. le Gouverneur Général, 25 October 1938, ANOM ALG/GGA 8 CAB 19.

11. Letter from Si Kaddour to Gouverneur Général, 7 October 1938, ANOM ALG/GGA 8 CAB 19.

12. Extensive investigations were conducted to ascertain whether a given imam or mufti could truly be relied upon to be loyal to the administrations paying his salary. These investigations took on added urgency when a Muslim religious figure was suspected of nationalist sympathies. Even when intelligence services did not formally intervene, Si Kaddour brought problematic cases to the attention of the administration in Algiers or the Ministry of the Interior. For example, he requested that Saadi ben Mohammed Zerrouki, the imam of the cimetière musulman de Bobigny and

the Mosquée's muezzin, be asked to return to Algeria as quickly as possible, where "it would be easier to monitor his activities" than it was proving to be in occupied Paris. He accused Zerrouki of trading in tombstones and requiring payments for the recitation of prayers, though it seems that Si Kaddour's real objections were based in Zerrouki's support for the ENA and other groups which "present danger to French sovereignty in North Africa." See letter from Vichy's Office Administratif du Gouvernement Général de l'Algérie to the Gouverneur Général, 6 October 1942, ANOM ALG/GGA 8 CAB 19.

13. Renseignement: Les Nord-Africains à Paris, 21 May 1941, ANOM ALG/GGA 8 CAB 19.

14. A note prepared for the Sous-Direction de l'Algérie of the Ministère de l'Intérieur explained the complicated arrangements that had been made for the payment of imams in the metropole during the course of World War II: this note makes clear that "the Sous-Direction de l'Algérie was never responsible for the payment of Muslim *agents du culte* in the Metropole (it had no budget to do so)" except for certain moments of crisis due to the war in which the Ministère de l'Intérieur paid certain salaries with a special account set up by the Algerian administration. From 1941 to 1942, the Governor General paid the Mosquée's imam's salary by mandate since the Mosquée did not have the money in its budget. In 1943, another special account was set up to pay the salaries of two imams in Marseille and Bordeaux who were dispatched by the Mosquée. During 1944 and 1945, the Algerian administration continued to pay the salaries of the Mosquée's official imams in Paris, Marseille, and Bordeaux, as well as agreeing to provide an additional subvention to allow for the staffing of additional provincial Muslim religious sites. The note specifies that all the *agents du culte* in the metropole were to be selected by the Mosquée's leadership with the approval of the Ministère de l'Intérieur. See "Note pour M. le Directeur," Sous-Direction de l'Algérie, January 1946. ANOM 81F 832.

15. As we have already seen, this "exceptional" measure in fact defined the legal administration of Islam in Algeria after the passage of the law of 1905.

16. Governor-General of Algeria to the Minister of the Interior, Sous-Direction de l'Algérie. 23 April 1945, ANOM 81F 832.

17. Letter from Ministre de l'Intérieur to Gouverneur Général d'Algérie, 26 September 1945, ANOM 81F 832.

18. Letter from Gouverneur Général d'Algérie to Ministre de l'Intérieur, 17 October 1945, ANOM 81F 832.

19. Letter from Si Kaddour to the Chief of Social Services of the Moroccan Office, 26 May 1948, AMAEE Afrique-Levant/Levant 1944–1952/Questions Islamo-Arabes, Généralités 1944–1952/47.

20. Letter from the Ministre de l'Intérieur to the Ministre des Affaires Etrangères, 1 December 1945, ANOM 81F 832. The Ministry of Foreign Affairs was responsible for coordinating Morocco and Tunisia's contributions as they were protectorates and not colonies.

21. The Secours National was placed under Pétain's command by the law of 4 October 1940. This "state within a state" was supposed to have a monopoly over all humanitarian and charitable works in France, making it illegal for private organizations to solicit donations. The Secours National was thus solely responsible for allotting funds to different charitable projects, whose requests were not always

granted. The agency's main focus was programs that provided food and clothing. See Jean-Pierre Le Crom, "De la philanthropie à l'action humanitaire," in *La Protection sociale sous le régime de Vichy,* ed. Jean-Philippe Hesse and Jean-Pierre Le Crom (Rennes, France: Presses Universitaires de Rennes, 2001).

22. See Si Kaddour's defensive "Note sur l'activité de l'Institut Musulman et de la Mosquée de Paris pendant la période d'occupation, Juin 1940 à Août 1944" [undated, probably 1944], AMAEE Afrique-Levant/Levant 1944–1952/Questions Islamo-Arabes, Généralités 1944–1954/47. The Letter from the Chef du SAINA to the Préfet de Police, 13 December 1941, is found in APP E^b 125/Aïd El Khébir.

23. The myriad coping strategies devised by devastated populations to deal with wartime and postwar food shortages make clear the extent to which questions of daily food intake defined everyday life in this period. See, for example, Lynne Taylor, "The Black Market in Occupied France, 1940–1944," *Contemporary European History* 6, no. 2 (July 1997): 153–76, and *Between Resistance and Collaboration: Popular Protest in Northern France, 1940–1945* (New York: St. Martin's Press, 2000).

24. Letter from Si Kaddour to the Secrétaire d'Etat au Ravitaillement, 13 December 1941, APP E^b 125/Aïd El Khébir.

25. The Muslim journalists of *Er Rachid* were notoriously opposed to Si Kaddour and the Mosquée because of their rapport with the French state. Nevertheless, their accusations of shady practices by the Mosquée's leadership were often echoed by other critics and sometimes even acknowledged by French officials. This particular accusation is found in a news brief in issue 5, 20 May 1943. The author wrote, "The Quran forbids Muslims to absorb pig flesh, especially in a mosque. But in Paris, under the beautiful Ile-de-France sky, the verse which discusses this is filed in the accessory drawer, since this question is treated 'liberally.'"

26. The emphasis on providing "traditional" foods spanned this entire period, in both its non-*laïc* and *laïc* years.

27. Note, 11 October 1942, APP E^b 125/Aïd El Khébir.

28. Note, 17 December 1942, APP E^b 125/Aïd El Khébir.

29. Note, 1 October 1943, APP E^b 125/Aïd El Khébir.

30. Note, 7 December 1943, APP E^b 125/Aïd El Khébir.

31. Letter from Sous-Direction de l'Algérie, Ministère de l'Intérieur to the Préfet de Police, 10 August 1945, APP E^b 125/Aïd El Khébir.

32. Letter from the Directeur de la Police Economique to the Préfet de Police, 13 November 1945, APP E^b 125/Aïd El Khébir.

33. See the Ministry of the Interior's Algerian Affairs' notes on these celebrations: 18 August 1947 and 15 October 1948, ANOM 81F 833. The ceremonial visits by French officials took place either during the afternoon, several hours after the religious ceremony and lunch had concluded, or the following day.

34. Note au sujet de la fête de l'Aïd el Kébir à Paris, 23 April 1952, ANOM 81F 833.

35. Note au sujet de la fête de l'Aïd el Kébir à la Mosquée de Paris et Note au sujet de la Réception à l'Institut Musulman de Paris à l'occasion de la fête de l'Aïd el Kébir, 23 September 1950, ANOM 81F 833.

36. Denise de Fontfreyde, "L'Aïd el Kébir." *Er Rachid* 1 (January 1943). This article is remarkable not only for what it tells us about the perceptions of French observers of Muslim religious ritual, but because it is one of the very few sources

from this period produced by a woman. De Fontfreyde explicitly mentions the gender dimensions of religious observance at the Mosquée when she writes that "the women, pitilessly set apart from their very entrance, are grouped in a small gallery from which they are only authorized to leave for the distribution of pastries, when the ceremony at the Mosquée is over. They will see, however, from their glass prison, all the French and Muslim personalities." However, whatever the basis for her feminist critique of women's place in Islam, she still seemed to be swept away by the pageantry she witnessed at the Mosquée.

37. André Levant, "L'Aïd el Kébir," *Er Rachid* 19 (20 December 1943): 7.

38. E.M., "Notre Aïd el Kébir et l'autre," *Er Rachid* 19 (20 December 1943): 8.

39. Letter from the Minister of the Interior to the Secrétaire Général de Ravitaillement, 6 August 1947, ANOM 81F 833. The minister's use of the word *tradition* to describe the state's policy of providing food for the holidays is suggestive, almost as though this act was part of the religious ritual itself.

40. In August 1947, this organization received: 3,400 kg of couscous, 400 kg of dry vegetables, 650 kg of sugar, 80 kg of tea, 160 kg of coffee, 80 kg of butter, and 60 l of oil, which were to be distributed to poor Muslim families in the Paris region. This letter from the Ministry of Foreign Affairs to the Ministry of the Interior explains neither the state's nor this particular agency's definition of "poor," so the socioeconomic position of the families who would ultimately receive these goods is unclear. 22 August 1947, ANOM 81F 833.

41. Letter from Monscouri, Okkaki, Ouarara, Belkacem, and Djafrani to the Directeur du Service de Ravitaillement, 28 July 1947, ANOM 81F 833. Their request was taken very seriously by the Service because cafe and restaurant owners were often social, political, and economic leaders in North African neighborhoods with "a real influence" over their fellow immigrants. See "Note sur Ravitaillement en couscous des restauranteurs Algériens de Paris," 31 July 1947, ANOM 81F 833.

42. M.E., "Couscous, barbaque et tripaille." *Er Rachid* 4 (5 May 1943): 6.

43. Letter from J. Bourgeois, Chef du BSNA St Etienne to Ministre du Travail, 29 August 1946, ANOM 81F/833/Fêtes musulmanes.

44. One of the commission's members, Colonel Messal, "deplored that the Commission's work be limited to the Paris region for holiday celebrations," a sentiment that was apparently shared by his fellow members, as the "entire Commission voiced the wish that in 1948 they have the means to extend their work to benefit all the Muslims who have come to France." This task would be difficult, they admitted, given the large numbers of North African workers in the metropole. See the Séance du 6 October 1947, ANOM 81F 833.

45. This man, Roger Valroff, also happened to be the son of the Secrétaire Général of the Mosquée de Paris.

46. The holiday packages (families received 150 g couscous, 70 g sugar, 10 g coffee, and 25 g dried beans; *foyers* received 150 g couscous, 25 g sugar, 100 g meat, 10 g coffee, 10 g oil, 10 g butter, and 25 g dried beans; and patients in hospitals received a 3-kg package containing jam, sugar, dates, sardines, tomato paste, and tobacco) were distributed to families in Paris and Nanterre, Colombes, and Argenteuil; to the Mosquée and the Hôpital Franco-Musulman; to prisoners; and to SAINA centers.

47. The German officers' desire to take photos of "this beautiful Mosque" were thwarted by Si Kaddour, however, who refused permission on the grounds that "at

the Mosquée de Paris we don't engage in politics or propaganda." See Si Kaddour's "Note sur l'activité de l'Institut Musulman et de la Mosquée de Paris pendant la période d'occupation, Juin 1940 à Août 1944," AMAEE Afrique-Levant/Levant 1944–1952/AMAEE Afrique-Levant/Levant 1944–1952/Questions Islamo-Arabes, Généralités 1944–1954/47. Of course, Si Kaddour had no objections to the Mosquée or himself appearing in propaganda films made by the French government before and after the Vichy years.

48. Only non-Muslim visitors were charged admission fees.

49. See Si Kaddour's reports on the budgets of 1939, 1944, and 1945. AMAEE Afrique-Levant/Levant 1944–1952/Questions Islamo-Arabes, Généralités 1944–1954/47. A Pakistani visitor to the Mosquée in 1952 wrote for a British newspaper that "I purchased some picture postcards from [a man in the Mosquée] and made a bargain. He said if I did not ask for a receipt he would charge me less. I agreed. Later, I came to know that the mosque has a *hammam,* a restaurant, some shops, a cafe where North African Andulus music may be heard." See Ahmed Hasan, "The Paris Mosque," *Dawn,* 23 March 1952. Hasan's comments are suggestive not only because of the hint that the amounts listed in the budget for revenues from postcards may not have reflected actual sales but also because he only came to learn *after* his visit to the complex that it also contained all the auxiliary services. This suggests two intriguing possibilities: that the restaurant and *hammam* had really fallen into disuse (other than the occasional use of the restaurant for receptions during holidays) and were thus not highlighted by the Mosquée's paid tour guides, or else these same guides were directed to take visitors only to the purely religious areas of the Mosquée complex and did not include the other sites on the tour. Though it is entirely possible and likely that the tour has changed, as of the summer of 2005, the Mosquée tour takes the visitor through the gardens, the patio in front of the *salle de prière* (visitors can look into the room but not enter), and the library. It does not include the shop, the *hammam,* or the café, nor does the guide make reference to them. Regardless of the official tours provided by the guides, however, that Hasan was completely unaware of the Mosquée complex's other offerings, in addition to his anecdote about him asking passersby to direct him to the Mosquée and no one being able to provide him with directions, suggests that these sites were not as successful as tourist attractions as the metropolitan and colonial administrations may have liked.

50. Charles-Edmond Sée, "Les bains-douches: Bains-douches de la Ville de Paris, rue Lacépède." *La Construction moderne* 44 (29 July 1934): 818–28.

51. Jean Arroy Thialat, director, *A l'ombre de la Mosquée.* Paris: Force et voix de France, producer, 1946.

52. For information on Vichy-era propaganda, see Pascal Blanchard and Gilles Boëtsch, "La France de Pétain et l'Afrique: Images et propagandes coloniales," *Canadian Journal of African Studies* 28, no. 1 (1994): 1–31; and Brett Bowles, "Newsreels, Ideology, and Public Opinion under Vichy: The Case of *La France en Marche.*" *French Historical Studies* 27, no. 2 (Spring 2004): 419–63.

53. Si Kaddour, in explaining the Mosquée's financial problems in 1948 to the minister of foreign affairs, wrote explicitly that "if this Institution is open to Muslims from all over the world, we must not forget that it was for the Muslims of North Africa that the French government gave its financial and moral support to the creation of this Foundation." See his "Note pour Bidault expliquant les difficultés financières

de la Mosquée," 14 June 1948, AMAEE Afrique-Levant/Levant 1944–1952/Questions Islamo-Arabes, Généralités 1944–1954/47. On the other hand, when asking the minister for overseas France for financial support, he wrote that one of the founding members of the Société des Habous was Si Abdelhamid Abdou Kan of Dakar and that "AOF has always been part of the foundation of the Institut Musulman and Mosquée de Paris." See his letter to the Minister, 5 October 1949, ANOM FM 1 affpol/2258/2.

54. "Note au sujet du scénario "A l'ombre de la Mosquée," 3 September 1946, AMAEE Afrique-Levant/Levant 1944–1952/Questions Islamo-Arabes, Généralités 1944–1954/47.

55. Letter from the Minister of Foreign Affairs to Minister of France Outre-Mer, 7 October 1949, AMAEE Afrique-Levant/Levant 1944–1952/Questions Islamo-Arabes, Généralités 1944–1954/47. The High Commissioner of AOF eventually agreed to an annual subvention of 300,000 francs, which the Minister of France Outre-Mer said was in proportion to the contributions of the North African territories. The latter also pointed out to his ministerial colleague that "in fact AOF is not a uniquely Muslim territory, and the number of its Muslim citizens in France is rather limited." See letter from Minister of Overseas France to Minister of Foreign Affairs, 26 January 1950 [which can be found in the same dossier].

56. A *mahakma* is a Muslim law tribunal.

57. Letter from Scelles to Minister of Foreign Affairs, 17 March 1951, AMAEE Afrique-Levant/Levant 1944–1952/Questions Islamo-Arabes, Généralités 1944–1954/47.

58. The Judiciary Committee also added that the *mahakma* would have to take into account the different rites followed by Muslims living in France: most Algerians followed the Malekite rite, though the other Orthodox rites were within the French Empire, especially Hanefite. See Commission d'Etudes de l'Union française, Comité Juridique, "Note sur la création d'une Mahakma à Paris," 31 March 1949, ANOM FM 1affpol/2258/2.

59. There were also, of course, countless requests that the government fund the construction of a mosque or *salle de prière* that did not receive favorable responses. Sometimes Muslim delegations approached the local MONA offices to present their plans to build a religious site and ask for financial support. One example is the city of Alès, whose Comité musulman asked the head of Alès's MONA office to inform Si Kaddour and the Ministry of the Interior that they had found an empty one-bedroom apartment that had formerly been used as a shop, measuring 2m50x4 and 3m50x4. It was owned by a miner named Mohamed Boumerzoug, "a Marabout of the Alaouite sect," who used it "for his religious exercises and those of some of his *confrérie*'s members." Boumerzoug was prepared to rent his space to the Comité musulman to make an "official *salle de prière*" for 400 francs a month. The committee members wanted to know if the Mosquée would be responsible for appointing and paying an imam, and whether the Ministry of the Interior would provide them with a subvention to transform the space into their vision of a *salle de prière*. Unfortunately, the archives do not tell us whether the Comité musulman received the financial support they sought or not. See letter from Chef du Bureau de la MONA à Alès to Si Kaddour, 15 February 1945, ANOM 81F/832.

60. Jarrassé, *Une histoire des synagogues françaises,* 286–88.

61. Ibid., 290–91.

62. Ibid., 296–99.

63. Letter from Sous-Directeur de l'Algérie to Si Kaddour, 6 August 1943, ANOM 81F 832.

64. Letter from the Préfet de la Loire to Ministre de l'Intérieur, 23 January 1945, ANOM 81F 832.

65. Rapport sur l'Inauguration du Cimetière Musulman et de la Kouba à Marseille, 21 November 1945, ANOM 81F 834. A different document says that this incident took place between a Jewish funeral procession and the Muslims lined up in prayer.

66. Note autour du Cimetière Musulman de St Pierre, 23 July 1945, ANOM 81F 834. For a discussion of contemporary French Muslim burial practices, see Yassine Chaïb, *L'émigré et la mort: La mort musulmane en France* (Paris: Edisud, 2000). Chaïb explains that while there is no religious obligation to be buried in Muslim territory, the act of repatriating the body of the deceased to North Africa holds great symbolic meaning for members of France's immigrant communities.

67. Rapport sur l'Inauguration.

68. Letter from Chérif Si Madani El Mekki to Gouverneur Général, 4 December 1941, ANOM ALG/GGA 8 CAB 19.

69. Ibid.

70. Letter from the Gouverneur Général to the Mayor of Nice, undated, ANOM ALG/GGA 8 CAB 19.

71. Note pour M. le Secrétaire Général du Gouvernement, 8 January 1942, ANOM ALG/GGA 8 CAB 19.

72. Letter from J. B. Jondet, Fatimi Laraki, Mohamed Bey Khalil et al. to Maire de Vichy, September 1947, ANOM 81F 832. It is interesting to note that the first signatory to this letter is the director of one of Vichy's hotels, which lends credence to the idea that as in Nice, Vichy's mosque was envisioned by local politicians and businessmen as a potential tourist site.

73. "Note pour M. le Directeur des Affaires Générales, Eréction d'une mosquée à Vichy" [undated, probably November 1947], ANOM 81F 832.

74. Si Kaddour would later write to the Ministry of the Interior that he had never opposed the project to build a mosque in Vichy. As he explained it, "some twenty years ago" a Tunisian who was being treated at Vichy began promoting the idea and wrote a letter on Mosquée letterhead that Si Kaddour leaves one to understand was used when he raised funds among Muslims in France and North Africa. When he was asked, Si Kaddour denied any connection between the Mosquée and this project, but "never manifested the desire to be hostile to the construction of a mosque in Vichy. On the contrary, I think a religious center in Vichy, city of waters visited by many Muslims annually, would produce an excellent effect in North African and Oriental Islam." Letter from Si Kaddour to Ministre de l'Intérieur, 2 December 1947, ANOM 81F 832.

75. Letter from Ministre de l'Intérieur to the Préfet de l'Allier, 16 January 1948 (?), ANOM 81F 832.

76. In fact, Marseille's Muslim associations and Mayor Gaudin announced on 7 July 2006, that construction for the city's mosque would begin in 2007 or 2008, only seventy years after the initial plans were created. The mosque will be built on the old abat-

toirs in the 15th *arrondissement* on 11,150 square meters of land donated by the *mairie.* The mosque's construction will cost 6 million euros and will be financed by private donations, though the Muslim associations have been charged with restricting foreign donations to protect the site from external interference. See "Après des années de tergiversations, Marseille aura sa grande mosquée," *Le Monde,* 7 July 2007.

77. See Michel Renard, "Les débuts de la présence musulmane en France et son encadrement," in *L'Islam et les musulmans en France,* 732–34.

78. Letter from the Préfet Régional de Marseille to the Gouverneur Général, 26 February 1942, ANOM ALG/GGA 8 CAB 19.

79. Extrait des registres des déliberation de la Délégation Municipale, Séance du 19 décembre 1944. Urbanisme: Construction d'une mosquée à Marseille, AMAEE Afrique-Levant/Généralités 1944–1952/48.

80. Ibid.

81. Ibid.

82. André Devin, "Mosquée de Marseille, Avant-Projet. Description Sommaire," [undated, but from 1942], AMAEE Afrique-Levant/Généralités 1944–1952/48, emphasis added.

83. Si Kaddour, "Note sur la Mosquée et l'Institut Musulman," 14 June 1948, AMAEE Afrique-Levant/Levant 1944–1952/Questions Islamo-Arabes, Généralités, 1944–1952/47.

84. "Réunion à Rabat de la Société des Habous des Lieux Saints de l'Islam les 26 et 27 Janvier 1946," AMAEE Afrique-Levant/Levant 1944–1952/Questions Islamo-Arabes, Généralités, 1944–1952/47.

85. This phrase is taken from a letter from Maurice Papon, then minister of the interior, to the minister for foreign affairs, 1 December 1945, ANOM 81F 832.

86. M.E., "Couscous, barbaque et tripaille." *Er Rachid* 4 (5 May 1943): 6.

87. Note au sujet de la fête de Moulay Yacoub à Gennevilliers (Seine), 11 August 1952, ANOM 81F 833.

88. Note, 5 October 1943, APP E[b] 125/Aïd El Khébir.

89. Invitation, Association Marocaine de Bienfaisance, 17 July 1950, ANOM 81F 833.

90. Note au sujet de la soirée artistique organisée le 30 juin à 21h30 à la Grange-aux-Belles, à l'occasion du 27ème jour du Ramadan, 26 June 1951, ANOM 81F 833.

91. Letter from the Gouverneur Général to the Minister of the Interior, 6 December 1949, AN 5046.

92. "Situation des Musulmans dans la Département de la Seine," 17 August 1948, APP H[a] 7/Etudes générales sur la présence des Nord-Africains en Métropole (1938–1957).

93. Colonel Frandon, Section Afrique de l'Etat-Major, Général de la Défense Nationale to Gouverneur Général de l'Algérie and Résident Général du Maroc, "Aperçu sur la situation des Nord-Africains de la Région Parisienne," 2 September 1945, ANOM ALG/GGA 10 CAB/221/Musulmans de France.

94. On the population increase, see Jacques Simon, *L'immigration algérienne en France. Des origins à l'indépendance* (Paris: Paris-Méditerannée, 2000).

95. "Repartition des Musulmans Nord-Africains dans le département de la Seine," 17 November 1949; "La population Nord-Africaine de Paris et du Départe-

ment de la Seine," 1952, APP H[a] 7/Etudes générales sur la présence des Nord-Africains en Métropole (1938–1957).

96. This reference is taken from a 1953 headline: Madeleine Chapsal, "Les Algériens à Paris: Dans leur fief de la Goutte d'Or, ils se taisent quand on cherche leur parler politique," *L'Express,* 18 October 1953.

97. The reference to the "physiognomy" of a given neighborhood is taken from a police report on the Goutte d'Or and Chappelle neighborhoods, Roger Guenne, Commissaire de Police des Quartiers de la Chapelle et de la Goutte d'Or, "Physionomie des quartiers de la Chapelle et de la Goutte d'Or en 1954," APP H[a] 8/Immigration nord africaine en métropole. A detailed historical sociology of the neighborhood shows that the 18th *arrondissement* has the second largest population of immigrants in Paris from 1911 to 1921 and that the working-class nature of the district and the constant new waves of immigration made for an "easy penetration" of foreign populations and "favorized spatial 'absorption.'" Goutte d'Or, in particular, was made up of Swiss, Belgians, Italians, Spanish, Russians, Romanians, and Poles in addition to Algerians, who, in 1926, made up 11% of the population. That 11% was divided almost equally across three streets, meaning that the entire Algerian population, though it was overall in the minority, might have appeared to dominate the rue de la Charbonnière, the rue de la Goutte d'Or, and the rue de Chartres. See Jean-Claude Toubon and Khelifa Messamah, *Centralité Immigrée: Le quartier de la Goutte d'Or, Dynamiques d'un espace pluri-ethnique: succession, compétition, cohabitation* (Paris: L'Harmattan, 1990), 126–48.

98. Préfecture de Police, Service des Renseignements Généraux, Services des Jeux, "Rapport au sujet des cantines algériennes à Paris et banlieue," 6 April 1918, APP B[a] 2247/Ouvriers étrangers en France.

99. "Structures de la Migration algérienne" [undated, early 1950s], APP H[a] 8/ Immigration nord africaine en métropole.

100. Colette Pétonnet, *Espaces habitées: Ethnologie des banlieues* (Paris: Editions Galilée, 1982), 20.

101. See Robert Badinter, *Un antisémitisme ordinaire: Vichy et les avocats juifs (1940–1944)* (Paris: Fayard, 1997), 41.

102. See Leora Auslander, "Coming Home? Jews in Postwar Paris," *Journal of Contemporary History* 40 (2005): 237–59.

Chapter 5

1. Letter from Minister of the Interior to the Préfet de Police, "Achat de débits de boissons, de restaurants, d'hôtels et de meublés par des français-musulmans," 20 September 1957, APP H[a] 15/Commerçants nord-africains, dispositions générales (1952–1962).

2. On the mechanisms of these distinctions, see Shepard, *Invention of Decolonization.*

3. For an overview of the War of Algerian Independence, see Sylvie Thénault, *Histoire de la guerre d'indépendence algérienne* (Paris: Flammarion, 2005). On the FLN in particular, see Gilbert Meynier, *Histoire intérieure du FLN, 1954–1962* (Paris: Fayard, 2002).

4. James McDougall, "S'écrire un destin: l'Association des 'ulama dans la revolution algérienne," in *Institut d'histoire du temps present, Bulletin 83 (Repression, contrôle et encadrement dans le monde colonial au XXe siècle).*

5. The split between the "centrists" in the MTLD who wanted to join the CRUA and the "Messalistes" who wanted to maintain an independent nationalist movement was held by many to be responsible for the organization's failure to provide a viable alternative to the FLN. FLN sympathizers condemned the MNA more harshly for "forcing" the FLN into a "fratricidal war" and proving to French authorities that continued repression in Algeria was necessary to avoid a civil war. For an example of this attitude, see Ali Haroun's memoir of his role in the FFFLN, *La 7e Wilaya: La guerre du FLN en France 1954–1962* (Paris: Seuil, 1986), 252–53.

6. The FFFLN published a scathing critique of the MNA in the form of a small brochure in 1959, entitled "From Counter-Revolution to Collaboration, or the Treason of the Messalistes." In the short introduction to the collection of reprinted communiqués exposing the faults of the MNA and Messali Hadj in particular, the editors wrote the following:

> How an adventurous movement which brought together demagogues with deeply primitive politics could slide bit by bit into counter-revolution, then into hidden collaboration which was finally overt, with the worst French colonialists, that is the evolution which is shown in these pages, written while we watched Algerian patriots fall under the blows of treason.
>
> Hundreds of Algerians killed and thousands wounded testify against Messali and his friends who never hesitated to use the worst methods. The machine-gunnings of Algerian cafés in France aren't even justified by the alibi of fighting a political adversary. It is terrorism in its purest state, since there is no designated victim.
>
> But on whom are the Messalist killers firing? On any Algeria who doesn't adore the "Bearded Mage," who doesn't bow down before "Rasputin," as he is called by the FLN militants in France (3).

According to the FLN, the MNA's "treason" was expressed as the Messalistes' desire to "sit at the negotiating table [with] prefabricated representatives of the occupation army" and to paint the FLN as authoritarian and totalitarian. See *De la contre-révolution à la collaboration, ou la trahison des Messalistes. Études et documents édités par le Front de Libération Nationale (Fédération de France),* Paris, 1959.

7. Cited in Ruedy, *Modern Algeria,* 159.

8. Kateb Yacine, *Le Polygone étoilé* (Paris: Seuil, 1966), 143.

9. Paul A. Silverstein, *Algeria in France: Transpolitics, Race, and Nation* (Bloomington: Indiana University Press, 2004), 69–70.

10. This particular formulation is taken from an official letter from the FLN to the chief rabbi of Algiers, October 1956. Cited in Benjamin Stora, *Les Trois exils: Juifs d'Algérie* (Paris: Stock, 2006), 142.

11. Ibid.

12. See Guy Pervillé, "The Frenchification of Algerian Intellectuals," in *Franco-Arab Encounters: Studies in Memory of David C. Gordon,* ed. L. Carl Brown and Matthew S. Gordon (Beirut: American University of Beirut, 1996), 433.

13. See Seddak Sellam, *La France et ses musulmans: Un siècle de politique musulman, 1895–2005* (Paris: Fayard, 2006), 172.

14. Frémeaux, "Les ambiguïtés de l'idéologie coloniale," in *Histoire de l'islam et des musulmans en France du Moyen Age à nos jours,* ed. Mohamed Arkoun (Paris: Albin Michel, 2006), 533.

15. James McDougall locates the crucial turning point when the Ouléma rallied to the side of the FLN in 1956 at its annual Congress. For a detailed discussion of this, see "S'écrire un destin: L'Association des 'ulama dans la revolution algérienne."

16. See Mounira M. Charrad, *States and Women's Rights: The Making of Postcolonial Tunisia, Algeria, and Morocco* (Berkeley: University of California Press, 2001), 174.

17. The title of the FLN's journal, *El Moudjahid* ("The Warrior") comes from the same root as *jihad,* with its strong religious connotations. According to Monique Gadant's analysis of the place of Islam in FLN discourse as seen in its newspaper, other potential names for the paper included *L'Algérien* and *El Moukafih,* the latter of which also means "warrior" but without the religious connotation. FLN leadership chose the Islamically inflected title in spite of the potential for misunderstanding the revolution's goals. See Monique Gadant, *Islam et nationalisme en Algérie* (Paris: L'Harmattan, 1988), 22–23.

18. Matthew Connelly, *A Diplomatic Revolution: Algeria's Fight for Independence and the Origins of the Post-Cold War Era* (Oxford: Oxford University Press, 2002), 36.

19. Gadant, *Islam et nationalisme en Algérie,* 11.

20. Le Pautremat, *La Politique musulmane de la France au XXe siècle,* 430–31. See also Charles-Robert Ageron, "Une dimension de la guerre d'Algérie: les 'regroupements' de populations," in *Militaires et guérilla dans la guerre d'Algérie,* ed. J.-C. Jauffret and M. Vaïsse (Brussels: Editions Complexe, 2001).

21. René Gallissot, "La guerre et l'immigration algérienne en France," in *La Guerre d'Algérie et les Français,* ed. Jean-Pierre Rioux (Paris: Fayard, 1990), 344.

22. Ruedy, *Modern Algeria,* 168. The curfew was also a tool used often by police in major metropolitan cities: it was imposed on North African residents of the Département de la Seine on 27 August 1958 and afterwards in many other cities. See Stora, *Ils venaient d'Algérie,* 364.

23. For discussions of the *harkis,* see Charles-Robert Ageron, "*Les supplétifs algériens dans l'armée française,*" *Vingtième siècle* 48 (October–December 1995): 3–20; and Mohand Hamoumou, *Et ils sont devenus harkis* (Paris: Fayard, 1993).

24. Le Pautremat, *La Politique musulmane de la France au XXe siècle,* 448–49.

25. This infamous attack on Parisian Algerians was orchestrated by none other than Maurice Papon, the préfet de Police, who would eventually be put on trial for his role in the deportation of French Jews under the Vichy administration. The link between French state violence against Jews and Muslims is explored in Didier Daeninckx's novel *Meurtres pour mémoire* (Paris: Gallimard, 1998). On the events of 17 October 1961, see Paulette Péju, *Ratonnades à Paris* (Paris: Editions François Maspéro, 1961); and Jean-Luc Einaudi, *La Bataille de Paris: 17 Octobre 1961* (Paris: Seuil, 1991). On the FLN's organization of the demonstration, see Ali Haroun, *La 7ème Wilaya: La guerre du F.L.N. en France. 1954–1962* (Paris: Seuil, 1986); and Jim House and Neil MacMaster, "La Fédération de France du FLN et l'organisation de la manifestation du 17 octobre 1961," *Vingtième siècle. Revue d'histoire* 82 (July–September 2004): 145–60.

26. Stora, *Ils venaient d'Algérie* 335–36.

27. French communist Henri Alleg, a victim of torture at the hands of the French army, was one of the first to speak of his experiences in *La Question* (Paris: Minuit, 1961).

28. See Raphaëlle Branche, *La torture et l'armée pendant la guerre d'Algérie 1954–1962* (Paris: Gallimard, 2001). Kristin Ross's "Starting Afresh: Hygiene and Modernization in Postwar France," *October* 67 (Winter 1994): 22–57, considers the way in which the "dirty war" in Algeria, which included torture, was the distorted mirror image of a reconstructed metropolitan France obsessed with cleanliness.

29. The laws of 26 June 1889 and 22 July 1893 instituted automatic naturalizations for European residents of Algeria, which transformed a colony in which Spanish nationals, for example, outnumbered French citizens by as many as four to one in certain regions, into one in which all Europeans were "French."

30. Jean-Jacques Jordi, "Les pieds-noirs: constructions identitaires et réinvention des origines," *Hommes et migrations* 1236 (March–April 2002): 14–25.

31. *Journal officiel,* 28 December 1961.

32. Décret du 10 mars 1962.

33. Ordonnance no. 62-400, 11 April 1962.

34. See also Jean-Jacques Jordi and Emile Témime, eds., *Marseille et le choc des décolonisations* (Aix: Edisud, 1996); and Jeannine Verdès-Leroux, *Les Français d'Algérie de 1830 à nos jours* (Paris: Fayard, 2001).

35. Doris Bensimon, "La guerre et l'évolution de la commaunté juive," in *La Guerre d'Algérie et les Français,* ed. Rioux, 542.

36. See Shepard, *Invention of Decolonization,* ch. 6: "Repatriation Rather than Aliyah: The Jews of France and the End of French Algeria," especially 180–82.

37. Michel Abitbol, "The Integration of North African Jews in France," *Yale French Studies* 85 (1994): 251. Abitbol also adds that unlike earlier Eastern European Jewish immigrants in the 1920s and 1930s, these Algerian Jews were not forced to rely primarily on the aid of French Jewish associations for their insertion into French society.

38. Joëlle Bahloul, *La maison de mémoire: Ethologie d'une demeure judéo-arabe en Algérie (1937–1961)* (Paris: Métailié, 1992), 194–95.

39. Approximately 180,000 Algerians formally supported the French army during the war, of which approximately 70,000 served as *harkis,* from *harka,* Arabic for "movement." They were officially constituted as *unités supplétives* in 1956 even though they had been active from the beginning of the conflict. The 7 November 1961 Statut des Harkis mandated, among other things, that *harkis* were to be engaged by monthly contracts that could be renewed but also canceled for any reason without notice and that their benefits were limited to one-time payments for injury or death. The *harkis* were not considered to be soldiers in the French army and were thus ineligible for the veteran's benefits and pensions that their metropolitan counterparts would get at the war's end. For a contemporary discussion of questions relating to the *harkis*' status immediately following the war, see C. Brière, *Qui sont les harkis?* (Prades, France: Amicale des Rapatriés et originaires français d'Afrique du Nord, 1975).

40. Michel Roux, *Les Harkis: Les oubliés de l'histoire, 1954–1991* (Paris: La Découverte, 1991), 214–17.

41. Stora, *Ils Venaient d'Algérie,* 400.

42. Benjamin Stora, among others, would argue that France still bears the scars of the Algerian War and, more broadly, of centuries of colonialism. See his *La gangrène et l'oubli: La Mémoire de la guerre d'Algérie* (Paris: La Découverte, 1991).

43. "Note pour le Secrétaite d'Etat au sujet de la Mosquée de Paris," Ministère des Affaires Etrangères, Sous-Direction du Maroc, 24 March 1956, Archives d'Histoire Contemporaine, Institut des Etudes Politiques/Fonds Alain Savary/SV12/Dr2.

44. Alain Savary, the Secrétaire d'Etat aux Affaires marocaines et tunisiennes under Guy Mollet, explained that the Ministre des Affaires marocaines et tunisiennes supported Si Ahmed as the Mosquée's new *recteur* because of his "qualities of devotion and loyalty," which "constituted the best guarantee for the French government." The ministry was impressed by Si Ahmed's achievements during his tenure as the site's temporary leader given the difficult circumstances of his arrival, though it was noted that his ability to lead was helped by his Moroccan title of *chancelier-adjoint des Ordres Chérifiens*. This connection gave Si Ahmed "the prestige necessary to perform his new functions in a dignified manner, and to maintain the Moroccan tradition at the Mosquée de Paris in spite of certain oppositions." See the letter from Alain Savary to the Haut Commissaire de France à Rabat, 7 May 1956, Archives d'Histoire Contemporaine, Institut des Etudes Politiques/Fonds Alain Savary/SV12/Dr2.

45. Letter from Alain Savary to the Ministry of the Interior, Affaires Algériennes, 22 June 1956, Archives d'Histoire Contemporaine, Institut des Etudes Politiques/Fonds Alain Savary/SV12/Dr2. The candidature of Si Mammeri was also supported by the Moroccan sultan.

46. Ibid.

47. Note au sujet de la Succession de Si Ahmed Ben Ghabrit à la Mosquée de Paris, Ministre des Affaires Etrangères, Sous-Direction Maroc, 7 September 1956, Archives d'Histoire Contemporaine, Institut des Etudes Politiques/Fonds Alain Savary/SV12/Dr2.

48. Ibid.

49. Ibid.

50. A series of legal battles ensued contesting Si Hamza's assumption of the role of *recteur*, but the Tribunal de Grande Instance de la Seine confirmed his right to the post in a decision on 31 May 1967.

51. Sellam, *La France et ses musulmans*, 257.

52. Note au sujet de la fête musulmane de l'Aïd el Kébir, 7 August 1954, ANOM 81F 833.

53. Ministère de l'Intérieur, Note: Les Marocains de la Région Parisienne et l'Aïd el Kébir, 9 August 1954, ANOM 81F 833.

54. Messali Hadj had again been subject to repressive measures by French authorities since 1952 and at the time was restricted to living in Angoulême, Charente. Note au sujet de la fête musulmane de l'Aïd el Kébir, 7 August 1954, ANOM 81F 833.

55. Note: Célébration de "l'Aïd el Kébir" à la Mosquée de Paris, 9 August 1954, ANOM 81F 833.

56. Note au sujet de la célébration de l'Aïd el Kébir à la Mosquée de Paris, 10 August 1954, ANOM 81F 833.

57. Note au sujet de la Cérémonie de la Mosquée de Paris à l'occasion de l'Aïd es-Seghir, 23 May 1955, ANOM 81F 833.

58. Note: Récéption à la Mosquée de Paris à l'occasion de "l'Aïd es-Seghir," 26 May 1955, ANOM 81F 833.

59. Note au sujet de la célébration de l'Aïd el Kébir, 29 July 1955, ANOM 81F 833.

60. Note: Cérémonie à la Mosquée de Paris à l'occasion de "l'Aïd el Kébir," 30 July 1955, ANOM 81F 833. Radiodiffusion Française (RDF) was the state-run public radio service.

61. Note: Récéption à la Mosquée de Paris à l'occasion de l'Aïd el Kébir, 2 August 1955, ANOM 81F 833.

62. Matthew Connolly argues that once Moroccan and Tunisian independence became inevitable, the French government's policy became isolating Algeria by conceding "independence within interdependence" to the two neighboring protectorates. French politicians hoped not only to prevent their former territories from supporting the Algerian struggle but also to enlist Moroccan and Tunisian cooperation in ending the revolution. See Connelly, *Diplomatic Revolution,* 8.

63. I should note here that I am not using "*Islam algérien*" in the same sense as Raberh Achi when he describes the Ouléma's rejection of the "official" Islam sponsored by the French colonial administration in Algeria, derided as *islam algérien.* See Raberh Achi, "'L'islam authentique appartient à Dieu, "l'islam algérien" à César': La mobilisation de l'association des oulémas d'Algérie pour la séparation du culte musulman et de l'État (1931–1956)," *Genèses* 4, no. 69 (2007).

64. The FFFLN was headed by the Federal Committee, which oversaw the activities of the seven wilayas, gave orders, maintained discipline, and controlled the budget. The committee was directly responsible to the GPRA, the Algerian government in exile, which gave the FFFLN its orders. See Stora *Ils venaient d'Algérie* 326.

65. Cited in Stora, *Ils Venaient d'Algérie,* 343.

66. Letter from Minister of the Interior to Prefects, 10 February 1958, AN AN F1[a] 5035/Circulaires importantes concernant les Affaires musulmanes, 1943–1967.

67. Stora *Ils venaient d'Algérie* 328.

68. See Ali Haroun, *Le 7ème Wilaya: La guerre du FLN en France* (Paris: Seuil, 1986).

69. Ibid., 343.

70. Note au sujet du Ramadan, 28 March 1957, ANOM 81F 833.

71. The FFFLN also indicated that not only should Algerians refuse to give money to MNA militants who would be conducting a fund-raising drive but they should also indicate the MNA's members to FFFLN leadership.

72. Note au sujet du déroulement du Ramadan, 3 April 1957, ANOM 81F 833.

73. No notice seems to have been taken of the new presence of West African Muslims at the Mosquée. As we have seen, the site was conceived aesthetically as Moroccan and was imagined, in theory, to serve North African Muslims. Sub-Saharan Muslims never featured significantly in the imaginations of the Mosquée's founders, French and Muslim alike.

74. Ibid.

75. Judith Surkis, "Hymenal Politics: Marriage, Secularism, and French Sovereignty," *Public Culture* 22 no. 3 (2010): 553. On the longer history of French interest in the "oppression" of Muslim women, see, for example, Julia Clancy-Smith, "Islam, Gender, and Identities in the Making of French Algeria, 1830–1962," in *Domesticating The Empire: Languages of Gender, Race, and Family Life in French and Dutch Colonialism, 1830–1962,* ed. Julia Clancy-Smith and Frances Gouda (Charlottesville: University Press of Virginia, 1998).

76. See, for example, Ryme Seferdjeli, "French 'Reforms' and Muslim Women's Emancipation during the Algerian War," *Journal of North African Studies* 9 no. 4 (Winter 2004): 19–61; Neil MacMaster, *Burning the Veil: The Algerian War and the "Emancipation" of Muslim Women, 1954–1962* (Manchester: Manchester University Press, 2010); Diane Sambron, *Les femmes algériennes pendant la colonisation* (Paris: Riveneuve, 2009).

77. Letter from Président du Conseil, Secretaire général pour les affaires algériennes) to the Ministre de Justice, undated, ANOM Fonds Ministériels 14 CAB 233/ Opinions des personnalités consultées

78. See MacMaster, *Burning the Veil,* 286. He suggests that the terms of the ordinance were inspired by Habib Bourguiba's reform of Tunisian family law, which went further than the French reforms by banning polygamy.

79. The Simoneau commission of 1957 was supposed to propose legislation reforming women's status in Algeria but shelved the project until it was taken up again in 1958 under de Gaulle's instructions. Neil MacMaster argues that the same tensions that animated the Simoneau commission—fears of FLN reaction versus a desire to bring Algerian law in line with its Maghrébin neighbors—continued to plague the debates of 2008–9. See MacMaster, *Burning the Veil,* 82.

80. *Commission d'étude de la situation de la femme musulmane,* 5 December 1958, ANOM FM 14 CAB/233/Opinions des personnalités consultées.

81. MacMaster, *Burning the Veil,* 82.

82. *Rapport de M. le Professeur Hamza Boubakeur, Directeur de l'Institut Musulman de la Mosquée de Paris sur le Projet de réforme du statut personnel de la femme musulmane et de la femme Kabyle en Algérie,* ANOM FM 14 CAB/233/Opinions des personnalités consultées.

83. Ibid.

84. MacMaster, *Burning the Veil,* 290–91.

85. Ibid., 300–302. The existing inadequacies of regional bureaucracies were worsened because of the war.

86. See Alfred Dittgen, "La forme du mariage en Europe. Cérémonie civile, cérémonie religieuse. Panorama et évolution," *Population* 2 (March–April 1994): 339–68.

87. Cited in Stora, *Trois exils,* 45–46.

88. Direction Générale des Affaires Politiques et de l'Administration du Territoire, Service des Affaires Musulmanes, Ministère de l'Intérieur. Note au sujet de l'Etablissement et validité des actes de mariages contractés en France par des ressortissants algériens, 20 Juin 1963, AN F1[a] 5035/Circulaires importantes concernant les Affaires musulmanes, 1943–1967.

89. "Reglement concernant les mariages suivant le droit musulman," undated pamphlet produced by the FFFLN, AN F1[a] 5125/Mariages des Algériens, textes de base, 1951–1965.

90. Ibid.

91. The *fatiha* is the first sourate of the Quran.

92. "Les Nord-Africains et leurs problèmes juridiques en métropole," *Les Cahiers Nord-Africains* 46 (1955): 37.

93. Letter from Bouezza to de Gaulle, 11 December 1959, AN F1[a] 5125/Mariages des Algériens, textes de base, 1951–1965.

94. As the *Cahiers Nord-Africains* pointed out, the consequences for North Africans who did not marry by French law were many, such as the fact that any children born in the interval between their religious and civil marriages would be considered illegitimate in the eyes of the French state.

95. Letter from Si Hamza to the Directeur des Affaires musulmanes, Ministère de l'Intérieur, 31 May 1965, AN F1[a] 5125/Mariages des Algériens, textes de base, 1951–1965.

96. It appears that such a report was in fact issued by the Ministry of Justice, but it is unfortunately unavailable for consultation.

97. Letter from Si Hamza to the Directeur des Affaires musulmanes, Ministère de l'Intérieur, 31 May 1965, AN F1[a] 5125/Mariages des Algériens, textes de base, 1951–1965.

98. Letter from Minister of Justice to Si Hamza, 31 May 1960, AN F1[a] 5125/Mariages des Algériens, textes de base, 1951–1965.

99. Préfecture de Police, Direction des Renseignements Généraux, "La Communauté Algérienne du Département de la Seine," 21 June 1965, AN F1[a] 5016/Documentation du SLPM.

100. The Amicale represented a transformation of the "comités de soutien" of the FFFLN, which the FLN officially dissolved in November 1962. It was created as a 1901 *association,* and proclaimed its activities to be associative, educative and cultural. See Stora, *Ils Venaient d'Algérie,* 418–19.

101. Letter from Service des Affaires Musulmanes et de l'Action Sociale to Secrétaire Général pour les Affaires Algériennes, 5 February 1960, ANOM 81F 832.

102. "Action social en faveur des Nord-Africains dans la region parisienne," January 1959, AN F[1a] 5056/Action sociale du Ministère de l'Intérieur, 1953–1964. Social assistance programs for North Africans living in France were organized at the national level by the Comité interministériel d'action sociale pour les Français musulmans d'Algérie en métropole, created by decree on 8 December 1958, which answered directly to the président du conseil. The committee's members included representatives from SAMAS and the Ministries of Labor, Public Health, Construction, Education, Armies, and Veterans. Its mission was to "propose social action programs and strategies to implement them to the président du conseil; these programs must address action in favor of families and youth, housing, professional training, and employment in particular." See *Journal Officiel,* 2 December 1958, Décret 58-1148 du 1er décembre tendant à organiser l'action sociale pour les Français musulmans d'Algérie en métropole.

103. "Guide de l'Action sociale au Bénéfice des Nord-Africains en Métropole," [undated], AN F[1a] 5056/Action sociale du Ministère de l'Intérieur, 1953–1964.

104. Exercise du budget 1961, ANOM 81F 832.

105. Letter from Ministre de l'Intérieur to Ministre d'Etat chargé des Affaires Algériennes, 10 March 1961, ANOM 81F 832.

106. Exercise du budget 1961. According to Si Hamza, the Institut's library had never been adequately stocked. A collection was created covering 1926 through 1938, but nothing was added from then until 1957; in fact, the existing collection was plundered by a former imam who sold most of the works to individuals. Thus not only did the library need to be brought up to date on two decades' worth of research, but the classic works which made up the initial collection needed to be replaced.

107. See Lucine Endelstein's interesting account of the growth of kosher restaurants and businesses in contemporary Paris: "Les juifs originaires d'Afrique du Nord, acteurs du développement du commerce cacher aujourd'hui. Itinéraires professionnels et stratégies de localisation (Paris, 19ème)." *Actes de l'histoire de l'immigration*, Ecole Normale Supérieure 2003.

108. Service de Coordination des Affaires Algériennes, Section de Renseignements. Objet: Tous renseignements sur cinq personnes interpellées lors de l'attentat à l'intérieur de la Mosquée de Paris, le 25 mai 1961, 17 June 1961, APP H^{1b} 23. Aside from the three French women, the rest of the thirty-three people brought in for questioning were male, Muslim, and of North African origin. The only exception was the women's Lebanese classmate. Of the men, four were Algerian, four were Tunisian, and the rest were Moroccan, which confirms that Algerians were even more scarce than usual at the Mosquée during the war.

109. Ibid.

110. "Paradoxically," Si Hamza noted, these pieces of furniture were easily found in Paris. Nevertheless, he was disappointed by many members of the Muslim elite who, finding themselves settled in Paris, chose to "deprive themselves" of the "traditional" decor they were used to and replace their furniture and decoration with "modern knicknacks."

111. Exercise du Budget 1961.

112. These accusations are taken from Colonel Amirouche of Wilaya III's letter to Si Hamza, dated 11 November 1958, APP Hb 23.

113. Si Hamza took on French nationality in March 1963.

Chapter 6

1. In 1973, the Algerian state halted emigration to France, and in 1974, France suspended labor immigration while allowing for "*regroupement familial,*" which permitted families to join relatives already present in the metropole. By 1976, there were 872,000 Algerians, 304,000 Moroccans, and 164,000 Tunisians living in France, with much of that population residing in the Paris region and Marseille. West Africans made up a smaller percentage of immigrants from France's former colonies, with 80,000 individuals from the entire region present in the metropole by 1976.

2. Secrétariat d'état aux travailleurs immigrés, *La nouvelle politique de l'immigration* (Paris, 1976), 25–27.

3. Ibid.

4. On the politics of this agreement, see Alexis Spire, *Étrangers à la carte: L'administration de l'immigration en France* (Paris: Grasset, 2005), 208.

5. Ibid., 213. Spire and Todd Shepard explain that the principle of freedom of movement was intended for the benefit of French citizens living in Algeria, but the principle of reciprocity demanded that it also be extended to Muslim residents of France's former colony. See also Shepard, *Invention of Decolonization,* 156.

6. President Boumedienne explained this decision by denouncing the "insults, provocations, assassinations and other discriminatory measures" that constituted daily life for Algerians in France. He further stated that Algerians residents of the metropole should be proud of their "Arabo-Islamic authenticity" as a way of resisting any desire to integrate into French society. See Stora, *Ils venaient d'Algérie,* 422.

7. On racist violence against people of North African origin, see Gérard Noiriel, *Immigration, racism et antisémitisme en France* (Paris: Fayard, 2007). Between 1971 and 1977, approximately seventy Algerians were the victims of racist attacks in France.

8. "*Ratonnade,*" a violent physical attack on Maghrébins, is derived from *raton* (baby rat), a derogatory term used to refer to North Africans.

9. Ibid.

10. France's suspension of immigration was not only a reaction to the Algerian government's own decree: it was issued in the context of the 1973 oil crisis and recession and applied to all immigrants, not only those from Algeria. See Patrick Weil, *Qu'est-ce qu'un Français? Histoire de la nationalité française depuis la Révolution* (Paris: Grasset, 2002), 166–67.

11. See Catherine Wihtol de Wenden, "L'intégration des populations musulmanes en France, trente ans d'évolution," in *Histoire de l'islam et des musulmans en France du Moyen Age à nos jours,* ed. Mohammed Arkoun (Paris: Albin Michel, 2006), 800–821.

12. On earlier programs designed to cope with immigration, see Amelia H. Lyons, "Social Welfare, French Muslims, and Decolonization in France: The Case of the Fonds d'action sociale." *Patterns of Prejudice* 43, no. 1 (2009): 65–89. One example is that of the Fonds d'action sociale (FAS), created during the Algerian War to cope exclusively with Algerian immigrants (the FAS was renamed in 1964 as the Fonds d'action sociale pour les travailleurs étrangers). On the place of culture in immigration policies, see Angéline Escafré-Dublet, "L'État et la culture des immigrés, 1974–1984," *Histoire@Politique* 4, no. 1 (2008).

13. Secrétariat d'état aux travailleurs immigrés, *La nouvelle politique de l'immigration* (Paris, 1976), 37.

14. Ibid., 41.

15. Ibid., 83.

16. The Algerian state was also concerned about the effects of immigration on their emigrants, though these fears were born out of the hope that these workers would eventually return to Algeria to build up the newly independent country. To this end, the government sponsored educational programs (Arabic lessons, classes about Islam) for the children of Algerian immigrants living in France.

17. For a discussion of the development of migration as an object of sociological study in the 1960s, see Noiriel, *Immigration, antisémitisme et racism en France,* chapter 7.

18. *La nouvelle politique de l'immigration,* 111.

19. Ibid., 83.

20. Ibid., 115.

21. Ibid., 118.

22. Ibid.

23. Comité d'information et d'études sur les migrations méditerannéenes. "L'Islam en France, Enquête sur les lieux de culte et l'enseignement de l'arabe" (Paris: 1978) 46–47.

24. A *circulaire* is a ministerial text interpreting recent legislation to provide directives to the ministry's public servants on new procedures.

25. Programme "Lieux de culte," circulaire du 2 septembre 1976.

26. "L'Islam en France," 49.

27. Ibid.

28. Ibid.

29. Ibid., emphasis added.

30. Ibid., 47.

31. Gilles Kepel, *Les banlieues de l'Islam: Naissance d'une religion en France* (Paris: Seuil, 1991).

32. Originally the SONACOTRAL (*Société nationale de construction de logements pour les travailleurs algériens,* with the final "al" representing Algerian workers), the group became SONACOTRA after 1962 and Algerian independence.

33. Marie-France Moulin, *Machines à dormir: Les foyers neufs de la sonacotra, de l'adef et quelques autres* (Paris: Maspero, 1976), 53.

34. Mireille Ginesy-Galano, *Les immigrés hors la cité* (Paris: L'Harmattan, 1984), 83.

35. Alexis Spire traces the careers of former colonial administrators in the post-colonial metropole in his *Etrangers à la carte.* SONACOTRA was but one of many state agencies staffed by former colonial agents. In 1972, for example, no less than 95% of foyer directors were former military men stationed in Indochine, Africa, or the Maghreb. These directors were specially recruited by SONACOTRA administrators for their colonial experience. See Spire, *Etrangers à la carte,* 210–11. See also Choukri Hmed, "Loger les étrangers 'isolés' en France. Socio-histoire d'une institution d'Etat: la Sonacotra (1956–2006)," Ph.D. dissertation, Université de Paris I, 2006; and "'Tenir ses hommes': La gestion des étrangers 'isolés' dans les foyers Sonacotra après la guerre d'Algérie," *Politix* 76, no. 4 (2006): 11–30.

36. The study, completed before the strikes, was never made public. See the GISTI's response to the SONACOTRA's brochure explaining the strike: "'*Grève des loyers' Re-mise au point. Replique du G.I.S.T.I. à la SONACOTRA,*" *CIEMM* 5 (January 1979): 6.

37. Ginesy-Galano, *Les immigrés hors la cité,* 129. During the strikes, a collective of foyer managers published a booklet in which they anonymously described their backgrounds and thoughts on their roles at SONACOTRA in order to dispute their characterization as racist. Claudius-Petit, who wrote a brief introduction to the piece, painted a picture of the directors as unsung heroes: "Three hundred directors live alone with their families in the SONACOTRA foyer-hotels for foreign workers. Illegal aliens, drugs, girls, fights, this is everyday life in the foyers. One out of every three is currently not paying rent. The directors earn an average of 4500 francs per month. They have one day off per week. Two out of every three are former military men. At the beginning, they were the only ones who could or would cope with immigrant workers. Now, the recruitment is more diversified: overseers, workers, farmers, employees, priests . . . their work requires multiple skills and most particu-

larly management skills and readiness to 'put their hands to the wheel.' . . . When people talk about them, outside, far from the trash bins which need to be emptied every morning, it's to call them 'fascists' or 'racists.'" As one foyer director explained, "What I like [about the job] are the relationships that can exist between men. As Director, I see a lot of guys who come through my office, to talk about everything and nothing. 'I have a little girl,' 'I have a little boy, he'll be named Mohammed. What do you think?' Another—like Ali—has a father who's died. Work accident. He came to see me, in tears. Soon, I cried with him. And we talked, the two of us, trying to come up with a plan to figure out what to do with the body. . . . I've learned a lot about what immigrants are like, especially Arabs, Arab culture—because the foyer is mostly Arab." See POGURE, *Non aux Gérants racists* (Paris: Les Editions du cerf, 1979), preface and 26–27.

38. The *salles de prière* differed in each *foyer*: occasionally a room was permanently designated as a Muslim religious site, while in other cases a multipurpose room could be used for prayers on some occasions. Over the course of the strikes, the following SONACOTRA foyers acquired *salles de prière*: Meaux, Massy I and II, Aulnay-sous-Bois, Bagnolet, Bobigny, Montreuil, Romainville, Saint Denis, Sevran, Villemomle, Elancourt, Gargenville, Clichy, Colombes, Gennevilliers, Nanterre, Argenteuil, and Cormeilles-en-Parisis. "Foyers et Services" brochure published by SONACOTRA, 1978. Archives de l'Archeveque de Paris 3K1/13/SITI.

39. Ginesy-Galano, *Les immigrés hors la cité,* 54.

40. Moulin, *Machines à dormir,* 44.

41. The serving of alcohol was forbidden in a fair number of foyers not out of respect for Muslim religious restrictions, but because foyer directors argued that the consumption of alcoholic beverages led to fights and problems among residents.

42. "Non à l'Amicale briseuse de grèves," *La Voix des Travailleurs Algériens* (June 1976): 8. The same article attacks the Amicale for negotiating with SONACOTRA, who had turned to the Algerian and Moroccan consulates in hoping they would help break the strike. "The Algerian bourgeoisie is trying to keep its control over us. It sends us to work but it has to guarantee our docility to the French bourgeoisie. On the other hand, it is also scared that the experience we gain in the struggles we're waging here with our French and immigrant comrades may one day serve us to put into question the way it exploits our brothers still in the homeland."

43. The MTA was created in 1972 by a group of intellectuals and workers who were members of the former Comités de Palestine in Paris and Marseille. These associations, created in response to the expulsion of the PLO from Jordan in 1970, were comprised of members of the radical left, Maoists, and students. The MTA declared itself to "orientation, direction, and unification" for the "Arab national conscience," yet it was also implicated in pursuing the rights of undocumented workers, deportees, and others. See Rabah Aissaoui, "Le discours du Mouvement des travailleurs arabes (MTA) dans les années 1970 en France: Mobilisation et mémoire du combat national," *Hommes et migrations* 1263 (September–October 2006): 105–19.

44. Kepel, *Les banlieues de l'Islam,* 133.

45. Ibid., 128–29.

46. *Non aux gérants racists!* 103. Other directors described their attempts to provide foyer residents with North African cultural *and* religious celebratory events, sometimes seeming to blend the two. They often used funds from the FAS (Fonds

d'action sociale) for this purpose. One director organized a "gigantic couscous" for residents: "We made a couscous and gathered everyone downstairs, in the main room, the one with the TV, and we put out a big white table. . . . My wife went to get all the vegetables at the market with the North Africans: Tunisians, Algerians, Moroccans. . . . Some Senegalese and Malians had nothing to do, so I suggested they be the butchers. They slaughtered, skinned, and butchered the three sheep" (96–97). As we will see below, this director has (perhaps) unconsciously alluded to the divisions in the foyers between North and West Africans, while trying to unite them all with a culturally North African meal. Another director explicitly chose to celebrate a Muslim religious holiday, Aïd el Kébir. He began delegating responsibilities for the festive preparations a month before the holiday, saying that "for my wife and me, it was a rite of passage. We told ourselves, 'If it works, we'll stay, if it doesn't work, we're off.'" The director claims the men experienced "pleasure and joy" at the holiday celebration in spite of the mayor's drunken speech, which he feared would upset them. It is interesting to note that the director's carefully planned meal, including sheep ordered a full month ahead of time to be slaughtered, also included "a good Bordeaux, 28 francs a bottle," on every table (99–101). Unfortunately, I do not know what residents thought of their director's insistence on certain elements of Muslim religious celebrations coupled with ignoring the far more serious prohibition on alcohol.

47. Jacques Barou, in CNRS-RNUR, *Les OS dans l'industrie automobile* (Paris, 1986), 139–40.

48. Jacques Barou, Moustafa Diop, and Subhi Toma, "Des musulmans dans l'usine," in *Ouvriers spécialisés à Billancourt: Les derniers témoins,* ed. Renaud Sainsaulieu and Ahsène Zehraoui (Paris: L'Harmattan, 1995), 131–61. Not all employers were as accommodating of their Muslim employees' religious observances or identities; many workers complained that their work routines left them little room for prayer or holiday observances. This large-scale insensitivity toward the needs of some immigrant workers also played itself out on a small scale. As a woman who taught a French class for recent immigrants criticized one factory director in an open letter in reference to the Christmas gift he had decided to give all his employees: a bottle of aperitif, a bottle of wine, a pork pâté, and a box of chocolates, which most of his Muslim employees would not consume. "Wouldn't it have been possible, in planning these gifts, to think about the people who would be receiving them? Maybe you didn't think about it? Maybe you could care less?" "Monsieur le directeur," *Paris-Babel* 13 (January 1972): 9.

49. Ibid., 133.

50. French sociologist Jean-Hughes Déchaux notes that these sites also offered factory owners and managers the opportunity to negotiate with imams, possibly side-stepping elected union officials. See "Les immigrés dans le monde de travail: un nouvel âge d'immigration?" *Revue de l'OFCE* 36, no. 36 (1991): 85–116.

51. The imam in the second *salle de prières* was associated with the Faith and Practice (Foi et pratique, or Jama'at al Tabligh) pietist movement, which will be discussed later in this chapter.

52. Barou, Diop, and Toma, "Des Musulmans dans l'Usine," 157.

53. The West African *jalbab* blends local fashions with either North African or Middle Eastern–style djellabahs. For a fuller discussion of choices in male Muslim religious clothing in the postcolonial West African context, see Ousman Kobo's *Promoting the Good and Forbidding the Evil* (forthcoming).

54. "L'Islam en Afrique noire," *Croissance de l'Eglise* 34 (April 1975): 13.

55. "Pourquoi prier seulement en Arabe?" *France-Islam* 1 (March 1967): 9.

56. Ibid.

57. See Manara Kamitenga's narrative, written in Saint-Ouen, 25 April 1978, AN Fonds Claudius-Petit 538AP/99.

58. Michel Samuel, *Le prolétariat africain noir en France* (Paris: Maspero, 1978), 128–29.

59. Ibid., 129.

60. Moustapha Diop and Laurence Michalak. "'Refuge' and 'Prison': Islam, Ethnicity, and the Adaptation of Space in Workers' Housing in France," in *Making Muslim Space in North America and Europe,* ed. Barbara Daly Metcalf (Berkeley: University of California Press, 1996), 79.

61. Samuel, *Le prolétariat africain noir en France*, 146.

62. Ibid.

63. Kamel Djaider, "La Haine de l'émigré," *El Moudjahid* 21–22 (March 1971): 4.

64. "Dossier: L'offensive de haine contre les algériens émigrés en France," *El Moudjahid* (1 June 1971): 1.

65. The MTA was created in Marseille in 1970 and was responsible for much of the mobilizing that took place beginning in 1973 around immigrant workers' rights.

66. Poster, Mouvement des travailleurs arabe, "Contre le racisme, 2 journées d'information les 26–27 avril 1975," BDIC.

67. The association's leader was a Muslim from Réunion. That he came from neither North nor West Africa was perhaps what enabled him to try to create a Muslim association that reflected Islam's universalist aspirations.

68. El Mountaqid, "Les Musulmans en France: Faux problèmes et problèmes réels," *France-Islam* 103–106 (September–December 1975): 1.

69. Gérard Noiriel argues in his most recent book, *Immigration, antisémitisme et racisme en France,* that on the contrary, racist words and discourse have been instrumental in the propagation of racist and xenophobic sentiments in French history.

70. All citations from Hamza Boubakeur, "Autour d'une manifestation antiraciste," *Le Monde* (22 September 1973).

71. "Une lâche aggression devant la Mosquée de Paris," *France-Islam* 42–44 (August–October 1970): cover page.

72. The ad in question, which was reproduced in the article criticizing Boubakeur (with the name of the company omitted so as not to provide it with further publicity), showed a display of rugs arranged in front of the archway of the Patio/Cour d'honneur: "The Mosquée de Paris transformed into an advertising background set while its administration's heavies forbid youth from studying the Quran before the Friday prayers." Djebali Ali, "Offense intolerable à l'Islam," *France-Islam* 52 (June 1971): back cover. The Amicale had a similar response to charge that Si Hamza was selling non-*halal* meat within the Mosquée complex: "His Imam, thus, can continue every Friday to blare his slogans in favor of the House's business from the height of the Mimbar, while his henchmen keep the faithful from opening their mouths, even to glorify their Creator, in the Mosquée." See "Hamza Boubakeur et la viande halâl," *France-Islam* 68–70 (October–December 1972): cover page.

73. References to the Association culturelle islamique's distribution of prayer schedules for the month of Ramadan abound in immigrant association newsletters

and bulletins, such as the Service intérdiocesain des travailleurs immigrés' bulletin *Paris-Babel,* which suggests that these schedules were widely distributed. It is likely that the student distributing the free schedules at the Mosquée was a member of the ACI, which would also explain his ejection by Si Hamza.

74. Djebali Ali, "Les aggressions à la Mosquée de Paris se suivent et ne se ressemblent pas," *France-Islam* 4546 (November–December 1970): back cover. Ali was the president of the Association des étudiants islamiques en France (AEIF, founded in 1963), an apolitical, pietist, and ritualist association. The AEIF originally enjoyed the support of the Mosquée de Paris, which saw an opportunity to make a gesture toward other currents in Parisian Muslim life. After the incident in question, however, the AEIF moved into a small space in the 15th *arrondissement* with the help of Professor Muhammad Hamidullah, a CNRS scholar of Pakistani origin and founder of the Centre culturel islamique. The center was intended to serve an academic audience, with conferences and publications; Kepel argues that Hamidullah's audience increased through his association with the AEIF. See Kepel, *Les banlieues de l'Islam,* 96; and Sellam, *La France et ses musulmans,* 118–19.

75. Ibid.

76. Boubakeur's translation included the verses made famous by Salman Rushdie as "the satanic verses," which describe the goddess Al-Lat. The Amicale took the scholars of Al-Azhar University in Cairo to task for their positive review of his translation.

77. Rodinson, one of France's premier orientalist scholars and historian of religion was a professor at the Ecole des hautes études en sciences sociales. A Marxist of Jewish origin, he published his *Mahomet* in 1961.

78. "Hamza Boubakeur, l'homme au chapeau magique et quelques interrogations," [Winter 1974].

79. "Le despotisme de la direction de la Mosquée de Paris," *France-Islam* 45–46 (November–December 1970): 2.

80. On Muslim-Jewish tensions in France, see Ethan Katz, "Jews and Muslims in the Shadow of Marianne: Conflicting Identities and Republican Culture in France, 1914–1985," Ph.D. dissertation, University of Wisconsin, 2009; and Maud Mandel, *Beyond Antisemitism: Muslims and Jews in Contemporary France* (forthcoming, Princeton University Press).

81. "Manifestation à la Mosquée de Paris contre Hamza Boubakeur," *El Moudjahid* (January 4, 1974).

82. The document is signed by the Mosquée de Belleville, de Nanterre, D'Argenteuil, de Clichy, and de Montfermeil as well as by "workers and Maghrebin students."

83. Citations from this tract come from "Manifestation à la Mosquée de Paris contre Hamza Boubakeur," *El Moudjahid* (January 4, 1974), which reprinted it in full.

84. M. Farah, "Le pacha de Paris," *El Moudjahid* (4 January 1974).

85. Ibid.

86. Ibid.

87. B.N., "Hamza Boubakeur ou l'incarnation de la trahision," *El Moudjahid* (12 January 1974): 3.

88. Ibid.

89. Les Associations religieuses Islamiques de France, "Hamza Boubakeur, l'homme au chapeau magique et quelques interrogations," tract distributed during the winter of 1974 [n.d.].

90. "Johnny Hallyday champion de la lutte contre le racisme et l'antisémitisme," *France-Soir,* 2 February 1972.

91. See Daniel Gordon, "Juifs et musulmans à Belleville (Paris 20e) entre tolérance et conflit," *Cahiers de la Méditerrannée* 67 (2003); and Michel Abitbol, "The Integration of North African Jews in France," *Yale French Studies* 85 (1994): 248–61.

92. An extract from this letter was printed in the Union Musulmane Internationale Bulletin no. 26.

93. Communiqué à la presse, 31 January 1974. The Muslim religious authorities who signed this statement included the Egyptian Cheikh Amer, the grand muphti of France; Si Hadj Abderrahman Henni, the inspecteur général des imams de France and imam de la Gironde et de la Vienne (no nationality listed); the Algerian Si Hadj Ali Benhamida, imam of l'Hérault and of the Pyrénées; the Moroccan Hadj Chellaf, imam of Paris and delegate of the Alaouiyya Brotherhood in France; the Tunisian Abdelkader Farfour, imam social at the Mosquée de Paris and in the suburbs; the Senegalese Cheikh Moussa Touré, of the Tidjaniyya Brotherhood; the Algerian Mohamed Benouaou, imam social in Paris; Hadj Tahar Hamdaoui, imam of La Charente and head of the Khadiriyya Brotherhood in France (no nationality given); and the religious delegates of l'Aube, l'Eure, Normandy, and Loire-Atlantique. The press release, of course, does not give us any insight into the discussions that took place at the meeting of the Amicale (headquartered at the Mosquée de Paris) and whether there was dissension among the religious leaders in terms of support for Si Hamza. The diversity of nationalities and religious tendencies among those who signed this text is intriguing, but I would argue that the fact of such a varied group of Muslim leaders publicly voicing support for Si Hamza is less indicative of broad-based support in the diverse Muslim communities of France than a sign that the Mosquée's subordinates were following their leader's party line. Those Muslim religious figures who openly attacked Si Hamza did so from independent positions, not from posts in Paris or the provinces that depended on the Parisian institution for funding and support.

94. The "party" in question refers to the FLN.

95. Philippe Bernert, "Il se bat pour sauver la Mosquée de Paris," *L'Aurore* (26 February 1974).

96. John Ruedy argues that in the years immediately following independence, the Algerian government emphasized the compatibility between Islam and socialism and devoted significant financial support to the construction of religious sites, Islamic education, and the training and salaries of Muslim religious leaders. The government also appropriated symbols of Islam by incorporating religious observances into public life. But the Ministry of Religious Affairs maintained strict control over the country's religious personnel, even going as far as to distribute "suggestions" for Friday sermons. See Ruedy, *Modern Algeria,* 224–25.

97. G. D., "Croyants en dispersion vus par un travailleur social," *Missi (Magazine d'information spirituelle et de solidarité internationale)* 9 (November 1976): 280–83.

98. "Des migrants comme nous sont à la recherche du Dieu-Vivant," *Croissance de l'Eglise* 34 (April 1975): 9.

99. G. D., "Croyants," 281.

100. For descriptive explanations of Muslim holidays for a non-Muslim audience, see for example "Regard sur l'Islam," a special issue of *Fêtes et saisons* 315 (May 1977).

101. Gaston Pietri, "*Tous fils d'Abraham*," *Paris-Babel* 96 (November 1980): 7.

102. The Jama'at al Tabligh movement was founded in India in 1927. Its goal was to bring India's Muslims back to Islam and away from their ties to Hinduism through outreach with a simple message, intense personal engagement, and group cohesion. The principles of the Tablighi movement are as follows: the profession of faith, prayer, the acquisition of the knowledge of God, respect for all Muslims, sincere intentions, the devotion of time for preaching, and abstention from all futile or worldly words or actions. The Tablighis would leave the AIB's mosque due to a schism between the two groups and go on to establish an important mosque in Clichy in 1970. 1973 marked the beginning of their presence on rue Jean-Pierre Timbaud, in Paris' 11th *arrondissement,* which was followed by the opening of mosques all over Ile-de-France and in provincial centers with large Muslim populations. See Kepel's chapter "Foi et Pratique" in *Les Banlieues de l'Islam.*

103. *La Croix* (16 September 1975), cited in Kepel, *Les Banlieues de l'Islam,* 97–98.

104. See letter from the Service interdiocésan des travailleurs immigrés (SITI), 15 March 1976. Archives historiques de l'Archdiocèse de Paris Dossier N.D. de la Croix de Ménilmontant.

105. Ibid.

106. A letter from Père Loubier to Church officials attempted to reassure them that the arrangement was a temporary one and that the entry to the crypt was completely separate from those to the church. He emphasized the Muslims' respect for their Catholic hosts' sensibilities, saying that the only negative reaction from a parishioner had come from a *pied noir.* However, Loubier worried that "in spite of these explanations, our initiative won't please everyone, and racist reactions may yet come." However, he was confident that the ONCPI would come to the church's aid if need be. Letter dated 4 May 1976, AHDP Dossier N.D. de la Croix de Ménilmontant.

107. "A Paris, la crypte de l'église de Ménilmontant accueille la mosquée du quartier Belleville." *Missi* 9 (November 1976).

108. "Ramadhan à Paris," *L'Algérien en Europe* 113 (15–29 November 1970): 21.

109. "Ramadan 1396 à Paris," *Paris-Babel* 58 (October 1976): 14.

110. See "Retour du pélérinage," *Fêtes et Saisons* 22.

111. Alain Boyer, *L'Institut Musulman de la Mosquée de Paris* (Paris: La Documentation française, 1992), 48. The Mosquée had begun to go into debt by the beginning of Si Hamza's tenure as *recteur.* In an interview with French sociologist Mohammed Telhine, he explained that Si Ahmed had been guilty of financial mismanagement during his brief period as the institution's leader and brought formal charges against him. He claimed to have eventually abandoned the charges of financial wrong-doing he laid against Si Ahmed at the request of the French government. See Mohammed Telhine, *L'islam et les musulmans en France: une histoire des mosquées* (Paris: L'Harmattan, 2010), 207–8.

112. Ibid., 208–9.

113. Legally, as it turned out, this decision was not binding because the association would have had to declare its own dissolution and the transfer of its patrimony in the *Journal Officiel,* followed by a *décret d'autorisation,* at which point a notary would

have been able to register the transfer. Since this procedure was not followed, the 4 August 1982 decision had no legal value but was nevertheless treated as binding by the Algerian government in staking its claim on the site.

114. This announcement was made on 16 September 1982.

115. Cited in Boyer, *L'Institut Musulman de la Mosquée de Paris,* 51.

116. In 1989, French political scientist Bruno Étienne estimated the total Muslim population to be approximately 2.5 million people by counting immigrants from Muslim countries and French citizens with origins in one or more Muslim country, with the addition of European converts and undocumented immigrants. See Bruno Étienne, *La France et l'islam* (Paris: Hachette, 1989). More recent estimates put the figure at approximately 5 million people, of whom half are North African Arabs, the rest divided between a majority of Berber North Africans and smaller groups of Turks, West Africans, Madagascarians, Comorians, South Asians, and European converts.

117. For an interesting discussion of the difficulties of identifying "Muslim" in France historically or in the present, given the prohibitions on census questions about race and religion, see the introduction to Jonathan Laurence and Justin Vaïsse's *Integrating Islam* (Washington, DC: Brookings Institution Press, 2006). In conducting their own research, they explain that for their population estimates they considered "potential Muslims," that is to say, people of "Muslim origin" at least some of whose ancestors were "Muslim" because of their place of birth and European converts to Islam. They also note that they consider to be Muslim people who might not consider themselves to be Muslim and would identify as atheist or members of another religion or would simply refuse to identify themselves as religious or not since they consider themselves first and foremost republicans. Their inclusion of these "sociological Muslims" offers a telling example of the extent to which race and national origin have been conflated with Muslimness by social scientists. They also provide a typology of generational investment in Muslimness, ranging from the immigrant workers of the 1970s to their children, the *beurs* of the 1980s concerned with racism and social justice, and then finally the "Muslims" of the 1990s, who identify themselves explicitly as Muslim and demanded rights as such. See Laurence and Vaïsse, *Integrating Islam,* 25–27.

Conclusion

1. The project was originally known as the Institut des cultures musulmanes.

2. These citations, as well as those that follow, are taken from the Paris City Hall's *Projet de Mission: Assistance à la Maîtrise d'Ouvrage pour la définition du programme de réalisation d'un "Institut des cultures musulmanes" dans le quartier de la Goutte d'Or* (23 November 2005).

3. Ibid.

4. For concise discussions of the headscarf controversies and analyses of their implications, see Joan Wallach Scott, *The Politics of the Veil* (Princeton: Princeton University Press, 2007); and John Bowen, *Why the French Don't Like Headscarves: Islam, the State, and Public Space* (Princeton: Princeton University Press, 2007). On other dimensions of the controversies, see, for example, Leora Auslander, "Bavarian Crucifixes and French Headscarves: Religious Signs and the Postmodern European

State," *Cultural Dynamics* 12, no. 3 (2000): 183–209; Françoise Gaspard and Farhad Khosrokhavar, *Le foulard et la République* (Paris: La Découverte, 1995); and Cécile Laborde, *Critical Republicanism: The Hijab Controversy and Political Philosophy* (Oxford: Oxford University Press, 2008). For the reflections of the father of the Lévy sisters, at the heart of the controversies in 2003, see Laurent Lévy, *La Gauche, les noirs et les Arabes* (Paris: Fabrique, 2010).

5. See Bowen, *Why the French,* 84; and Scott, *Politics of the Veil,* 21–24. Scott and Bowen both point to the intentional slippage in language used by the French media, intellectuals, politicians, and associations, in which the move from headscarf (*foulard*) to veil (*voile*) was made very quickly, and even to the *chador*, associated with the Iranian Revolution (even though none of the girls in question were fully covered).

6. Henri Tincq, "Un entretien avec le cheikh Tedjini Haddam recteur de la Mosquée de Paris: 'Je lance un appel à la dédramatisation et au dialogue,'" *Le Monde* (24 October 1989).

7. Many teachers, dismayed by the law's vagueness, complained about not knowing how they were to determine whether a particular article of clothing or accessory was "ostentatious" or not. See Bowen, *Why the French,* 141.

8. The first citation is taken from "Dalil Boubakeur hostile aux manifestations; L'UMP cherche à durcir le projet de loi sur la laïcité à l'école," *Le Monde* (8 January 2004), the second from Caroline Monnot, "Des réactions contrastées qui traversent les familles de pensée; Port du foulard à l'école," *Le Monde* (14 October 2003).

9. Boubakeur said that he opposed the expulsions because he did not think all possibilities of compromise had been investigated, but he did not support the girls who refused to remove their scarves in class.

10. The French parliament passed a law (2010-1192) on 11 October 2010 that began to be applied on 11 April 2011 "prohibiting concealment of the face in public space." Exceptions are to be made for people concealing their faces for health or professional reasons, or for sporting activities, or in the case of festivals or "artistic or traditional" events. There are no references in the text of the law to either burqas or niqabs, but the French press universally refers to this law as the "anti-niqab" law.

11. *Commission de reflexion sur l'application du principe de laïcité dans la République, Rapport au Président de la République,* 11 December 2003, 46, available at http://lesrapports.ladocumentationfrancaise.fr/BRP/034000725/0000.pdf.

12. The reasons girls and women give to explain their head coverings vary widely. Those who study the question agree that in addition to religious motivations, some girls explicitly say they veil themselves out of solidarity with their brothers.

13. In addition to Tedjini Haddam, the Mosquée's *recteur,* CORIF members included Khalil Merroun, the *recteur* of the mosquée d'Évry-Courcouronnes and a member of the FNMF; Mohand Hadj Allili, *recteur* of the mosquée du Bon Pasteur de Marseille; and Omar Lasfar, *recteur* of the mosquée of Lille-Sud and a member of the UIOF as well as Muslims who held political office, two Muslim university professors, one member of Millî Görüs, and two members of the FFAIACA. See Franck Frégosi, *Penser l'islam dans la laïcité* (Paris: Fayard, 2008), 224–26.

14. Laurence and Vaïsse, *Integrating Islam,* 181–82.

15. In the first election, there were 4,042 delegates, hailing from approximately one thousand mosques, of which 210 represented "major" prayer sites while the rest were considerably smaller. Small mosques tended to vote with the federations rather

than with the Mosquée. It was not necessary to be a French citizen or to be elected as a member of the CFCM to participate in the vote.

16. This fear was realized in 2008, when the Mosquée refrained from voting in the elections and lost much of its power. It also boycotted the elections of 2011. Interestingly, Dalil Boubakeur explains his refusal to participate in elections as a protest of the fact that the CFCM has contributed to the "ethnicization" of Islam in France while at the same time claiming to represent "the Algerian sensibility in French Islam." See "*Dalil Boubakeur, figure incontournable de l'islam en France,*" *Le Monde* (4 June 2011).

17. For further information on the CFCM, see Bernard Godard and Sylvie Taussig, *Les musulmans en France: Courants, institutions, communautés, un état des lieux* (Paris: Robert Laffont, 2007). See also the following articles in *French Politics, Culture and Society* 23, no. 1 (Spring 2005): Alain Boyer, "La représentation du culte musulman en France" (8–22), Jonathan Laurence, "From the Elysée Salon to the Table of the Republic: State-Islam Relations and the Integration of Muslims in France" (37–64), and Claire de Galembert and Mustapha Belbah, "Le Conseil français du culte musulman à l'épreuve des territoires" (76–86).

18. Bowen, *Why the French,* 58–59.

19. Louise Couvelaire, "Islam parisien, Croissant haut," *Le Nouvel Observateur: Paris Ile-de-France* 2185 (21–27 September 2006): 4–5.

20. In 2005, Nicolas Sarkozy wrote an article in *Le Monde* in which he introduced the possibility of rethinking *laïcité*'s contours. This was necessary, he argued, in order to allow Muslims the same rights as all other French citizens. As he explained, "To argue that Islam is incompatible with the Republic is no more or less than to prohibit certain Frenchmen from living an engagement permitted to others. This is discrimination at the least, and racism at worst. Islam's believers must be able to live their faith, publicly, never clandestinely. Thus each Muslim's identity will be recognized. He will no longer feel the need to live his faith confrontationally, feeling it to be challenged. Islam must be in the Republic, not next to it! If the right to religion, or its absence, is recognized, there is nevertheless no right to different treatment under the law. This is to say that the Republic's laws are not applied by variable geometry according to whether one is Muslim or not." Of course, as we have seen, French law was in fact applied differently for Muslims throughout the twentieth century. See his "Vers une nouvelle citoyenneté français," *Le Monde* (April 30, 2003).

21. "Objectifs de l'opération." Projet de Mission, 1.

22. The 2010 brochure begins with the language of compensation: "In the aftermath of WWI . . . the Grande Mosquée de Paris' edification was decided with the participation of the city government of Paris, in recognition of the Muslims who had died for France."

23. L'Institut des cultures d'Islam, brochure, 2010.

24. "Projet de mission," 2.

25. Ibid.

26. "Note préparatoire pour la réunion du Conseil Scientifique du 4 mai, 2007."

27. "Projet de Mission," 3.

28. Ibid.

29. Although Devin's mosque will never be built, Marseille should have its mosque by 2011, as Marseille mayor Jean-Claude Gaudin, over his initial objections,

finally approved a building permit for the site in 2009. The new mosque, designed by architect Maxime Repaux, will be the largest in France and one of the largest in Europe. Its twenty-five-meter minaret "will be a lighthouse . . . diffusing the call to prayer with a ray of light, a symbolic gesture," explained Repaux. The vocal call to prayer will only be audible within the mosque. The city of Marseille provided a *bail emphytéotique,* but the mosque still requires 22 million euros for its construction. For Repaux's comments, see Aliette de Broqua, "Marseille: la plus grande mosque de France en 2011," *Le Figaro* (6 November 2011). For a discussion of the Marseille mosque's present in light of its history, see Marcel Maussen, "Islamic Presence and Mosque Establishment in France: Colonialism, Arrangements for Guest Workers and Citizenship," *Journal of Ethnic and Migration Studies* 33, no. 6 (August 2007): 981–1002.

30. Dalil Boubakeur and Virginie Malabard, *Non! L'Islam n'est pas une politique* (Paris: Desclée de Brouwer, 2003), 84–85.

31. On the question of unexceptional citizenship, see Mayanthi Fernando, "Exceptional Citizens: Secular Muslim Women and the Politics of Difference in France," *Social Anthropology/Anthropologie Sociale* 17, no. 3 (2009): 379–92.

32. Cécile Laborde, *Critical Republicanism,* 4.

33. Scott, *Politics of the Veil,* 112–19.

34. Éric Aeschimann, "'Le Front national est un front antinational,'" *Libération* (14 July 2011).

Bibliography

Archives and Libraries

Archives de l'Archdiocèse de Paris (AAP), Paris
Archives de l'Assistance Publique/Hôpitaux Publics (AAP/HP), Paris
Archives départementales de Seine-Saint Denis (AD S-SD), Bobigny
Archives de l'Institut des études politiques (AIEP), Paris
Archives du Ministère des Affaires étrangères et européennes (AMAEE), Paris
Archives Nationales (AN), Paris
Archives Nationales d'outre-mer (ANOM), Aix-en-Provence
Archives de la Préfecture de Police (APP), Paris
Archives du Vicariat de la solidarité (AVS), Paris
Association Génériques, Paris
Bibliothèque administrative de la ville de Paris (BAVP), Paris
Bibliothèque du Centre culturel algérien (CCA), Paris
Bibliothèque de documentation internationale contemporaine (BDIC), Nanterre
Bibliothèque historique de la ville de Paris (BHVP), Paris
Bibliothèque nationale de France (BNF), Paris
Société histoirque de l'Armée de la Terre (SHAT), Vincennes

Newspapers and Periodicals

L'Algérien en Europe, Paris
L'Aurore, Paris
Croissance de l'Eglise, Paris
La Croix, Paris
En Terre d'Islam, Paris
Fêtes et Saisons, Paris
France-Islam, Paris
France-Soir, Paris
L'Illustration, Paris
Libération, Paris
Missi, Paris
Le Monde, Paris
El Moudjahid, Algiers
El Ouma, Paris
Paris-Babel, Paris
Le Petit Journal, Paris
Er Rachid, Paris
La Voix des Travailleurs Algériens, Paris

Published Primary Sources

Alleg, Henri. *La Question.* Paris: Editions de Minuit, 1961.

Bachetarzi, Mahieddine. *Mémoires 1919–1939.* Algiers: SNED, 1968.

Benaïcha, Brahim. *Vivre au paradis: d'un oasis à un bidonville.* Paris: Desclée de Brouwer, 1992.

Boubakeur, Dalil, and Virginie Malabard. *Non! L'Islam n'est pas une politique.* Paris: Desclée de Brouwer, 2003.

Bourdarie, Paul. "L'Institut musulman et la Mosquée de Paris." *La Revue Indigène* (October–November 1919).

Brière, C. *Qui sont les harkis?* Prades, France: Amicale des Rapatriés et originaires français de l'Afrique du Nord, 1975.

Buchet, Georges. "La Mosquée de Paris." *En Terre d'Islam* 34 (January 1930): 28–32.

——. "Les Musulmans en France: Enquête. Gennevilliers: La Cité Arabe." *En Terre d'Islam* 33 (December 1929): 36–48.

Bugeaud, Thomas-Robert. *Par l'épée et par la charrue, écrits et discours de Bugeaud.* Paris: PUF, 1948.

De Caix, Robert. *L'Afrique française.* November 1900.

Le Châtelier, Alfred. *L'Islam dans l'Afrique occidentale.* Paris: Steinheil, 1899.

Comité d'information et d'études sur les migrations méditeranéennes. "L'Islam en France. Enqûete sur les lieux de culte et l'enseignement de l'arabe." Paris: 1978.

Commission de Reflexion sur l'Application du Principe de Laïcité dans la République. *Rapport au Président de la République.* 11 December 2003. Available at http://lesrapports.ladocumentationfrancaise.fr/BRP/034000725/0000.pdf, accessed 15 October 2011.

Daeninckx, Didier. *Meurtres pour mémoire.* Paris: Gallimard, 1998.

Dermengham, Emile. "Musulmans de Paris." *La Grande Revue* 799 (December 1934): 15–21.

Descamps, Henri. *L'Architecture moderne au Maroc.* Paris: Librairie de la Construction moderne, 1931.

Doutté, Edmond. *L'Islam algérien en l'an 1900.* Algiers: Girault, 1900.

——. *Magie et religion dans l'Afrique du Nord.* Paris: Maisonneuve, 1984.

"Du douar à l'usine: La religion musulmane." *Cahiers Nord-Africains* 11 (1956).

Durand, Jacky. "'Parler de l'islam radical et montrer des gens en train de faire la prière, c'est dramatique.' Entretien avec Abdelhak Eddouk." *Libération,* 1 November 2005.

Emonet, M. le Capitaine. *La Grande Mosquée de Meknès.* Paris: Imprimerie nationale, 1917.

Etcherelli, Claire. *Elise ou la vraie vie.* Paris: Denoël, 1967.

Front de Libération Nationale (Fédération de France). *De la contre-révolution à la collaboration, ou la trahison des Messalistes. Études et documents édités par le Front de Libération Nationale.* Paris, 1959.

Goissaud, Antony. "L'Institut musulman et la Mosquée de Paris." *La Construction moderne* 3 (2 November 1924): 50–55.

Haddad, Malek. *Je t'offrirai une gazelle.* Paris: Julliard, 1959.
Haguenauer, P. "Lettre d'un aumônier." *Archives israélites,* 19 October 1916.
Haldd, Sylvain. "Jewish Participation in the Great War." *American Jewish Yearbook* 21 (1919–1920).
Hardy, Georges. *Portrait de Lyautey.* Paris: Bloud et Gay, 1949.
Hulman, Max. "L'Hôpital Franco-Musulman de Paris et du Département de la Seine." *La Presse médicale* 74 (14 September 1935): 1443–45.
"L'Islam en Afrique noire." *Croissance de l'Eglise* 34 (April 1975): 13.
Justinard, Pierre. "La Mosquée de Paris." M.A. thesis, Ecole Nationale de la France d'Outre-Mer, 1944.
Madras, Didier, and Boris Maslow. *Fès, Capitale artistique de l'Islam.* Casablanca, Morocco: Editions Paul Bory, 1948.
Marçais, Georges. "Nouvelles remarques sur l'esthetique musulmane." *Annales de l'Institut d'études orientales* 6 (1942–1947): 31–52.
Martial, René. *L'Immigration continental et transcontinentales.* Paris: Baillière, 1933.
Maslow, Boris. *Les Mosquées de Fès et du Nord du Maroc.* Paris: Les Editions d'Art et d'Histoire, 1937.
Massignon, Louis. *Opera Minora: Textes recueillis, classés et présentés avec une bibliographie.* Paris: PUF, 1969.
——. *Situation d'Islam.* Paris: Geuthner, 1939.
Mauco, Georges. *Les étrangers en France: leur rôle dans l'activité économique.* Paris: Armand Colin, 1932.
Ministère du Travail, de l'Emploi et de la Population. *L'Office national d'immigration: sa mission, ses résultats.* 1970.
"Les Nord-Africains et leurs problèmes juridiques en métropole." *Les Cahiers Nord-Africains* 46 (1955).
A l'ombre de la Mosquée. Dir. Jean Arroy Thialat. Force et voix de France, 1946.
Paon, Maurice. *L'Immigration en France.* Paris: Payot, 1926.
Péju, Paulette. *Ratonnades à Paris.* Paris: Editions François Maspero, 1961.
Quinet, Edgar. *Du génie des religions.* Paris: Charpentier, 1842.
Récéption à l'Hôtel de Ville de Son Altesse Mohamed El Habib Pacha Bey, Possesseur du Royaume de Tunis, 13 juillet 1923. Paris: Imprimerie Lapine, 1923.
"Le régime de l'Algérie au début du XXe siècle." *La Revue des deux mondes,* 1 April 1903.
De Rochebrune, Renaud, ed. *Les mémoires de Messali Hadj 1898–1938.* Paris: Editions J.-C. Lattès, 1982.
Royer, Jean. *L'urbanisme aux colonies et dans les pays tropicaux.* La Charité-sur-Loire, France: Delayance, 1932.
Sécretariat d'état aux travailleurs immigrés. *La nouvelle politique de l'immigration.* Paris, 1976.
Sée, Charles-Edmond. "Les bains-douches: Bains-douches de la Ville de Paris, rue Lacépède." *La Construction moderne* 44 (29 July 1934): 818–28.
De Tocqueville, Alexis. *Sur l'Algérie.* Paris: Flammarion, 2003.
Le Tourneau, R. "L'évolution des villes musulmanes d'Afrique du Nord au contact de l'Occident." *Annales de l'Institut d'études orientales* 7 (1954): 199–222.
Van Gennep, Arnold. *En Algérie.* Paris: Mercure de France, 1914.

Weiss, René. *Réception à l'Hôtel de Ville de Sa Majesté Moulay Youssef, Sultan du Maroc, Inauguration de l'Institut Musulman et de la Mosquée de Paris.* Paris: Imprimerie Nationale, 1927.

Yacine, Kateb. *Le polygone étoilé.* Paris: Seuil, 1966.

Secondary Sources

Abitbol, Michel. "The Integration of North African Jews in France." *Yale French Studies* 85 (1994): 248–61.

Abu-Lughod, Janet. *Rabat: Urban Apartheid in Morocco.* Princeton: Princeton University Press, 1980.

Achi, Raberh. "'L'islam authentique appartient à Dieu, "l'Islam algérien" à César': La mobilization de l'association des oulémas d'Algérie pour la separation du culte musulman et de l'État (1931–1956)." *Génèses* 69, no. 4 (2007): 49–69.

——. "La séparation des Eglises et de l'Etat à l'épreuve de la situation coloniale. Les usages de la dérogation dans l'administration du culte musulman en Algérie (1905–1959)." *Politix* 17, no. 66 (September 2004): 81–106.

Ageron, Charles-Robert. "Enquête sur les origines du nationalism algérien. L'émir Khaled, petit-fils d'Abd El Kader, fut-il le premier nationaliste algérien?" *Revue de l'Occident musulman et de la Méditerranée* 2 (1966): 9–49.

——. *France coloniale ou parti colonial?* Paris: PUF, 1978.

——. *Les Algériens musulmans et la France.* Paris: PUF, 1968.

——. "Une dimension de la guerre d'Algérie: les 'regroupements' de populations." In *Militaires et guérilla dans la guerre d'Algérie,* edited by J.-C. Jauffret and M. Vaïsse. Brussels: Editions Complexes, 2001.

——. "L'immigration maghrébine en France: un survol historique." *Vingtième siècle* 7 (July–September 1985): 59–70.

——. "*Les supplétifs algériens dans l'armée française.*" *Vingtième siècle* 48 (October–December 1995): 3–20.

Allouche-Benayoun, Joëlle. "Les enjeux de la naturalisation des Juifs d'Algérie: du dhimmi au citoyen." In *Le choc colonial et l'islam: Les politiques religieuses des puissances coloniales en terres d'islam,* edited by Pierre-Jean Luizard. Paris: La Découverte, 2006.

Almi, Saïd. *Urbanisme et colonisation: Présence française en Algérie.* Sprimont, Belgium: Mardaga, 2002.

Amselle, Jean-Loup. *Vers un multiculturalisme français: l'empire de la coutume.* Paris: Flammarion, 2001.

Arkin, Kimberly. "Rhinestone Aesthetics and Religious Essence: Looking Jewish in Paris." *American Ethnologist* 36, no. 4 (2009): 722–34.

Asad, Talal. *Formations of the Secular: Christianity, Islam, Modernity.* Stanford: Stanford University Press, 2003.

——. *Genealogies of Religion: Discipline and Reasons of Power in Christianity and Islam.* Baltimore: Johns Hopkins University Press, 1993.

——. *The Idea of an Anthropology of Islam.* Washington, DC: Center for Contemporary Arab Studies, Georgetown University, 1986.

Auslander, Leora. "Bavarian Cruxifixes and French Headscarves: Religious Signs in the Postmodern European State." *Cultural Dynamics* 12, no. 3 (2000): 283–309.

——. "Beyond Words." *American History Review* 110 (October 2005): 1015–45.
——. "Coming Home? Jews in Postwar Paris." *Journal of Contemporary History* 40, no. 2 (2005): 237–59.
Auslander, Leora, and Thomas C. Holt. "Sambo in Paris: Race and Racism in the Iconography of the Everyday." In *The Color of Liberty: Histories of Race in France,* edited by Sue Peabody and Tyler Stovall. Durham, NC: Duke University Press, 2003.
Badinter, Robert. *Un antisémitisme ordinaire: Vichy et les avocats juifs (1940–1944).* Paris: Fayard, 1997.
Bahloul, Joëlle. *La Maison de mémoire: Ethnologie d'une demeure judéo-arabe en Algérie (1937–1961).* Paris: Métailié, 1992.
Balibar, Etienne, and Immanuel Wallerstein. *Race, Nation, Class: Ambiguous Identities.* London: Verso, 1991.
Bancel, Nicolas, and Pascal Blanchard. "Les origines républicaines de la fracture coloniale." In *La fracture coloniale: La société française au prisme de l'héritage colonial,* edited by Pascal Blanchard, Nicolas Bancel, and Sandrine Lemaire. Paris: La Découverte, 2005.
Barou, Jacques. *Les OS dans l'industrie automobile.* Paris: CNRS-RNUR, 1986.
Barou, Jacques, Moustapha Diop, and Subhi Toma. "Des Musulmans dans l'Usine." In *Ouvriers spécialisés à Billancourt, les derniers témoins,* edited by Renaud Sainsaulieu and Ahsène Zehraoui. Paris: L'Harmattan, 1995.
Baubérot, Jean. *Laïcité 1905–2005, Entre passion et raison.* Paris: Seuil, 2004.
——. *Vers une nouvelle pacte laïque?* Paris: Seuil, 1990.
Bayoumi, Moustafa. "Shadows and Light: Colonial Modernity and the Grande Mosquee of Paris." *Yale Journal of Criticism* 13 (2000): 267–92.
Beau, Nicolas. *Paris, capitale arabe.* Paris: Seuil, 1995.
Béguin, François. *Arabisances: décor architectural et tracé urbain en Afrique du Nord, 1830–1950.* Paris: Dunod, 1983.
Benbassa, Esther. *Histoire des Juifs de France de l'Antiquité à nos jours.* Paris: Seuil, 1997.
Bencheikh, Soheib. *Marianne et le Prophète: L'Islam dans la France laïque.* Paris: Grasset, 1998.
Bendifallah, Smail. *L'immigration algérienne et le droit français.* Paris: R. Pichon and R. Durand-Auzias, 1974.
Benkheira, Mohamed Hocine. *Islâm et interdits alimentaires: juguler l'animalité.* Paris: PUF, 2000.
Bensimon, Doris. "La guerre et l'évolution de la communauté juive." In *La Guerre d'Algérie et les Français,* edited by Jean-Pierre Rioux. Paris: Fayard, 1990.
Betts, Raymond F. *Assimilation and Association in French Colonial Theory.* Lincoln: University of Nebraska Press, 1960.
Birnbaum, Pierre. *Les fous de la République: histoire politique des juifs d'etat, de Gambetta à Vichy.* Paris: Fayard, 1992.
——, ed. *Histoire politique des juifs de France: Entre universalisme et Particularisme.* Paris: Presses de la Fondation nationale des sciences politiques, 1990.
Blanc, M. "Le logement des travailleurs immigrés en France: après le taudis, le foyer, et aujourd'hui le HLM." *Espaces et sociétés* 42 (1983): 129–40.

Blanchard, Pascal, and Gilles Boëtsch. "La France de Pétain et l'Afrique: Images et propagandes coloniales." *Canadian Journal of African Studies* 28, no. 1 (1994): 1–31.

Blévis, Laure. "Sociologie d'un droit colonial. Citoyenneté et nationalité en Algérie (1865–1947): une exception républicaine?" Ph.D. dissertation, Institut d'Etudes Politiques, Aix-en-Provence, 2004.

De Bonneville, Françoise. *Le livre du bain.* Paris: Flammarion, 2001.

Boubekeur, Amel, and Abderrahim Lamchichi. *Musulmans de France.* Paris: L'Harmattan, 2006.

Bourdieu, Pierre, and Abdelmalek Sayad. *Le déracinement: la crise de l'agriculture traditionnelle en Algérie.* Paris: Editions de Minuit, 1964.

Bowles, Brian. "Newsreels, Ideology, and Public Opinion under Vichy: The Case of *La France en Marche.*" *French Historical Studies* 27, no. 2 (2004): 419–63.

Boyer, Alain. *L'Institut Musulman de la Mosquée de Paris.* Paris: La Documentation française, 1992.

——. *L'Islam en France.* Paris: Presses universitaires de France, 1998.

——. "La représentation du culte musulman en France." *French Historical Studies* 23, no. 1 (2005): 8–22.

Bowen, John R. *Can Islam Be French? Pluralism and Pragmatism in a Secularist State.* Princeton: Princeton University Press, 2010.

——. *Why the French Don't Like Headscarves: Islam, the State, and Public Space.* Princeton: Princeton University Press, 2007.

Branche, Raphaëlle. *La Torture et l'armée pendant la guerre d'Algérie 1954–1962.* Paris: Gallimard, 2001.

Brown, Wendy. *Regulating Aversion: Tolerance in the Age of Identity and Empire.* Princeton: Princeton University Press, 2008.

——. "Tolerance and/or Equality? The 'Jewish Question' and the 'Woman Question.'" *Differences* 152 (2004): 1–31.

Brubaker, Rogers. *Citizenship and Nationhood in France and Germany.* Cambridge: Harvard University Press, 1992.

Bunle, Henri. *Mouvements migratoires entre la France et l'étranger.* Paris: PUF, 1943.

Camiscioli, Elisa. "Producing Citizens, Reproducing the 'French Race': Immigration, Demography, and Pronatalism in Early Twentieth-Century France." *Gender and History* 13 (November 2001): 593–621.

——. *Reproducing the French Race: Immigration, Intimacy and Embodiment in the Early Twentieth Century.* Durham, NC: Duke University Press, 2009.

——. "Reproducing the French Race: Immigration, Reproduction and National Identity in France, 1900–1939." Ph.D. dissertation, University of Chicago, 2000.

Cantier, Jacques. *L'Algérie sous le régime de Vichy.* Paris: Odile Jacob, 2002.

Çelik, Zeynep. *Displaying the Orient: Architecture of Islam at Nineteenth-Century World's Fairs.* Berkeley: University of California Press, 1992.

——. *Empire, Architecture, and the City: French Ottoman Encounters, 1830–1914.* Seattle: University of Washington Press, 2008.

——. *Urban Forms and Colonial Confrontations: Algiers under French Rule.* Berkeley: University of California Press, 1997.

Cesari, Jocelyne. *Etre musulman en France: Associations, militants et mosquées.* Paris: Karthala, 1994.

——. *Musulmans et républicains: les jeunes, l'Islam et la France.* Brussels: Editions Complexe, 1998.

Chachoua, Kamel. *L'islam kabyle: religion, état et société en Algérie.* Paris: Maisonneuve and Larose, 2001.

Chaïb, Yassine. *L'émigré et la mort: La mort musulmane en France.* Paris: Edisud, 2000.

Charrad, Mounira. *States and Women's Rights: The Making of Postcolonial Tunisia, Algeria, and Morocco.* Berkeley: University of California Press, 2001.

Chevillard-Vabre, Josiane. "Histoire de l'Hôpital Franco-Musulman." MD dissertation, Faculté de Médecine Saint-Antoine Paris, 1982.

Clancy-Smith, Julia. "Islam, Gender, and Identities in the Making of French Algeria, 1830–1962." In *Domesticating the Empire: Race, Gender, and Family Life in French and Dutch Colonialism*, edited by Julia Clancy-Smith and Frances Gouda. Charlottesville: University of Virginia Press, 1998.

——. *Rebel and Saint: Muslim Notables, Populist Protest, Colonial Encounters (Algeria and Tunisia, 1800–1904).* Berkeley: University of California Press, 1997.

Clifford, James. *The Predicament of Culture: Twentieth-Century Ethnography, Literature, and Art.* Cambridge, MA: Harvard University Press, 1988.

Cohen, Jean-Louis. "Architectural History and the Colonial Question: Casablanca, Algiers and Beyond." *Architectural History* 49 (2006): 349–68.

Coller, Ian. *Arab France: Islam and the Making of Modern Europe, 1798–1831.* Berkeley: University of California Press, 2010.

Collot, Claude. *Les institutions de l'Algérie Durant la période coloniale (1830–1962).* Paris: CNRS, 1987.

Colonna, Fanny. *Les versets de l'invincibilité: Permanence et changements dans l'Algérie contemporaine.* Paris: Presses de Sciences Po, 1995.

Conklin, Alice L. *A Mission to Civilize: The Republican Idea of Empire in France and West Africa, 1895–1930.* Stanford, CA: Stanford University Press, 1997.

Connelly, Matthew. *A Diplomatic Revolution: Algeria's Fight for Independence and the Origins of the Post–Cold War Era.* Oxford: Oxford University Press, 2002.

Cooper, Frederick. *Colonialism in Question: Theory, Knowledge, History.* Berkeley: University of California Press, 2005.

Costa-Lascoux, Jacqueline, and Emile Témime, eds. *Les Algériens en France: Genèse et devoir d'une migration.* Paris: Publisud, 1985.

Costa-Lascoux, Jacqueline, Geneviève Dreyfus-Armand, and Emile Témime, eds. *Renault sur Seine: Hommes et lieux de mémoire de l'industrie automobile.* Paris: Découverte, 2007.

Le Cour Grandmaison, Olivier. *Coloniser, Exterminer: Sur la guerre et l'Etat colonial.* Paris: Fayard, 2005.

Courtois, Stéphane, and Gilles Kepel. "Musulmans et prolétaires." In *Les musulmans dans la société française,* edited by Rémy Leveau and Gilles Kepel. Paris: Presses de la Fondation nationale des sciences politiques, 1987.

Le Crom, Jean-Pierre. "De la philanthropie à l'action humanitaire." In *La Protection social sous le régime de Vichy,* edited by Jean-Philippe Hesse and Jean-Pierre Crom. Rennes, France: Presses Universitaires de Rennes, 2001.

Cross, Gary. *Immigrant Workers in Industrial France: The Making of a New Laboring Class.* Philadelphia: Temple University Press, 1983.

Daly, Barbara Metcalfe, ed. *Making Muslim Space in North America and Europe.* Berkeley: University of California Press, 1996.

Derder, Peggy. *L'immigration algérienne et les pouvoirs publics dans le département de la Seine 1954–1962.* Paris: L'Harmattan, 2001.

Diop, Moustapha, and Laurence Michalak. "'Refuge' and 'Prison': Islam, Ethnicity, and the Adaptation of Space in Workers' Housing in France." In *Making Muslim Space in North America and Europe,* edited by Barbara Daly Metcalfe. Berkeley: University of California Press, 1996.

Dittgen, Alfred. "La forme du mariage en Europe. Cérémonie civile, cérémonie religieuse. Panorama et évolution." *Population* 2 (1994): 339–68.

Dorlin, Elsa. *La matrice de la race: Généalogie sexuelle et colonial de la nation française.* Paris: La Découverte, 2006.

Dubois, Laurent. *A Colony of Citizens: Revolution and Slave Emancipation in the French Caribbean, 1787–1804.* Chapel Hill: University of North Carolina Press, 2004.

Einaudi, Jean-Luc. *La Bataille de Paris: 17 Octobre 1961.* Paris: Seuil, 1991.

Endelstein, Lucine. "Les juifs originaires d'Afrique du Nord, acteurs du développement du commerce cacher aujourd'hui." In *Petites entreprises et petits entrepreneurs étrangers en France, 19e-20 siècles,* edited by Anne Sophie Bruno and Claire Zalc. Paris: Publibook, 2006.

De l'Estoile, Benoît. *Le goût des autres: de l'Exposition coloniale aux arts premiers.* Paris: Flammarion, 2007.

Etienne, Bruno. *La France et l'Islam.* Paris: Hachette, 1989.

——. *L'Islam en France: Islam, état et société.* Paris: CNRS, 1990.

Fassin, Didier, and Éric Fassin, editors. *De la question sociale à la question raciale?* Paris: La Découverte, 2006.

Fernando, Mayanthi L. "Exceptional Citizens: Secular Muslim Women and the Politics of Difference in France." *Social Anthropology* 17, no. 3 (2009): 379–92.

——. *French Citizens of Muslim Faith: Islam, Secularism, and the Politics of Difference in Contemporary France.* Ph.D. dissertation, University of Chicago, 2006.

——. "Reconfiguring Freedom: Muslim Piety and the Limits of Secular Law and Public Discourse in France." *American Ethnologist* 37, no. 1 (2010): 19–35.

Ferré, Jean-Noël. *La religion de la vie quotidienne chez les marocains musulmans.* Paris: Karthala, 2004.

Fogarty, Richard S. *Race and War in France: Colonial Subjects in the French Army, 1914–1918.* Baltimore: Johns Hopkins University Press, 2008.

Fourcaut, Annie. *Bobigny, Banlieue rouge.* Paris: Les Editions ouvrières, 1986.

Frégosi, Franck. *La formation des cadres religieux musulmans en France: approaches socio-juridiques.* Paris: L'Harmattan, 1998.

——. *Penser l'islam dans la laïcité.* Paris: Fayard, 2008.

Frémeaux, Jacques. "Les ambiguïtés de l'idéologie coloniale." In *Histoire de l'islam et des musulmans en France du Moyen Age à nos jours,* edited by Mohamed Arkoun. Paris: Albin Michel, 2006.

——. *La France et l'Islam depuis 1789.* Paris: PUF, 1991.

Gadant, Monique. *Islam et nationalisme en Algérie.* Paris: L'Harmattan, 1988.

De Galembert, Claire, and Mustapha Belbah. "Le Conseil français du culte musulman à l'épreuve des territoires." *French Historical Studies* 23, no. 1 (2005): 76–86.

Gallissot, René. "La guerre et l'immigration algérienne en France." In *La Guerre d'Algérie et les Français,* edited by Jean-Pierre Roux. Paris: Fayard, 1990.

Gaspard, Françoise, and Farhad Khosrokhavar. *Le foulard et la République.* Paris: La Découverte, 1995.

Geertz, Clifford. *Islam Observed.* New Haven: Yale University Press, 1968.

Gilroy, Paul. *"There Ain't No Black in the Union Jack": The Cultural Politics of Race and Nation.* Chicago: University of Chicago Press, 1987.

Ginesy-Galano, Mireille. *Les immigrés hors la cité.* Paris: L'Harmattan, 1984.

Godard, Bernard and Sylvie Taussig. *Les musulmans en France: Courants, Institutions communautés, un état des lieux.* Paris: Robert Laffont, 2007.

Grabar, Oleg. "Symbols and Signs in Islamic Architecture." In *Architecture and Community: Building in the Islamic World Today,* edited by Renata Holod. Millerton, NY: Aperture, 1983.

Grandhomme, Hélène. "Connaissance de l'islam et pouvoir colonial: L'exemple de la France au Sénégal, 1936–1957." *French Colonial History* 10 (2009): 171–88.

Green, Nancy. *The Pletzl of Paris: Jewish Immigrant Workers in the "Belle Epoque."* New York: Holmes and Meier, 1986.

Gresh, Alain, and Michel Tubiana. *1905–2005, les enjeux de la laïcité.* Paris: L'Harmattan, 2005.

Guénif-Souilamas, Nacira. "La réduction à son corps de l'indigène de la République." In *La fracture coloniale: La société française au prisme de l'héritage colonial,* edited by Pascal Blanchard, Nicolas Bancel, and Sandrine Lemaire. Paris: La Découverte, 2005

Hammadi, Rodolphe, and Marie-Jeanne Dumont. *Paris arabesques: Architectures et décors arabes et orientalisants à Paris.* Paris: Editions Eric Koehler, 1988.

Hamoumou, Mohand. *Et ils sont devenus harkis.* Paris: Fayard, 1993.

Harbi, Mohamed. "Les immigrés maghrébins entre le passé et l'avenir." *Les Temps Modernes* 452–454 (March–May 1984): 1697–1706.

Hargreaves, Alec. *Immigration, "Race," and Ethnicity in Contemporary France.* New York: Routledge, 1995.

Haroun, Ali. *Le 7ème Wilaya: La guerre du F.L.N. en France, 1954–1962.* Paris: Seuil, 1986.

Harrison, Christopher. *France and Islam in West Africa, 1860–1960.* Cambridge, U.K.: Cambridge University Press, 1988.

Harvey, David. *Paris: Capital of Modernity.* New York: Routledge, 2003.

Haut Conseil à l'Intégration. *L'Islam dans la République.* Paris: La documentation française, 2001.

Heffernan, Michael J. "The Parisian Poor and the Colonization of Algeria under the Second Republic." *French History* 3, no. 4 (1989): 377–403.

Hermon-Belot, Rita. "La genèse du système des cultes reconnus: aux origines de la notion française de reconnaissance." *Archives de sciences sociales des religions* 129 (January–March 2005): 17–35.

Hervo, Monique. *Chroniques du bidonville Nanterre en Guerre d'Algérie 1959–1962.* Paris: Seuil, 2001.

Hifi, Belkacem. *L'immigration algérienne en France: origines et perspectives de non-retour.* Paris: L'Harmattan, 1985.

Hmed, Choukri. "Loger les étrangers 'isolés' en France. Socio-histoire d'une institution d'Etat: la Sonacotra (1956–2006)." Ph.D. dissertation, Université de Paris I, 2006.

——. "'Tenir ses hommes': la gestion des étrangers 'isolés' dans les foyers Sonacotra après la guerre d'Algérie." *Politix* 76, no. 4 (2006): 11–30.

House, Jim, and Neil MacMaster. "La Fédération de France du FLN et l'organisation de la manifestation du 17 octobre 1961." *Vingtième siècle* 82 (2004): 145–60.

Hyman, Paula E. *The Jews of Modern France.* Berkeley: University of California Press, 1998.

Jarrassé, Dominique. *Une histoire des synagogues françaises: Entre Occident et Orient.* Arles: Actes Sud, 1999.

Jennings, Eric. *Vichy in the Tropics: Pétain's National Revolution in Madagascar, Guadaloupe, and Indochina, 1940–1944.* Stanford, CA: Stanford University Press, 2001.

Jordi, Jean-Jacques. "Les pieds-noirs: constructions identitaires et réinvention des origines." *Hommes et migrations* 1236 (2002): 14–25.

Jordi, Jean-Jacques, and Emile Témime, eds. *Marseille et le choc des décolonisations.* Aix-en-Provence: Edisud, 1996.

Kaspi, André. *Le Paris des étrangers.* Paris: Imprimerie nationale, 1989.

Katz, Ethan. "Jews and Muslims in the Shadow of Marianne: Conflicting Identities and Republican Culture in France, 1914–1985." PhD dissertation, University of Wisconsin, 2009.

——. "Secular French Nationhood and its Discontents: Jews, Muslims, Public Religion, and Ethnicity in Occupied France." Unpublished paper.

Keller, Richard. *Colonial Madness: Psychiatry in French North Africa.* Chicago: University of Chicago Press, 2007.

Kepel, Gilles. *Les banlieues de l'Islam: Naissance d'une religion en France.* Paris: Seuil, 1991.

Khellil, Mohand. *L'Intégration des maghrébins en France.* Paris: PUF, 1991.

Kidd, William. "Representation or Recuperation? The French Colonies and 1914–1918 War Memorials." In *Promoting the Colonial Idea: Propaganda and Visions of Empire in France,* edited by Tony Chafer and Amanda Sackur. New York: Palgrave, 2002.

Krieger-Krynicki, Annie. *Les musulmans en France: Religion et culture.* Paris: Maisonneuve and Larose, 1985.

Kruger, Steven. *The Spectral Jew: Conversion and Embodiment in Medieval Europe.* Minneapolis: University of Minnesota Press, 2006.

Laborde, Cécile. *Critical Republicanism: The Hijab Controversy and Political Philosophy.* Oxford: Oxford University Press, 2008.

Lamchichi, Abderrahim. *Islam et muuslmans de France: Pluralisme, laïcité et citoyenneté.* Paris: L'Harmattan, 1999.

Laurence, Jonathan. "From the Elysée Salon to the Table of the Republic: State-Islam Relation and the Integration of Muslims in France." *French Historical Studies* 23, no. 1 (2005): 37–64.

Laurence, Jonathan, and Justin Vaisse. *Integrating Islam: Political and Religious Challenges in Contemporary France.* Washington, DC: Brookings Institution Press, 2006.

Laurens, Henry. *Orientales II: La Troisième République et l'Islam.* Paris: CNRS, 2004.

Lawrence, Denise L., and Setha M. Low. "The Built Environment and the Spatial Form." *Annual Review of Anthropology* 19 (1990): 453–505.

Lebovics, Herman. *True France: The Wars over Cultural Identity, 1900–1945.* Ithaca: Cornell University Press, 1992.

Leff, Lisa Moses. *Sacred Bonds of Solidarity: The Rise of Jewish Internationalism in Nineteenth-Century France.* Stanford: Stanford University Press, 2006.

Le Goff, Jacques, and René Remond, eds. *Histoire de la France religieuse: Tome IV: Société sécularisée et renouveaux religieux.* Paris: Seuil, 1992.

Leveau, Rémy, and Khadija Mohsen-Finan. *L'Islam en France et en Allemagne: Identités et citoyennetés.* Paris: La Documentation française, 2001.

Lévy, Laurent. *La gauche, les noirs et les arabes.* Paris: Fabrique, 2010.

Lewis, Mary D. *The Boundaries of the Republic: Migrant Rights and the Limits of Universalism in France, 1918–1940.* Stanford: Stanford University Press, 2007.

Liauzu, Claude. "Immigration, colonisation et racisme: Pour une histoire liée." *Hommes et migrations* 1228 (November–December 2000): 5–14.

——. *L'Islam de l'Occident: la question de l'Islam dans la conscience occidentale.* Paris: Arcantère éditions, 1989.

Lorcin, Patricia. *Imperial Identities: Stereotyping, Prejudice, and Race in Colonial Algeria.* London: I. B. Tauris, 1995.

Luizard, Pierre-Jean. "La politique coloniale de Jules Ferry en Algérie et en Tunisie." In *Le choc colonial et l'islam: Les politiques religieuses des puissances colonials en terres d'islam,* edited by Pierre-Jean Luizard. Paris: La Découverte, 2006.

Lunn, Joe. "'*Les races guerrières*': Racial Preoccupations in the French Military about West African Soldiers during the First World War." *Journal of Contemporary History* 34, no. 4 (1999): 517–36.

Lyons, Amelia. "Invisible Immigrants: Algerian Families and the French Welfare State in the era of Decolonization." Ph.D. dissertation, University of California at Irvine, 2004.

Kaltenbach, Jeanne-Hélène, and Michèle Tribalat. *La République et l'islam: Entre crainte et aveuglement.* Paris: Gallimard, 2002.

MacMaster, Neil. *Burning the Veil: The Algerian War and the "Emancipation" of Algerian Women, 1954–1962.* Manchester: Manchester University Press, 2010.

——. *Colonial Migrants and Racism: Algerians in France, 1900–1962.* New York: St. Martin's Press, 1997.

——. "Imperial Facades: Muslim Institutions and Propaganda in Interwar Paris." In *Promoting the Colonial Idea: Propaganda and Visions of Empire in France,* edited by Tony Chafer and Amanda Sackur. New York: Palgrave, 2002.

McDougall, James. *History and the Culture of Nationalism in Algeria.* Cambridge, U.K.: Cambridge University Press, 2006.

——. "The Secular State's Islamic Empire: Muslim Spaces and the Subjects of Jurisdiction in Paris and Algiers, 1905–1957." *Comparative Studies in Society and History* 52, no. 3 (2010): 553–80.

——. "S'écrire un destin: L'Association des 'ulama dans la revolution algérienne." *Bulletin de l'Institut d'histoire du temps present* 83 (2004): 38–52.

Mahmood, Saba. *Politics of Piety: The Islamic Revival and the Feminist Subject.* Princeton: Princeton University Press, 2005.

Mann, Gregory, and Baz Lecoq. "Between Empire, *Umma,* and the Muslim Third World: The French Union and African Pilgrims to Mecca, 1946–1948." *Comparative Studies of South Asia, Africa, and the Middle East* 27, no. 2 (2007): 367–83.

Masuzawa, Tomoko. *The Invention of World Religions.* Chicago: University of Chicago Press, 2005.

Maussen, Marcel. "Islamic Presence and Mosque Establishment in France: Colonialism, Arrangement for Guest Workers, and Citizenship." *Journal of Ethnic and Migration Studies* 33, no. 6 (August 2007): 981–1002.

Mayeur, Jean-Marie. *La séparation des églises et de l'état.* Paris: Les Editions Ouvrières, 1991.

Mbembe, Achille. "La République et l'impensé de la 'race.'" In *La fracture coloniale: La société française au prisme de l'héritage colonial,* edited by Pascal Blanchard, Nicolas Bancel, and Sandrine Lemaire. Paris: La Découverte, 2005.

El Mechat, Samya. *Les États-Unis et l'Algérie: de la méconnaissance à la reconnaissance. 1945–1962.* Paris: L'Harmattan, 1996.

Merad, Ali. *Le réformisme musulman en Algérie de 1925 à 1940.* Paris: Mouton, 1967.

Merle, Isabelle. "*De la 'légalisation' de la violence en contexte colonial. Le régime de l'indigénat en question.*" *Politix* 17, no. 66 (2004): 137–62.

Merleau-Ponty, Maurice. *Phénoménologie de la perception.* Paris: Gallimard, 1945.

Messner, Francis, Pierre-Henri Prélot, and Jean-Marie Woehrling. *Traité de droit français des religions.* Paris: Litec, 2003.

Meynier, Gilbert. *L'Algérié révelée. La guerre de 1914–1918 et le premier quart du XXe siècle.* Geneva: Droz, 1981.

——. *Histoire intérieure du FLN, 1954–1962.* Paris: Fayard, 2002.

Mitchell, Timothy. *Colonising Egypt.* Berkeley: University of California Press, 1988.

——. "The World as Exhibition." *Comparative Studies in Society and History* 31, no. 2 (April 1989): 217–36.

Morton, Patricia A. *Hybrid Modernities: Architecture and Representation at the 1931 Colonial Exposition, Paris.* Cambridge, MA: MIT Press, 2003.

Moulin, Marie-France. *Machines à dormir: Les foyers neufs de la sonacotra, de l'adef et quelques autres.* Paris: Maspero, 1976.

Naylor, Philip. *France and Algeria: A History of Decolonization and Transformation.* Gainesville: University of Florida Press, 2000.

Ndiaye, Pap. *La condition noire: Essai sur une minorité française.* Paris: Calmann-Lévy, 2008.

Neaimi, Sadek. *L'Islam au siècle des Lumières: Image de la civilisation islamique chez les philosophes français du XVIIIe siècle.* Paris: L'Harmattan, 2003.

Noiriel, Gérard. *Le creuset français: Histoire de l'immigration XIXe–XXe siècle.* Paris: Seuil, 1988.

——. *Immigration, antisémitisme et racisme en France (XIX–XXe siècles): Discours publics, humiliations privées.* Paris: Fayard, 2007.

Le Pautremat, Pascal. *La Politique musulmane de la France au XXe siècle: De l'Hexagone aux terres d'Islam, Espoirs, réussites, échecs.* Paris: Maisonneuve and Larose, 2003.

Peabody, Sue, and Tyler Stovall, eds. *The Color of Liberty: Histories of Race in France.* Durham, NC: Duke University Press, 2003.

Pena-Ruiz, Henri. *Qu'est-ce que la laïcité?* Paris: Gallimard, 2003.

Perrot, Michelle. "Les 'Apaches', premières bandes de jeunes." *Les marginaux et les exclus dans l'histoire, Cahiers Jussieu* 5, 1979.

Pervillé, Guy. "The Frenchification of Algerian Intellectuals." In *Franco-Arab Encounters: Studies in Memory of David C. Gordon,* edited by L. Carl Brown and Matthew S. Gordon. Beirut: American University of Beirut, 1966.

Pétonnet, Colette. *Espaces habitées: Ethnologie des banlieues.* Paris: Editions Galilée, 1982.

Powers, Paul. "Interiors, Intentions, and the 'Spirituality' of Islamic Ritual Practice." *Journal of the American Academy of Religion* 72, no. 2 (June 2004): 425–59.

Prochaska, David. *Making Algeria French: Colonialism in Bône, 1870–1920.* Cambridge, U.K.: Cambridge University Press, 1990.

Rabinow, Paul. *French Modern: Norms and Forms of the Social Environment.* Cambridge, MA: MIT Press, 1989.

Raymond, André. "Islamic City, Arab City: Orientalist Myths and Recent Views." *British Journal of Middle Eastern Studies* 21, no. 1 (1994): 3–18.

Recham, Belkacem. "Les musulmans dans l'armée française, 1900–1945." In In *Histoire de l'islam et des musulmans en France du Moyen Age à nos jours,* edited by Mohamed Arkoun. Paris: Albin Michel, 2006.

Régnier, Faustine. "Spicing up the Imagination: Culinary Exoticism in France and Germany, 1930– Châtelier 1990." *Food and Foodways* 11 (2003): 189–214.

Renard, Michel. "Les débuts de la présence musulmane en France et son encadrement." In *Histoire de l'islam et des musulmans en France du Moyen Age à nos jours,* edited by Mohamed Arkoun. Paris: Albin Michel, 2006.

——. "Gratitude, contrôle, accompagnement: le traitement du religieux islamique en métropole, 1914–1950." *Cahiers de l'IHTP* 83 (June 2004): 54–69.

Rivet, Daniel. *Lyautey et l'Institution du protectorat français au Maroc 1912–1925 Tome II.* Paris: L'Harmattan, 1988.

——. *Le Maghreb à l'épreuve de la colonisation.* Paris: Hachette, 2002.

——. "Quelques propos sur la politique musulmane de Lyautey au Maroc." In *Le choc colonial et l'islam: Les politiques religieuses des puissances colonials en terres d'islam,* edited by Pierre-Jean Luizard. Paris: La Découverte, 2006.

Robinson, David. *Paths of Accommodation: Muslim Societies and French Colonial Authorities in Senegal and Mauritania, 1880–1920.* Athens: Ohio University Press, 2000.

Robinson, David, and Jean-Louis Triaud. *Le temps des marabouts: Itinéraires et stratégies islamiques en Afrique occidentale française v. 1880–1960.* Paris: Karthala, 1997.

Rosenberg, Clifford. *Policing Paris: The Origins of Modern Immigration Control between the Wars.* Ithaca: Cornell University Press, 2006.

Ross, Kristin. *Fast Cars, Clean Bodies: Decolonization and the Reordering of French Culture.* Cambridge, MA: MIT Press, 1995.

——. *May '68 and Its Afterlives.* Chicago: University of Chicago Press, 2004.

——. "Starting Afresh: Hygiene and Modernization in Postwar France." *October* 67 (1994): 22–57.

Roux, Michel. *Les Harkis: Les oubliés de l'histoire, 1954–1991.* Paris: La Decouverte, 1991.

Roy, Olivier. *La laïcité face à l'islam.* Paris: Stock, 2005.

——. *Vers un islam européen.* Paris: Esprit, 1999.

Ruedy, John. *Modern Algeria: The Origins and Development of a Nation.* Bloomington: Indiana University Press, 2005.

Saada, Emmanuelle. *Les enfants de la colonie: Les métis de l'Empire français, entre sujétion et citoyenneté.* Paris: La Découverte, 2007.

Sambron, Diane. *Les femmes algériennes pendant la colonization.* Paris: Riveneuve, 2009.

Samuel, Michel. *Le prolétariat africain noir en France.* Paris: Maspero, 1978.

Sayad, Abdelmalek. "Les trois actes de l'émigration algérienne en France." *Actes de la recherche en sciences sociales* 15 (1977): 59–77.

Sbaï, Jalila. "La République et la Mosquée: génèse et institution(s) de l'Islam en France." In *Le choc colonial et l'islam: Les politiques religieuses des puissances coloniales en terres d'islam,* edited by Pierre-Jean Luizard. Paris: La Découverte, 2006.

Schnapper, Dominique. *Juifs et israélites.* Paris: Gallimard, 1980.

Schor, Ralph. "Le facteur religieux et l'intégration des étrangers en France." *Vingtième Siècle* 47 (July–September 1995): 103–15.

——. *L'Immigration en France 1919–1939.* Nice: Centre de la Méditerranée Moderne et Contemporaine, 1986.

Schreier, Joshua. *Arabs of the Jewish Faith: The Civilizing Mission in Colonial Algeria.* New Brunswick, NJ: Rutgers University Press, 2010.

Schroeter, Daniel J., and Joseph Chetrit. "Emancipation and its Discontents: Jews at the Formative Period of Colonial Rule in Morocco." *Jewish Social Studies: History, Culture, and Society* 13, no. 1 (Fall 2006): 170–206.

Schwarzfuchs, Simon. *Du juif à l'israélite: Histoire d'une mutation, 1770–1870.* Paris: Fayard, 1989.

Scott, Joan Wallach. *Only Paradoxes to Offer: French Feminists and the Rights of Man.* Cambridge, MA: Harvard University Press, 1996.

——. *Parité! Sexual Equality and the Crisis of French Universalism.* Chicago: University of Chicago Press, 2005.

——. *The Politics of the Veil.* Princeton: Princeton University Press, 2007.

Seferdjeli, Ryme. "French 'Reforms' and Muslim Women's Emancipation during the Algerian War." *Journal of North African Studies* 9, no. 4 (Winter 2004): 19–61.

Seligman, Adam B., et al. *Ritual and its Consequences: An Essay on the Limits of Sincerity.* Oxford: Oxford University Press, 2008.

Sellam, Sadek. *La France et ses musulmans.* Paris: Fayard, 2006.

Shepard, Todd. *The Invention of Decolonization: The Algerian War and the Remaking of France.* Ithaca: Cornell University Press, 2006.

Sherman, Daniel. *The Construction of Memory in Interwar France.* Chicago: University of Chicago Press, 1999.

Sibeud, Emmanuelle. "Un ethnographe face à la colonization: Arnold Van Gennep en Algérie (1911–1912)." *Revue d'Histoire des Sciences Humaines* 10 (2004): 79–103.

Silverman, Maxim. *Deconstructing the Nation: Immigration, Racism, and Citizenship in Modern France.* New York: Routledge, 1992.

Silverstein, Paul A. *Algeria in France: Transpolitics, Race, and Nation.* Bloomington: Indiana University Press, 2004.

Simon, Jacques. *L'immigration algérienne en France des origines à l'indépendence.* Paris: Editions Paris-Méditerranée, 2000.

Spire, Alexis. *Etrangers à la carte: L'administration de l'immigration en France.* Paris: Grasset, 2005.

Stoler, Ann Laura. *Race and the Education of Desire: Foucault's* History of Sexuality *and the Colonial Order of Things.* Durham, NC: Duke University Press, 1995.

Stora, Benjamin. *La gangrène et l'oubli: La mémoire de la guerre d'Algérie.* Paris: La Découverte, 1991.

——. *Histoire de l'Algérie coloniale, 1830–1954.* Paris: La Découverte, 2004.

——. *Ils venaient d'Algérie.* Paris: Fayard, 1991.

——. "Locate, Isolate, Place under Surveillance: Algerian Migration to France in the 1930s." In *Franco-Arab Encounters: Studies in Memory of David C. Gordon,* edited by L. Carl Brown and Matthew S. Gordon. Beirut: American University of Beirut, 1966.

——. *Les trois exils: Juifs d'Algérie.* Paris: Stock, 2006.

Stovall, Tyler. "The Color Line behind the Lines: Racial Violence in France during the Great War." *American Historical Review* 103, no. 3 (June 1998): 737–69.

Le Sueur, James. *Uncivil War: Intellectuals and Identity Politics during the Decolonization of Algeria.* Philadelphia: University of Pennsylvania Press, 2001.

Surkis, Judith. "Hymenal Politics: Marriage, Secularism, and French Sovereignty." *Public Culture* 22, no. 3 (2010): 531–56.

Taguieff, Pierre-André. "Face à l'immigration: Mixophobie, xénophobie ou sélection: Un débat français dans l'Entre-deux-guerres." *Vingtième Siècle* 47 (July–September 1995).

——. "Les métamorphoses idéologiques du racisme et de la crise de l'anti-racisme." In *Face au racisme, Tome II: Analyses, hypothèses, perspectives,* edited by Pierre-André Taguieff. Paris: La Découverte, 1991.

Taylor, Lynne. *Between Resistance and Collaboration: Popular Protest in Northern France, 1940–1945.* New York: St. Martin's Press, 2000.

——. "The Black Market in Occupied France, 1940–1944." *Contemporary European History* 6 (July 1997): 153–76.

Taylor, Katherine Fischer. *In the Theater of Criminal Justice: The Palais de Justice in Second Empire Paris.* Princeton: Princeton University Press, 1993.

Ternisien, Xavier. *La France des mosquées.* Paris: Albin Michel, 2002.

Thénault, Sylvie. *Histoire de la guerre d'indépendence algérienne.* Paris: Flammarion, 2005.

Thompson, Elizabeth. *Colonial Citizens: Republican Rights, Paternal Privilege, and Gender in French Syria and Lebanon.* New York: Columbia University Press, 2000.

Timera, Mahamet. *Les Soninké en France: d'un histoire à l'autre.* Paris: Karthala, 1996.

Todorov, Tzvetan. *Nous et les autres: la réflexion française sur la diversité humaine.* Paris: Seuil, 1989.

Toubon, Jean-Claude, and Khelifa Messamah. *Centralité immigrée: Le quartier de la Goutte d'Or, Dynamiques d'un espace pluri-ethnique: succession, compétition, cohabitation.* Paris: L'Harmattan, 1990.

Triaud, Jean-Louis. *La légende noire de la Sanûsiyya: Une confrérie musulmane saharienne sous le regard français (1840–1930).* Paris: Editions de la Maison des sciences de l'homme, 1995.

——. "Politiques musulmanes de la France en Afrique subsaharienne à l'époque coloniale." In *Le choc colonial et l'islam: Les politiques religieuses des puissances coloniales en terres d'islam,* edited by Pierre-Jean Luizard. Paris: La Découverte, 2006.

Trumbull, George R. IV. *An Empire of Facts: Colonial Knowledge, Cultural Power, and Islam: Algeria, 1871–1914.* Oxford: Oxford University Press, 2009.

Verdès-Leroux, Jeannine. *Les Français d'Algérie de 1830 à nos jours.* Paris: Fayard, 2001.

Ware, Rudolph III. "*Njàngaan*: The Daily Regime of Qu'ranic Students in Twentieth-Century Senegal." *International Journal of African Historical Studies* 37, no. 3 (2004): 515–38.

Weil, Patrick. *How to Be French: Nationality in the Making since 1789.* Durham, NC: Duke University Press, 2008.

Wilder, Gary. *The French Imperial Nation-State: Negritude and Colonial Humanism between the Two World Wars.* Chicago: University of Chicago Press, 2005.

Wieviorka, Michel. *La France raciste.* Paris: Seuil, 1992.

Withol de Wenden, Catherine. "L'intégration des populations musulmanes en France, trente ans d'évolution." In *Histoire de l'islam et des musulmans en France du Moyen Age à nos jours,* edited by Mohamed Arkoun. Paris: Albin Michel, 2006.

Wright, Gwendolyn. *The Politics of Design in French Colonial Urbanism.* Chicago: University of Chicago Press, 1991.

Zarka, Yves Charles, Sylvie Taussig, et al. *L'Islam en France.* Paris: Presses universitaires françaises, 2004.

Zeghal, Malika. "La constitution du Conseil Français du Culte Musulman: reconnaissance politique d'un Islam français?" *Archives de sciences socials des religions* 129 (January–March 2005): 97–113.

Zehraoui, Ahsène. *Les travailleurs algériens en France: Etude sociologique de quelques aspects de la vie familiale.* Paris: Maspero, 1971.

Index

Note: Pages numbers followed by *f* indicate figures and photographs.